HARVARD–RADCLIFFE FINE ARTS SERIES

MEDIEVAL STUDIES
IN MEMORY OF
A. KINGSLEY PORTER
VOLUME II

LONDON: HUMPHREY MILFORD
OXFORD UNIVERSITY PRESS

MEDIEVAL STUDIES

IN MEMORY OF

A. KINGSLEY PORTER

EDITED BY WILHELM R. W. KOEHLER

VOLUME II

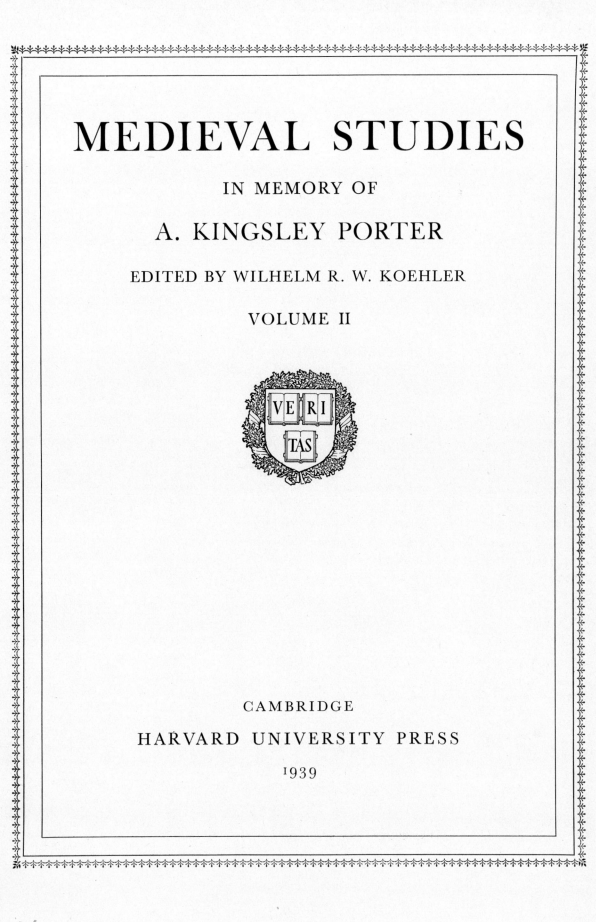

CAMBRIDGE

HARVARD UNIVERSITY PRESS

1939

PRINTED AT THE HARVARD UNIVERSITY PRESS

CAMBRIDGE, MASS., U. S. A.

CONTENTS

VOLUME II

V. MEDIEVAL ART IN FRANCE

VI. MEDIEVAL ART IN GERMANY AND SWITZERLAND

VII. MEDIEVAL ART IN SCANDINAVIA AND THE BRITISH ISLES

V. MEDIEVAL ART IN FRANCE

A. KINGSLEY PORTER ET LA BOURGOGNE

CHARLES OURSEL

SANS examiner, ce que d'autres ont fait ou feront, la valeur définitive des travaux et des thèses de Kingsley Porter dans les divers domaines de l'archéologie médiévale où il a porté son extraordinaire activité, nous voudrions attirer l'attention sur les titres qu'il s'est acquis à la reconnaissance des fervents de l'art bourguignon.

Avant lui, certes, aucun historien de l'art, aucun archéologue ne contestait l'existence en Bourgogne, dans une contrée aux frontières géographiques et politiques assez vagues, d'une école romane originale, puissante et féconde. Mais ni les caractères exacts, ni l'évolution vraie de cette école et de ses formes architecturales n'avaient été définis avec une rigoureuse certitude. On peut même ajouter que la place réservée à l'école de Bourgogne dans le développement général de l'art français était mesurée avec quelque parcimonie. En effet, tout l'art roman de Bourgogne est dominé par le nom de Cluny, par imitation ou par réaction; et le problème de Cluny était mal posé. Les incontestables excès de la théorie clunisienne de Viollet-le-Duc avaient, par contraste, produit une antithèse non moins exagérée, mais beaucoup plus dangereuse et funeste par ses conséquences. A peine le nom de Cluny survivait-il, ou, plus exactement, ce nom évoquait l'idée d'un monument à coup sûr remarquable, mais sans aucun rayonnement. Cluny était l'une des églises de l'école romane de Bourgogne, assez tard venue; sa sculpture, la conclusion de la sculpture romane de Bourgogne. Ni les communications et le gros livre du savant abbé Terret sur la sculpture de Cluny, ni les mémoires profonds du vicomte Pierre de Truchis dans les *Congrès archéologiques* de France ou dans le *Bulletin monumental* n'avaient vraiment réussi à faire sortir les archéologues des chemins battus, dans lesquels ils égaraient leur critique.

C'est à Kingsley Porter que nous devons d'être sortis de l'ornière. Il ne s'agit pas de chercher si, sans lui, le progrès normal des études aurait fini par aboutir à nos conclusions actuelles. Il s'agit simplement de savoir s'il a, en fait, été l'initiateur et l'artisan principal de la rénovation des études clunisiennes, avec toutes les conséquences qu'a comportées cette rénovation. Il n'est pas inutile d'insister sur ce point puisque, dans un article récent du *Bulletin monumental*[1] sur "Le Rôle de Cluny," le nom de Kingsley Porter n'est même pas cité en forme ou par allusion.

Un simple article de la *Gazette des Beaux-Arts* a produit cette révolution. Les discussions et controverses nées des études sur la sculpture lombarde dans la *Lombard Architecture* et sur l'antériorité respective des écoles de Lombardie et de Languedoc amenèrent l'archéologue américain à chercher une origine commune

---

[1] Deshoulières, "Le Rôle de Cluny," dans le *Bulletin monumental*, t. XCIV (1935).

à deux arts qui, selon lui, manifestaient des identités, et cette origine, il la trouva
en Bourgogne et plus spécialement à Cluny. Tout le système est établi dans "La
Sculpture du XIIe siècle en Bourgogne." [2] L'auteur bouleverse de fond en
comble la chronologie traditionnelle de la sculpture romane en Bourgogne, et
il la fait graviter essentiellement autour des célèbres chapiteaux de l'abside de
l'abbatiale Saint-Pierre et Saint-Paul de Cluny. En assignant à ces oeuvres ad-
mirables la date même de la construction du monument, 1088–1095, il les place
en tête et à l'origine de la sculpture bourguignonne, alors que leur caractère et
leur perfection les faisaient communément regarder comme la conclusion de
toute l'école et comme son plein épanouissement. Si déjà les problèmes de
l'architecture et de la sculpture lombarde n'avaient agité l'opinion des érudits, si
déjà les théories de Porter n'avaient attiré l'attention par quelques apparents
paradoxes, peut-être son article sur la sculpture romane de Bourgogne eût-il
passé à peu près inaperçu. Mais il avait trop accoutumé l'érudition française à
veiller sur ses doctrines pour que la nouvelle thèse ne suscitât pas elle-même une
réfutation.

M. Paul Deschamps [3] se chargea de cette tâche, avec une telle vigueur et une
telle fermeté de principes que la théorie américaine parut un instant frappée de
mort et de stérilité. Le savant archéologue affirmait avec netteté la certitude de
l'enseignement traditionnel en France et rétablissait, selon la doctrine de l'école,
la chronologie officielle de la sculpture romane de Bourgogne.

La question cependant ne pouvait laisser indifférents les érudits bourguignons.
Sans doute n'eussent-ils pas d'eux-mêmes provoqué la discussion; nul indice du
moins ne le laissait supposer. Mais puisqu'ils étaient, sans le vouloir, et sans
l'avoir désiré, partie au procès, rien d'étonnant qu'ils aient cherché à leur tour
la solution du problème posé. Et ainsi le système de Kingsley Porter reçut un
appréciable renfort; la controverse en fut ranimée; elle n'est pas encore tout à
fait close. Elle déborda d'ailleurs le domaine assez étroit dans lequel elle était
primitivement enfermée. De la sculpture, on en vint à l'architecture, puis à la
peinture et à l'iconographie.

Et ainsi commença de s'affermir, dans l'opinion commune des historiens de
l'art, l'influence prépondérante de l'abbaye de Cluny. Nul n'a contribué plus
puissamment à ce retournement progressif de la doctrine commune en France que
l'un des élèves de Kingsley Porter, le minutieux et savant Kenneth Conant, par
son exploration méthodique du sol dévasté et des ruines de la grande abbatiale
de saint Hugues.

Quelles sont les conséquences de tout ce mouvement? D'abord la Bourgogne
romane a pris ou repris dans l'étude de l'art roman en France, et même hors de
France, une valeur plus considérable. La critique de ses monuments a été re-
nouvelée, la chronologie de ses églises plus exactement définie, les rapports de
ses édifices religieux et de leur ornementation avec Cluny [4] plus rigoureusement

---

[2] *Gazette des Beaux-Arts*, août-septembre 1920.

[3] "Notes sur la sculpture romane en Bourgogne," dans la *Gazette des Beaux-Arts*, juillet-août 1922.

[4] La réédition récente du livre capital de Jean Virey, *Les Églises romanes de l'ancien diocèse de Mâcon*
(Mâcon, Protat, 1934), et l'ouvrage nouveau de Marcel et Christiane Dickson, *Les Églises romanes de l'ancien*

et plus scientifiquement déduits et établis; tout cet effort interne, si l'on peut ainsi parler, a vraiment eu pour origine les travaux de Porter; pour en mesurer l'autorité, il a bien fallu revoir les textes, réviser les classifications anciennes, et savoir comment s'opérait la concordance des sources écrites et des monuments construits. Mieux connue, la Bourgogne romane, architecture, sculpture et peinture même, a offert pour les études d'archéologie comparée un terme plus assuré et plus critiquement vérifié. Si l'on veut bien considérer que notre connaissance du XIᵉ et du XIIᵉ siècle demeure encore souvent bien vague et bien incertaine, ce premier bénéfice n'est pas négligeable.

Mais il n'est pas le seul. Tant que Cluny demeurait inclus et comme enfermé dans l'école romane de Bourgogne, comme un simple élément de cette école, un peu plus brillant que d'autres sans doute, mais sans véritable originalité propre, il était loisible de n'attacher à ce prodigieux édifice qu'une sorte d'intérêt de curiosité. Et il n'était vraiment pas nécessaire de se référer à l'abbatiale de saint Hugues comme à un de ces monuments qui déterminent une évolution générale, qui sont, si l'on peut ainsi s'exprimer, l'un des pôles de l'histoire générale de l'art en Occident. Il n'est plus aujourd'hui possible de garder cette attitude négative. La connaissance définitive et complète de Cluny importe essentiellement à l'idée que nous pouvons nous faire de l'art médiéval, de sa formation, et de son développement.

Et par voie de conséquence, puisque Cluny n'est pas simplement un monument bourguignon comme les autres, se pose la question de ses origines architecturales. D'où vient cette église? Où le constructeur en a-t-il pris le modèle? D'où en a-t-il tiré les éléments? De France, ou hors de France? Même problème et même recherche pour la sculpture. Il ne suffit plus de comparer étroitement Cluny à Toulouse et à Moissac, de s'ingénier à démontrer simplement la primauté du Languedoc sur la Bourgogne, ou inversement, d'affirmer que Moissac et Toulouse sont aux origines de la renaissance de la sculpture en France et en Occident. Il faut bien rechercher si, comme pour l'architecture, d'autres sources ne seraient pas à explorer; en particulier si la brillante civilisation rhénane, issue des traditions de l'empire carolingien et de la dynastie ottonienne n'aurait pas fourni quelque apport; si les abbés de Cluny n'ont rien tiré de leurs voyages constants en Italie, en Lombardie, à travers les Alpes et dans le bassin du Rhin. Les limites de l'investigation reculent et s'étendent. Lorsque le tour d'horizon aura été achevé, peut-être pourra-t-on substituer à des formules faciles des démonstrations précises, et prendre de l'histoire de nos églises romanes, et de la plus magnifique d'entre elles, une connaissance plus approfondie et plus exacte. C'est bien en vérité une page de la civilisation occidentale qui s'écrit ainsi. Mais qui, pour l'écrire, a mis la plume à la main des archéologues et des érudits? Qui a contraint aux révisions nécessaires? La fécondité de l'action ne se mesure pas à quelques erreurs certaines, mais à l'intensité du travail créé, et à la valeur des notions nouvelles que ce travail a permis et permettra encore d'acquérir.

---

diocèse de Chalon (Mâcon, Protat, 1935) ont reçu tous deux un sous-titre tout à fait symptomatique: *Cluny et sa région.*

THE THIRD CHURCH AT CLUNY

KENNETH JOHN CONANT

ARTHUR KINGSLEY PORTER'S name will never be forgotten by those who are concerned with Cluny studies because of his beautifully appreciative writing on the role of the great Burgundian abbey, and because excavation of its site was suggested — indeed, necessitated — by the questions raised in Mr. Porter's bold solution of the Cluny problem. It is a work of what he called "creeping scholarship" to follow where his intuition led the way. A careful review now in progress, based on evidence accumulated since Mr. Porter wrote in 1923, seems to confirm his vision of Cluny as the key and culminating point of the artistic revival of the eleventh and early twelfth centuries. The present study, generously sponsored by the Mediaeval Academy of America, is so detailed that no definitive publication can be made for a number of years, though current results are presented in the Academy's journal, *Speculum* (July 1928 ff.). The older church and monastery buildings at Cluny are as yet imperfectly known; however, secure results have been achieved in the investigation of the wonderful third church, for which Mr. Porter cared so much, and these results are here summarized, with the Academy's permission, in this volume published to honor Mr. Porter's memory.

The church called Cluny III formed a part of a general rebuilding which took place at the monastery under the great sixth abbot, Hugh of Semur. The buildings raised by his predecessors, Mayeul (954–994) and Odilo (994–1049), and known to us through the Farfa Consuetudinary, proved insufficient for the growing community, which had about seventy professed monks in 1042, about two hundred in 1083, and about three hundred in 1109 at the death of Abbot Hugh. For them a vast new infirmary was built about 1075–1080; the refectory was rebuilt on a large scale, probably between 1077 and 1083, and a new oratory of the Virgin almost as large as the old abbey church of *c.* 955–981 was dedicated in the autumn of 1085. Excavated foundations show that the masonry of this Lady Chapel was very much like that of the new abbey church, and it may be that the construction crew was transferred thither for preparatory works as soon as the chapel was finished. (Figs. 1, 2.)

As Peter the Venerable says, the great church was begun by Alfonso VI, King of Spain, on an admirable plan which distinguished it from all other churches on the globe; and it is assumed that Alfonso's generosity came as a thank-offering for the capture of Toledo, May 25, 1085. The building which resulted was a magnificent epitome of Romanesque architecture, based, to be sure, on earlier progress in Burgundy, but entirely transcending any local style, and eminently worthy of the powerful and widely ramified Cluniac Benedictines, then at the zenith of their influence and effectiveness. The design had an im-

perial majesty of scale, but its variety and its skillful combination were truly
French in spirit, and so remarkable that even the earliest account of it (1113) is
tinged with the miraculous. Gunzo, former abbot of Baume retired at Cluny,
is said to have seen the plan in a vision. It is easy to imagine that the Cluniacs
were put on their mettle by the recent accomplishment at Montecassino, visited
by Abbot Hugh in November 1083, when the splendid Desiderian monastery
was newly built, and when Desiderius' notable school of carvers, painters, and
other artisans was ready to be drawn upon. Hezelo, the architect who put
Abbot Hugh's building into execution, came, however, from Liège.

Since it is possible that the preparatory work for the great new church at Cluny
began as early as 1086, the recorded *fundatio* may mark a ceremonial beginning
of the superstructure, following the analogy of Santiago cathedral, where the first
beginnings go back to *c.* 1075, and the ceremonial beginning dates from V Ides of
July 1078. Similarly, two dates are given for Peterborough Cathedral — March
12, 1117, and March 8, 1118. There is no precise information regarding
the state of the works in Cluny at the date of the constituent act, II Kalends of
October (September 30) 1088.

This must be the approximate date of a letter of Alfonso VI, assigned to 1060
by Baluze and to 1080 by Bruel, in which the King, "engaged in pacifying the
cities of Spain," probably after the capture of Toledo, refers to an archbishop
(probably Bernard of Toledo, elected December 18, 1085) and pledges all de-
sired aid toward the church which Abbot Hugh has under construction. The
bearer of this letter was charged with a gift of ten thousand talents, perhaps the
equivalent of some thirty-five thousand dollars in gold. Hugh and Alfonso met
in Burgos at Eastertide 1090, and thenceforth Alfonso doubled the former annual
tribute to Cluny, paying two thousand gold *mancales* (some two hundred ounces,
now worth seven thousand dollars) yearly as a thank-offering for his success in
establishing himself as a ruler in Spain; and he required his successors to continue
the subsidy. The buying power of the grants, though large, is not easy to determine. A somewhat unsatisfactory reference in the Gallia Christiana (IV,
col. 1132: *sic narrat Bertholdus ad an. 1093*) indicates a great gift from Alfonso VI
in the year named. Certainly he was the chief patron of the building until his
death (July 1, 1109), for Abbot Hugh speaks of the new church *quam ipse de
propriis facultatibus construxisse videtur.*

The great later patron of the church was Henry I, King of England from
1100 to 1135. In 1129 he made a grant of one hundred marks of silver annually
from the revenues of London and Lincoln, and two manors, worth a hundred
marks a year, were granted at the same time. The first-named grant was confirmed by Innocent II at Rouen in 1131 and commuted for the manor of Let-
comb Regis in 1136. According to a petition of Abbot Jean de Bourbon to
Henry VI (1458), Henry I sent special gifts of money and jewels — presumably
in the interval 1101–1129? — but nothing is known in detail concerning these
contributions. The value of two hundred marks is given as £133 4*s.*

Alfonso VI was connected with the English royal family through his betrothed, Agnes, for whose patroness the northernmost chapel of the minor transept at Cluny was named. King Stephen's son, Henry de Blois, was sent to Cluny about 1110 and brought up there. Henry I recalled him to be abbot of Glastonbury in 1126, and three years later he became bishop of Winchester. He and Henry I's daughter Matilda were great benefactors of the abbey.

Late writers, Robert de Torigny (1139) and Ralph de Sully (1176), attribute the larger part of the church to Henry I's generosity. Their statements can be reconciled with Abbot Hugh's on the basis that the most essential parts of the edifice were finished by Alfonso, but conspicuous works like the narthex, the western part of the nave, and several of the towers owed much to Henry I.

The remains of this noblest of Romanesque buildings have been carefully investigated by the Mediaeval Academy's mission. A new master plan of the excavations, set up by Mr. Frédéric Palmer and checked with utmost care, gives trustworthy information about the construction campaigns and the dimensions. A value of 187.31 metres is indicated for the exterior length of the church, measured on the axis from a point between the western tower buttresses to the plinth of the central absidiole. It is interesting to note that the clear interior length of St. Peter's in Rome is officially given as 186.36 metres, whereas the comparable dimension at Cluny was 125.2 metres. The master plan discloses several axial bends marking out irregular sections which indicate successive moments in the construction, thus making it clear that the church proper was built in two main campaigns, and the antechurch in two more, of which the chronology is indicated in Figure 2.

Construction undoubtedly began with the chevet (Fig. 1) and the north flank of the church. The first major campaign included the sanctuary, both transepts, and five bays of the nave. Indications in the plantation of the piers, in the buttress system, and in the molding profiles show that the work was done in three nearly equal parts, and probably with little or no real interruption. There is contemporary evidence for the remarkable speed with which the building went forward; in the fall of 1095, seven years after the *fundatio*, the sanctuary was usable and perhaps complete (Fig. 3). Five of its altars, belonging to the liturgical group of principal or special altars (*de praecipuis*) of the Cluniac use, are mentioned as ready — *parata sunt* — on VIII Kalends of November (October 25) 1095, when three were dedicated by members of the suite of Pope Urban II and two by the pontiff himself. Urban dedicated the matutinal altar in the eastern part of the sanctuary to the particular honor of St. Mary, and he dedicated the high altar in honor of Our Lord Jesus Christ's Resurrection, the blessed and ever-virgin Mary, the holy Apostles Peter and Paul, and the Protomartyr Stephen, stipulating that the final dedication of the building should take place on the same day of the year as had this consecration of five altars. A lost inscription in the chapel of St. James recorded that the altar there was built by the Cluniac monk and bishop Dalmatius of Santiago. Strictly, this would imply a gift made after the transfer of the see of Iria to Compostela (December 5, 1095), but the dating is very close in any event, for the bishop died on December 13, 1095, after a pontificate of only two years. No other altar of the chevet is mentioned in the earliest sources, although there were seven in all.

Surviving fragments of two or three of these altars have been identified. They are beautiful architectural carvings which could hardly be improvised for a dedication, and would not normally be installed until the heavy structural work of the apse was completed. The minor transept had places for six altars which were not ready for consecration; probably the transept itself was not entirely ready to receive them for a year or two. It is most reasonable to suppose that the ceremony of October 25, 1095, resembled a Greek ᾽ανοιξηθύρια, when an unfinished but usable church building is thrown open for worship, and the liturgy performed at its altar, although there is no anointing of walls and columns as at the dedication of a completed structure.

On the apse vault above the matutinal altar at Cluny there was an impressive painting of Christ in glory, with the symbols of the Evangelists and the celestial choir. Its precise date is unknown, but since the studies of MM. Virey, Oursel, and Mercier, we know that painters using the same methods and materials executed a similar design of great beauty at the near-by Cluniac obedience of Berzé-la-Ville about the year 1104. The work was Byzantine in character and showed Italian influence, according to M. Mercier.

There is quite general agreement that the great transept at Cluny (Fig. 4) was finished about 1100, except the large towers. Pedro de Roda, Cluniac reforming bishop of Pamplona from 1084 to 1114, consecrated the still surviving chapel of St. Gabriel in the square tower. The bishop visited Cluny between 1094 and 1104 (probably in 1100) bearing gifts from Peter I of Aragon, and his own gifts, as shown by Miss Rose Graham.

Abbot Hugh devoted the masses of an altar of the special group *de praecipuis* to the builder-king Alfonso in a document which appears to mark the beginning of the new church as center for the monastery's worship. There is no mention of spiritual benefits for the queen, as in the charter of 1090; thus the later charter may belong to the period of Alfonso's widowerhood (*c.* 1102–1105); in any event, it is not later than 1107 or 1108.

We are informed that services in the new church were disturbed in the time of Abbot Hugh by visitors to a healing spring which is still represented by a well in the nave of the great church; we know also from Gilo's account (1113) that the abbot was buried in a *mausoleum* beyond the matutinal altar a few days after his death (April 28, 1109).

It will be observed that with the construction of the Porta Galilea the new nave could be entered processionally from the old cloister in a normal way. This was doubtless the goal of the first major construction campaign (1088–1108).

But before the death of Abbot Hugh preparations had probably been made to build the original west front of the church, for Abbot Hugh is connected by legend with the Great Portal, and one of its sculptors clearly belongs to the group which created the oldest sculptures in the sanctuary (1088–1095), whereas another certainly worked on the great abbot's tomb (*c.* 1109 — Figs. 5, 6, 7). However, the southern part of the façade is out of line. From this fact it may be suspected that the west portals and the façade were completed after an interruption, and probably after Abbot Hugh's death. It remained for Abbot Pontius (1109–1122) to clear away old structures on the south side of the nave, to complete the aisles (about 1109–1115) and (about 1115–1120) the remaining bays of the high vault, involving a length of from thirty-five to seventy metres. Thus the second construction campaign was brought to a close.

The scheme just presented takes into account many peculiarities of layout revealed in the excavations, and it reconciles several difficult texts, as explained below.

(1) The main part of the church, though incomplete, must have reached as far as the west front in the time of Abbot Hugh. The familiar statement, "He raised so great a basilica in twenty years that if an emperor had built it in so short a time the accomplishment would be considered worthy of admiration" — written in 1113 or 1114 by Abbot Hugh's biographer, the monk Gilo — was echoed by Bishop Hildebert of le Mans and others who knew the church during the whole decade following Abbot Hugh's death. However, Gilo, in speaking of the capacity of the church, says that it is suitable to accommodate a thousand of the brethren, making no special reference to length, or to a multitude which might be gathered in the nave west of the monks' choir. This permits the supposition that the nave was not fully in use in 1113.

(2) An inscription of c. 1740 set up in the church gave the building as "the work of twenty-five years"; according to this it was brought to some measure of completion in 1113, unless the double interval 1088–1108 plus 1125–1130 was meant.

(3) Geoffrey, bishop of Amiens (1104–1115), consecrated an altar in 1104 or some few years later.

(4) A new cloister walk and the Chapel of the Abbot were under construction south of the nave from about 1115 onward, for the chapel was consecrated on August 16, 1118, by Guy de Bourgogne, the future Pope Calixtus II. Certainly the advanced state of the nave permitted artisans to be transferred to this new work, for the monk Hugh, writing to Abbot Pontius in 1121, says that since the new church, wonderfully wrought, "was constructed in his days" he ordered the older one (Cluny II) to be demolished and the cloister to be enlarged.

(5) Calixtus II was not far from Cluny on October 25, 1119, engaged with Abbot Pontius on the interviews which preceded the Council of Reims (October 27–30). A detour and a slight change in the Council's date would have enabled Calixtus to dedicate the great church, if it had been ready, on the day specified by Urban II. Possibly this means that the vault was not complete in October 1119.

(6) Peter the Venerable, writing after 1130 of Pope Innocent II, states that several of his predecessors would have liked to consecrate the church. Pope Calixtus' visit was made from December 29 or 30, 1119, to January 7, 1120. He canonized Abbot Hugh at that time.

(7) St. Bernard, in his Apology to William of St. Thierry in 1124, writes of *immoderatas longitudines* in the Cluniac churches: by inference in the mother church at Cluny itself.

(8) Orderic Vital, who visited Cluny in 1132, says in his Ecclesiastical History that the gigantic nave was "recently built" in 1125 when it collapsed. No one was hurt in the fall, a circumstance which suggests that the bays over the monks' choir were not involved, but rather the newly finished open nave west of them. The failure was probably due to the over-bold design of the clearstory, which lacked lateral buttressing; but there is also the possibility of hasty construction, the too early removal of centering, and the use of unsuitable second-hand material from the demolition of Cluny II. The vault may have brought down some parts of the clearstory and triforium with it when it fell, but the aisles were far too sturdy to be affected.

Only the nave of the old church Cluny II was in fact demolished under Pontius. This venerable sanctuary was begun shortly after 954 by Abbot Mayeul, coadjutor of Abbot Aymard, who was buried there in 963. It had enshrined relics of SS. Peter and Paul since its dedication (February 14, 981). Flanking the group of three middle apses were side compartments known as *cryptae* where the monks could retire for ascetic devotion. To this purpose the whole apse was assigned by Pontius, and the necessary rebuilding was apparently complete by 1121, if not before (Fig. 2). The old apse survived until about 1718, the transept until shortly before 1682, when the old galilee was also demolished; thus it happened that the crossing tower of the old church, the galilee, and one of its two towers were represented in Louis Prevost's view of Cluny, made about 1670. This was republished in the Album of the Millénaire de Cluny as Plate II and is reproduced here, in part, as Figure 8 (see N). It may be said parenthetically that present studies based on the excavations, although not yet ready for publication, clearly show that Cluny II furnished the inspiration for the general lines of such Burgundian churches as St. Vincent des Prés, Chapaize, Charlieu, and Gigny; thus we have an earlier *école clunisienne* to put beside the familiar group of monuments radiated from the third church. There is little evidence for an upper story in the galilee of Cluny II; nevertheless it bore some resemblance to that of St. Philibert at Tournus (*c.* 950 or 960–*c.* 1019).

The galilee continued to serve as the setting for the processional station between the cloister and the monastic church, even though Cluny III had replaced Cluny II. Its function of vestibule before the main door of the old church probably suggested the construction of the narthex which served as vestibule for Cluny III.

A third campaign of construction begins for the great church with this narthex, which represents a definite augmentation of the original scheme of the building. Perhaps it was begun as early as 1118, when Pontius finished his Chapel of the Abbot, but the initiative may have come from Abbot Peter the Venerable (1122–1156). The general design of the façade and certain peculiarities in the excavated masonry show that as late as 1109 no antechurch was projected. But we may be sure that the third major building campaign, involving this narthex, was under way by 1125, for the interior elevation (Fig. 9) of its two easternmost bays shows that originally a pointed barrel vault above a clearstory like that of the church nave, was intended. A ribbed groin vault with ramping penetrations was built instead, and provided with flying buttresses of archaic form, obviously as a result of the lessons taught by the crash of 1125. It seems likely that the nave had been repaired and its vault strengthened: it is possible that two bays of the narthex had been enclosed, when Innocent II performed the definitive consecration of the church on October 25, 1130. But the dedication was to some extent a political gesture of Peter the Venerable, who wished to advertise his support of Pope Innocent II against the schismatic Anacletus II, a former monk of Cluny. This we gather from Peter's biographer, Abbot Ralph de Sully, who wrote in 1173–1176. Insofar as the dedication was a matter of politics we are uncertain that the church was fully ready for the ceremony.

Ralph de Sully speaks of the church as if it were wholly built by Peter the Venerable. Most if not all of the antechurch was built by him; it was surely he who repaired the ruin in the nave and built two or three of the major towers. These and the narthex were probably under construction in 1132, for one of the new statutes of the Order drawn up in that year, and codified in 1146, mentions the *chantier* of the church; silence was not required there. It may be inferred that the portions under construction were isolated from the older parts and also that works were in progress in 1146. Perhaps a dozen years (1135–1147) were sufficient to carry the three western bays of the narthex to completion, in spite of the misfortunes of the abbey at the period. Indeed, one of the petitions of Jean de Bourbon to Henry VI of England (1458) says that the abbey was heavily in debt on account of the building before the return of Henry de Blois, nephew of Henry I and bishop of Winchester (1149), who then conferred immeasurable benefits on the abbey by putting its economy in order, making necessary loans without interest, and bestowing great gifts. In 1155 he brought his treasure to Cluny, and he did considerable building. He had passed his boyhood and young manhood at Cluny while the great church nave was being constructed, and was an intimate friend of Peter the Venerable. We may fairly surmise that if anything remained to be completed in the antechurch after 1149, he carried it forward or finished it. He administered the abbey from the passing of Peter the Venerable (December 25, 1156) to the accession of a successor (1158) and returned more than once before his death (1171).

We hear of an active prior, Otger, under Abbot William d'Angleterre, but no work on the fabric of the church is credited to him (1176–1179). It was a beginning of better days for the abbey; conditions were further ameliorated under Abbots Hugh of Clermont (1180–1204) and Hugh of Anjou (1204–1207). The still unviolated tomb of this latter Hugh was visited, but not profaned, in the course of the excavations carried out by the Mediaeval Academy of America. Abbot Gerald of Flanders (1215–1220) was generous, and under him the abbey was again prosperous. His successor, Roland of Hainault (1220–1228), built or rebuilt the west wall of the narthex, which was thus provided with a round-arched Gothic portal, a Gothic triforium, and a Gothic rose window; and the vault received attention, if that was needful. Perhaps some of this work was due to an earthquake which occurred in 1215. In the inscription of *c.* 1740 affixed to the wall of the church near the entrance to the sacristy, Abbot Roland was wrongly credited with building the entire narthex, where older walls of Romanesque construction may even now be seen. The narthex portal was restored (perhaps merely painted) under Abbot Eudes de la Perrière (1424–1457), and it may be that a handsome polychrome tonsured head recovered in the excavations belonged to the statue of St. Stephen on the north jamb of this exterior portal.

The fourth major building campaign of the church was concerned with the construction of a pair of western towers which formed no part of the original project of the church; nevertheless, they did carry on the tradition of the towers of Cluny II, and they were executed in a curious belated Romanesque style for harmony with the older parts of Cluny III. The south tower, begun perhaps before 1200, was carried up and roofed by Abbot Pierre de Chastellus (1322–1342); its mate and a wooden porch between the towers were built by Eudes de la Perrière, thus finally completing the enlarged scheme of the church.

A certain amount of rebuilding and three minor additions on the north side of the church remain to be noticed. The chapel of St. Orens was added to the northern great transept at an undetermined period in the twelfth or thirteenth century; a porch was built for the Porta Germanorum in the thirteenth or fourteenth, and a line of flying buttresses was added to support the aisle vaults (which were perhaps themselves repaired) by Abbot Jean de Bourbon (1457–1481). The chapel of St. Denis had meanwhile been rebuilt in the Gothic style (between 1351 and 1360, or between 1389 and 1397?); so also the chapel of St. Martin (about 1420?) and the chapel of St. Martial (between 1322 and 1342). Jean de Bourbon himself rebuilt the curious chapel of St. Eutrope, while the corresponding chapel of St. Agatha at the other end of the minor transept was rebuilt under Abbot Emmanuel-Théodose de la Tour d'Auvergne about the year 1700. Eudes de la Perrière began a campaign of works on the towers in the middle part of the church; he worked at the north transeptal tower. Before the end of Jean de Bourbon's abbacy all four major towers had received steep pyramidal roofs. Their rapid slope and their covering of slate were out of harmony with the original design, but nevertheless very chic and handsome.

It is not clear when the high vault was strengthened by blocking up many of the windows, including two-thirds of the clearstory. Perhaps this occurred in the eighteenth century, when general repairs were undertaken, and the new monastery was built (*c.* 1718–1789); but would Mabillon in 1682 have spoken of the church as *subobscura* if it still had over three hundred windows?

The addition of a belfry stage to the stair tower of the south great transept (1750), the reconstruction of the central spire, the refreshing of the whole exterior by a coat of stucco; whitewash, minor repairs, and a general renewal of the liturgical furniture on the interior complete the tale of works done on the church by the monks in the eighteenth century. The mournful fragments which survived the demolition of 1798–1815 have had fair care and some restoration since 1823.

Technical studies on aspects of the third church at Cluny which are important for the general history of the fine arts are being carried on in conjunction with the work of discovering its forms and chronology. Thus it will be necessary to investigate the relationship of the reconstructions of 1125–1130 to the development of Gothic architecture. It may be that the new ribbed high vault of the narthex was one of the earliest of its kind in France; moreover, it was abutted by pierced buttresses over the aisle roofs, as was the reconstructed vault of the nave, where a complete range of such buttresses was built. Even though pointed arches, ribbed vaults, and archaic flying buttresses may have been present together at Cluny, it is nevertheless certain that an essential element of Gothic structure, the cut-stone vaulting-web with a surface of double curvature, did not develop in Burgundy.

The great portal at Cluny, dated 1109–1115 by common accord, was clearly the first medieval church doorway of majestic scale which was decorated with elaborate figure sculpture arranged according to a lucid iconographical scheme. The fragments recovered by excavation make it perfectly evident that the carvings possessed rare beauty, and also the monumental quality required of the elements in a composition which measured about twenty metres in height and fourteen metres in width. There is sufficient data for a satisfactory restoration of the gorgeous polychromy. Color and reliefs are both being studied in minute detail by Miss Helen Kleinschmidt with a view to constructing an accurate painted model. Much information comes from a description, a drawing (Fig. 9), and an engraving, all made before the destruction of this part of the church by gunpowder on May 8, 1810.

The uppermost register of the portal was an arcade enclosing painted figures of eight abbots. Their somewhat exposed situation raises the question as to whether they were a part of the original scheme, or whether, indeed, the portal was painted at all before it was closed in by the narthex. Except for the doorvalves, the rest of the decoration was in relief. The spandrels each had two figures of Evangelists, and the angles of the tympanum were filled by their symbols; the eagle of St. John has been preserved, and is in the Louvre (Fig. 5). A series of medallions on an outer archivolt contained heads of the four and twenty Elders and of God the Father, while an inner archivolt was made up of fifteen horseshoe cusps, each enclosing an angel. The vast central tympanum contained a figure of Christ enthroned in an oval glory upheld by two standing angels, and set off by two plunging seraphs underneath. The lintel had a Virgin in the center, with one of the Men in White and six Apostles to either side, posed to show that the Christ above was considered as part of an Ascension scene. Here we have an obvious reminiscence of the symbolical Galilee station before the door of the older church, and this same processional station of the Cluniac liturgy would seem to account for the choice of an Ascension for the tympanum relief at Charlieu, oldest known occurrence of this form (about 1090). The motive was elaborated according to the Acts of the Apostles (1: 9–11) at Cluny, and according to St. Matthew's Gospel (28: 19 ff.) at Vézelay. At Cluny the ends of the lintel were carved with the visit of the Holy Women to the tomb (left) and perhaps Christ in Limbo (right). The door-valves were of painted wood, but probably arranged in panels with figures, like contemporary bronze and niello doors.

The stonework of the portal was beautifully painted in tempera, with a predominance of earthen colors. The background of lintel, tympanum, and cusped archivolt was cobalt blue, and the figures were brought out by painting in natural tints within a restricted palette like that used in the apse of Berzé-la-Ville, or in contemporary illuminated manuscripts. Some of the carvings in the upper part of the design were enriched by gilding. A considerable use was made of red: the Christ, set against an oval *mandorla* of orange and gold, was vested with a deep red mantle shaded in green. The wide channels containing border ornaments were brightened with red. Leafage and other channeled borders were colored green, and rosettes appeared in red, ochre, and green. Marbled effects were used, and apparently the flanking shafts were painted also. Modulations were made sometimes by mixing the basic pigments and sometimes by overlay.

The architect of the Cluny portal was obviously indebted to earlier French, Roman, and Moorish designs. But the painting was doubtless influenced by the Cassinese school and so were the architectural forms. Perhaps novelty and beauty dictated the choice, but sentimental ties with St. Benedict's own monastery on that noble south-Italian hill doubtless counted for something. Portals like that of the cathedral of Salerno (1084–1099) and others which issued from Montecassino (1066–1071) offer likely forerunners for many features of the Cluny design. Moreover, the pointed arch and vault came, in all likelihood, to Cluny from Montecassino, whither they were brought by Amalfitan builders inspired by Moslem architecture. Two of their vaults dated about 1075 still exist in company with bullseyes like those which flanked the apse at Cluny (Figs. 3, 10). The interior elevation of the apse itself was inspired from Italy also: a drawing which came to light in 1935 (Fig. 11) shows pilasters and medallions having only-too-obvious connections with the nave of S. Paolo fuori le Mura at Rome. From this venerable church came relics of SS. Peter and Paul to Cluny II shortly before 981, and there the great churchman Hildebrand was prior before his elevation to the papacy in 1077.

The most conservative French archaeologists teach that the Cluniac primacy in sculpture was inaugurated by the carvings of the gigantic portal with its multitude of figures, rather than by the lovely capitals of the sanctuary at Cluny. That Cluny created the accomplished twelfth-century sculptural style, as Mr. Porter believed, is now generally admitted, and the question of his date (1095) for the ambulatory capitals is henceforth one of detail, but the chronology of these capitals must nevertheless be settled on account of the importance and beauty of the pieces (Figs. 11, 12, 13, 14).

All of the evidence gathered in the excavations and in the course of the new studies has, without exception, fortified the thesis and dating proposed by Mr. Porter. His opinion, a sensational novelty in 1920, is now predominant, and may be considered as almost established — especially since the excavations of 1936 and 1938 have yielded fragments of the cloister built by Abbot Pontius in 1115–1118, precisely the date ascribed by conservative archaeologists to the sanctuary capitals. For the style of Pontius' carvings is more advanced — is, indeed, the forerunner of the style of the outer portal at Charlieu (Fig. 15). The character of the stone, the manner of cutting it, the use of drill-holes, and the bobbin profiles of the bells all differ from the corresponding features of the great capitals, and the latter are unquestionably older.

Several other lines of proof have developed since Mr. Porter presented his case. The prototype found at S. Paolo fuori le Mura is a powerful new argument for the artistic unity of the Cluny sanctuary. Its structural unity has been proved by the foundations, the profiles, and the materials used, as well as by the discovery of impost blocks which would surely have betrayed traces of a replacement or a recutting of the capitals (Figs. 16, 17). Now it is admitted on all sides that the blocks for the capitals were set by 1095, and that the imposts above were original. If, as some conservative archaeologists suppose, the capitals were placed but not finished when the sanctuary was first built, then certainly the soffits of the preserved impost blocks ought to show traces of the final finishing. There are no such traces. Not only do the tops of the capitals show strokes which could not be made after the impost was placed (Fig. 18), but the careful rubbing process which gave the sculptures their final delicate surface was in several cases carried up tangent to the top of the capital, obviously before the impost blocks were set in position (Fig. 19). Thus the capitals were studio works, as their delicate scale indicates. They were provided with lewis holes for handling, so that it was possible to place them without danger to their delicate detail. The boldly overhanging impost blocks, once they were in position, provided excellent shelter against accidents, and the slenderness of the columns suggests that the ambulatory arches were built immediately for stability's sake. These are the essentials of the proof that the Cluny capitals were carved when the great apse was building, and consequently before Urban II's consecration of 1095.

Precise studies on the portal (1109–1115) have demonstrated that the figures there were not relatively flat and calligraphic like those on the great capitals, but were instead practically in the round, and much more elongated than the figures on the sanctuary carvings. That alone is enough to prove that the sanctuary carvings are earlier, as they would be if the sculpture was carried along *pari passu* with the building in the natural way. The excavations have yielded fragments of the decorative carvings of the ambulatory wall (Fig. 20) and these works prove to be in exactly the same style as the great capitals, made of the same stone, carved and finished in the same way. One could perhaps imagine scaffolding put up (to a height of nine metres, by the way) for a later carving of the eight great capitals, but it stretches credulity to suppose that scaffolding would also be put up, long after the original construction, for the numerous small sculptures of the ambulatory wall (Figs. 12, 21). Iconographically these smaller sculptures, representing Vices and a Psychomachia, are a foil to the Virtues of the great capitals; and the whole group, large and small, must have been in position, and carved, by 1095.

Is it more natural to suppose that the accomplished twelfth-century sculptural style originated in the sanctuary than that it sprang into existence with the vast portal? Many archaeologists have been accustomed to think of the wonderful Moissac portal as such an apparition. The minor sculptures of the Cluny ambulatory offer a much better explanation. The grace and finish of these sculptures suggest ivory carving; the rubbing process by which the surfaces were finished is actually used on ivory. The minor sculptures were a natural place for experiment and practice in the new style, as a preparation for the far larger and more conspicuous compositions which encircled the altar. The sculptor must have been familiar with fine illuminations, with ivory and marble carvings, with stuccoes and metalwork. Such works were surely represented among the treasures gathered at Cluny; however, it is not past belief that a brilliant young sculptor was sent out as a journeyman to form his style. Whether German, Italian, or Byzantine works lie back of his achievement, surely it was a great personal creation, which he transmitted to his fellow workers and their followers at Cluny and far afield. His rightful place is with the architects and the painters who first labored to create a church of surpassing beauty at Cluny.

None denies that their glorious fabric deserved the beautiful words of the chronicler, "If it could be believed that human abiding-places of this sort are pleasing to the dwellers on high, then this would be called a place where angels tread," and the joy of bringing its lineaments back from the place where exiled beauty dwells has sustained the Mediaeval Academy's mission in the course of a long and intricate archaeological study.

FIG. 1. LALLEMAND VIEW OF THE ABBEY (*c.* 1787)

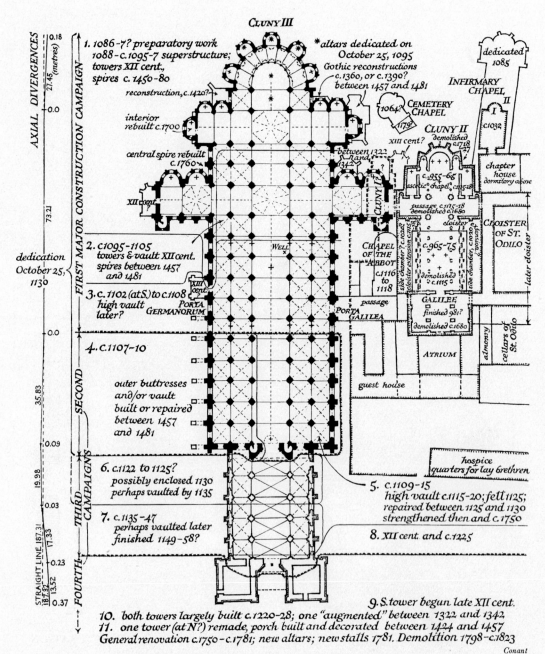

CLUNY III

1. 1086-7? preparatory work
1088-c.1095-7 superstructure;
towers XII cent.,
spires c.1450-80

reconstruction, c.1420?

interior
rebuilt c.1700

central spire rebuilt
c.1760

XII cent.

2. c.1095-1105
towers & vault XII cent.
spires between 1457
and 1481

3. c.1102 (at S.) to c.1108
high vault
later?

4. c.1107-10

outer buttresses
and/or vault
built or repaired
between 1457
and 1481

6. c.1122 to 1125?
possibly enclosed 1130
perhaps vaulted by 1135

7. c.1135-47
perhaps vaulted later
finished 1149-58?

AXIAL DIVERGENCES
0.18
27.46 (metres)
0.0

FIRST MAJOR CONSTRUCTION CAMPAIGN
73.21

dedication
October 25,
1130

SECOND
0.0

35.83

THIRD CAMPAIGNS
0.09

19.98
0.03

FOURTH
17.33

STRAIGHT LINE 187.31
0.23
13.52
187.31
0.37

WELL

XIII cent.
PORTA
GERMANORUM

PORTA
GALILEA

passage

CHAPEL OF THE ABBOT
c.1116
to
1118

*altars dedicated on
October 25, 1095
Gothic reconstructions
c.1360, or c.1390?
between 1457 and 1481

CEMETERY CHAPEL
1064?
XIII cent?
1791

CLUNY II
demolished
c.1718-27

between 1322
and
1342

c.955-68
ascetic° chapel c.1518

passage c.1115-18
demolished c.1680

cloister

c.965-75

Demolished
c.1115

GALILEE
finished 981?
demolished c.1680

ATRIUM

guest house

INFIRMARY CHAPEL
dedicated
1085
II
I
c.1032

CLUNY II
demolished
c.1718-27

chapter house
dormitory above

side chamber? c.1002
cloister extension c.1156

side chamber, cross c.1156
& cloister c.1090?

CLOISTER OF ST. ODILO

later cloister

almonry

cellars of St. Odilo

hospice
quarters for lay brethren

5. c.1109-15
high vault c.1115-20; fell 1125;
repaired between 1125 and 1130
strengthened then and c.1750

8. XII cent. and c.1225

9. S. tower begun late XII cent.

10. both towers largely built c.1220-28; one "augmented" between 1322 and 1342.
11. one tower (at N?) remade, porch built and decorated between 1424 and 1457
General renovation c.1750-c.1781; new altars; new stalls 1781. Demolition 1798-c.1823

Conant

FIG. 2. ANALYTICAL PLAN OF CLUNY II AND III
Tenth and earlier eleventh century buildings in ragged line; original plan of Cluny III, full black; augmentations of Cluny III, double line; reconstructions and other auxiliary structures, single line

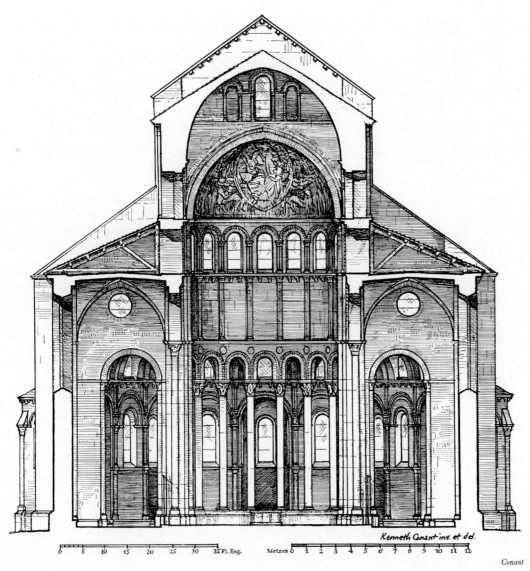

FIG. 3. TRANSVERSE SECTION OF THE SANCTUARY, PRELIMINARY RESTORATION

Conant

FIG. 4. TRANSVERSE SECTION OF THE NAVE, PRELIMINARY RESTORATION

FIG. 5. EAGLE FROM THE TYMPANUM
LOUVRE, PARIS

Loury photo.

FIG. 6. HEAD OF WINGED MAN FROM TYMPANUM, COMPARED WITH HEAD OF
EVE FROM CAPITAL 10

Conant

FIG. 7. ELEVATION OF ORIGINAL WEST FRONT, PRELIMINARY RESTORATION

FIG. 8. PREVOST VIEW (*c.* 1670)

From left to right: Tour Ronde, Infirmary, Infirmary Chapel, Dormitory, western tower of Galilee, Galilee, crossing tower Cluny II (N); entrance arcade to Atrium of Cluny II (I–I), Apse Cluny III

FIG. 9. LALLEMAND VIEW OF THE NARTHEX (*c.* 1787)

FIG. 10. THE APSE IN DEMOLITION (DRAWING, *c.* 1812)

┌MONASTIC LIFE┐ ─── VIRTUES ─── ┌DIVINE PRAISE┐

Adam | Corinthian | Beehive | Palaestra | Theological Virtues and Justice | Prudence Spring, Summer | Cardinal Virtues (Four Rivers) | I Plainsong | II Plainsong | Sacrifice of Abraham
and Eve

Conant

FIG. 11. DETAIL OF FIG. 10. CAPITALS IN ORDER, WITH ICONOGRAPHIC SCHEME

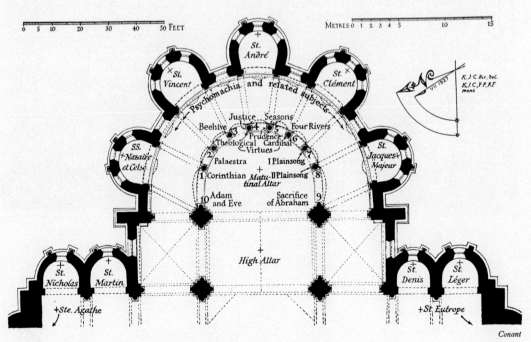

FIG. 12. PLAN OF THE APSE

Conant

FIG. 13. THE APSE ARCADE, RESTORED OVER A PHOTOGRAPH OF A FULL–SIZE
REPRODUCTION

FIG. 14. CAPITAL FROM THE APSE ARCADE WITH
OLD IMPOST BLOCK AND NECKING

MUSEUM AT CLUNY

FIG. 15.   ELEMENTS OF ABBOT PONTIUS' CLOISTER, FOUND IN THE EXCAVATIONS
OF 1936

Loury photo.

FIG. 16. SOFFIT OF IMPOST BLOCK (FIG. 14), WITH MORTAR OF THE ORIGINAL
JOINT STILL ADHERING

FIG. 17. SOFFIT OF IMPOST BLOCK FROM OUTER WALL OF AMBULATORY
SHOWING NO TRACES OF FINISHING OF CAPITAL

[353]

FIG. 18.   TOP OF CAPITAL OF THE FOUR RIVERS OF PARADISE, SHOWING LEAFAGE
AND APPLES CARVED BEFORE PLACING OF IMPOST BLOCK

Loury photo.

FIG. 19. TOP OF PRUDENCE CAPITAL, SHOWING THAT FINISHED SURFACE OF
FLEURONS RUNS UP TO A TANGENT WITH THE IMPOST

FIG. 20. FRAGMENTS FROM THE CAPITALS OF THE AMBULATORY WALL

FIG. 21. DRAWING OF THE AMBULATORY (*c.* 1787)

THE SCULPTURES OF SOUILLAC

MEYER SCHAPIRO

THE SCULPTURES now preserved in the inner west wall of the abbey church of Souillac (Fig. 1) are the fragments of a larger whole which we can no longer reconstruct. The largest of these (Fig. 2) — the relief of the story of Theophilus — is still intact,[1] though possibly removed from its original architectural field. It is so irregular in design that we are led to suppose at first that this relief, too, has been subject to a later reconstruction and loosely transformed. The parts seem as oddly fitted to each other as the whole to its modern field. If Porter could admire its inner composition, another writer has spoken of its mediocre architectural design.[2] The expected Romanesque adherence to an embracing architectural frame is violated throughout the work. But a more detailed analysis will show that the apparently "accidental" design is a deeply coherent arrangement, even systematic in a sense, and similar to other medieval works. In the course of this analysis, I will indicate the existence of a type of medieval design which has received little attention from investigators, though important for a correct account of medieval art.

I

The relief is composed of nine main slabs in three stepped horizontal rows of three (Fig. 3). This sustained three-part scheme resembles the inner divisions of the objects, the zones and the content of the sculpture. The story of Theophilus, which includes three actors — the *vidame*, the devil, and the Virgin —, is recounted in three episodes. There are also three angels issuing from the trefoil arch, and the great central field is flanked by two saints. But the actual fields of the masonry do not correspond strictly to the figures applied to them. For the joints intersect them at points which are not genuine terminations either in meaning or in form. The horizontal joints of the central slabs cross the breasts and arms of Theophilus and the devil, and the joints of the slabs at the sides intersect the legs of the abbot Benedict and the thighs of Peter (Fig. 2).

On the other hand, the extremities of the figures are relatively independent of the larger frame. The four heads of the devil and the sinner in the central field are unframed and unconnected with the salient elements of the adjoining fields. The heads of Benedict and Peter are similarly unenclosed. And if we observe the feet of these six figures, we encounter again a conception of the field and the frame as an unarchitectural mosaic or marquetry.

---

[1] Mâle (*L'Art religieux du XIIe siècle en France*, Paris, 1922, p. 434, n. 1) says of these blocks: "quelques-unes de ces pièces doivent nous manquer." But it is sufficient to observe the continuity and perfect connection of carved forms across the joints, especially the wing and right arm of the central descending angel and also the Virgin's scroll, to conclude that no piece is missing from the relief of Theophilus.

[2] Cf. A. Ramé (*Gazette archéologique*, 1885, p. 231), "son mérite d'architecte est des plus contestables."

In this relation of the masonry and the carving, as in many other respects, the relief of Souillac agrees with the sculptures of Moissac;[3] the common stylistic types are bound up with common technical procedures. But in Souillac, even more than in Moissac, the lack of a strict accord between the composition

Kunstgesch. Seminar Marburg

FIG. 1. SOUILLAC, ABBEY CHURCH, WEST WALL

of the sculpture and the composition of the material field corresponds to the nature of the sculptural composition. For within the latter, also, there is a discrepancy between the frame of the whole and the enclosed elements.

The trefoil arch above the scene is designed as a symmetrical structure embracing a field with a corresponding symmetrical three-part form. Yet the axes of the two symmetrical sets do not correspond. The central arch-segment

[3] See my analysis in *Art Bulletin*, XIII (1931), pp. 468, 469, 493, 499, n. 127.

is indeed placed directly above the central scene. But the two pairs of Theophilus and the devil are unequal in breadth; the right is broader than the left, so that the vertical compositional axis is a little to the left of the geometrical axis of the field. More important are the inequalities of the segments of the trefoil arch. The left one extends considerably beyond the figure of Benedict below, whereas the right is tangent to the frame of Peter. This inequality is sustained

Kunstgesch. Seminar Marburg

FIG. 2. STORY OF THEOPHILUS

by the fine differences in the curvature of the flanking segmental arches and by the variant levels of the two terminal points of the central arch. The frame thus appears to be modeled on a freehand drawing of a frame, and is not a typical constructed shape; it is an eccentric, irregular, flattened trefoil without a supporting form. The central arch is above the irregular, uncentralized composition of the central field, and the flanking, irregular arch-segments are above the rigid, stabilized figures of Benedict and Peter. The seated frontal saints are thus placed at the sides, and the central field is occupied by the more active and uncentralized profile figures. This arrangement negates the usual conception of an arched Romanesque field, as in Moissac and Chartres, where the central area is occupied by a stable, even rigid, frontal figure and the sides by more active profile figures. In Souillac the central turbulent figures are even reduced in size; the flanking, detached Peter and Benedict are the largest in the whole relief. But their rigid axes find no prolongation or conclusion in the segments above them, for the central axes of the latter are diagonal and converge toward the main field. And even if we should isolate a vertical axis in the area spanned by each lateral segment, it would not coincide with the axis of the rigid figure below. In fact, the sculptor has consciously marked such an axis in the symmetrical convergence of the voluted ornament on the crowns of the segmental arches. On the right it is far to the left of Peter's axis; on the left, it is slightly to the right of Benedict's.

II

We shall call this discrepant relationship of corresponding parts "discoördinate." By discoördination we mean a grouping or division such that corresponding sets of elements include parts, relations, or properties which negate that correspondence. A simple example of a discoördinate design is a vertical figure in a horizontal rectangle or a horizontal figure in a vertical rectangle.[4] The frame corresponds to the figure in its rectangular form, but its major axis

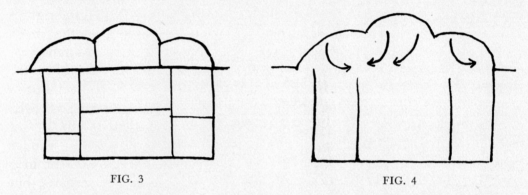

FIG. 3　　　　　　　　　　　　　　　　　　　FIG. 4

is opposed to the major axis of the enclosed figure. Such arrangements are not "errors" of taste or artistic judgment; they occur in works of high quality in the Middle Ages and must be seen in detail to be understood.

Consider the grouping of the figures directly under the trefoil arch in Souillac. Each segment includes a descending angel; but these angels, instead of tieing the three members of the frame to the corresponding fields below, destroy this implied coördination. The left angel descends diagonally toward the central rather than the lateral field; the diagonal of his wings points downward to Theophilus, and his extended scroll completes the chain in repeating the direction of his arm and the curve of the wing of the descending angel of the central field. He is completely detached in gesture and movement from Benedict below, although their adjacent forms are plastically similar, with an analogous roundness and salience.[5]

We should expect — given the symmetry of the arched frame and the fields

[4] Like the symbol of Luke in the Book of Durrow. See K. Pfister, *Irische Buchmalerei* (1927), Pl. 22. I hope to deal with this aspect of Hiberno-Saxon art elsewhere.

[5] In this analysis I have omitted reference to plastic qualities, to relations of modeling, relief, and surface, in order to isolate more sharply the compositional or inner "topographical" relations of the sculpture.

below — that the angel emerging from under the right segment would be turned
to the left as the symmetrical counterpart of the first angel. On the contrary,
he descends to the right and poses a book above the head of Peter, repeating the
movement of the left angel, but also negating the latter's relation to Benedict,
the corresponding seated figure. The diagonal slope of his wings, exactly as in
the left angel, confirms the unsymmetrical repetition of the figures. Thus we
have within a symmetrical group a left to right movement, instead of a convergence of counterpart elements (Fig. 4). The three-part structure of the upper
zone of the relief is therefore discoördinate with respect to the three-part structure of the lower zone, a discoördination already implied in the relation of the
arched frame to the field below.

A similar relation may be found in the cloud-forms and the trefoil, but it is
less significant than the relation of the two lateral angels to the central pair of
descending figures, the Virgin and the third angel. This pair may be seen in two
ways: moving diagonally to the left in opposition to the flanking twin pair of
angels, who move diagonally to the right, or as two figures, of which the right is
the symmetrical counterpart of the adjacent right angel and the left is the counterpart of the left angel. I believe that the first is the more significant and preg-
nant view of the whole, especially since the central figures, embraced by the
dominant arch-segment, are tied to each other by shape and meaning. But in
either view the static symmetry of the centralized three-part scheme is destroyed
and a violent opposition created within the heart of the larger symmetrical
structure. Just as the lateral components of the symmetrical series are similar
rather than counterparts and thus introduce a left to right movement in a
symmetrical group, the central figures are also similar, not counterparts, but
introduce a lateral movement in the opposite direction.[6] Even the subordinate
structure isolated in the second way of seeing the group has a similar character;
for then two new axes are produced at the meeting of the arch-segments (Fig. 4).
At the right, the angel moving rightward and the Virgin moving leftward form
a *diverging* symmetrical pair with respect to the juncture of their two segments;
while on the other side the two descending angels form a second (though less
rigorous) pair *converging* to each other. The two individually balanced pairs are
not counterparts of each other; they are simply juxtaposed, even overlapping,
structures, one convergent, the other divergent, but made up of roughly similar
elements.

The reference to the junctions of the segments as alternative axial points is
confirmed by the divergent spiral or voluted tips at these junctions. Moreover,
the fine voluted ornament of the trefoil segments is designed symmetrically with
respect to both the crowns of the arches and the junctions. And in the cloud
forms we can observe within the seemingly unordered, freely improvised lines
differentiated pairs of volutes, convergent at the issuing point of the left angel,
divergent above the central angel, and parallel above the Virgin and the right
angel.

[6] For a related conception of paired figures in Moissac, see *Art Bulletin*, XIII (1931), p. 473.

If the two outer angels were converging counterparts rather than parallel figures directed to the right, there would result a predominance of movements to the left, since three of the four figures would have that direction. We can see then how the present discoördinate arrangement is a necessary balanced scheme; but its balance depends on the negation of the usual order of the symmetrical three-part scheme of central and flanking elements implied in the trefoil frame. It corresponds to those single Romanesque figures with arms turned one way,

Kunstgesch. Seminar Marburg   Kunstgesch. Seminar Marburg

FIG. 5. JOSEPH   FIG. 6. ISAIAH

head and legs the other way, like the Joseph in Souillac (Fig. 5). In the Isaiah (Fig. 6) the crossed symmetrical legs and the arms are turned to the left, and the central dominant mass of the head to the right. In the upper group of the angels and Mary a movement is balanced, not by a directly confronting mass, but by elements on both sides, as by a larger active milieu. The central figures move in one way; their *surrounding* attendants all move in the opposite way. The extension of the trefoil at the left may be regarded as an adjustment of the contrast of these directions.

It is possible to discover other schemes within the four upper figures, more clearly symmetrical than the grouping described above. But these newer groupings are also tied to the larger discoördinate scheme. Thus we can see the left arms of the central angel and the Virgin, plus the head of the angel, as a convex arched form opposed to the concave loops of the bodies of the lateral angels, and the three curves as a symmetrical counterpart scheme corresponding to the trefoil above (Fig. 7). But within this scheme the four heads create a discoördinate structure; the heads of the central pair are considerably to the left of the main axis of the relief, the heads of the outer angels are shifted as markedly to the right.

III

The peculiarities of the four upper figures and their relations to the enclosing forms recur in the flanking saints (Figs. 9, 10). How Benedict is placed centrally below his arched segment and Peter eccentrically below the other, has already

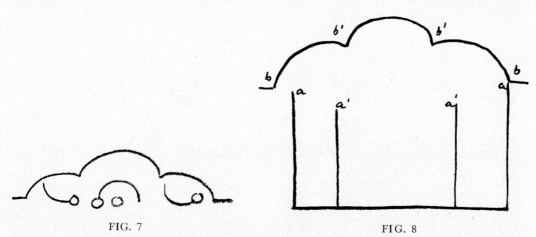

FIG. 7   FIG. 8

been observed. This asymmetry reappears within the narrower field of each saint in the enclosing shafts, which are of unequal height; it corresponds to the asymmetry of the arch above. But these inequalities are ordered in a counter-part sense, forming a larger symmetrical frame, a–a', a'–a, like the trefoil as a whole (Fig. 8). The enclosed saints, however, are disposed like the two lateral angels, as repeated rather than counterpart elements, and thereby contradict — though to a lesser degree — the order of their frames. Thus each holds a book in the left hand and an appropriate symbol in the right. The common position of the books and the identity of form, even to the placing of the clasp, create a pronounced rightward deviation from the axis of the whole relief, opposed to the leftward extension of the trefoil above. But the common diagonal inclination of the crozier and keys produces a counter-movement to the left. This movement is also upward because of the diagonal relation of the levels of the two attributes. In opposition to these repeated forms, the right arms, which would maintain a common form if they agreed with the system of repeats, are flexed as symmetri-cal counterpart shapes, the arm of Benedict being turned outward, of Peter, inward.

In truth, the two figures are thoroughly differentiated and contrasted in de-tail, contrary to the larger correspondences described. In Peter the diagonal of the right arm is repeated in the band across the breast and shoulder, opposed in turn by the huge keys. In accord with this X-scheme the draperies of the torso

and the legs are zigzag, pervasively diagonal and symmetrical, like the legs and
feet. But in Benedict a more compact, placid, cubical form is created, with pri-
mary vertical and horizontal accents and with prolonged lines. Hence the
elongated crozier, the book, the vertical folds of the garment, the clear horizontal edges, the inward turn of the crozier and the left hand. The silhouette
is less richly indented than Peter's, the mass less skeletalized; hence the relaxed
quality of Benedict in contrast to the tension and rigidity of Peter. Both figures
seem to hold identical books, but the book of Peter rests only partly on his diagonal thigh. It projects beyond the body, while Benedict's book is held firmly on
the foreshortened thigh. The difference in conception may be verified finally
in the hands and feet. Peter's left hand is turned slightly away from the body,
Benedict's, inward. Peter's feet are bare and claw-like, with multiplied diagonal
forms which resemble the clawed feet of his throne; Benedict wears shoes which
form a simpler, broader, more stable mass. The distinction between the beardless and bearded faces is an element in this sustained contrast.

Even the beasts under the feet of the two figures maintain the formal oppositions above them. Under Peter two dragons are crossed in an X, biting each
other's tails; the wing of the left dragon points diagonally upward, the parallel
wing of the right, inversely downward. Under Benedict a more compact,
rounded, serpentine monster is deployed horizontally across the field in three
coilings (Fig. 11). From the summits of the coils issue three grotesque human
figures which form a roughly symmetrical, centralized group in horizontal
alignment, like the three groups of pleats at the edge of Benedict's robe. But the
two left figures, torsos of devils, are isolated as an independent pair with converging wings and corresponding ribs, inwardly and outwardly symmetrical.
The axis of this pair coincides with the juncture of the two left coils from which
the demons emerge. These coils, however, are neither symmetrical counterparts nor repetitions of each other; one is the inverse rather than reverse of the
other. The outer left coil has as its veiled counterpart the third coil at the extreme right; but the magnificent head issuing from the latter is turned to the
right like the first figure, rather than to the left as its proper counterpart. Thus
the scheme of the angels of the upper trefoil field, with the rightward turn of the
outer figures and the leftward of the inner angel, is repeated below at the feet of
Benedict. But whereas in the trefoil the leftward movement of a central pair is
balanced by the rightward movement of surrounding figures, here a symmetrical
pair at the left is balanced by the accented rightward direction and magnitude
of a single head at the right. In distinction from the upper group which sur-
mounts the entire centralized field of the sculpture, the lower group is simply a
lateral element and is adjusted to its restricted marginal place below by the predominance of the lateral head. In the double scale of this head and the two little
demons, the sculptor reproduces the contrast of the figures of the central field
and the great lateral saints. Further, this large head maintains the direction of
the serpent's body (which corresponds to the order of the diabolical scenes in the
central field), in opposition to the twisted head of the serpent below. These two

FIG. 9. ST. BENEDICT

FIG. 10. ST. PETER

FIG. 11. DETAIL OF ST. BENEDICT

heads are turned divergently, unlike the two confronted demons at the left; and, also unlike the latter, they are superposed vertically rather than set horizontally beside each other. Finally, this large head reëmbodies within the fantastic bifurcation of the beard the inner oppositions of the two demons.

Because these groups of monstrous beasts under the ledges supporting Benedict and Peter are so small and so minor an element in the whole, they reveal to us all the more deeply in their minute distinctions and powerful fantasy and in the pervasive contrast of corresponding parts the sculptor's independence of an *a priori* architectural form and his conscious method of design, with its virtuosity in variation and intricate juggling of symmetrical schemes.

IV

Let us turn now to the central field (Fig. 2). The relative frequency of the protagonists suggests a schematized hierarchical grouping. Theophilus appears three times, the devil twice, the Virgin once. But these numerical relations are hardly disposed in a symbolic sense and play little part in the actual composition. The system of repeated and contrasted pairs is more crucial for the structure of the whole. Below, the devil first offers the contract to Theophilus; then, at the right, the same group is repeated, but the devil grasps Theophilus by the hands to make him his liege man. The simple succession from left to right, the repetition of the broad structure of the first scene in the second, corresponds to the grouping of the outer angels above; and this correspondence is accented by the parallelism of the devil's and the angels' wings. The two scenes produce a chiasmic symmetry, with Theophilus and the devil back to back in the center of the field, and the devil and Theophilus face to face at the sides of the field. The order of the inner divergent pair is reversed in the outer pair, and by this very means the opposition of man and devil is varied and sustained. Reading the group as a, b, a', b', we can isolate four symmetrical pairs, a–b, a'–b', b–a', a–b', in every one of which appear the opposed Theophilus and the devil. If for the sake of a larger symmetry of the two scenes, the sculptor had grouped the figures, a, b, b', a', the second scene would be the counterpart of the first, but the opposition of Theophilus and the devil would then be less pervasive.[7] The symmetrical pairs, a–b, b–b', a–a', b'–a', include only two in which the protagonists are opposed, a–b, b'–a'. This alternative system is evoked, however, in one detail of the present arrangement, the relation of the arms. In the left group the devil's arm is raised higher, Theophilus', lower; in the right group this order is reversed, so that an a–b, b–a scheme results. In the actual design the chiasmic form is maintained throughout the two groups by the mimetic play of the diverging and converging limbs in energetic diagonal schemes of which the linear elements are diffused in the ribs, the zigzag, hairy waistband, and the wings of the devil and in the draperies of Theophilus.

---

[7] The actual grouping was perhaps influenced by the idea that the devil's proper place is always at the left, as the evil and sinister side; but in the three scenes of the Temptation of Christ in Beaulieu, the devil appears twice at the right, with Christ at the left.

With a passionate feeling for the expressive pantomime, the sculptor has varied the two pairs according to the meanings of the episodes, the left showing a more relaxed and compact confrontation of the figures, like the adjoining Benedict, and the right, a more tense and vehement combination, like Peter. These qualities appear in the relations of hands and heads as well as in the major limbs, and finally in the spiral, cable column between the figures at the right. The column, of which the diagonal coils move upward toward Theophilus, concentrates the aggressive energy of the devil's forward movement in a single intermediate member, expanding also the motif of the diagonally grasping hands. The devil's wings are diagonal in both episodes and point downward to Theophilus, but while in the left scene the inner wing passes behind Theophilus as an embracing form and is obscured, it is pointed fixedly like a sword in uninterrupted movement toward Theophilus at the right. In both groups there is a sustained correspondence of lines down to the smallest details, but the form is different in each scene according to the underlying content of the figures. Yet transcending these differences is a common movement that pervades the relief, without culminating, however, in a central or surmounting object. Observe, for example, how the two heads are turned to each other in the left group, how the intervening wing bridges their forms, but, originating in the devil, maintains a dominant left-to-right movement; and how, in the second group, the whole physiognomy of the devil has changed with the turn of the head, assuming a more predacious character by an astonishing conversion of the features into flamboyant, centrifugal, tentacular curves, related to the forms of the clouds above. This inventiveness and energy of expression is maintained in the adjacent elements which unite the devil's and the *vidame*'s heads. The lines of the devil's jaw and snout flow into the curves of the capital surmounting the column, and thus to the bowed, not opposed, head of Theophilus. In the first group, the figures are linked by a continuous convex curve; in the second, which represents not only agreement but an asserted possession and submission, the heads are united by an undulating curve with a central concavity, a curve issuing from the monstrous active snout of the devil.

The sculptor's conception of contrast as both a principle of arrangement and a quality of antagonistic or divided objects appears also in the rendering of the devil's feet. They are different in the two episodes, as if to indicate a development in the devil who changes in the course of the action. At first he has the clawed feet of a predacious quadruped; then the feet are distinguished from each other: the right is clawed like a bird's, the left is a cloven hoof. This inner change corresponds to the contrast of Benedict's and Peter's feet which has already been observed; but the internal asymmetry of the devil in the second scene is a progressive revelation of the demon, a final emergence of his lowest nature and ugliness, as in the changing shape of his head.

For the solution of the drama, which includes a third act — the repentance of Theophilus and miraculous intervention of Mary —, the sculptor had to introduce the new figures in a sequence which breaks with the established order of episodes. The final scene is not placed at the extreme right to continue the left-to-right movement of the story, but above the left scene in an ambiguous temporal relation to the others. Theophilus is prostrate above the first scene, but the church in which he prays (according to the legend) is above the second, and is in part an element of the latter. The image, however, is more than a succession of incidents to be identified by the spectator; their arrangement depends on devices of expressive composition applied according to the artist's judgment of the significant content of the story. For the medieval spectator the reconstruction of the sequence of moments was a simple matter which flowed from his understanding of the objects. The religious and dramatic values, the inner gradations of action, were more important; and it was from these that the artist derived his liberty of arrangement. The third incident with its transcendent persons had to be placed above; as a culminating moment it was centralized and elevated to the zone of angels. But it is not a dominant theme for the sculptor. Its elevation and centrality, as will be shown later, are more conventional than expressive.

It is more difficult to describe this region of the sculpture than any other, not merely because it is more irregular or complex in arrangement but because the third figure of Theophilus, as a mediating element between the upper and lower zones, belongs at the same time to so many distinct configurations.

Thus the recumbent sleeping Theophilus is balanced in his own horizontal field by the masses of the adjoining church, with its attached vertical and slightly inclined horizontal blocks, and may be seen together with them as the base of the apical pair of the Virgin and angel. But he is also the counterpart of the second Theophilus swung through an arc of 90°. The two figures, with their corresponding heads, arms, and thighs, are symmetrical with respect to a diagonal line bisecting the left building and tangent to the devil's snout (Fig. 12). The divergent wings of the devil have a related symmetry; and if the right wing is above the arm of the second Theophilus, and the left wing below the arm of his counterpart, the variation corresponds to the interplay of the mantle and the arm in the two figures. At the right, Theophilus' left arm issues from under the mantle; in the upper figure the corresponding right arm extends above the mantle.

Finally, the praying Theophilus is tied to the lower band of figures. He emerges directly from behind the first devil and the raised wing of the second; no border or frame divides the upper from the lower band. By this interception of the legs Theophilus is bound to the movement of the figures below. His body appears to be an arched form spanning the first and the second devil and surmounting the first Theophilus, as if the latter were a central figure. The two devils are bound in turn by the embracing mass of the penitent, just as the wing in the first scene connects the heads of the devil and Theophilus. The right leg of the penitent prolongs the right arm and torso of the first devil, and the right arm of the former parallels the right arm of the second devil. The rear wing of each devil rises to the body of the penitent. The leftmost wing meets the de-

scending wing of the central angel, and thus the uppermost and lowest groups
are brought into contact. But this is a minor contact beside the more decisive
mediation of the penitent's right arm, which resembles the general form of the
bent limbs below. It corresponds also to the arms of the upper lateral angels,
and belongs to the same scale of arched forms as the arms of the central angel
and the Virgin. The common obtuse angle of these rhythmically distributed
arms in the three zones of the relief distinguishes them as elements of a single
scheme, distinct from the acutely flexed arms of Peter and Benedict.

The correspondence of the penitent figure and the buildings before him has
also a mediating character. The upward-tending, emergent mass of the figure
is opposed by the upward-tending and emergent buildings at the right. They

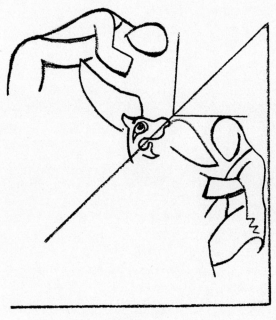

FIG. 12

form the only directly confronting symmetrical pair on the axis of the large field.
The devil and Theophilus below are divergent, back to back; the angel and the
Virgin above are turned in one direction. But the relation of figure and building is approximately, not rigidly, symmetrical, and then only with respect to
an axis considerably to the right of the main axis of the relief. The axis of the
three superposed pairs is therefore roughly zigzag in form, like the contact of the
central adossed pair of Theophilus and the devil. The rightward movement of
the penitent Theophilus, who reaches across the axis of the field and is prolonged
by the ascending scheme of knobs on the buildings and the throne of Peter at
the right, is opposed to the asymmetrical leftward turn of the Virgin and angel
above, but repeats the rightward disposition of the lateral angels and the order
of the scenes below. The meander ornament under the central field is also directed to the right.

Thus the interwoven contrasts and discoördinate relations of the trefoil and the upper row of suspended figures are continuous finally with the middle and lower zones of the relief. The three episodes become a single differentiated action of three groups.

V

Although we are uncertain whether the figures of Isaiah and Joseph (Figs. 5, 6) were originally placed below the relief of Theophilus, as they are today, their coherence with the latter is proved by numerous correspondences. They are paired symmetrically with respect to the doorway; Joseph's head is turned to the left, Isaiah's to the right, and their arms, in similar opposition to the heads, are extended in counterpart patterns to the doorway. But in contrast to these symmetrical relations the legs are all turned in the same leftward direction; and this contrast, which resembles the systematic discoördinate oppositions of the relief above, is maintained in the opposed rightward movement of the meandering ribbons under their feet. Thus the arms of Joseph are directed like the devil's, and the arms of Isaiah, like the sinner's; but if the general direction of the upper pair is from left to right, in the lower pair it is from right to left. The counterpart of Isaiah's scroll appears, however, in the hands of the devil at the left.

The two figures are tied still more intimately to the large relief in their fine inner differences which correspond to the contrasted elements above. Both are internally asymmetrical and mobile, with head turned one way, arms or feet, the other way; but Isaiah is the more skeletal, angular, and tense, like Peter and the devil; Joseph, the more stable, compact, and relaxed, like Benedict and Theophilus. Isaiah is similar in these respects, as well as in energy of movement, to the group of Theophilus and the devil at the right. Even the swirling diagonal edge of Isaiah's robe that encircles the right leg reappears in the second Theophilus. The latter's posture and drapery agree in other details with Isaiah's; his head, however, is bent submissively, in contrast to the independent turn of the announcing prophet's. On the other side, Joseph's body is like Theophilus' at the left, but his arms correspond to the devil's rather than the sinner's. The former's scroll reappears, however, in Isaiah's hands, not Joseph's. Finally, the separate but counterpart symmetrical gestures of the two figures below reënact the transacting gestures of the devil and the sinner at the left.

If we accept Joseph and Isaiah as parts of a larger scheme including the relief of Theophilus — and I think this is justified by the intimate correspondences, which imply a purposive connection — then we have an added evidence of the formal method of the sculptor. The procedure of discoördinate pairing, of repetitions in counterpart elements, of oppositions in repeated units, recurs in the two figures below. Yet they are no duplicate of any of the pairs above, but form a distinct variation of the common theme of the paired figures. They are flanking elements like the two seated saints above, and are also active like Theophilus and the devil; parallel, however, rather than opposed, in their motion, like the upper lateral angels. But more essential, each is divided internally in his motion unlike any of the figures above, and thereby resumes within himself as an isolated single being the contrasting structures which pervade the larger groups and the work as a whole.

VI

This internal contrast reappears in the fabulous *trumeau* (Fig. 13). Here it is raised to a higher power in paired figures which are not merely confronted, like Isaiah and Joseph, but diagonally crossed. The motif underlying the frantic confusion of struggling, devouring, intertwining figures is the repeated pair of crossed beasts with a common victim. Their bodies diverge, but their heads are turned back to face each other. Isolate this chiasmic unit and the whole will emerge ordered and clear. Tie it, however, to its architectural frame — the parallel columns around which the beasts twist their necks — and the whole will appear inextricably involved (Fig. 14).

A remarkable intrigue animates these opposed predacious beasts. They are of different species, the one, a monstrous quadruped with the wings and head of a bird, the other, a kind of Romanesque lion. Their foreparts are mounted on each other's backs, but their bodies are turned in opposite directions, as if awaiting other prey. Then reversing the divergent movements of their bodies, they turn their heads and find a common prey behind their crossed backs.

Even this paradoxical return is obstructed and indirect. The necks are twisted around constricting colonnettes. The violence is therefore devious, improvised, and constrained; the weak victim is caught between the opposed monsters, like the latter between the slender colonnettes. In their common enlacement of the colonnettes, the monsters are distinguished again; the outer one twists his neck around the obstacle from within, the other, from without. The contrast of the two upper victims, with bent, resisting forms, to the lower ones, with rigid bodies, and the repetition within these pairs, also recall the formal method of the large relief.

In the diagonal crisscross and knotted forms, the functional, structural lines of the *trumeau* are completely obscured. There is no sustained vertical element in the design. On the contrary, if the two lower victims are vertical, they are unstable, unresisting figures, held momentarily in place between the jaws of the monsters. And if the colonnettes are conceived as quasi-structural members which appear to support the impost above and hence the whole mass carried by the *trumeau*, we are shown this function in the very process of its disturbance by the action of more powerful, non-architectural forces. The vertical colonnettes are bent inward at four levels by the lateral pull or tension of the excited beasts; the latters' force, greater than the architectural load, deforms the supporting colonnettes. Another pull, and the whole structure will topple down into a shapeless heap.

The sculpture is therefore an undemountable form. We cannot isolate the figures without disrupting the architecture. The contorted animals must first be unwound from their frame; and the frame will change its shape, it will return to a vertical, when the figures are removed.[8]

The pattern of the *trumeau* is not simply a network of abstract, ornamental lines to which the figures have been submitted. The beasts are twisted, entangled,

Kunstgesch. Seminar Marburg

FIG. 13. SOUILLAC, TRUMEAU

and unbalanced by their own rapacious energy. Every motion issues naturalistically from its opposite. The intensity of the beasts, their almost supernatural vehemence, lies in the deforming oppositions generated by impulsive movements. In his divided posture the beast acquires a human complexity and inwardness,

[8] The flexibility of the colonnettes recalls in the scalloped forms the "unarchitectural" disposition of

a suggestion of conflicting motives, like a Christian with his double nature. The diagonal crisscross pattern, the interlaced scheme, and the scalloped verticals are the inspired devices of this tense, congested struggle. They are material aspects of the beasts, or physical elements, like the sagging colonnettes, real situations of tension, instability, obstruction, and entanglement, even if repeated in the sense of ornament. The beast is not unstable because fitted into a diagonal scheme; he is presented diagonally because the sculptor wishes an unstable figure. This

FIG. 14

realism of design corresponds to the powerful reality of representation in the animals, and to the rich variety in the repeated units, which transcends the norms of ornament.[9]

VII

The relation of the content of the large relief to the formal characteristics and method of design analyzed above is more difficult to state, since we must refer to meanings which are hardly as explicit to us as the forms of the sculpture. To approach this relation fruitfully we must begin, I think, not with the episodic

the trefoil frame of the relief of Theophilus. It is related, however, to the common practice of the builders of Quercy and Limousin, who prolonged the tenuous colonnettes of their portals and windows as a torus of the spanning archivolt, often without an intermediate impost, so that the continuity of colonnette and curved torus is accentuated. (See Enlart, *Manuel d'archéologie française, l'architecture religieuse*, 2e éd., 1919, I, pp. 353, 396; and R. Fage, in *Bulletin archéologique*, 1920, pp. 378 ff.) It is also the same builders who gave a cusped or scalloped form to the jambs of a portal and the engaged colonnettes — examples at Moissac, La Souterraine, Noailles, Vigeois, etc. (see Fage, *loc. cit.*, p. 382).

[9] The realistic aspect of the represented animals was recognized by Viollet-le-Duc (*Dictionnaire raisonné de l'architecture*, Paris, 1854–1869, VIII, p. 197), who, at the same time, compared the underlying design with the interlaced, deformed animals of the Cross page of the Lindisfarne Gospels (*ibid.*, p. 186, Fig. 33). We cannot deal here with the relationships of Souillac to northern and eastern art indicated by Viollet-le-Duc, and observed also on the iconographic side by Arthur Kingsley Porter (*The Crosses and Culture of Ireland*, New Haven, 1931, pp. 126, 127). In our own view, these relations — which we should have to qualify

details of the story of Theophilus, but with the broader, even formal, aspects of the story.[10]

We have already observed that in contrast to such works as the tympana of Moissac and Chartres, and, in fact, to most monumental medieval sculptures, the theme in Souillac is so disposed that the religiously inferior figures (Theophilus and the devil) occupy the central field, and the Virgin, angels, and saints, the peripheral fields. The center consists, moreover, of the mobile, episodic figures, and the sides, of the stable, hierarchically elevated figures. The contingent, the temporal, and inferior are centralized in Souillac, the stationary and elevated are marginal. As a result, the chief formal devices of showing transcendental objects — namely, magnitude, stability, centrality, and elevation — are unconnected here. The figures grow smaller as they approach the crown of the field.[11] This suggests compositions of the later Renaissance, like El Greco's "Burial of Count Orgaz"; but the contraction of forms in Souillac is without perspective value. It creates no optical illusion of distance and transcendence. No figure in the lower zone looks upward or toward a central object. There is, in fact, no fully central object, only an implicit axis, the junction of two figures who stand back to back. And correspondingly, in the upper zone, the religiously transcendent figure of the Virgin is shown, not enlarged and enthroned, but reduced, unstable, descending, and suspended from an angel's arms. The flanking angels, far from constituting a symmetrical retinue, are directed toward the right, rather than toward the center. With the two enthroned figures at the sides, the normal hierarchical relations become merely accessory and conventional. Finally, it is the heavenly figures, the Virgin and the angels, who are incomplete, being intercepted by the frame.

These aspects of the larger form may therefore be seen as a conception of the content, a devaluation of absolute transcendence. In the episodic trinity of the man, the devil, and the Virgin, the central figure is not the Virgin, but the apostate-penitent Theophilus.[12]

---

severely — are not the result of a direct influence of a distant art on Souillac, but of a long tradition or of descent from a common source. The crossed animals of Souillac are an old oriental theme which is fairly common in Quercy and other parts of southwestern France, appearing in manuscripts of Limoges (Paris, Bibl. nat. lat. 8 and lat. 254) and Toulouse (British Museum, Harley MS. 4951), and in capitals in Saint-Savin, Monsempron, Carennac, Moissac, etc. The motif is related to the figures with legs crossed in X, and even to the more uncommon theme of the crossed columns (St. Amand-de-Boixe). Mâle (*op. cit.*, p. 19), in comparing the *trumeau* with an ornament of the tenth century in the Limoges Bible, Paris Bibl. nat. lat. 5, which lacks precisely the crossed form and the intertwining of animals with their enframing bands, has overlooked not only the northern examples but also the true parallels of such animal and band interlace in South French manuscripts of the late eleventh and twelfth century — Bibl. nat. lat. 7, 254, 2154, 5056, etc.

[10] We have already referred to meanings in the formal analysis in so far as our judgment of "directions" and movements depends on our interpretation of the action of the figures.

[11] This diminution is further accentuated by the greater distance of the upper figures from the spectator. It is also worth observing that the central arch-segment of the trefoil frame appears to be the most shallow and the smallest, though the spans of all three are identical.

[12] The exact opposite of this formal conception of a sculpture dedicated to the Virgin is the south portal of the west façade of Chartres, where the axes of both tympanum and lintel correspond rigidly to the Virgin and Child.

It may be asked whether the sculpture of Theophilus was not perhaps an accessory relief beside a

A similar relation governs the content of the *trumeau*. If themes of violence and conflict are represented on the sides, they are the more restrained, human, and religious motifs. (On the right, three superposed pairs of embracing and wrestling figures of an old man and a youth; on the left, Abraham about to sacrifice his son, and an angel descending with a ram to stay the hand of the patriarch.)[13] The more violent struggles of the monsters are applied to the broader frontal face, and it is the latter which are most intricately articulated and most capable of divided movements. But within the dominant outer groups the central element is always the weakest figure, the helpless prey caught between the powerful beasts. As on the great relief of Theophilus, the traditional values of centrality and symmetry have been inverted. In Oriental and Romanesque art, the heraldic beasts paired beside a central object are protecting or adoring figures; here they destroy the inferior prey. The adossed beasts who turn their heads are like the familiar apocalyptic escorts of the enthroned Christ in Majesty in Carolingian and Romanesque art. On the *trumeau* of Souillac they become predacious monsters devouring the immobilized central victim.[14]

This devaluation of the central and the immobile and of the absolute hierarchical order is already present in the meanings of the sculpture of Theophilus,

---

larger, more emphatically centralized sculpture of Christ or the Virgin in glory, like the accessory moral and narrative reliefs in Moissac and Beaulieu. I lack the data for a reconstruction of the original arrangement of the portal; but judging by the dimensions of the porch and of the sculptures and by their relation to the other portals of the same school (Moissac, Beaulieu, Cahors), it seems to me highly improbable that the sculpture of Theophilus was a subordinate pendant or flanking relief. But even if it were only a secondary relief, the characters described would still be significant. In other versions, of a still smaller scale or lesser rank in a whole, the theme is centralized and dominated by the Virgin. Cf. Fig. 15 of this article, and a miniature of the early thirteenth century by Conrad von Scheyern in Munich Clm. 17401 (Boeckler, *Jahrbuch für Kunstwissenschaft*, I, 1923, pl. 25).

[13] Reproduced by A. K. Porter, *Romanesque Sculpture of the Pilgrimage Roads* (1923), ill. 350–352.

[14] It should be observed further that the theme of Abraham and Isaac, which is not only a symbol of salvation and of the Crucifixion but also has the value of an instance of submission to authority, Abraham preparing to sacrifice his son at God's command and Isaac submitting to his father — this theme is parodied on the opposite side of the *trumeau* by images of conflict between a youth and an old man, wrestling pairs who resemble Abraham and Isaac. Some writers (cf. Porter, *Crosses and Culture of Ireland*, pp. 126, 127) have identified them as Jacob wrestling with the angel. This is doubtful for the following reasons. The pair is shown three times, but in no case with attributes consistent with the distinction of Jacob and the angel. They are both naked to the waist, and neither has wings. Nor is there reference to Jacob's thigh, weakened by the angel's blow, as told in *Genesis* XXXIII : 25 and illustrated in Trani. It has been supposed that the praying gesture of the boy in the upper zone indicates the blessing of Jacob by the angel; but why should this bearded angel clutch Jacob by the hair, as in the scene of Abraham and Isaac on the other side? In the middle zone, the tail of a monster on the front of the *trumeau* is wound tightly around the necks of the wrestlers. This is evidently a *drôlerie*, and the intriguing contrast of the wallet hanging from the boy's belt and the key from the old man's seems to confirm this interpretation. From the viewpoint of the formal peculiarity of the sculptures of Souillac we might even hazard the guess that the wallet and key pertain to an episodic intrigue formed like the sculptural pattern, wallet and key being complementary opposites, each incomplete in itself, like the wrestling, interlocked figures. In Beaulieu, too, a young and an old man are juxtaposed as caryatids on the *trumeau* of the portal. Playful fantasies of force and conflict underlie the conception in Souillac, rather than a theological idea. If anything, it is a counter-theological idea. The parody or secular inversion of the Abraham-Isaac theme in these wrestling figures in Souillac corresponds to the marginal inversion of the Daniel theme on the impost of a capital in the cloister of Moissac (*Art Bulletin*, XIII, 1931, p. 334; Rupin, *L'Abbaye et les cloîtres de Moissac*, Paris, 1897, pp. 293, 294). There a little figure, no prophet or saint, but a droll layman, strangles two giant birds with his arms, pulls the tail of one lion and stabs another in the jaws with a comical bravado and irreverent self-confidence which deflates the theme below of Daniel protected by God from the lions.

in the positive concern with the religious and moral struggles of a single lay individual. The sense of the story of Theophilus is much richer than appears from
the simple moral of salvation through Mary. In its twelfth century form [15] we
can distinguish the following contemporary interests and motives:

1. The secular concern with position and wealth in the very bosom of the
church, the church being one of the great feudal powers, a corporate land-
holder with a functional stratification of rank. The *vidame*, Theophilus, the lay
administrator of the church funds,[16] has declined the office of bishop through
humility. But once he is removed from his own office by the new bishop, he is
deeply distressed and attempts to recover his old position. The presence of Peter
and Benedict [17] at the sides of the relief pertains to the administrative, ecclesiastical context of the affair: Benedict is the great abbot, Peter, the first bishop. I
know of no other image of Theophilus in which this context of authority is
emphasized through the figures of the two saints.

2. The apostasy or heresy of Theophilus. To regain his position, he renounces
Christ and the Virgin and accepts the devil as his lord. The intermediary is a
Jew. The legend probably originated in Asia Minor [18] during the early Christian
period at a moment of heresies and controversies over the nature of Mary as the
mother of God. But in the twelfth century the apostasy of Theophilus, his adherence to the devil, had a local significance in southern France, the classic

[15] For a summary of the history of the story, with a bibliography of the numerous vernacular versions,
see Karl Plenzat, *Die Theophiluslegende in den Dichtungen des Mittelalters* (Germanische Studien, Heft 43, Berlin,
1926), the edition of *Rutebeuf, Le Miracle de Théophile*, by Grace Frank (Champion, Paris, 1925), pp. iv–x, and
Ramé, *loc. cit.*, pp. 228, 229. For Latin versions of the Romanesque period (eleventh and twelfth centuries),
see the sermon of Fulbert of Chartres, Migne, *P.L.*, v. 141, col. 323, 324; the chronicle of Sigebert, *ibid.*,
v. 160, col. 102; the poem *Historia Theophili Metrica*, attributed to Marbodus, *ibid.*, v. 171, col. 1593 ff.;
Honorius of Autun, *ibid.*, v. 172, col. 992–994. When this article was in press, I learned of Alfred C.
Fryer's "Theophilus, the Penitent, as Represented in Art," *Archaeological Journal*, XCII (1936), pp. 287–333.
E. Faligan, "Des formes iconographiques de la légende de Théophile," *Revue des traditions populaires*, v (1890),
pp. 1–14, lists several versions of the thirteenth century, but ignores Souillac.

[16] On the *vidame* (Latin, *vicedominus*) see A. Luchaire, *Manuel des institutions françaises* (*Période des Capé-
tiens directs*), Paris, 1892, pp. 288, 289. The *vidame* was appointed by the bishop to exercise episcopal juris-
diction in certain temporal matters, to look after the property of the church, to represent the bishop in the
feudal courts, to protect the episcopal palace, etc. It was often a hereditary office, with a seigneurie consisting of a house in the city and a piece of land. In some literary versions, Theophilus is a merchant or layman and is prompted by a desire for wealth (cf. Plenzat, *op. cit.*, pp. 43, 231).

[17] The identity of this figure is not altogether certain. It is unlikely that it represents St. Stephen
(as Porter supposed), in spite of the prominent dalmatic, the maniple, and the youthful face. The crozier
excludes a deacon; it is more properly the attribute of a bishop or abbot, who are sometimes shown, as
here, with dalmatic and maniple and without chasuble and mitre. The omission of the chasuble in the relief
may have been a formal necessity, the V-shape being unsuited to the design at this point.

What particular saintly abbot or bishop was represented is difficult to decide. The following come into
question: St. Eligius (Eloi), bishop of Noyon, who was mistakenly regarded as the founder of the abbey
(see *Gallia Christiana*, I, p. 179) and whose feast and translation were celebrated in Souillac (but it is unknown whether this tradition and cult already existed in the twelfth century); St. Gerald, abbot of Aurillac, founder of the abbey of Aurillac to which the monastery of Souillac belonged, and the donor of the
site of Souillac to this abbey (909); finally, St. Benedict, the founder of the order itself. Benedict is represented on the portal of Moissac, but without the crozier. He holds the latter on a capital in St. Benoît-sur-
Loire (Porter, *Pilgrimage Roads*, ill. 1420) and in other Romanesque works. Of these three possibilities,
Benedict seems the most plausible counterpart to Peter, and we provisionally assign his name to the figure.

[18] In the literary versions Theophilus is described as a *vidame* of the church of Adana in Cilicia in the
sixth century. The Latin accounts can be traced back in part to a Greek version by one Eutychianos who
pretends to be an eyewitness.

region of medieval "Manichaean" heresy which regarded the church as a creation of Satan.[19] A grievance of the heretics against the church was the sinfulness
of its great wealth and offices; they demanded a cheap religion compatible with
the ideals of poverty and a pure devotion.

3. The acquisition of rank through a written charter, feudal in nature,
whereby the individual obtains a privilege or benefit by conceding something
in turn to a seigneur and by becoming his vassal. The signing of the charter
plays an important part in the story in the literary versions of the Romanesque
period.[20] In Souillac the feudal moment is enacted ceremonially in the gesture
of feudal homage; the devil takes the hands of Theophilus between his own.[21]

4. The conception of the feudal contract as a fatal trap. The vassal sells
himself; he is in the power of the seigneur. This aspect of the feudal relation we
suppose was significant in Souillac because of the secular lords of the churches
and abbeys in the diocese of Cahors, to which Souillac belonged. The cathedral
of Cahors and the abbeys of Moissac and Beaulieu, among others, were continu-
ally disturbed in the late eleventh and early twelfth century by the claims of
nobles of the region, the so-called "secular-abbots," on whom they had once
relied for protection in return for feudal privileges.[22]

5. The rescue of the vassal through the intervention, not of God, but the
Virgin, i.e., the powerful lady who is superior to the seigneur-devil; she is also
the patroness of the abbey of Souillac. In the Middle Ages, the queen or noblewoman could intercede for a guilty person and was regarded as an especially
influential protector of the suppliant.[23]

6. The intercession of Mary is personally solicited in this story, outside the
normal channels of administered liturgy; but it is effectively won only in the
church and through a canonical penance of forty days. Hence the church satis-
fies through this legend the popular demands, so crucial to the protestants of the
twelfth and later centuries, for an individual, unmediated relation to God and
for an inexpensive piety. But it encloses them within the physical framework of
the organized, orthodox religion.

7. Salvation, finally, by a material device, through return of the contract,
a salvation in this world and by everyday juridical means. The devil has no
power over Theophilus when the latter has regained the document with his

[19] On the heresies in southern France, see I. von Döllinger, *Beiträge zur Sektengeschichte des Mittelalters*, I
(Munich, 1890), and J. Guiraud, *Histoire de l'Inquisition au Moyen Age*, I (Paris, 1935).

[20] See the Latin texts cited in n. 15 above.

[21] On this ceremony, see Luchaire, *op. cit.*, p. 185. In Gothic art, Theophilus kneels before the devil.
In the Greek text, Theophilus is kissed by the devil, as in the ceremony of homage in the Byzantine court.
This detail is omitted in the early Latin translation (Plenzat, *op. cit.*, p. 18, n. 13).

[22] On these *abbates-milites* in Moissac and Beaulieu, see A. Lagrèze-Fossat, *Études historiques sur Moissac*,
I (Paris, 1870), pp. 115–142, and M. Deloche, *Cartulaire de l'abbaye de Beaulieu en Limousin* (*Collection de documents inédits sur l'histoire de France*), Paris, 1859, pp. xix ff.

[23] On the analogy of the noblewoman as intercessor, see the medieval text cited by Coulton, *Five Centuries of Religion*, I, 140. In France the conception of the Virgin as the interceding queen of heaven was undoubtedly conditioned by the important administrative and even judicial role of the queen in the French
monarchy, especially since the rising monarchy during the twelfth century had the support of the
church.

signature.[24] Neither the confession nor the death of the penitent, which follows soon after, appears in the relief.

Of all these possible meanings and interests, only certain ones were essential to the designers of the relief. The chief moments in the sculpture are the contract, the submission to the devil as seigneur, and the liberation from the contract through the Virgin's aid. But these episodes are enclosed by figures of church authority, Benedict and Peter, and by the mediating angels.

The subject of the great relief is therefore not the supervening Christ-Savior, dogmatically centralized and elevated, but an individual rescued from the devil, from apostasy, from material, feudal difficulties and his own corruption within the political body of the church, through the direct intervention of the mother of Christ, opposed as a woman to the loathsome male devil. Theophilus is a layman, whose pact with the devil and change of fortune have an essentially secular nucleus,[25] comparable to the later adventure of Faust. The antitheses of rank and privation, of the devil and the Virgin, of apostasy and repentance, create a psychological depth — the counterpart of a world of developing secular activity and freedom, more complex than the closed field of Christian piety represented in the dogmatic images of the majestic Christ on Romanesque portals. In the themes of individual salvation and intercession, the relief of Souillac anticipates the Gothic tympana of the Last Judgment in which the Christian spectator could identify himself and his fellows. It goes far beyond these, however, since the judgment of Theophilus is isolated from the Resurrection of the dead and the divinity of the crucified Christ; the incident is localized on this earth as the dramatic vicissitude of a single intriguing individual. But the fortunes of this individual at every point depend on his relations to the feudal church.

VIII

The school of the diocese of Cahors (or the region of Quercy and southeast Limousin) to which the sculptures of Souillac, Moissac, and Beaulieu belong, shows a remarkable evolution of themes within the short period of fifteen years between about 1115 and 1130. Each of these portals is a highly original or, at least, untraditional work: we know no earlier example of a tympanum or painting with the *crowned* Christ among the seated elders, as in Moissac; no earlier Last Judgment with the naked torso and outstretched arms of Christ, as in Beaulieu; and no prior image of the story of Theophilus.[26] If we consider merely

[24] Cf. the version by Fulbert of Chartres: "She (Mary) consoled the grieving man, promising him indulgence: and that he should not doubt her promise, she tore the charter from the devil and returned it to the captive as a token of his liberty. When, upon awakening, he found it on his breast, what joy he felt, with what pious feeling he uttered sounds of exultation and confession!" (Migne, *P.L.*, v. 141, col. 323, 324.)

[25] This sense of Theophilus is indicated in the representation of the story in a wheel of fortune in the de Brailles psalter in the Fitzwilliam Museum, Cambridge. See Fryer, *op. cit.*, pl. IX, opp. p. 300.

[26] Mr. Charles Niver has called my attention to a drawing of Theophilus in Paris, Bibl. Nat. MS. Latin 11750, f. 51, a manuscript of the mid-eleventh century from St. Germain-des-Prés, and has kindly permitted me to reproduce it in this article (Fig. 15). But here we see only the figure of Theophilus imploring the Virgin seated between angels; the compact with the devil is not represented. The real subject of the drawing is the Virgin, who is elevated, centralized, and enthroned, and retains her hierarchical majesty.

FIG. 15. PARIS, BIBLIOTHÈQUE NATIONALE, LAT. 11750,
FOL. 51: THEOPHILUS AND THE VIRGIN

the broad external aspect of the iconography, the familiar names like the Last
Judgment, the Vision of Christ and the Elders, the Legend of Theophilus and the
Virgin, by which these sculptures are designated in the books, we will hardly see
more than a superficial relation between them. But if we observe the fuller
range and connection of subjects within each portal, common themes and a continuous growth will be evident, and the local peculiarity and originality of the
school will seem even greater.

In Moissac the dominating scene is already secular and realistic in tendency.
The enthroned royal Christ — whom the natives have identified with Clovis
(*Reclobis*), the legendary founder of the abbey — is surrounded by a court of
lesser kings with an independent mobility of posture, with luxurious costume and
the instruments of courtly entertainment. The hierarchical relations of Roman
Christianity, the temporal claims of the church, are presented here in terms of the
most advanced conceptions of centralized feudal power possible at that moment.
The scenes below, which form uncentralized, episodic groups, display an even
greater iconographic realism. They pertain to history and morality — the
domestic, maternal moments of the Christian legend, the punishment of Avarice
and Unchastity by the monstrous devils, and the banquet of Dives and the
reward of the beggar Lazarus in heaven.

In Beaulieu [27] the moral, individual reference is developed further. The royal
Christ becomes the resurrected, crucified figure, with naked torso and tensely
outstretched arms, surrounded by the material instruments of the Passion. His
absolute formal centrality is compromised by the competing cross held behind
him at the side by two angels; and throughout the tympanum the apostles and
resurrected figures are grouped as independent gesticulating pairs detached from
the central Christ. The hierarchical stratification of Moissac disappears under
the intercepted zones and overlapping figures — signs of a contingent, uncon-
fined activity of single individuals. The historical themes of the porch of Moissac
are lacking; but the tormented figures of Avarice and Unchastity reappear beside new themes of moral conflict and divine intervention. Whereas Moissac
shows only the sin as an accomplished fact in the reliefs of Avarice and Unchastity punished by the devil, Beaulieu adds the psychological episodes of the
Temptation of Christ by the demon. And whereas in Moissac the contrast of
torture and bliss is absolute and still located in the afterlife, in Beaulieu the sculptor creates also a transitive scene of divine intervention; he represents the angel
bringing Habakkuk to Daniel, who sits unharmed among the lions.

In Souillac these marginal human aspects of Beaulieu and Moissac become
central. The subject is the individual sinner, his temptation, intrigue and repentance, his psychological torment and deliverance within this world. Theophilus
confronts the devil twice, like Christ in the Temptation; he is rescued by the Virgin, who is brought by an angel, like Habakkuk to Daniel in Beaulieu, and like
the ram to Isaac in Abraham's Sacrifice on the *trumeau* of Souillac. The fear of
violent destruction, which is embodied in the mythical story of Daniel in the

   [27] Reproduced by A. K. Porter, *Romanesque Sculpture of the Pilgrimage Roads*, ill. 409–420.

lion's den, is evoked in Souillac directly and with overwhelming power by the monstrous beasts actually devouring their victims.

The iconographic development disengaged above from these three portals does not correspond strictly to the temporal order of the works, but to three stages which are evident in the school at different rather than successive moments within a short period of time. The dates of the portals are uncertain; but it is commonly admitted today that the tympanum of Moissac is the oldest of the three, and Beaulieu the most recent. The reliefs below the tympanum of Moissac seem to me to be later than those of Souillac, and contemporary with, or a little later than, Beaulieu.[28] But whatever the exact dates of the sculptures, we may consider their subjects as expressions of new religious and secular interests current in this region during the first third of the twelfth century.

The portal of Moissac, with its incipient realism, is still tied to the dogmatic, centralized iconographic types of earlier medieval art; the tympanum of Beaulieu points to Gothic iconography; but the relief of Souillac looks even farther forward and anticipates in some respects the Renaissance and the end of the Middle Ages. In every one of these, however, there is a moralistic reference to the Christian individual. The spiritual conceptions have a secular axis; they embody the most recent attitude of the church to questions and demands posed under a changing feudalism by the people of the towns and by critical elements within the church. If the majesty of Christ is pictured concretely in Moissac as a royal structure in a feudal world of small, individual vassal-rulers, the moral subjects betray the concern with individual activity outside the confines of traditional Christian piety — Avarice being the accumulation of wealth by the burghers, and Unchastity the libertinism of the towns and the new aristocratic culture. In denouncing these vices and in representing Christ as a king of kings, as the ideal apex of temporal powers, the church was not only asserting its superiority to the feudal lords,[29] but was also defending itself against the charges of the heretics and burgher enemies — especially numerous in southern France — who deplored its wealth and demanded a humble and inexpensive Christianity, a church restricted to its spiritual sphere.

In Beaulieu the Last Judgment becomes increasingly concrete. It portrays the humanity of the judging Christ and assigns a prominent place to the individual sinners and the blessed and to their actual emergence from the tomb. If the wealthy abbey of Moissac in a spirit of counter-reform condemned the avaricious burgher and recommended poverty and charity in the person of the beggar Lazarus, Souillac pictured the quasi-simoniac official as an un-Christian apostate, but finally a repentant sinner, saved by the indulgent Virgin after his prolonged prayer in the church. In Beaulieu we see on one side of the porch

[28] I date the tympanum of Moissac about 1115, the sculptures of Souillac about 1115–1120, the porch of Moissac, including the jamb figures of Isaiah and Peter, about 1120–1130, and Beaulieu about 1125–1130. The reasons are too complex to be presented here.

[29] Such an image of the supreme king expressed also the monarchical sympathies of the church, the centralized, monarchical state being the necessary political counterpart of the expanding centralized church and its ally in the common struggle against the local feudal nobility.

Christ refusing the devil's offer of the riches of the world, on the other, Daniel protected from the lions and nourished in the den by the miraculously transported Habakkuk, the type of the priest who administers communion.

Thus the church glorifies poverty as a Christian virtue and admits a personal relation to a higher being, the mother of God; at the same time, answering those who deny the value of the Eucharist, it represents individual salvation, physical and spiritual, as finally dependent on the instrumentality of the church. The themes of Daniel, the Temptation of Christ, and the Last Judgment were known long before in art, and Theophilus, Avarice, and Unchastity in literature. But in the face of new conditions the church does not simply reaffirm its older doctrines. It presents new versions or rearrangements which isolate the aspects of these themes relevant to its mediating function, its power, and its interests in the changing society of which the church is a sensitive part. In Souillac the individual ecclesiastic moral episode replaces the symbolic, hierarchical Christ as a central theme. The protagonist is a secular functionary of the church.[30]

The accompanying stylistic changes cannot be deduced simply from the new content of religious art. They are shaped finally in a wider field of social and cultural conditions, although certain of the formal peculiarities of the sculpture of Souillac are solutions of a problem of religious representation posed uniquely in Souillac. The decentralizing episodic forms and discoördinate schemes, the antithetic mobility of the figures, the concreteness and energy of presentation, in contrast to the traditional centralized, symbolic designs, presuppose the broader conception of the active, morally divided individual, at once Christian and secular, whose struggles are resolved in the religious legends of the church. The social and economic development which indirectly evoked the new programs of imagery in the church also promoted the freedom of the sculptor and suggested to him within the framework of spiritualistic and ascetic conceptions more naturalistic forms, a more articulated and flexible composition, to satisfy the new norms of lay experience. Throughout his work the sculptor displays in the intricate design and variety of detail an independent virtuosity of manipulation, beyond the needs of traditional, symbolic imagery. (In this he resembles the vernacular lyric poets of the time whose freedom as artist-craftsmen, affirmed in numerous comments on their own art, depends also on their service in the entertainment of the feudal nobility.) The specialized autonomy of the sculptor as an artisan entrusted with great enterprises by the church appears not only in the prominence of original carved ornament beside the religious subjects, but in the tendency of the sculptor to transform this ornament into images of action and daily life abounding in realistic detail. Even if it is possible that the beasts of the pillar of Souillac were already interpreted as Christian symbols in the

---

[30] It is not a theme issuing from the "people"; its popularity, as M. Mâle has observed, is due to the importance given to the story by the church, which introduced it into the liturgy as early as the eleventh century. It is worth citing here the observation of Plenzat (*op. cit.*, p. 236) that none of the vernacular versions of the legend is by a nobleman; they were all written by poets from the clergy or the lower classes, and abound in secular-pagan elements. In several of the poems, the Virgin is relatively unimportant and the action terminates, as in Souillac, with the return of the contract.

twelfth century, it is hardly likely that they were designed as such from the very first. The fear of violence or the respect for aggressive force which was usually sublimated in mythical themes of divine protection, like Daniel in the lions' den, or of the heroism of a religious figure, like Samson, is here embodied directly in a nonreligious fantasy of rapacious beasts. The very existence of the *trumeau* implies that sculpture has begun to emerge as an independent spectacle on the margins of religious art, as a wonderful imaginative workmanship addressed to secular fantasy. But this fantasy is governed by the content and material levels of social experience. The *trumeau* is a passionate *drôlerie*, brutal and realistic in detail, an elaboration of themes of impulsive and overwhelming physical force, corresponding to the role of violence at this point in the history of feudal society. They are like the dreams of animal combat which foretell the ferocious human battles in the contemporary *chansons de geste*.

The secular tendency evident in the sculpture of Souillac within the framework of the church issued from a moment in social development which was apparently very brief. We lack the documents to reconstruct the formative factors in Souillac itself. The local peculiarities of the history of neither Souillac [31] nor the region [32] are sufficiently clear. And the economic and social movement of Quercy during this period has yet to be described from a viewpoint broad enough to permit us to grasp directly the interplay of classes, institutions, traditions, and culture, and to account for the differences between the local art and that of other regions. We know simply that in the later eleventh and early twelfth century, after a long period of restricted agricultural economy and anarchic feudal struggles, this region experienced an intense economic development. The growing communes acquired vernacular written codes of municipal law; and the monasteries themselves, which had accumulated great landed properties and moved beyond the sphere of merely local interests, were affected in some measure by the rise of the towns and the burgher class, profiting by the growth of trade and amassing wealth from their tolls, rents, and agricultural enterprises. The strength of the local nobility declined, while the power of the abbeys became broader and more centralized, sustained by Cluny, the bishops and popes, and sometimes by the towns. The abbeys of Moissac, Souillac, and Beaulieu were all situated on important streams and derived from their feudal rights over the river traffic and the fishing a considerable income and influence over the towns.[33] The abbey of Souillac was the feudal seigneur of the town, to which she owed a part of her revenues, but was herself undisturbed by the rival feudal powers — unlike Moissac, where the townsmen achieved a high degree of municipal independence early in the twelfth century, and the secular "cavalier-abbots" intervened for a

---

[31] The book of Abbé P. Pons, *Souillac et ses environs* (Souillac, 1923) summarizes the scanty older literature on this period; see p. 205 for a bibliography of manuscripts and printed literature.

[32] The chief work remains the first volume of Guillaume Lacoste, *Histoire générale de la province de Quercy* (Cahors, 1883). For the history of Moissac and Beaulieu, see n. 22 above.

[33] The wealth of the merchants of Souillac during the Middle Ages seems to have issued from their monopoly of the salt trade in Corrèze, Auvergne, and part of Quercy. They shipped timber to Bordeaux by way of the Dordogne and brought back salt in exchange. See Pons, *op. cit.*, p. 11.

time in the affairs of the monastery. With their many dependent priories (some over a hundred miles away), their cultivated lands, projects of reclamation and construction, and constant jurisdictional disputes, these great abbeys, as administrative centers of an expanding corporate power, promoted the practical attitudes, the calculations, and the everyday realism familiar to the merchants of the time. The abbots of Moissac were respected for their sagacity and leadership in temporal affairs.

The fact that so many of the great churches of the region, including the cathedral of Cahors, were built in the beginning of the twelfth century long before the cathedrals of the North, is itself a sign of the material expansion in Quercy at this moment. And the very character of the Romanesque churches of Souillac, Moissac, and Cahors, as single-aisled domed buildings, untraditional in plan and method of construction,[34] also points to the force of novel conditions. However original and peculiar to Aquitaine are the complete buildings, the conception of the unit bay with dome, pendentives, and salient piers was borrowed directly from the art of a distant eastern region with which the West had just renewed commercial and political relations after a gigantic military effort. Instead of the prolonged vista focussed on the choir and altar, instead of the succession of nave bays flanked by subordinate aisles, these churches present a shorter series of independent, self-contained domical bays to which the choir is added as a subordinate terminal niche. When we enter the nave, we are not drawn to the distant sacred space of the apse by the endless rhythmical procession of arches and supports, but each of the two or three gigantic bays appears to us a complete individual with its own domical focus. The domed churches are a sharp deviation from the historical line leading from Romanesque to Gothic architecture and foreshadow late medieval, Renaissance, and Protestant churches. The broad proportions of these novel buildings, their diffuse, undramatic lighting, the explicitness and accented materiality of the prismatic and concave forms are secular in suggestion. Nothing in Romanesque architecture is more remote from the

[34] On these buildings see Raymond Rey, *La Cathédrale de Cahors et les origines de l'architecture à coupoles d'Aquitaine* (Paris, 1925). On pp. 194 ff. he attributes the domed church of Moissac (of which only the lower nave walls, narthex, and porch survive) to the period of 1150 to 1180. This attribution rests largely on an equivocal document concerning the attendance of the bishop of Oloron at the dedication of the church of Moissac in 1180, but is not supported by the detailed comparative study of the moldings and ornament. The church is more likely of the first third of the twelfth century. Excavations have shown that the foundations of the preceding Romanesque church (mid-eleventh century) did not extend as far as the present narthex and porch, which are no later than the first third of the twelfth century. The west wall of the nave which masks the narthex and tower was erected only soon after, and so soon after, that the courses of the upper north side could coincide with the western part of the adjoining nave wall which was progressing toward the narthex at this time. The moldings of the porch, the narthex, the exterior of the tower, and the windows of the nave are very similar, and in some details identical. The same atelier produced the capitals of the nave windows, various modillions of the tower of Moissac and capitals and modillions of the domed church of Cahors, which M. Rey attributes to the first quarter of the century. (On pp. 162, 163 he assigns to the same period the domed church of Souillac which in some respects is more developed toward the later types than either Moissac or Cahors.) It is therefore highly unlikely that the similar construction in Moissac belongs to the second half of the century, and is fifty or more years later than its own narthex. More relevant to the date of construction than the reference of 1180 is the papal bull of 1132 which granted forty days' indulgence to those who visited Moissac on the feast of the dedication of its church (Lagrèze-Fossat, *op. cit.*, III, pp. 234–235).

Gothic cathedrals which inspire, through their steep proportions, their hierarchical subdivisions, their mysterious contrasts of light and dark and network of ascending and receding lines, apprehensions of an intangible, pervasive but transcendent order, everywhere reaching out to subdue and absorb the individual. The domed churches are clear in form and unmystical in expression, especially in the spaces of the nave reserved for the congregation. The nave is amplified and liberated from the compulsive apsidal focus, just as the monumental design of Theophilus disenthrones the absolutized Christ.

We cannot pursue here the similarities in the development of the architecture and the sculpture of the region. The parallelism is quite general and limited to aspects in which common factors operate; for the two arts have their special functions and conditions at this moment and therefore respond differently to the great historical changes of the time. The forms of the domed churches of Aquitaine have been explained, together with the three-aisled churches, as a *direct* reflection of the heretical movements of southern France.[35] But no evidence connects the particular buildings directly with the heretics, and it is in a region outside the main centers of heresy in Languedoc that the domed churches arise. The secular attitudes expressed in the heresies were not limited, however, to the new religious sects; the latter were themselves the result of special circumstances in the opposition to the church. The secular tendencies which under some conditions promoted the heresies were part of a more general development of society of which the effects appear also in political forms like the communes, in new moral ideas, in vernacular literature and science — in that whole complex of worldly interests which is sometimes called the proto-renaissance. The paganism of this culture does not exclude the ascetic ideals of the heretics, just as the later Protestantism with its puritan virtues is an aggressive middle-class religious counterpart of the humanism of an aristocratic culture. The domed architecture of Aquitaine was affected, like the living church itself, by the social and economic conditions which were also the fruitful ground of anti-ecclesiastical, puritan, heretical beliefs. It illustrates how the church, despite its claim to an independent spiritual sphere, by virtue of its real dependence on earthly conditions adopted an architecture more adequate to sentiments of secular freedom. In the relief of Theophilus in Souillac the elements of the conflict between the older ecclesiastical claims and the new social relations are mythically transposed and resolved in a compromise form which entails, however, a new individual framework of Christian piety. Not in Souillac alone but throughout Romanesque art can be observed in varying degree a dual character of realism and abstraction, of secularity and dogma, rooted in the historical development and social oppositions of the time.

[35] Notably by Felix Witting, *Westfranzösische Kuppelkirchen* (Strassburg, 1904).

ADDENDUM: A drawing of the Last Judgment in Pembroke College (Cambridge) MS. 120, in which Christ is shown with naked breast and arms extended diagonally downward, seems to be of the same period as the sculpture of Beaulieu.

LES TRAITS ORIGINAUX DE L'ICONOGRAPHIE
DANS LA SCULPTURE ROMANE DE L'AUVERGNE

LOUIS BRÉHIER

ON NE SOUTIENT plus aujourd'hui, comme le voulait Quicherat, que les seuls procédés architecturaux distinguent les écoles régionales de l'art roman. On reconnait que leur originalité ne s'affirme pas seulement dans les plans d'édifices et les combinaisons d'équilibre, mais aussi dans leur ornementation sculptée, dont les méthodes, la technique et le style révèlent au même degré que l'architecture les qualités profondes et le génie d'une province. A ces éléments il convient d'ajouter les thèmes iconographiques, profanes ou religieux, traités par les sculpteurs. Dans l'immense programme encyclopédique de décoration, chaque région fit son choix et c'est ce choix qui manifeste le mieux l'originalité d'une école régionale, comme celles de Bourgogne, de Provence, de Lombardie, du Languedoc. C'est par les thèmes favoris traités dans ces régions que s'affirment leur tempérament, leurs préoccupations morales, religieuses et même parfois sociales.

C'est à ce point de vue que l'école d'art roman, qui a couvert de ses édifices la Basse-Auvergne, mérite d'être étudiée. Non seulement ses monuments sont remarquables par leur unité d'inspiration, mais le plus grand nombre des thèmes iconographiques traités par ses maîtres révèle une originalité profonde qui la distingue d'une manière saisissante des régions voisines, Haute-Auvergne, Limousin, Bourgogne, Velay, dont chacune a des traditions iconographiques différentes.

On peut diviser en trois classes les thèmes iconographiques de la Basse-Auvergne. Les uns lui sont communs avec d'autres provinces. D'autres, qui se trouvent dans le même cas, ont été adoptés par les Auvergnats avec une telle prédilection et reproduits si souvent qu'ils forment un des traits caractéristiques de l'art roman auvergnat. D'autres en fin ont été créés en Auvergne: on ne les trouve nulle part ailleurs et quelques uns sont des exemples uniques. Ce sont les plus intéressants et les plus savoureux. Ce sont ceux-ci surtout dont il sera question dans cette brève étude destinée à honorer la mémoire du grand archéologue que fut Kingsley Porter, avec qui l'auteur de ces lignes eut autrefois le grand honneur de visiter quelques uns des plus beaux monuments de l'Auvergne romane.

Le champ de l'iconographie. — On ne voit pas en Auvergne de grands ensembles iconographiques comparables a ceux des autres provinces. Le seul grand portail auquel aient travaillé des maîtres auvergnats, celui de Conques-en-Rouergue, est situé hors de la province. Ceux-mêmes, dont on trouve des traces en Auvergne (Ebreuil, Saint-Pourçain), situés aux frontières du pays, sont l'oeuvre de maîtres étrangers.

En Auvergne l'ornement sculpté se développe d'abord sur les linteaux en bâtière et parfois dans les arcs de décharge qui les surmontent. Les portails en plein cintre à voussures garnies de statuettes (Nonette, Mailhat) sont très rares. Mais ce sont surtout les corbeilles des chapiteaux sculptés, soit à deux faces aux demi-colonnes, soit sur leurs quatre faces, dans les chœurs entourés d'un déambulatoire, que se développent les thèmes iconographiques.

Iconographie et technique. — La méthode même avec laquelle ces thèmes sont disposés est le trait fondamental de l'originalité auvergnate. Les sculpteurs, qui ont traité presque exclusivement le chapiteau corinthien, lui ont, de parti pris, conservé ses lignes essentielles, même lorsqu'il est historié de figures. De là le souci de placer aux angles du chapiteau, soulignant les volutes de la corbeille corinthienne, des têtes de personnages, traitées presque en ronde-bosse et disproportionnées avec le volume et la taille de leurs corps. De là aussi une méthode de composition étrange qui consiste à placer dans un angle le personnage principal d'une scène, par exemple le Christ de la Transfiguration ou du Jugement Dernier à Saint-Nectaire, ou à répéter le même personnage aux deux extrémités d'une même face [1] (Adam à Notre Dame du Port de Clermont).

D'autre part, les compositions auvergnates sont soumises comme celles des autres provinces aux lois de la stylistique romane, si bien formulées par Henri Focillon et Jurgis Baltrušaitis. Sous la liberté apparente de la composition, on retrouve toujours le schéma géométrique qui l'a engendré. Lorsque le cadre est apparent, comme sur les linteaux en bâtière, ou bien la taille des personnages diminue progressivement du centre aux extrémités (parti naïf du linteau de Mozat), ou bien d'une manière plus savante, le sculpteur adapte la vraisemblance des poses aux dimensions du cadre (linteau du portail sud de Notre Dame du Port, dont les motifs sont si bien équilibrés et où le sculpteur, pour obéir aux exigences du cadre, a créé une belle variante iconographique, en agenouillant l'ange qui assiste au baptême de Jésus).[2]

Enfin c'est encore pour sacrifier au schéma géometrique et à la symétrie qui en résulte, que les sculpteurs n'ont pas hésité à redoubler sur le même chapiteau telle figure, comme celle du Bon Pasteur, qui n'a de sens que si elle est isolée. Ainsi c'est le point de vue décoratif qui prédomine dans l'art roman auvergnat et auquel doivent se soumettre les thèmes iconographiques eux-mêmes.

L'imitation de l'antique. — Nous laisserons de côté des thèmes que l'Auvergne possède en commun avec d'autres provinces, mais que ses maîtres ont reproduits si fréquemment, qu'ils constituent un trait caractéristique de l'école auvergnate: *aigles*, souvenir du symbolisme de l'art triomphal; *centaures*, presque toujours répétés et affrontés (sur certains chapiteaux le centaure, muni de longues oreilles est confondu avec le *minotaure*, comme l'indique l'inscription d'un chapiteau de Besse); *griffons* buvant dans un calice ou simplement affrontés; *atlantes* debout, accroupis, agenouillés et saisissant leurs pieds relevés avec leurs mains, ainsi que les *néréides*, *sirènes*, *tritons* qui sont aussi en nombre imposant.

---

[1] Kingsley Porter, *Romanesque Sculpture of the Pilgrimage Roads* (Boston, 1923), VIII, n°s 1172, 1201.
[2] K. Porter, *op. laud.*, n°s 1223, 1161.

Nous nous contenterons d'attirer l'attention sur des modèles plus rares et propres à l'Auvergne. Tel est le chapiteau sur lequel apparaissent trois masques au milieu de touffes d'acanthe, dont un modèle galloromain se trouve au musée de Reims.[3]

Exemplaires: Mozat, nef (Fig. 1: le plus près de l'antique, fermeté du style); *Notre Dame du Port*, nef (archaïque); *Saint-Nectaire*; *Volvic* (un seul mascaron au centre); *Glaine-Montaigut* (masques aux angles de la corbeille); *Aulnat* (masque barbu en cul-de-lampe).

FIG. 1. MOZAT, COLLATÉRAL NORD

Tels sont les chapiteaux décorés de lutteurs, toujours nus, lançant des balles (*Thiers*, église du Moûtier. — *Courpière*) ou pliant le genou comme s'ils exécutaient des mouvements rythmés (*Thiers*, même église. — *Mozat*). Des figurines semblables timbrent parfois les poteries rouges à reliefs fabriquées à Lezoux, non loin de Thiers.[4]

Un thème rare, qui rapelle le symbolisme triomphal est celui de la Victoire gravant des exploits sur un bouclier, sujet banal à l'epoque romaine. Les sculp-

---

[3] Espérandieu, *Bas-reliefs de la Gaule romaine*, t. v, n° 3746.
[4] Cf. Déchelette, *Vases céramiques de la Gaule*, t. I, pl. v, n° 69.

FIG. 2. CHAPITEAUX DU COLLATÉRAL SUD DE MOZAT

teurs auvergnats ont doublé la figure sur leurs corbeilles suivant les lois de la stylistique et placé les deux figures aux angles, les boucliers sur les faces.

Exemplaires: Mozat (Fig. 2); *Notre Dame du Port; Saint-Nectaire.*

Enfin un chapiteau du chœur de Notre Dame du Port est unique en son genre. Une de ses faces représente deux génies ailés affrontés, coiffés de casques

FIG. 3. CHŒUR DE NOTRE-DAME DU PORT

et vêtus de tuniques courtes, perçant symétriquement de leurs lances entrecroisées leur boucliers oblongs, heurtés l'un contre l'autre (Fig. 3).

Ethique et morale pratique. — C'est dans ce domaine que les sculpteurs auvergnats ont montré peut-être le plus de verve et d'invention.

On sait quelle vogue eut au moyen âge le poëme de Prudence de la Psychomachie. Les plus anciens manuscrits illustrés de cette oeuvre attribuent l'armure guerrière aux Vertus combattant contre les Vices. Les sculpteurs romans se sont inspirés de ces miniatures, mais la plupart du temps, comme dans l'ouest de la France, leurs Vertus sont allongées dans les voussures d'un portail (*Aulnay,*

Blasimon, Corme-Royal, Pont-l'Abbé, Chadenac, etc.). Il n'en est que plus intéressant de trouver des épisodes de la Psychomachie sur un chapiteau du chœur de Notre Damé du Port:

> *Largitas* et *Caritas* coiffées du casque hémispherique carolingien, vêtues de la lourde broigne, entrechoquant leurs boucliers et perçant de leurs lances entrecroisées les Vices terrassés; la *Colère,* femme nue, échevelée, aux bras de laquelle s'enroulent d'affreux dragons ailés, se perçant la poitrine d'une large épée; enfin le combat de *Miséricorde* (désignée par l'inscription tirée de Math. 29:39, gravée sur son bouclier), couverte de l'armure carolingienne et menaçant de sa large épée un démon barbu, l'*Avarice,* dont la tirelire, une marmite à deux anses, l'*aulula* de Plaute, gît à ses pieds.[5]

Sur une corbeille du chœur de Volvic les vertus cardinales, désignées par des inscriptions, sont figurées par des personnages symboliques: FORTITVDO par un chevalier tête nue, vêtu d'un haubert, la main sur un long pavois; VMILITAS par un évêque; IVSTITIA par un clerc tenant une balance; TEMPERANTIA par une lance dont la hampe est tenue par le chevalier et par l'évêque des faces précédentes. Ce sont là les vertus attribuées par ses panégyristes à l'évêque Saint Priest (sanctus Praejectus), assassiné à Volvic en 674.[6]

Un chapiteau particulier à l'Auvergne, où il est répandu à de multiples exemplaires, mais dont la signification est quelque peu énigmatique, représente un homme vêtu du bliaud et des chausses collantes du XIIe siècle, tirant de toutes ses forces sur une corde passée au cou d'un grand singe velu, au front fuyant, à la mâchoire bestiale. La seule hypothèse raisonnable c'est que le singe représente le démon vaincu et pris au piège, comme le montrent de nombreuses légendes médiévales. Dans la Tentation du Christ figurée à la Porte des Orfèvres de Santiago de Compostelle, le diable, monté sur le toit du Temple, ressemble au singe des chapiteaux auvergnats et les assimilations du singe au diable se rencontrent dans la litterature.[7]

> *Exemplaires: Notre Dame du Port; Mozat; Saint-Nectaire; Besse; Brioude; Pont-du-Château; Chauriat; Orcival; Maringues* (le personnage qui tient la corde est à cheval et couvert d'une armure); *Gergovie,* anc. *Merdogne* (deux singes aux angles tenus par trois personnages); *Combronde* (le chasseur est agenouillé); *Issoire* (sur la face le chasseur tient au lasso deux singes qui semblent résister).

Le thème si répandu est évidemment issu de quelque légende populaire dont le sens est aujourd'hui perdu. Au contraire un autre thème, non moins fréquent, a une signification très claire. Il représente au centre des corbeilles un usurier agenouillé, en général une grosse bourse pendue au cou, que tourmentent deux démons placés aux angles. Un cartouche portant la même inscription orne les exemplaires de Clermont et de Brioude: MILEARTIFEX SCRIPSIT TV PERIISTI VSVRA (l'être aux mille moyens — cf. le *polymechanos Odysseus* d'Homère — a écrit: Tu as péri par ton usure). On sait qu'au moyen âge le simple prêt à intérêt était regardé par l'Eglise comme usuraire, d'où peut-être ce thème de prédication morale

---

[5] K. Porter, n°s 1180–1182.

[6] K. Porter, n° 1207.

[7] Hugue de Saint-Victor, *De bestiis,* Migne, t. CLXXVII, col. 62. — Etienne de Bourbon, n° 335, édit. *Soc. Hist. de France,* p. 284–285.

destiné à flêtrir les usuriers notoires, Juifs, Lombards, et Cahorsins ; en Auvergne les transactions multiples qui eurent lieu au moment de la première croisade pour l'équipement des chevaliers amenèrent la formation d'une classe de banquiers et de prêteurs sur gage, ce qui explique peut-être l'insistance avec laquelle le thème y a été traité. Les sculpteurs romans ont d'ailleurs flêtri l'usure dans toutes les provinces, mais surtout aux portails (Moissac, La Graulière) et jamais sous la forme originale des chapiteaux auvergnats, dont le modèle est unique.

FIG. 4. CHAPITEAU D'ENNEZAT

Exemplaires: Notre Dame du Port et *Brioude* (avec l'inscription) ; *Saint-Nectaire; Saint-Paulien; Chanteuges* (démons remplacés par deux dragons) ; *Chatelmontagne; Mailhat* (portail sud) ; *Chauriat; Maringues; Volvic.*

Variantes: Issoire, Saint-Myon (un seul démon entraîne deux usuriers) ; *Lavaudieu,* cloître (l'usurier seul représenté la bourse au cou) ; *Orcival* (le coupable désigné par l'inscription: FOLDIVES, *riche insensé,* la bourse au cou, est entouré de deux démons à oreilles de chat qui lui enfoncent un épieu dans l'épaule) ; *Ennezat* (Fig. 4: l'usurier, bourse au cou, de face a les mains broyées par l'étreinte des deux démons. Sur les côtés deux petits diables écrivent avec un *calamus* sur une banderole qui entoure la corbeille, avec l'inscription: CANDO VSVRAM ACCEPISTI OPERA MEA FECISTI. Sous la banderole on aperçoit la marmite à deux anses du chapiteau de Notre Dame du Port) ; *Besse (la mort de l'avare,* repelle le thème traité à Moissac, avec les démons emportant l'âme du pécheur la tête en bas, mais avec le détail pittoresque du coffret à entonnoir placé sous le lit et vers lequel rampe un serpent).

Portraits de donateurs. — Dans beaucoup d'édifices romans des donateurs sont représentés, parfois en pied (l'abbé Durand au cloître de Moissac, Guillaume II de Sicile offrant à la Vierge le modèle de la cathédrale de Monreale), mais le plus souvent à genoux (le roi de l'autel d'Avenas) et presque toujours sur les tympans des portails, sous la forme d'humbles figurines prosternées. En Auvergne cette attitude est celle de l'abbé, qui figure sur un tympan de Mozat et qu'un saint présente à la Vierge.[8] Par contre on trouve sur deux chapiteaux des portraits de donateur de grandeur naturelle et représentés dans l'acte même de leur donation. A Notre Dame du Port sur la face du chapiteau de la Psychomachie donnant sur le chœur, on aperçoit à l'angle un personnage barbu qui porte le costume des bourgeois du temps, hautes bottines, chausses collantes, bliaud serré à la taille par une large ceinture. D'une main il tient un petit chapiteau à feuillages et il pose l'autre sur un livre ouvert tenu par un ange et sur lequel on lit : IN ONORE S (anctae) MARIA(e) STEFANVS ME FIERI IVSSIT. Etienne a donné probablement les chapiteaux du chœur, sculptés par le maître Robert, dont le nom figure sur le chapiteau voisin.[9]

A Volvic un chapiteau tout entier est consacré à la donation d'un Guillaume Debez, dont le nom est écrit en toutes lettres sur le tailloir, où on a reproduit les formules mêmes de la charte de donation, faite par lui en l'honneur de saint Priest pour le salut de son âme et de celle de son épouse : INCIPIT DONALIA SANCTI PRE(je)CTI QVE FECIT GVILLELMES DEBEZ PRO ANIMA SVA ET CO(njugis). Le donateur lui-même apparaît sur le fond d'un mur appareillé, posant la main sur une colonne dont le prieur de Volvic prend possession. Sur les autres faces des anges tenant une oriflamme et un encensoir entourent l'autel de l'église placé sous un ciborium.

Iconographie religieuse.   Thèmes retardataires. — Un des traits particuliers à l'iconographie auvergnate, c'est sa prédilection pour des thèmes très anciens, remontant parfois aux premiers temps chrétiens, et abandonnés depuis longtemps dans les autres provinces. Ce fait peut s'expliquer par l'ancienneté de l'école auvergnate, mais aussi par la fidélité à une tradition iconographique d'une haute antiquité. On est étonné par exemple de trouver sur les chapiteaux une des plus anciennes figures de l'art chrétien, le Bon Pasteur, conforme au type des catacombes romaines, portant sa brebis sur l'épaule, mais représenté en double suivant les lois de la stylistique.

Exemplaires: Issoire; Saint-Nectaire, Besse, Brioude; Volvic; Glaine-Montaigut; Chanteuge; Orcival; Lempdes; Thuret.

Sur un linteau triangulaire de *Champeix* la Trinité est figurée par les mêmes symboles que sur une peinture de la basilique élevée par Saint Paulin de Nole en l'an 402 : la main bénissante, l'agneau, la colombe avec l'inscription en latin barbare : TRES TRINVM SIGNA(nt) POLLEX PECVS ATQVE COLV(m)BA.

Un autre détail indiquant des sources anciennes caractérise les récits de la Passion figurés sur les chapiteaux, par exemple à Saint-Nectaire et à Issoire. La Crucifixion en est toujours absente, ainsi que la Déposition de Croix. Les crucifix sculptés en ronde-bosse ne manquaient pourtant pas en Auvergne à l'époque romane (Christ du Musée de Cluny à Paris, fragment provenant de Lavaudieu au Louvre), mais l'épisode ne figurait pas dans les sources utilisées par les sculpteurs. Comme à Saint-Apollinaire le Neuf, à Ravenne, on passait

---

[8] K. Porter, n° 1223.
[9] K. Porter, n° 1183.

directement des épisodes de la Passion à la Résurrection. Un seul chapiteau auvergnat, à notre connaissance, montre un Christ en croix, mais c'est à *Eglise-neuve d'Entraigues*, village situé sur les confins de la Haute-Auvergne et du Limousin, où ce sujet est parfois traité.

On pourrait relever dans la sculpture auvergnate bien d'autres traits archaiques, comme la croix que le Christ porte à la main quand il accomplit des miracles, comme la reproduction sur un chapiteau de Mozat des épisodes de la vie de Jonas empruntés visiblement à un sarcophage de Ve siècle, comme la fidélité au vieux thème de la visite des Saintes Femmes au tombeau du Christ, avec l'édifice du Saint-Sépulcre, les gardes endormis et revêtus de l'armure chevaleresque du XIIe siècle, l'ange assis à la porte de l'édifice, détails qui procèdent, sauf l'armure des soldats, de monuments analogues aux ivoires du Ve ou du VIe siècle.

Exemplaires: Mozat; Issoire; Saint-Nectaire.[10]

Au XIIe siècle, comme l'a si bien montré M. Emile Mâle,[11] l'iconographie religieuse s'est enrichie sous des influences diverses. L'Auvergne est restée rebelle aux innovations; elle a sans doute créé des thèmes nouveaux, mais qui ne sont guère répandus hors de ses frontières. Et, d'autre part, ses maîtres ont interprété d'une manière toute personelle les thèmes courants, tirés de l'Ancien et du Nouveau Testament.

Thèmes bibliques et évangéliques. — Ces sujets, relativement rares, ont été parfois inspirés, comme dans les autres provinces, par des peintures de manuscrits importés de l'Orient byzantin ou syriaque. Et c'est ce qui explique de curieuses similitudes entre telle sculpture auvergnate et telle peinture des églises rupestres de Cappadoce du Xe siècle (Arrestation de Jésus à Qaranleq-Kilisse et sur un chapiteau de Saint-Nectaire). Entre les deux oeuvres il y a eu l'intermédiaire d'un manuscrit, mais le maître auvergnat a exprimé sa personalité en interprétant les modèles à sa manière et en adaptant à la forme d'un chapiteau une composition picturale.

Parmi les thèmes de l'Ancien Testament, traités rarement ailleurs ou particuliers à l'Auvergne on doit citer:

Moïse sauvé des eaux (collatéral nord de *Saint-Nectaire*, avec le détail pittoresque des trois crocodiles à la gueule béante, qu'écarte un homme armé d'un bâton). *Ezéchiel obéissant aux ordres du Seigneur* (nef de *Royat*: interprétation litterale du texte d'Ezéchiel v, 14. Le prophète figuré deux fois, tenant le coûteau avec lequel il s'est rasé la barbe, puis la balance dans laquelle il l'a pesée. Le sens de ce thème a été découvert par E. Mâle, *Art du XIIe siècle*, p. 24, qui rapproche la scène d'une peinture de la Bible de Noailles, Paris, Bib. Nat. lat. 12302). *Histoire de Tobie* (nef de *Besse*: retour du fils de Tobie avec l'ange Raphaël; festin de Tobie, vieillard à longue barbe assis avec sa femme et son fils à une table servie).

Parmi les thèmes, rarement traités ailleurs, des Évangiles, mentionnons la *Rencontre du Christ avec Zachée* sur un chapiteau du déambulatoire de *Saint-*

---

[10] K. Porter, n°s 1190, 1225–1227.
[11] *L'Art du XIIe siècle en France.*

Nectaire, interprétation assez gauche d'un modèle semblable à une peinture de la chapelle rupestre de Qeledjlar en Cappadoce. Sur un chapiteau de *Maringues*, on assiste au miracle des dix lépreux (Luc XVII, 17). La composition suit de près le récit évangélique et est accompagné de l'inscription : NON(n)E DECEM MVNDATI S(un)T.

Un trait propre à l'Auvergne est le rapprochement sur deux chapiteaux voisins du thème de la *Tentation de Notre Seigneur* et de celui du *Combat de Saint Michel contre des démons* (*Notre Dame du Port, Saint-Nectaire*), inspiré des commentateurs de l'Apocalypse, qui expliquent que le dragon a essayé d'entraîner l'Église dans le péché, mais qu'il a été vaincu par les anges.[12]

Enfin on voit dans plusieurs églises des ensembles de thèmes évangéliques qui sont ce que l'Auvergne a produit de plus original; ils sont en général reservés aux corbeilles sculptées sur quatre faces, qui surmontent les colonnes du sanctuaire dans les chevets pourvus d'un déambulatoire.

Chœur de Notre Dame du Port. — Tous les chapiteaux historiés, sauf celui de la Psychomachie, sont destinés à la glorification de Marie, patronne de l'église. Tous appartiennent à l'atelier du sculpteur Robert, dont le nom figure sur une corbeille (Inscription : R(O)TB(er)TVS ME FECIT) et dont le style très particulier (personnages principaux aux angles, fonds d'architecture, notes malicieuses, d'esprit populaire, grand nombre d'inscriptions), se reconnaît sur toutes les corbeilles.[13]

C'est d'abord au nord-est le récit des épisodes qui précèdent la Nativité, empruntés aux premiers chapitres de Saint Luc et de Saint Mathieu :

Prédiction de la Nativité de Saint Jean Baptiste (sur la face temple de Salomon ouvert, aux angles l'ange apparaissant et Zacharie en costume sacerdotal, l'encensoir à la main). *Annonciation* (Gabriel à l'angle, Marie debout de face, maison de Nazareth au fond). *Visitation*, figurée sur la face. *Doutes de Joseph* (d'après Math. I, 19–21) (interprétation unique). Saint Joseph est un vieillard chauve, à longue barbe, vêtu du bliaud et des chausses collantes du XIIᵉ siècle. Il est vu de face, encadré par les ailes de deux anges, qui tiennent des banderoles, suivant le texte de Mathieu, et dont l'un tire irrespectueusement sa longue barbe.[14]

Deux autres chapiteaux voisins l'un de l'autre illustrent un véritable exposé théologique, destiné à démontrer que Marie est la nouvelle Eve, comparaison que la littérature religieuse du temps reproduit à satiété. Eve, instrument de la chute de l'homme est opposée à Marie, instrument de son rachat. D'un côté le paradis perdu, l'autre le paradis retrouvé. La double composition ordonnée comme une homélie comprend quatre points qui s'opposent d'un chapiteau à l'autre :

1. *La désobéissance.* Le serpent enroulé à l'arbre de la science aux larges feuilles, dont l'une cache le sexe d'Eve. Celle-ci tient une branche chargée de 3

1. *L'Assomption.* Le Christ, assisté de deux anges tenant des livres ouverts, tire le corps de Marie, enveloppé de bandelettes, d'un sarcophage, muni,

---

[12] Walafrid Strabo, Migne t. CXIV, col. 732; Rupert de Deutz, ib. t. CLXIX, col. 1464–1466.

[13] K. Porter, n° 1179.

[14] K. Porter, nᵒˢ 1175–1179.

grappes et en présente une autre à Adam. (Pas d'inscription.)[15]

2. *La Sentence.* Le Seigneur apparaît sur une face, tête à longue barbe, nimbe crucifère. D'une main il repousse Adam; de l'autre il tient un livre ouvert sur lequel on lit: ECCE ADAM CASI VNVS EX VOBIS F(actus) (Gen. III, 22).[17]

3. *L'expulsion du Paradis.* La face est occupée par un ange qui tire par la barbe Adam placé à l'angle gauche (cf. le geste de l'ange tirant la barbe de Joseph). Avant de quitter le Paradis Adam cueille une feuille de l'arbre de la science (point de départ de la légende de la croix) et saisit par les cheveux Eve agenouillée, à laquelle il lance en outre un brutal coup de pied.[19]

4. *Le Paradis fermé.* Les arbres du Paradis chargés de grappes. D'un tronc commun qui passe sous les jambes d'un ange aux ailes éployées, partent deux branches que celui-ci tient à pleine main et qui se terminent par des enroulements.[21]

comme ceux de l'époque, d'une logette pour la tête. Cette interprétation diffère du type habituel de Marie s'élevant au ciel et est unique dans l'art médieval. *Inscription:* MARIA HONORATA IN CELVM.[16]

2. *Marie sur le livre de Vie.* Un ange, vu de face, tient ouvert le Livre de vie chargé de l'inscription: ECCE LIBRO VITE ECCE MARIA NOBIS ASCRIPTA.[18]

3. *Marie conduite au paradis.* Partant du sarcophage, d'où le corps de Marie a été tiré, la procession des anges, dont l'un tient un gonfanon à trois flammes et sonne de l'olifant, un autre balance un encensoir, se dirigeant vers le Paradis.[20]

4. *Le Paradis ouvert.* Deux anges tirent à deux battants les portes chargées de pentures de fer du Paradis figuré comme une église avec l'autel drapé dans une abside éclairée par une lampe. Hautes fenêtres garnies de créneaux accostées de deux séraphins.[22]

On voit quel est le caractère original de cette série, absolument unique dans l'art du moyen âge, d'épisodes parallèles. On ne connait aucun autre exemple de cette manière de figurer l'Assomption corporelle de la Vierge et son entrée au ciel, mais il n'est pas indifférent de rappeler que Grégoire de Tours, un Arverne, décrit (*In gloria martyrum*, I, 8) la fête, que l'on célébrait de son temps à l'oratoire de Marsat, de l'introduction de la Vierge au paradis au milieu du chœur des anges. Il y a donc bien là une tradition régionale.

D'autre part le geste d'Adam, cueillant un rameau de l'arbre de la science, se rapporte à la légende d'après laquelle la croix du Golgotha aurait été fabriquée avec le bois de cet arbre.[23] Enfin la correction infligée à Eve, tirée d'une légende populaire, se trouve dans l'un des plus anciens mystères écrits en français, *le Jeu d'Adam.*

Chœur de Saint-Nectaire. — Les chapiteaux du chœur de Saint-Nectaire présentent les mêmes caractères, les mêmes procédés de composition, le même style que ceux du chœur clermontois. On ne peut les attribuer qu'à Robert ou tout au moins à son atelier. Cinq de ces chapiteaux illustrent l'Evangile:

---

[15] K. Porter, n° 1171.
[16] K. Porter, n° 1167.
[17] K. Porter, n° 1172.
[18] K. Porter, n° 1170.

[19] K. Porter, n° 1173.
[20] K. Porter, n° 1168.
[21] K. Porter, n° 1174.
[22] K. Porter, n° 1169.

[23] Voir Pauphilet, *Etude sur la Queste du Saint Graal* (Paris, 1921), p. 199–206.

1. *Miracles du Christ: Multiplication des pains* (scène simplifiée: le Christ entre deux apôtres tenant les pains et les poissons).[24] *Transfiguration:* Le Christ est à l'angle de la corbeille, le sceptre crucifère à la main. A sa droite Moïse et Elie déroulant des banderoles, placés sur la face voisine. A sa gauche, sur une autre face, deux apôtres endormis et Pierre debout, montrant les banderoles des prophètes. Aux pieds du Christ, les trois tentes figurées par les trois églises romanes élevées au XIIe siècle sur le Thabor.[25]

2. *La Passion: La Trahison.* Judas saisit à bras le corps de Jésus qu'un des soldats romains serre au poignet. De sa main libre le Sauveur recolle l'oreille du centurion Malchus que Saint Pierre saisit par les cheveux, mais qui élève une longue torche pour éclairer la scène (Fig. 5). *La Flagellation.* Le Christ est lié à la colonne par de grosses cordes, entouré des bourreaux qui portent l'armure du XIIe siècle. *Le Portement de Croix*, traité avec le même réalisme. A l'angle une femme nimbée, qui peut être la Vierge, regarde vers la scène suivante.[26] *L'Incrédulité de Saint Thomas*, avec le geste du Christ rejetant ses vêtements pour montrer ses plaies. L'absence de la Crucifixion, qui eût dû suivre logiquement, est remarquable.

3. *La Résurrection.* Trois faces sont consacrées à la visite des trois myrophores au tombeau, figuré par une église romane, reproduisant le type ancien, avec l'ange assis sur une pierre et les gardes endormis. Sur la quatrième face la *Descente aux Limbes*, sujet assez rare dans la sculpture romane.[27]

4. *L'Apocalypse.* A un angle, empiétant sur deux faces, le cavalier exterminateur lançant trois javelots sur les hommes qui s'enfuient (Apoc. 6, 8). A l'angle suivant l'ange armé d'une baguette marquant au front les justes endormis, tenant des palmes (Apoc. 7, 2–3). A un autre angle, Saint Michel tenant une balance, sujet qui ne figure pas dans l'Apocalypse. Tous ces détails sont rarement représentés sur les chapiteaux et jamais de cette manière.[28]

5. *Le Jugement Dernier.* Fidèle à sa méthode, le sculpteur fait apparaître le Christ à un angle, tenant de sa main gauche les clous de la Crucifixion, qu'il plaque au centre de la grande croix tenue par les anges sur la face voisine. A droite du Sauveur, les élus entre deux anges sonnant de l'olifant d'une main et de l'autre déployant des banderoles chargées d'inscriptions. A gauche les réprouvés exprimant naïvement leur douleur et à l'angle opposé un apôtre tenant ouvert un livre sur lequel on lit: ioan(n)es ivdi(cat) (v)os.[29]

Chœur d'Issoire. — Quatre chapiteaux du chœur de *Saint-Paul d'Issoire*, malheureusement restaurés et indignement peinturlurés, ont trait aussi à la Passion et aux apparitions du Christ après la Résurrection. Par leur composition et leur style ils révèlent un atelier différent. Les personnages ont le corps plus allongé que ceux du sculpteur Robert; leurs gestes sont moins désordonnés, leurs draperies plus sobres; les compositions sont plus calmes et plus claires; les personnages essentiels ne sont pas placés aux angles, mais sur les faces:

La Cène montre une disposition originale et naïve du Christ et des douze apôtres, figurés debout à une table qui court autour de la corbeille, de sorte qu'en réalité ils se tournent le dos; la table n'a pas de supports et on ne voit pas comment elle tient; Judas est désigné par l'absence de nimbe. *La Cène* est représentée de la même manière sur un chapiteau de Saint-Julien de Chauriat, mais précédée du *Lavement des pieds*. *La Passion:* Le chapiteau montre seulement *le Portement de croix*, avec un soldat coiffé du casque à

---

[24] K. Porter, n° 1200.
[25] K. Porter, n° 1203.
[26] K. Porter, n° 1204.

[27] K. Porter, n° 1190.
[28] K. Porter, n° 1193.
[29] K. Porter, n° 1191–1192.

nasal poussant Jésus de son bâton, la *Flagellation* et, sur deux faces, la *douleur des apôtres*, au nombre de six. *La Résurrection* figurée par le thème retardataire de la visite des Myrophores au sépulcre. *Les Apparitions du Christ:* apparition à Madeleine agenouillée; apparition à un apôtre; apparition aux disciples d'Emmaüs entrant avec le Christ à Jérusalem, ville avec tour crênelée et deux enceintes qui laissent voir le clocher d'une église. Le geste du Christ, prenant par la main l'un des disciples, est plein de naturel.[30]

FIG. 5.   CHŒUR DE SAINT-NECTAIRE

La Vie des saints. — On ne peut citer qu'un nombre assez restreint de chapiteaux ou de linteaux figurant d'une manière certaine des épisodes de la vie des saints, mais de nombreuses corbeilles dénuées de toute inscription présentent des sujets énigmatiques qui doivent se rapporter à l'hagiographie. Beaucoup de saints sont particuliers à l'Auvergne et leurs biographies constituent comme une autre légende dorée, contenue dans d'anciens bréviaires et surtout dans plusieurs manuscrits, dont un provient de l'abbaye de Saint-Allyre (Bibliothèque de Clermont, manuscrit 149, XIIᵉ siècle). Mais c'est surtout sur les verrières de la cathédrale de Clermont, exécutées au XIIIᵉ siécle qu'il faut chercher la narration détaillée de leurs faits et gestes.[31] Parmi les œuvres sculptées consacrées aux saints de l'Eglise universelle ou spéciaux à la région on peut citer:

[30] K. Porter, nᵒˢ 1212-1214.
[31] Voy, H. du Ranquet, *Les vitraux de la cathédrale de Clermont* (Clermont, 1932).

Linteau en bâtière a la façade de Chambon, figurant le martyre de Saint Etienne, transcription barbare d'une miniature carolingienne.[32] *Linteau de Mozat.* Saints entourant une Vierge en majesté, peut-être des abbés de Cluny, peut-être aussi le fondateur de l'église d'auvergne, Saint Austremoine, dont les reliques étaient conservées dans l'église.[33] *Chapiteau de Besse* montrant Saint André attaché à la croix par de grosses cordes disposées en X, avec l'inscription: PAS(S)IONEM SANCTI ANDREE, accusatif qui s'explique par le début du texte de la passion de Saint André propre au diocèse de Clermont. (Biblioth. de Clermont, mss. 148.) *Chapiteau de Saint-Nectaire*, représentant le martyre de Saint Sébastien, figuré dans une gloire en amande à la face principale, foulant au pied une tête qui ne peut être que celle de Dioclétien, qui l'a condamné; sur les autres faces, un archer lançant une flèche et les bourreaux achevant le saint à coups de fouet. *Chapiteau du chœur de Saint-Nectaire*, avec quatre épisodes de la vie du patron de l'église empruntés à sa légende: Saint Nectaire recevant de Saint Pierre la mission de convertir la Gaule, forçant le démon à lui faire traverser le Tibre, mort et rescussité par saint Pierre à Sutri, enfin rescussitant lui-même un certain Bradulus, avec un fond d'architecture représentant l'église Saint-Nectaire elle-même derrière une muraille crênelée. La légende raconte que le saint, retiré sur le mont Cornadore construisit une église pour son usage, "Monte Cornelio fabricavit sibi basilicam."[34] *Chapiteau du chœur de Mozat:* Saint Pierre délivré de sa prison par un ange (Act. Apost. 12).

Les Evangélistes. — Parmi les saints, les Evangélistes sont représentés en Auvergne sous la figure d'anges, déroulant ou non des banderoles indiquant leur nom. On ne trouve nulle part ailleurs cette figuration si curieuse, due peut-être sur les demi-chapiteaux tout au moins au goût de la symétrie qui a fait doubler un même personnage. Mathieu étant représenté par un ange, le sculpteur aurait redoublé simplement sa figure. Jamais d'ailleurs les évangélistes ne sont accompagnés de leurs symboles, comme dans toutes les autres provinces.

Exemplaires: Chœur de Volvic: quatre anges avec leurs noms sur les banderoles qu'ils tiennent: MATEVS–MARCVS–IOHANNES–LVCAS. *Chapiteau provenant de l'ancien chœur de Mozat.* Quatre évangélistes sous la figure d'anges. Sur leurs banderoles on lit le premier verset de chaque évangile (Fig. 6). Tous les autres spécimens sont des chapiteux de demi-colonnes ne comportant que deux figures: *Notre-Dame du Port*, nef: MARCVS–IOHANNES. *Besse*: LVCAS–IOHANNES. *Chauriat:* deux anges, mais une seule inscription: ANGELVS, qui désigne souvent Mathieu. *Cournon* (sans inscription). *Blesle* (sans inscription). *Brioude:* par une anomalie on lit sur l'une des banderoles: S. IVLIANVS. A *Sainte-Foy de Conques* où le travail de maîtres auvergnats est incontestable, aux quatre trompes d'angle de la coupole centrale, on voit quatre statues d'anges déroulant des banderoles, dont les inscriptions, peut-être peintes, ont disparu. Leur situation à cet endroit (cf. les évangélistes sur les pendentifs des coupoles byzantines) indique bien qu'il s'agit des quatre évangélistes et qu'ils ont été exécutés par un maître auvergnat.

En revanche deux archanges sont figurés avec leurs noms sur un chapiteau de *Maringues.* On lit sur leurs banderoles: ANGELVS MICHAEL–GABRIEL.

En dressant cet inventaire des thèmes iconographiques propres à l'Auvergne, nous ne pouvons nous flatter d'avoir épuisé le sujet. Beaucoup d'églises de campagne sont encore inexplorées et bien des chapiteaux dénués d'inscription n'ont pu être interprétés encore. Cependant les exemples que nous avons recueillis suffisent à montrer l'originalité profonde de l'inspiration, de caractère régional et populaire, qui s'est exercée sur cette iconographie.

[32] K. Porter, n° 1250.   [33] K. Porter, n° 1223.   [34] K. Porter, nᵒˢ 1194-1198.

FIG. 6. CHAPITEAU DE L'ANCIEN CHŒUR DE MOZAT

LES STATUES DU CHŒUR DE SAINT-MARTIN D'ANGERS AUJOURD'HUI AU MUSÉE D'ART DE L'UNIVERSITÉ YALE

MARCEL AUBERT

LES STATUES–COLONNES, dont j'ai montré autrepart [1] l'origine et le développement en Ile-de-France et dans le Domaine royal, puis peu à peu dans les différentes régions de France, dans la deuxième moitié du XIIe siècle et jusqu'au début du XIIIe, ne décoraient pas seulement les portails des églises. On les trouve aussi utilisées dans les arcatures qui ornent les façades et les tours, aux baies des clochers, aux arceaux des triforiums.

Un des exemples les plus anciens se voit à l'étage supérieur de la tour nord de la façade de Tournus.[2] La colonne centrale des deux piles qui séparent les trois baies est décorée d'une statue représentant un personnage barbu, raide, les bras au corps, la tête droite sous le chapiteau de l'archivolte; la prunelle des yeux est creuse et marquée par une boule de plomb ou de ciment noir. L'un des deux est un évêque ou un abbé, l'autre parait tenir dans la main un sceptre. Aux angles N.O. et S.O. du même étage se dressent deux statues-colonnes plus typiques encore, fortement allongées, cylindriques et terminées a leur partie inférieure, non par des pieds, mais par une base. Le profil des tailloirs — une gorge profonde entre deux tores — et des archivoltes, le décor des chapiteaux, et notamment les volutes très marquées aux angles de certains d'entre eux, le style des statues, ne permettent guère de vieillir ces sculptures au-delà du milieu ou même du troisième quart du XIIe siècle.

On voit encore des statues colonnes au XIIIe siècle au triforium de la cathédrale de Nevers, sous les bases des colonnettes de l'arcature au sommet de la tour nord de la cathédrale de Sens, à la façade de l'église de Mailly-le-Château (Yonne), où elles semblent plier, un peu à la manière des figures d'atlantes, sous le poids des hautes colonnes qu'elles portent.

On pourrait rapprocher aussi des statues-colonnes toutes ces statues raides, allongées, immobiles, qui décorent les façades des églises de l'Ouest, au milieu et dans la deuxième moitié du XIIe siècle et qui, souvent, se dressent de chaque côté des fenêtres ou des arcades décoratives, comme celles de Saint-Jouin de Marnes (Deux-Sèvres), ou le Saint Pierre et la Sainte Colombe de l'église de Sainte-Colombe (Charente). A Civray (Vienne), elles sont placées de chaque côté d'une haute colonne, disposition que l'on retrouve à l'intérieur de l'église d'Airvault (Deux-Sèvres),[3] entre les grandes arcades de la nef.

Mais, ce qui me parait le mieux prouver le goût qu'avaient les maîtres d'oeuvre d'alors pour les statues-colonnes qui affirmaient les lignes de la con-

[1] Marcel Aubert, *La Sculpture française au début de l'époque gothique, 1140–1225* (Paris, Panthéon, 1929).
[2] Repr. d'après une photographie de M. Altounian, dans le *Congrès archéologique de Dijon, 1928*, p. 382.
[3] A. Kingsley Porter, *Romanesque Sculpture of the Pilgrimage Roads*, I (1923), p. 258 note, et Pl. 898–900.

struction tout en les décorant, ce sont ces statuettes sculptées a la retombée des ogives croisées sous les voûtes, que l'on voit en Ile-de-France et surtout en Anjou et dans le bassin de la Loire, dans la seconde moitié du XIIᵉ siècle et au début du XIIIᵉ.

Il existe, dans quelques églises d'Ile-de-France, à la retombée de la voûte, de petites figures sculptées dans les assises basses des ogives. A la manière des

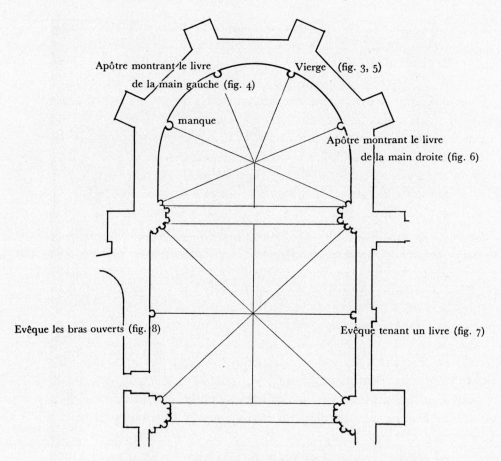

FIG. 1. PLAN DU CHŒUR DE SAINT-MARTIN D'ANGERS

atlantes antiques, elles semblent écrasées sous le poids de la voûte, ou lèvent les bras, comme pour porter les ogives. Parmi les plus anciennes, j'ai signalé [4] celles du croisillon sud de l'église de Cambronne (Oise) — l'une d'elles a été supprimée lors des agrandissements du XIIIᵉ siècle — et de la dernière travée du collatéral nord de l'église de Bury, voisine de Cambronne. On en voit encore au chœur de Lucheux (Somme).

Les artistes angevins reprendront ce motif dans la deuxième moitié du XIIᵉ siècle et au début du XIIIᵉ, et l'on retrouvera ces mêmes petites figures, anges, rois, reines, évêques et abbés, saints et saintes, généralement nimbés, raides et allongés, les bras près du corps, la tête droite, en tout semblables aux statues

[4] Marcel Aubert, *La Sculpture française au début de l'époque gothique*, pp. 42–43; *Les Plus Anciennes Croisées d'ogives, leur rôle dans la construction* (Paris, 1934), p. 82–83 (extr. du *Bulletin Monumental*, 1934).

colonnes, dressées contre les sommiers des ogives, sur le chapiteau des colonnes qui les reçoivent, et souvent abritées par un dais.[5] Il en subsiste encore à la croisée du transept de l'église d'Aigue-Vive et dans la salle du premier étage du clocher-porche de Saint-Aignan (Loir-et-Cher),[6] au chœur de l'église de Romorantin, où les quatre hautes statues appuyées aux ogives du fond du chœur et représentant les quatre Evangélistes, ont peut-être été refaites après le sac de

Archives Photographiques d'Art et d'Histoire, Paris

FIG. 2. LE CHŒUR DE SAINT-MARTIN D'ANGERS AVANT
LA RESTAURATION

l'église par les Hugenots en 1562 à la place des statues primitives; entre les fenêtres du fond du chœur de l'église de Levroux dans l'Indre;[7] à Saint-Epris, Crouzille et Cormery en Indre-et-Loire, au porche de Saint-Ours de Loches;

---

[5] On peut rapprocher de ces statues celles qui se dressent sous les grands arcs doubleaux du carré du transept de la Trinité de Vendôme et qui représentent l'Ange et la Vierge le l'Annonciation, saint Pierre et un évêque; repr. par A. Kingsley Porter, *Romanesque Sculpture of the Pilgrimage Roads*, Pl. 1516-1518.

[6] *Congrès archéologique de Blois, 1925*, p. 405.

[7] On a découvert, il y a quelques années, a Issoudun (Indre), et déposé au Musée une statuette de femme de style assez grossier, mais dont les vêtements à plis parallèles et la technique accusent la fin du XIIe siècle. Elle était peut-être placée aussi à la retombée des nervures des voûtes.

au chœur de l'église de la Couture au Mans,[8] à Angles en Vendée,[9] au chœur de Saint-Jouin de Marnes (Deux-Sèvres), dont les voûtes ont été remontées au début du XIIIe siècle sur des murs du début du XIIe, et où, de chaque côté de la fenêtre d'axe, se dressent deux statues au pied des ogives qui rayonnent sur l'abside, comme dans les chapelles du tour du chœur où de belles statues d'anges abritées sous des dais et posées sur des corbeaux sont adossées aux retombées des ogives, entre les puissants formerets qui encadrent les fenêtres.[10]

Un curieux exemple de cette disposition se voit encore sous les ogives montées au XIIIe siècle sur le chœur de l'église Saint-Didier de Langres.[11]

La série la plus remarquable peut-être se trouvait au chœur de Saint-Martin d'Angers.

Les fouilles exécutées dans ces dernières années à Saint-Martin par M. George A. Forsyth jr., de Princeton, qui complètent et précisent celles qu'avait faites M. le chanoine Pinier au cours de la restauration qu'il a exécutée avec grand soin de l'édifice,[12] montrent que le chœur de l'église carolingienne comprenait une travée droite terminée par un sanctuaire arrondi. Dans la deuxième moitié du XIIe siècle ce chœur fut agrandi et allongé vers l'Est d'une travée droite terminée par une grande abside circulaire à l'intérieur, à cinq pans à l'extérieur. Les travaux ont dû se terminer dans les dernières années du XIIe siècle. Deux fenêtres sont percées dans chacune des parois des travées droites, et une dans chacun des pans de l'abside. Les travées droites sont couvertes de voûtes d'ogives à liernes longitudinales et transversales,[13] et l'abside d'une voûte d'ogives simple complétée de deux nervures retombant vers l'Est de chaque côté de la fenêtre centrale: six branches d'ogives et une lierne rayonnent ainsi autour d'une clef centrale. Toutes ces ogives et les liernes transversales retombent sur des colonnes montant du sol et couronnées par de puissants chapiteaux aux larges tailloirs. Sur les quatre tailloirs de la partie circulaire de l'abside et sur ceux qui portent la colonne recevant la lierne transversale de la travée droite touchant à l'abside se dressaient de grandes statues colonnes. Les premières s'appuyaient contre la retombée de la nervure qui, taillée dans la même pierre qu'elles, se prolonge en une sorte de colonne dans leur dos, et les deux autres sur la colonne qui monte sous la retombée de la lierne.

Ces statues, qui avaient été repeintes en 1768[14]—elles portent encore des traces de ces peintures: brun, gris, noir, rouge brique, bleu — ont été fort mutilées à la Révolution; les têtes, la plupart des mains et des attributs ont été brisés, et l'une des statues, la première du côté nord de l'abside, a été complètement détruite. Les cinq qui subsistaient ont été transportées aux Etats-Unis en 1926

[8] Repr. dans *Congrès archéologique d'Angers — Saumur, 1910*, I, 286–287.

[9] Repr. *ibid.*, II, 241–244.

[10] Repr. *ibid.*, I, 114–117.

[11] On en pourrait citer également quelques exemples en Espagne, comme dans la nef de l'ancienne cathédrale de Salamanque, au porche de Saint-Martin de Ségovie et à Ciudad Rodrigo.

[12] *Congrès archéologique d'Angers — Saumur 1910*, I, 201–202.

[13] Marcel Aubert, *Les Plus Anciennes Croisées d'ogives* (1934), pp. 55–56 (extr. du *Bulletin Monumental*, 1934).

[14] Note du chanoine Pinier, dans *Congrès archéologique d'Angers — Saumur 1910*, I, 201–202.

Musée d'Art de l'Université d'Yale

FIGS. 3–8. STATUES PROVENANT DE SAINT–MARTIN D'ANGERS

et données par M. Maitland F. Griggs, au Musée d'art de l'Université d'Yale; [15]
elles décorent le fond de la grande salle du Musée. L'une représente une femme
assise, la Vierge portant l'Enfant, et les quatre autres, qui sont debout, deux
apôtres, les pieds nus, et deux personnages en costume épiscopal. [16]

La Vierge (fig. 3, 5) est assise sur un banc, une sorte de haut socle mouluré
d'une base à tore et d'une imposte ornée d'un tore, d'un cavet, d'un onglet et
d'un bandeau plat; le siège est légèrement incliné en avant. Ses longues jambes
se dessinent vigoureusement sous la robe et le manteau qui la couvrent. Elle
porte sur son genou droit, appuyé contre son bras droit, l'Enfant Jésus, à demi-
dressé contre sa poitrine. Les avant-bras qu'enveloppent étroitement le chainse
apparaissent dans l'ouverture des larges manches tombantes de la robe. L'Enfant Jésus, vêtu d'une robe légère et d'une sorte de manteau fendu sur le côté
droit, levait les bras. Un pan du voile de la Vierge tombe sur son bras gauche et
jusqu'au long du siège. La Vierge, svelte et mince, est fort élégante dans ses
vêtements qui font admirablement ressortir sa stature élancée; la robe retombe
légèrement sur le chainse dont il découvre les beaux plis groupés en éventail
entre les deux pieds, tandis que le manteau largement drapé sur les épaules et
les jambes, forme comme une chape derrière la Vierge. Malheureusement, les
têtes et les mains ont été brisées, ainsi que les pieds de l'Enfant. La statue mutilée
mesure 1m. 40 de haut. Cette Vierge de Saint-Martin d'Angers évoque à
l'esprit la fameuse statue de bois provenant de Saint-Martin des Champs à
Paris aujourd'hui conservée dans le chœur de Saint-Denis, notamment dans le
drapé des étoffes et la forme des plis, mais l'attitude est différente; dans la
statue de Saint-Martin des Champs, l'Enfant est encore assis sur les genoux de sa
mère, et esquisse à peine le geste de se lever, tandis qu'à Saint-Martin d'Angers,
il est déjà debout appuyé contre la Vierge et soutenu par son bras droit.

A la droite de la Vierge était une statue d'apôtre (fig. 4). Il mesurait 1m. 88
de haut, jusqu'au sommet du grand nimbe circulaire creusé en cuvette sur lequel
se détachait la tête; il est vêtu d'une longue robe sous laquelle se dessinent les
jambes et qui retombe en larges plis fortement marqués, et d'un manteau drapé
sur les épaules et relevé à la taille du côté gauche. Il porte dans la main droite
un livre qu'il maintient de la main gauche à demi couverte par un pli du manteau. Le socle qui le porte est bombé, et ses pieds nus s'inclinent en avant comme
dans les autres statues de ce groupe. Ce peut être un des évangélistes, saint Jean,
si l'on en croit les restes de l'inscription peinte en 1768.

A la gauche de la Vierge était une statue semblable à celle-ci, haute de 1m.
98 (fig. 6). Le nimbe est en partie brisé, la tête manque. Le manteau, entourant
le bras droit, et ramené à la taille par la main gauche, tombe en larges plis sur
les côtés et découvre le bas de la robe. Sur la main gauche est appuyé un livre
maintenu par la main droite. L'attitude est la même que dans la statue précé-

---

[15] *Bulletin of the Associates in Fine Arts at Yale University*, mars 1926, pp. 3–4.
[16] Le fait qu'ils ne portent pas de pallium n'empêche pas que ces personnages soient des évêques, comme
l'avait cru à tort M. Wolfgang Medding qui a publié récemment un article sur les statues d'Yale dans la
Gazette des Beaux-Arts, nov. 1934, pp. 170–173.

dente qui lui faisait pendant de l'autre côté de la Vierge, mais le geste est inversé. Ici encore, il s'agit d'un apôtre ou d'un évangéliste, peut-être saint Luc; il me parait difficile d'y voir saint André, comme on pourrait le croire d'après les traces encore visibles du nom peint en 1768 sur le socle.

Les deux autres statues (fig. 7, 8) etaient placées en vis-à-vis, dans la travée droite du chœur voisine de l'abside, contre les colonnes recevant les retombées des liernes transversales. Elles portent sur des socles moulurés aux angles abattus qui doublent le tailloir des chapiteaux placés au-dessous. Elles étaient nimbées. Les deux personnages sont chaussés et portent le costume épiscopal: l'aube aux nombreux plis s'écrasant sur le sol; la longue dalmatique aux manches demi-larges, descendant jusqu'au dessous des genoux et légèrement fendue sur le côté; la chasuble en étoffe souple relevée sur les bras et formant une pointe en avant et en arrière; les deux pans évasés de l'étole retombent jusqu'aux pieds; le manipule, de même coupe que l'étole, est pendu au bras gauche. Les fanons de la mitre sont encore visibles sur les épaules, comme le chef d'amict autour du cou. Les têtes manquent, et les mains d'une des statues. Ces personnages doivent être des évêques; ni l'un ni l'autre ne porte le pallium; on ne peut donc y reconnaître le patron de l'abbaye, saint Martin, qui fut archevêque de Tours.[17] Celui qui était au sud, du côté de l'épître, tient dans la main droite un livre ouvert dont il marque un passage de la main gauche; il porte, au medium de la main droite, l'anneau épiscopal gros et plat. Le fût de la crosse, qui passait sous son bras gauche, est encore en partie visible. Celui qui était au nord, du côté de l'Evangile, tend les bras en avant; les mains ont été brisées; il devait bénir de la droite et appuyait sans doute la gauche sur sa crosse — de bois ou de métal —, dont la pointe se posait sur un renflement réservé sans doute à cet effet sur le socle. Cette statue mesure 1m. 70 du bas du socle au cou, et celle qui lui fait pendant 1m. 67.

Toutes ces statues, raides, droites, élancées, sont traitées comme des statues-colonnes et s'appuient sur des colonnes ou des nervures dont la masse, relativement petite par rapport au volume de la statue, était engagée dans le mur. Nervures et colonnes sont pris dans le même bloc de pierre que la statue. Les longs plis, un peu secs mais profondément taillés, tombent droit, sans retroussis, en s'évasant entre les pieds et sur le côté. Les draperies sont traitées également par derrière, mais plus sommairement.

Ces statues se rattachent au groupe des statues-colonnes, dont le plus magnifique ensemble se voit au Portail royal de Chartres, mais elles sont moins allongées, moins raides; les étoffes sont plus souples, les plis moins parallèles et plus profondément creusés. Elles sont très proches, par leur style et leur exécution, des statues de la façade ouest de la cathédrale d'Angers qui ont dû être sculptées entre l'achèvement des voûtes de la nef par l'évêque Normand de Doué (1149-1153) et la reconstruction du transept commencée par l'évêque Raoul de Beaumont après 1177, c'est-à-dire entre 1160 et 1170 environ.[18] Même silhouette

---

[17] La statue qui a été arrachée et détruite à la Révolution, du côté nord de l'abside, représentait peut-être saint Martin.   [18] Marcel Aubert, *La Sculpture française au début de l'époque gothique*, Pl. 31-32.

générale des figures, mêmes attitudes, mêmes gestes, même manière de placer les mains, de poser les jambes fortement dessinées sous les draperies, même agencement des étoffes, mêmes plis, un peu secs, mais profonds et bien marqués. Les vêtements de la Vierge sont les mêmes que ceux des femmes de la façade de la cathédrale ; le grand pli oblique du manteau du Dieu de Majesté du tympan de la cathédrale se retrouve dans la statue de la Vierge de Saint-Martin ; les genoux et les jambes se dessinent de même, un peu maigres sous l'étoffe, dans les deux statues.

Cependant, une détente plus grande se manifeste dans les statues de Saint-Martin ; les attitudes sont plus libres, les gestes mieux observés, les étoffes plus souples, et elles sont certainement postérieures de quelques années à celles du portail de la cathédrale.

Je crois que l'on peut les dater des années 1180–1190, au moment où l'on exécutait, à la cathédrale de Senlis, le beau portail de la Vierge, terminé en 1191, et dont les grandes statues, aux attitudes variées, aux grandes draperies ramenées autour de la taille, comme à Angers, aux longs plis raides et secs profondément creusés, ne sont pas sans présenter quelque rapport avec celles de Saint-Martin. Les statues de Mantes et de Braisnes, celles du transept de la cathédrale de Chartres, montrent, au début du XIIIe siècle, un style plus avancé.

DAS TIER IN DER ROMANISCHEN PLASTIK FRANKREICHS

RICHARD HAMANN

WAS dem Reisenden in Frankreich an den romanischen Kirchen am meisten auffallen muss, ist der überwältigende Reichtum an bedeutungsvoller, künstlerisch sehr hochstehender Tierplastik. Das romanische Ornament ist Tierornament. Fehlt es, dann können wir auf Sonderbedingungen der romanischen Architektur schliessen, eine Renaissance der Antike etwa. Es gehört zur Natur des romanischen Stiles, sein Fehlen ist unnatürlich.

Treten wir vor ein Portal einer romanischen Kirche, dann finden wir, wie in St. Gilles, schon den Sockel der Säulen geschmückt mit Tierreliefs: Affen und Kamele breiten sich auf der Fläche aus, oder ein Hirsch wird von einem Centauren gejagt. Die Basen der Säulen selbst werden von Bären getragen, Löwen tragen die rankengeschmückten Pfeiler. Gehen wir an den Portalen der Kirche in Aulnay (Fig. 1) mit dem Blick hinauf zum Kapitell, dann verschlingen sich gespenstige Tierwesen, Köpfe mit Spinnenfüssen und Vögel zu einem gitterförmigen Ornament, Tiere und Menschen sind in wildem Kampf verwoben; auf der Deckplatte der Kapitelle im Kreuzgang von Moissac strecken sich wilde Tiere, ein Mensch wehrt sich gleichzeitig gegen eine vierfüssige Bestie und einen Riesenvogel. Die Pfosten der Portale sind zuweilen, wie in St. Denis, zu breiten Reliefstreifen ausgebildet und halten dem Eintretenden die Sinnbilder des Sternkreises entgegen, Widder, Stier, Löwe, Krebs, Skorpion. Ein Pfosten in Moissac, der den Türsturz trägt, ist aus Löwen kreuzförmig zusammengebaut, — ein Bestienpfeiler. In Souillac verschlingen sich an derselben Stelle in wildem Gewühl Tiere mit Menschen, die ihnen rettungslos verfallen sind. In den Bogenläufen der Portale, des Südportals von Aulnay etwa, ist als Türeinfassung, dem Blick am nächsten, eine Ranke, in der die Bilder von Tieren eingewoben sind, keine heiligen Tiere, Evangelisten-Symbole, sondern wilde Tiere; dann folgt auf zwei Reihen heiliger Personen als äusserster Rahmen wieder eine bestialische Welt, Stein auf Stein, ein ganzer Garten voll exotischer, fabelhafter, dämonischer Tiere. Geht der Blick noch weiter hinauf zu einem Gesims, das die Fassade teilt oder abschliesst — wieder Tiere an den Konsolen, die das Gesims tragen. Aber auch das Gesims bleibt nicht immer leer. Selbst wenn es schon profiliert ist, kommen, wie in St. Gilles, Tiere, Katzen, Hunde, Schlangen auf dem schmalen unteren Wulst entlanggelaufen oder ringeln sich in den Hohlkehlen. Treten wir in die Kirche ein, so begegnet uns dieselbe Welt wieder an den Basen, Kapitellen, Gesimsen. Wir schreiten zwischen Tieren hindurch, wie begleitet von ihren gierigen Blicken. Sie nisten sich ein in den Zwickeln zwischen den Arkadenbögen. Blicken wir empor, um ihnen zu entgehen, prallt der Blick an den tiergefüllten Schlussteinen wieder vor ihnen zurück. Suchen wir Schutz am Altar, finden wir die Schrägfläche der Tischkante des Altares mit dämonischen Streifen besetzt. Auch der Höchste der Priester, der Bischof, der uns entgegenkommt, hält uns einen Bischofstab entgegen, dessen Spitze sich als ein Schlangenleib krümmt und in einen Schlangenkopf endigt — eine Emailarbeit aus Limoges. Und nicht genug: durch diese Krümme huscht eidechsengleich ein Drache. St. Michael muss ihn bekämpfen. Auf dem Schrein des heiligen Ægidius in St. Gilles erhob sich ein Kreuz, das auf einem grossen Kristall stand. Dieser aber stellte dar einen grossen Fisch, mit der Schwanzflosse nach unten gerichtet. Und wenn wir schliess-

Marburger photo.

FIG. 1. AULNAY, ST. PIERRE, PORTAL DES SÜDLICHEN QUERSCHIFFS
1. HÄLFTE 12. JAHRHUNDERT

lich nur zu gleichgültigen Verhandlungen in die Sakristei eintreten, dann finden wir hinter dem Glas der Schränke Elfenbeinkästen, Elfenbeinhörner und als ihren Schmuck Tiere: Drachen, Kamele, Elefanten, Löwen. Wir können uns vor Christus und den Heiligen, vor Maria und den Engeln verbergen, wir können sogar dem Jüngsten Gericht am Portal entgehen, wenn wir schnell in die Kirche eintreten, vor dem Tier gibt es kein Entrinnen.

Diese dekorative Verwendung des Tieres scheint zunächst leicht als Erbe der Antike verständlich. Es ist antikes Barock, ein Zeichen von Spätkunst, so die Architektur zu verlebendigen, jede bauliche Funktion — das Tragen der Säule durch die Basis, den Kampf mit der Last im Kapitell, die Stützaktion einer Konsole, das Schliessen eines Bogens — durch Tiere mit kräftigem Rücken, durch

Vögel mit ausgebreiteten Schwingen oder durch Köpfe von Bestien auszudrükken. Vor allem ist es hellenistischer Dekorationsstil, die architektonischen Flächen mit Ranken zu überziehen, die den Stein wie in südlichen Gärten mit Rosen oder Weinranken überspinnen, in denen Vögel ihre Nester bauen. Die Jungen sperren ihre Schnäbel auf, die Alten fliegen ab und zu und bringen Würmer und Insekten, Eidechsen und kleine Schlangen huschen hindurch, zwischen den leichten Stämmen stehen, wie im Schilf, Vögel mit langen Hälsen, Ibisse, Kraniche, Störche. Es ist eine idyllische Welt, wie erfüllt von Blumenduft und Sonnenglanz. Solches Geranke, genugsam in den Resten der Antike vor Augen gestellt, schwebte den romanischen Künstlern vor, als sie ihre Tiere in die Ranken einwoben und deshalb unter den Tieren solche mit langem, biegsamem Hals, mit geschmeidigem Körper und mit langem Schweif bevorzugten, rankenhafte Tiere, sodass wir immer wieder auf Schlangen und Drachen stossen und auf Kombinationen von Vierfüsslern mit Schlangen und langhälsigen Vögeln. Es sind überwiegend Fabeltiere, die sich so miteinander verhaken lassen, über die Kapitellseiten hinüberbiegen oder, wenn sie zum Kapitellrand hinschreiten, wieder zur Mitte zurückbiegen lassen. Auch diese Fabeltiere waren antikes Erbgut, in Einzelheiten und im Prinzip aus der Antike übernommen: die Centauren, Sirenen, die Seepferdchen (Hippokampen), Greifen und Drachen, so falsch es andrerseits wäre, für jedes phantastische Tierwesen ein antikes Vorbild zu suchen. Die späte Antike, der Hellenismus und der römische Dekorationsstil liebten solche Fabelwesen, die in lineare Gebilde ausliefen und der dekorativen Verwendung erlaubten, zwanglos eine Verbindung von Tier und Pflanze, ein Übergleiten des tierischen Körpers in die vegetabile Ranke herzustellen. Die wildesten Tiere und mythischen Wesen wurden so zu einem leichten Spiel der Phantasie, in scherzhaftem Märchenton hingeplaudert, ovidische Metamorphosen.

Das aber ist ganz anders in der romanischen Kunst. Schon die Ranken und mit ihnen die eingewobenen Tiere huschen nicht über die architektonische Fläche hin, sondern fügen sich in sie ein, sie bilden recht eigentlich den schweren festen Block und drängen sich, die Fläche füllend, dicht zusammen. Der heitere, organische, aufgelöste Schwung stösst in einen geometrischen strengen Zug zurück. Mit den leichtesten, heitersten und freiesten Gebilden der Spätantike wird die ernste architektonische Masse, ihre Monumentalität hergestellt, mit lockerstem und durchsichtigem Gewebereichtum der feste unerschütterliche Kubus.

Die Tiere sind zwar bunt, märchenhaft, seltsam, aber zugleich wild und drohend. Ganz anders dicht als in der antiken Spätkunst drängen sie sich zusammen. Wäre nicht die himmlische Ordnung in diesem Reichtum, mit anderen Worten Architektur höchsten Ranges, dann könnte man oft an ein Knäuel von Schlangen oder Würmern denken, abschreckend, ekelhaft eher als schmückend. Man liebt auch keineswegs, obwohl es unter dem verführerischen Zwang der Vorbilder vorkommt, die Verbindung von Tier und Ranke, von Wesen und Schein; sondern man füllt die ganze Fläche mit Tieren, einem einzigen grossen herrischen Untier, oder beweist höchste Kunst, indem man nur Tiere unter

sich verflicht. Man lockert nicht auf, man drängt zusammen. Jeder Zoll
Getier!

Und was für Tiere! Würden wir sie aus ihrer Verflechtung und Vermischung
befreien, so blieben als Teile übrig Löwen, Leoparden, Bären, Wildschweine,
Adler, Geier, Schlangen — Raubtiere und Gifttiere, lauter Bestien, die dem
Menschen gefährlich werden, die sich selber bekriegen und auffressen, die auf
die Menschen mit ihren Schnäbeln einhacken, sie mit den Krallen zerreissen
und in ungeheueren Mäulern verschlingen. Wieder wird es Ernst gegenüber
der dekorativen Antike, blutiger Ernst.

Ursprünglich, in der spätantiken Kunst, zum Schmuck und zur Erheiterung
an Pfosten, Säulengliedern, Bogenläufen gedacht, stellt das Ornament jetzt dem
Eintretenden die furchtbare Macht des Tierischen entgegen, die wie wilde Hunde
den Eindringling, den Fremdling mit dem schlechten Gewissen, zurückscheucht.
Wie in der archaischen Kunst (Assyrien) wilde Tiere im Bilde die Palastfassade
bewachen, so auch hier. So ergibt sich ein Doppelgesicht der romanischen Tierplastik wie der romanischen Kunst überhaupt: eine innere Verwandtschaft mit
der das Tier scheu verehrenden archaischen Kunst, der ägyptischen und assyri-
schen, und eine äussere Beziehung zur spätantiken, hellenistischen Kunst, die
launisch und spielend die Tiere in den Schmuck ihres leichten Lebens einflocht.
Ornament und Sinn, Architekturschmuck und Darstellung streben nach zwei
verschiedenen Seiten — Scherz und Ernst. In diese graziöse und erhabene Zweideutigkeit der romanischen Kunst ist auch das Tier einbezogen. Vielleicht ist
die Tierplastik die grösste Zweideutigkeit. Durch die unnachahmlich reiche und
kostbare Ornamentik wird jedes Fenster, jede Tür ein festliches Portal, die Kirche
die gastlichste Stätte, allen freudig geöffnet; durch die architektonische Monumentalität aber, die Fülle und Wucht der tierischen Formen und durch die Bedeutung der Stellen, an denen sie stehen, wird schon hier die Kirche eine Stätte
der Scheu, des Kultus. Bezeugt nicht schon diese herrschende Fülle in den Or-
namenten, dass auch das Tier Gegenstand des Kultus ist? Die Analogie zu
den archaischen Skulpturen, die wir sonst kennen, lässt uns erwarten, dass auch
in dieser Zeit das Tier Gegenstand einer eingestandenen oder uneingestandenen
religiösen Verehrung ist. Wir brauchen nur an die Tiergottheiten Aegyptens, an
die religiöse Bedeutung zu denken, die der Ibis, das Krokodil in Aegypten
besassen, an die heiligen Tiere der Assyrer und die mythischen Tiere der griechi-
schen Religion. Was aber wäre andererseits der christlichen Lehre, ihrem rein
menschlichen Charakter, ihrer Abwendung von allen rein irdischen Mächten,
ihrer ethischen Haltung und ihrer Vergeistigung fremder, als ein ausgesprochener
Tierkult!

So ergab sich für die romanische Kunst die Situation, Vorwände zu finden,
diese Mächte, die die Seele bedrückten, den Sinn beherrschten und das Verhalten zu den unbekannten Kräften der Natur bedingten, dem Auge nahezu-
bringen und der Verkörperungssucht des kultischen Bedürfnisses zu genügen.
Die Möglichkeiten liegen im Guten wie im Bösen. Welchen Rang das Tier in der
Vorstellung dieses Zeitraumes der Geschichte, dieses Abschnittes der Kulturent-

wicklung einnimmt, ahnt man aus der überwältigenden Fülle und Fruchtbarkeit dieser Ornamentik. Aber die Darstellung des Tieres bleibt nicht auf diese beschränkt, sie drängt sich in die bedeutsamsten Stellen der Heiligenbilder und Heiligenverehrung, sie erobert sich im Evangelistensymbol den Platz unmittelbar neben Gott, vertritt in Gestalt des Lammes Gott selbst, sie masst sich den Platz an, den das Bild des Höchsten, des thronenden Christus einnimmt, wenn es im Tympanon erscheint.

Eine Möglichkeit, dem Tier einen Platz im Bilderkreis der Heiligengeschichte zu verschaffen und das Tier selbst dadurch zu heiligen, war gegeben durch jene Legenden, in denen das Tier die Heiligkeit eines Gottgeweihten spürt, durch die Scheu vor den sittlich religiösen Mächten die Wildheit und Grausamkeit seiner Tier-Natur aufgibt und zum Zeugen für die Macht des Geistes wird. Es muss in jedem Fall untersucht werden, wie weit bei jenen Legenden eine alte Überlieferung, eine antike oder vorchristliche (jüdisch-babylonische) Tradition mitgewirkt hat, ob also die Legende selbst schon unter dem Bedürfnis entstanden ist, dem Tier eine Rolle im Umkreis der kultischen Vorstellungen dieser Kulturstufe zuzuweisen. In der bildenden Kunst, das geht aus der Art der Darstellung hervor, bot das religiöse Motiv einen willkommenen Vorwand, die Macht des Tieres zu verherrlichen. Und wenn schon in vielen dieser Legenden Motive alter heidnischer Sagen wieder aufzuleben scheinen, die Darstellung kehrt noch stärker zu einem archaischen Glauben an das Tier zurück. Und wird die Kunst schon zweideutig dadurch, dass man an der Fülle und Bedeutung dieser Tierlegenden spürt, dass die Heiligengeschichte nur ein *Vorwand* ist, einen Tiermythus zu gestalten, so noch mehr durch die verschiedene Bedeutung, die der hinzugedachte und der sichtbare Sinn der Darstellung haben, die Heiligengeschichte und die Tierdarstellung.

Da ist die Leiche des Hl. Aventinus, irgendwo in der Wildnis versteckt. Ein Stier findet sie, begründet den Kult des Heiligen und führt zur Gründung heiliger Stätten für diesen Kult, wie die Kirche des Hl. Aventinus hoch oben in den Pyrenäen. Ein Relief verewigt diese Begebenheit (Fig. 2). Ein Stier in riesigem Ausmass, wild und roh, steht über dem Leichnam, der wie der Körper eines kleinen Kindes, eines Findlings, erscheint. Ein Engel schwebt hinter dem Stier, was bedeutet, dass, wie die Heiligen, auch dieser Stier von Engeln geleitet wird. Sinnbildlich galt die Darstellung der Bedeutung des Heiligen, seinem Bunde mit Gott und den Engeln, seiner Macht über die Tiere. Bildnerisch ist der Heilige nur Attribut des Stieres.

Die Hl. Magdalena ist gestorben. Ihr Nachbarheiliger Zosimos findet sie (Fig. 3), aber er ist selbst zu alt und schwach, ihr das Grab zu graben, und niemand sonst ist in der Wüste, der hier helfen könnte. Da kommt ein Löwe und schaufelt mit seinen Krallen das Grab. Dasselbe wird von dem Hl. Benedikt erzählt. Gross und bedeutungsvoll steht der Löwe im Zentrum des Bildes und gibt dem Tod und Begräbnis durch seine Anwesenheit eine höhere Bedeutung.

Am sinnfälligsten aber illustriert die physische Macht des Heiligen über die wilden Tiere die Geschichte von Daniel in der Löwengrube. Diese alttesta-

mentliche Erzählung ist vielleicht die beliebteste der romanischen Plastik
überhaupt, die Zahl der Beispiele ist unübersehbar. Sie ist so romanisch-mittel-
alterlich, gerade weil sie so beziehungsreich ist für die christlich-typologische
Deutung: das Bild eines Märtyrers und die Gewähr der Erlösung; so unchristlich
aber vor allem durch die Mehrzahl wilder Tiere, die sich hier im Bilde darstel-
len liessen — die Löwengrube. Man konnte ein herrliches Ornament aus einer
Vierzahl von Löwen entwickeln, wie an einem Kapitell in Saintes (Fig. 4): zwei
Löwen in der oberen Zone mit drohend zurückgewendetem Kopf und erhobener
Tatze, wie Wächter des Heiligen, aber auch wie Tiere, die im Genuss ihrer Beute
gestört werden; zwei im unteren Bezirk, die die Füsse Daniels lecken. Dieser sitzt

FIG. 2. ST. AVENTIN, KIRCHE, RELIEF AN LISENE
NEBEN PORTAL
2. VIERTEL 12. JAHRHUNDERT

majestasartig zwischen ihnen mit steif erhobenen Armen, wie ein Orant, durch
den Kranz von Tieren in eine furchtbare Glorie eingeschlossen, mit einer Geste,
die wie Gebet um Errettung wirkt. An einem Kapitell in Moissac (Fig. 5) stehen
die Tiere hoch aufgerichtet an Stämmen mit dem Rücken gegen den Heiligen,
wie Wappentiere, die den Adel des Menschen künden. Daniel hat dieselbe
Gebärde wie in Saintes. Die Gewalt und Majestät der Darstellung rührt her von
den Tieren; Daniel sitzt wie ein Gefangener zwischen ihnen. In Arles (Fig. 6)
ist die Szene aus der früh-archaischen Starrheit herausgewachsen und lebendiger
geworden. Riesige Löwen schreiten an den Seiten eines Fassadensockels aus der
Tiefe heraus und legen zähnefletschend dem Propheten die Tatzen auf die Knie.
Der Heilige sitzt bekümmert zwischen ihnen, das Haupt kläglich auf die Hand
gestützt, ein Bild des Jammers. Niemand würde der Darstellung ansehen, dass
Daniel über diese Bestien Gewalt hat. Die Macht der Darstellung gehört den

Löwen. Die Scheu des Betrachters ist nicht die Achtung vor dem Märtyrer, sondern die Angst vor der Bestie. Dabei muss man wissen, dass es Möglichkeiten gab, die Erzählung weniger monumental, weniger tierverherrlichend zu fassen, epischer, mit Angabe der Grube oder, wie es die altchristliche Kunst tat, die Löwen als kleines Beiwerk der Gestalt des Heiligen beigefügt, der allein als Vorbild einer Errettung für die Jenseits-Hoffnungen der Urchristen in Betracht kam.

Marburger photo.

FIG. 3. TOULOUSE, MUSÉE DES AUGUSTINS, KAPITELL
AUS KREUZGANG VON ST. ÉTIENNE
2. Viertel 12. Jahrhundert

Zu dem Kirchenvater Hieronymus kommt der Löwe als Bittsteller. Ihn quält ein Dorn. Der Heilige holt ihn heraus. Fortan begleitet ihn der Löwe wie ein Haustier. Diese rührende Geschichte von der Dankbarkeit des Löwen, eine Illustration, wie menschlich auch Tiere empfinden können, wird ein Lieblingsthema der Renaissance, die den Gelehrtenheiligen in seiner Häuslichkeit und den Löwen als biederes treues Haustier darstellt. In der romanischen Plastik Frankreichs kenne ich sie nur einmal, in der empfindsamen Kunst Autuns (Fig. 7). Und dennoch, wo ist hier das Gemütvolle der Szene geblieben!

FIG. 4. SAINTES, ST. EUTROPE, OBERKIRCHE, SÜDÖSTLICHER VIERUNGSPFEILER
1. HÄLFTE 12. JAHRHUNDERT

Marburger photo.

FIG. 5. MOISSAC, ST. PIERRE, KREUZGANG, KAPITELL AN NORDSEITE
DES WESTTRAKTES, UM 1100

Zwischen Bäumen und dem schüchtern gekrümmt sitzenden Heiligen richtet sich der Löwe im Zentrum des Kapitells empor, grösser und mächtiger als der Mensch. Er brüllt und streckt die mächtige Tatze dem Heiligen entgegen. Wie eine Schlange windet sich sein langer dicker Schweif nach der dem Heiligen abgewandten Seite. Der Monumentalität der Darstellung entsprechend ist der Dorn

Marburger photo.

FIG. 6.   ARLES, ST. TROPHÎME, WESTPORTAL,
SÄULENSOCKEL

MITTE 12. JAHRHUNDERT

ein kräftiger Stab, wie ein Pfeil oder eine Lanzenspitze. Der Löwe ist trotz seines Unglücks der überragende Held der Geschichte.

Dann gibt es Tiere, die für die Würde Gottes und seiner Zeichen mehr Gefühl haben als die Menschen, heilige Tiere gleichsam. Bileam, der ausgeritten ist, den Israeliten zu fluchen, trifft auf dem Wege den Engel Gottes, der ihm Halt gebietet. Er treibt den Esel zur Eile an, dieser aber, gläubiger und gehorsamer als der Mensch, sinkt in die Knie, sodass Bileam selbst nach vorn sinkt und sich, um nicht herunterzufallen, auf den Stab stützen muss, mit dem er eben noch das Tier gezüchtigt hat. So zeigt ihn ein herrliches Kapitell in Autun in einem dickwolligen Reisemantel, der in der dreieckigen Kapuze und dem schild-

förmigen Zipfel in archaischer Weise scheibenförmig verhärtet ist (Fig. 8). Auch
der Esel ist in eindrucksvoller Flächigkeit und kraftvoller Silhouette auf einem
kahlen Grunde ganz beherrschend dargestellt, gross wie in einem Denkmal. Ein
einziger dicker Stengel mit stilisierten Blüten bedeutet die Landschaft und verstärkt durch die Gegenwendung die ausdrucksvolle plötzliche Bewegung des Esels.
In Arles aber ist noch statuarischer oder denkmalshafter Bileam auf seinem Esel

Marburger photo.

FIG. 7.   AUTUN, KATHEDRALE, VORHALLE, KAPITELL DES
MITTLEREN WESTPORTALS

1. VIERTEL 12. JAHRHUNDERT

ganz allein auf einer Kapitellseite gegeben (Fig. 9). Die Plastik hat sich entwik-
kelt, die Formen sind gerundeter, die Haltungen energischer, und so entsteht von
neuem ein Lieblingsbild der personenverklärenden Kunst dieser Zeit: das
Reiterdenkmal. Im Sinne dieser Bileamsgeschichte wird man auch das merkwürdige Kapitell in Vézelay deuten müssen, wo streng rituell in symmetrischer
Entsprechung sich zwei Tiere, ein Bock und ein Schwein, vor einer Kreuzscheibe
aufrichten — wie ein Hund, der schön macht — und schneller als die Menschen
daneben die Heiligkeit dieses christlichen Symbols verstanden zu haben scheinen.

In der Geschichte des Eustachius ist es das Tier selbst, das über seinem Kopf
das Kreuz Christi trägt und so zum heiligen Tier, zum Träger und Symbol
Christi, wird. Das ganze ist eine Bekehrungs-Geschichte wie die des Paulus.
Das Kapitell in Vézelay überging dieses wichtigste Moment und machte ein
herrliches Jagd- und Reiterbild daraus. Das Kapitell in Autun (Fig. 10), das dem
in Vézelay vorausgeht und die Grundlage für dieses bildet, stellt zwar den Hl.
Eustachius dar, wie er vom Pferde abgesessen ist und betend sich in einer zarten,

Marburger photo.

FIG. 8. AUTUN, MUSÉE LAPIDAIRE, TÜRPFOSTENKAPITELL
VOM MITTLEREN WESTPORTAL DER KATHEDRALE

1. Viertel 12. Jahrhundert

Marburger photo.

FIG. 9. ARLES, ST. TROPHÎME, NORDTRAKT
DES KREUZGANGS, 1. JOCH, KAPITELL, UM 1130

schüchternen und kindlichen Haltung vor dem Hirsche beugt. Aber wäre nicht
die Gestalt des Heiligen in die Mitte gerückt, so würde sie kaum in Erscheinung
treten zwischen all den Tieren, dem Hirsch, Pferd und Hund, die sich hier
aneinanderdrängen. Das Pferd füllt ganz die eine Kapitellseite; und der jagd-
kundige Verfasser hat nicht vergessen, die auf die Jagd bezüglichen Einzelheiten
genau anzugeben: der Heilige hat hinter dem Pferd den Spiess eingerammt und
das Hifthorn daran aufgehängt. Symbolisch eine Heiligen-Geschichte, ist es
künstlerisch ein Tierkapitell.

Mit dem Motiv, dass wilde Tiere den Heiligen als Sockel dienen — ähnlich wie
die Sockel die Kirchensäulen tragen, denn auch die Apostel und Kirchenväter
sind Säulen der Kirche — wird dem Tier selbst schon eine Doppelbedeutung
zugeschrieben. Einerseits sind es die Tiere dieser Heiligen, Ort und Träger des
Heiligen und dadurch in den Kult dieser Heiligen einbezogen. Die Auslegung
konnte deshalb in ihnen Kräfte und Eigenschaften dieser Heiligen sehen, wie
es später an den Grabmälern geschah, bei denen die Verstorbenen ihre Füsse
auf Löwen, Hunde oder Drachen legen. Stärke, Treue, Klugheit liess sich aus
ihnen deuten. Oder sie versinnbildlichten, wie bei Daniel, Hieronymus, die
Macht des Heiligen ganz allgemein, seinen Sieg und Triumph über die natur-
haften Kräfte der Bestien, so wie Konstantins Sieg über das Heidentum durch eine
Figur symbolisiert wird, die unter den Füssen seines Pferdes liegt. Auf solchen
Tieren stehen die Propheten und Apostel in Moissac. Die grossartigste, vielleicht
auch früheste Ausprägung hat das Motiv in St. Gilles gefunden, nach dem es
schwächer und schlechter in Arles nachgebildet ist. Hier sind die Löwen halb
stilisiert, halb naturalistisch mit stärkster Angabe der Knochen und Muskeln
in ihrer ganzen physischen Gewalt geschildert; sie haben Menschen und Tiere,
Widder oder Schafe in ihren Fängen, die sie mit ihren Krallen zerreissen und mit
ihrem gewaltigen Gebiss zerfleischen. Es gibt wenige Darstellungen, in denen
die Furchtbarkeit dieser Tiere so überzeugend und so blutrünstig geschildert ist.
Für den Anblick triumphieren die Bestien. Dem naiven Betrachter müsste das
Herz stillstehen bei diesem Anblick. Und wenn er sich mit bebender Scheu den
Aposteln nahte, so verdanken diese ihre sichtbare Macht den Tieren. In der
Deutung überwinden sie diese und ihre Gewalt, in der Darstellung kommen sie
nicht gegen sie auf.

Sieht man, mit welcher Unermüdlichkeit des Schaffens und welcher grandio-
sen Fruchtbarkeit der Phantasie an Kapitellen, Gesimsen, in Tympana, an
Basen und Konsolen immer neue Motive der Überwältigung von Menschen
durch Bestien erfunden werden, dann wird einem ganz deutlich, wie unmittelbar
hier noch die Angst des primitiven, besonders des auf dem Lande und in Wäldern
lebenden Menschen vor wilden Tieren zum Ausdruck kommt. Diese Angst und
Scheu bewirkt, dass unter den Tieren alle wilden Tiere, alle Raubtiere be-
vorzugt werden und alle Fabeltiere oder fremden, exotischen Tiere, die mit dem
Geheimnis des Fremden und Wunderbaren umgeben waren und an heiliger
Stätte die Atmosphäre des Mythischen und des Zaubers schufen. Diese Tiere
und Fabelwesen sind deshalb nicht heiteres Spiel der Phantasie — als solche

FIG. 10. AUTUN, KATHEDRALE, VORHALLE, KAPITELL DES
MITTLEREN WESTPORTALS
2. Viertel 12. Jahrhundert

waren sie ererbt — sondern tiefer, furchtbarer Ernst, oder vielmehr wiederum beides in derselben reizvollen und reichen Durchdringung wie alles in der Kultur des Mittelalters. Wir haben sie deshalb noch nicht erklärt, wenn wir die Quellen für die einzelnen Fabelwesen und exotischen Tiere in der Antike nachweisen und die Wege der Überlieferung durch spät-antike Bücher, wie den Physiologus und die mittelalterlichen Bestiarien, oder durch die byzantinische und islamische Kunst aufzeigen, durch Werke der Kleinkunst und durch Stoffe des Orients. Vorlagen und Anregungen sind nicht die Ursache für die Tierdarstellungen im Mittelalter, sondern liefern nur das Material dem kultischen Bewusstsein, das, wie bei der heiligen Geschichte, sich gern auf ein Buch, eine Überlieferung berief. Gerade weil man an diese Tiere glauben wollte, mussten sie durch die Schrift, die Tradition beweisbar sein, mussten sie existieren. Die eigentliche Ursache ihrer Existenz in der romanischen Kunst Frankreichs ist die archaische Geisteshaltung, der geheime Kult des Tieres. Dass das Tier überall da ist, oder wo es ist und wie es ist, ist das Wichtige, nicht die Quelle für das Motiv im Allgemeinen. Denn selbst wenn sich jede seltsame Bildung auf ein Vorbild zurückführen liesse — was nicht einmal der Fall ist, da die Überlieferung für die Stärke dieses Bewusstseins zu arm war —, entscheidend ist, wie in jedem einzelnen Fall ein altes Motiv neue, grossartige, dämonische Form gewinnt, und welcher Sinn im Zusammenhang des Ganzen und der künstlerischen Prägung herrscht. Und das ist ganz eigen und ist in diesem Ausmass weder vorher schon da, noch nachher noch da.

Wenn wir also die einzelnen Darstellungen auf ihre Abkunft hin betrachten, dann müssen wir uns bewusst bleiben, dass wir die wilden Tiere, die wir an den Gliedern und Wänden der Kirchen finden, anders ansehen müssen als nur als Beweise für die Kenntnisse literarischer oder steinerner Überlieferungen oder irgendwelcher anderer Anregungen und auch nicht als Äusserungen einer harmlosen Welt- und Erdkunde. Sehen wir am Sockel von St. Gilles Affen und ein Kamel nebeneinander gestellt, dann ist es lehrreich, daran zu denken, dass zur Zeit, als diese Skulpturen entstanden, die Kreuzfahrer sich in St. Gilles nach dem Heiligen Lande einschifften und diese Verbindung zwischen dem Orient und Occident eine unmittelbare Anschauung und Kenntnis dieser Tiere vermittelt haben kann. Die Löwen aber, die viel häufiger als diese Tiere vorkommen, waren seit dem Altertum dem Blick und Wissen zugänglich in den ungezählten Löwenreliefs und Freiplastiken, die aus der spätantiken Kunst hinterlassen waren. Die Kenntis von Bären, die wir an einem anderen Sockel treffen, konnten damals die heimischen Wälder liefern. Aber auch für den Bären bot die Überlieferung Anregungen. Es ist ein altes Motiv; der Bär wird gerne in der Rolle verwendet, in der er für die Menschen eine nützliche Arbeit verrichtet, z.B. die Walze oder den Pflug über den Acker zieht (Coulonges) oder die Stämme zum Bauen aus dem Wald transportiert, wie schon in karolingischer Zeit auf dem Elfenbeinrelief des Hl. Tutilo in St. Gallen. Auch das geduldige Tragen einer Säule an einer Kirche, wie es die Bären ebenfalls an einem Sockel in St. Gilles tun, ist eine solche Arbeit. Wenn man an einem Kapitell in Nevers (Fig. 11) einen Bären über einen Menschen herfallen sieht, wie sonst meist die Löwen, dann wundert man sich, warum er so gemächlich schreitend auf dem Rücken des Mannes spaziert, und denkt mehr an eine Gauklerszene als an einen Kampf des Tieres mit dem Menschen. So gemächlich aber schreiten auf einem antiken Relief die Bären, die in einen Garten eingedrungen sind und von dem Besitzer mit Stein-würfen verjagt werden (Fig. 12). Es liegt also nahe, hier sogar einmal eine direkte antike Vorlage anzunehmen, auch wenn an Naturwahrheit die Nachbildung über das Original hinausgeht. Wir werden uns auch fragen, wenn wir an einem Kapitell in Mozac Affen finden, die an einer Leine von einem Jüngling gehalten werden, ob nicht die Anregung zu dieser Darstellung von den ornamental durch

Marburger photo.   *Marburger photo.*

FIG. 11. NEVERS, MUSÉE   FIG. 12. VIENNE, MUSÉE LAPIDAIRE IN
LAPIDAIRE, KAPITELL   ST. PIERRE, ANTIKES RELIEF
AUS ST. SAUVEUR

2. VIERTEL 12. JAHRHUNDERT

Bänder verflochtenen Affen ausgegangen ist, die wir in St. Gilles sehen, und wer-den auch noch andere Beziehungen zwischen den Kunstwerken hier und dort suchen.

Auch sind wir natürlich besonders froh, dass wir aus den Bestiarien die Namen der Tiere erfahren, vor allem gewisser Fabeltiere, die wir schwer aus der Antike belegen können, oder den Sinn von Situationen, die wir nicht ohne Weiteres verstehen. Wir lernen dabei, dass das delphinartige Wesen, auf dessen Rücken sich Menschen befinden und Feuer anzünden, ein Walfisch ist, dessen grosser Rücken eine Insel vortäuschte. Die Fischer glaubten an Land zu steigen und zünden auf ihm ein Feuer an. In demselben Augenblick taucht der Fisch unter und zieht die ganze Mannschaft mit sich in die Tiefe. Es ist also eine Geschichte ähnlich der von der Meersirene, dem Fischweibchen, das mit Fischen in der Hand und vielleicht mit seinem Gesang die Fischer im Kahn ins Verderben lockt (Fig. 34).

Aber wir dürfen nicht glauben, dass wir damit diese Bestien in der romanischen Kunst schon verstanden haben. Für die Bedeutung im Bewusstsein der Zeit ist wichtig, dass jener Bär in Nevers eben nicht im Früchtegarten herumtrottet, sondern sich als wildes Tier wie ein Löwe auf einen Menschen stürzt, dass in St. Gilles Affen und Dromedar in einer Reihe erscheinen, in der Löwen Menschen zerfleischen, und dass unmittelbar neben ihnen Nothelfer der Menschen (Symbole der Erlösung), David, Goliath, St. Michael, erscheinen, und dass die Heiligen auf den Tieren gegen diese Bilder der Gefahr angerufen werden können. Man muss darauf achten, dass die Tiere besonders gross wie Urtiere geschildert werden, eine Eidechse so gross wie ein Dromedar und alle grösser als die Menschen. Oft reiten auf einem Vogel kleine nackte Gestalten und erwecken die Vorstellung eines Riesenvogels, der imstande wäre, Menschen zu entführen und in finstere Schluchten zu tragen, zum Frass für seine Jungen.

Es muss uns auffallen, dass die fremden Tiere, Löwe, Affe usw., in einer Reihe mit den Fabeltieren erscheinen, dass sie also so erregend, so geheimnisvoll waren wie diese, und dass diese für so wirklich gehalten wurden wie jene, dass also auch der Wert der Bestiarien wesentlich darin besteht, uns von der Tiergläubigkeit der Zeit zu überzeugen. Denn Tierkataloge gab es auch in Stein, wie jene Säule in Souvigny oder die Kapitellreihe in Nevers, die, von Inschriften begleitet, ein Tierlexikon wie einen Heiligenkatalog geben und, weil in der Kirche befindlich, eine Mahntafel für das sind, was man glauben soll. Man muss darauf achten, wie ernst diese Tiere genommen werden, wenn sie im wildesten Kampf mit dem Menschen und unter sich geschildert werden. Eine Archivolte in Angoulême, die die Apostel umrahmt, hallt förmlich wider vom Angstgeschrei der Menschen, die von adlerartigen Untieren zerfleischt werden, vom Getrapp der Hufe und vom Geklirr der Waffen jener Ritter und Reiter, die den Kampf mit den Untieren aufnehmen (Fig. 13). Wenn wir in den Bestiarien diese Stimmung nicht wiederfinden, tun wir besser, die Sagen der Zeit, die Kämpfe von Rittern mit den Drachen in finsteren Wäldern zu lesen, um zu verstehen, dass hier nicht gewöhnliche, gefahrbringende Jagdszenen dargestellt sind, sondern gezeigt wird, wie sich in einer von Kampf und Jagd beherrschten Kulturstufe die feindlichen Mächte, die mythischen Kräfte der Welt zum Bilde von übermenschlichen bösen Gewalten steigern und umso übermenschlicher, je unbekannter oder unerkennbarer sie sind.

Wenn wir die Fabelwesen durchsehen, so ist uns sicherlich wertvoll festzustellen, dass der Greif mit Vogelkopf, Flügeln und Tierleib aus der Antike stammt, dass die antike Chimäre, halb Ziege, halb Löwe, hier wiederkehrt, dass das Tier, aus dessen Leib kleinere Tiere gleicher Art herauskriechen (Beaulieu), die Viper ist, von der der Physiologus berichtet, dass sie stirbt, wenn sie Junge hervorbringt, die lebendig aus ihrem Leibe hervorgehen, oder dass das Tier mit den vielen Hälsen und Köpfen das Tier der Apokalypse oder der Vision Daniels ist. Aber wichtiger ist zu konstatieren, dass diese Tiere nicht mehr Visionen sind, sondern greifbarste, nächste Wirklichkeit, nicht daran denken zu sterben, sondern ihre gefährliche unheimliche Lebendigkeit verstärken durch Vervielfältigung mit neuen, jüngeren Leibern, und dass man sich nicht genug tun kann, den widerlichen, unheimlichen Anblick eines Schlangenkopfes mit der züngelnden, gespaltenen Zunge den Gliedern eines Tieres anzuhängen und die Quaste des Schweifes damit zu dämonisieren. Wir würden deshalb bei diesen Tieren viel besser den Namen Fafnir oder Lernäische Hydra aussprechen oder irgendeinen Namen, bei dem man sich dreimal bekreuzigt, um seiner Bedeutung gerecht zu werden.

Wieder unterstützt die monumentale Form der Darstellung diese Bedeutsamkeit und macht die abgegriffenen, ewig wiederholten Symbole der Antike, diese Adler und Schlangen, diese Dekoratiosstücke und Götterattribute, die, wie

Marburger photo.

FIG. 13. ANGOULÊME, KATHEDRALE,
MITTELPORTAL DER WESTFASSADE
1. HÄLFTE 12. JAHRHUNDERT

unsere Adler auf den Münzen, inhaltlich nichts mehr besagten, wieder gewichtig und eindringlich, nagelt das Abgleitende wieder fest, erzeugt es in jedem Augenblicke wieder neu aus der Angst vor der dämonischen Kraft der für wirklich genommenen Bilder und steigert und vervielfältigt es zu dämonischer Wirkung.

Dass in jedem archaischen Kulturzustand die mythische Bedeutung des Tieres hauptsächlich aus der Angst geboren ist und in jeder Entwicklung der Augenblick kam, wo die dunklen Tierdämonen durch die menschlichen Götter des Lichts überwunden wurden, ein Zustand, dessen Wiederkehr sich hier in den vielen Kämpfen zwischen Mensch und Tier und in der Lichtgestalt des Hl. Michael verrät, erleichterte der kirchlich-christlichen Deutung, diese Tiere moralisch statt mythisch zu nehmen, sinnbildlich auf die Gefahren hinzudeuten, die der christlichen Seele aus den Verlockungen der Welt ständig drohten, und das

Reich des Bösen an ihnen zu erläutern. So wird das Mysterium des gefürchteten und mit heimlicher Scheu verehrten Tieres zum Symbol des Lasters, ohne dass diese allegorische Verflüchtigung so wenig wie die dekorative Verwendung dem Anblick die ursprüngliche Erhabenheit rauben konnte.

Wenn z.B. Löwen, die von beiden Seiten einer Kapitellseite an der Kapitellkante zusammengeführt werden und dort nur einen Kopf haben oder in der Mitte einer Kapitellseite zu einem Kopf zusammenwachsen, oder wenn auch einmal ein Tierleib aus dekorativen Gründen sich nach oben in zwei Köpfe auseinanderlegt, so ist es sicherlich auf der einen Seite die dekorative Spielerei der antiken Spätkunst gewesen, die diese Verachtung der Natur unterstützt hat. In den sassanidischen Kleinkunstwerken, in persischen Miniaturen und orienta-

Marburger photo.

FIG. 14.   ANZY–LE–DUC, ABTEIKIRCHE,
KAPITELL AN LANGHAUSPFEILER
1. Viertel 12. Jahrhundert

lischen Teppichen oder Stoffen, die in den Kirchen des Mittelalters als Vorhänge, als Kirchengewänder, als Hülle von Reliquien und Körpern der Heiligen in den Särgen und Schreinen mannigfach verwendet wurden, lässt sich die zunehmende Unbekümmertheit um die naturwissenschaftlich mögliche Form solcher tierischen Doppelwesen konstatieren. Ebenso gewiss aber ist es, dass die zunehmende Wundergläubigkeit und mythenbildende Kraft der urtümlicheren nachantiken Kulturen solche Mischbildungen förderten und den Willen, sie darzustellen, stärkten, dass aus der dekorativen Freiheit und Skepsis, die als Erbe den Reichtum des Dekorativen in romanischer Kunst bedingten, allmählich auch wieder ein Glaube an die Schöpfungen der Phantasie getreten war, dessen Wurzeln viel tiefer in das religiöse Bewusstsein reichten als in ein reines Schmuckbedürfnis.

Nur geht aus diesem dekorativen, geschmackvollen Erbe der Spätantike, das sich mit dem furchtbaren Ernst des primitiven Tiermythus mischt, wieder ein Doppelcharakter, eine Zweideutigkeit der romanischen Tierdarstellung hervor, das dämonisch Fratzenhafte im Spiegel heiterster, dekorativer Schönheit gesehen, das Abscheuerregende, überblendet von der Anziehungskraft des künstlerisch freisten Spieles.

Wiederum wäre es falsch aus der Ähnlichkeit romanischer Motive in der Plastik mit solchen aus orientalischen Stoffen, so interessant es ist, solche zu konstatieren, mehr herauszulesen, als dass das Weiterleben der antiken Spätkunst und der Zusammenprall dieser Endkunst mit der Frühkunst unverbrauchter und jüngerer Völker ein Phänomen ist, das natürlich viel weiter reicht als über das

Marburger photo.

FIG. 15.   ST. PARIZE–LE–CHÂTEL, SÄULEN-
KAPITELL DER KRYPTA

1. Hälfte 12. Jahrhundert

Herrschaftsgebiet romanischer Plastik in Frankreich hinweg, und dass diese Bewegung im Ganzen und jedes Motiv im Einzelnen seine Geschichte hat, die nach Rom, Byzanz, dem Orient führt und zurück bis in die frühesten Zeiten der Erstarrung der freiesten aller antiken Äusserungen, des Hellenismus. Man würde sehen, wie mit dem Eindringen unentwickelterer Bewusstseinsschichten den Randvölkern des römischen Imperiums altorientalische oder altgriechische Traditionen, die gerade an diesen Rändern der alleinstehenden Kultur fortleben, von Neuem lebendig werden und manche archaischen Motive ganz rein wieder verwendet werden konnten. Aber das alles doch nur, um wiederum festzustellen, wie innerlich verwandt diesen archaischen oder archaisierenden Kulturen die der romanischen Kunst zugrunde liegende Kultur ist. Das begierige Aufgreifen und Annehmen sowohl solcher alt- wie neuorientalischer Dekorationsstücke besagt doch nur die Stärke und Richtung des eigenen Produktionswillens, der das Verwandte als Stoff für seine Formungen auch am ehesten gebrauchen konnte. Dann aber beginnt erst die eigentliche Aufgabe, zu zeigen, wie weder quantitativ noch qualitativ eine solche Weite und Fülle neuer Schöpfungen wie in dieser französischen Kunst in irgendeiner der anderen zu finden ist, vor allem

Marburger photo.

FIG. 16. AUTUN, KATHEDRALE, WESTLICHES KAPITELL
DES 4. SÜDLICHEN LANGHAUSPFEILERS
1. VIERTEL 12. JAHRHUNDERT

nirgends eine so rücksichtslose und konsequente Verschmelzung des graziös-dekorativen Stiles der Spätkunst mit dem Monumentalen und Dämonischen der Frühkultur, nirgends eine so vollständige Umbildung eines festlichen Schmuckes in eine mythische Personifikation. Man wird immer finden, dass in der byzantinischen Kunst die Heilige Geschichte nach der Seite der strengen Stilisierung und formalen Verbildlichung vieles der monumentalen Menschendarstellung im Romanischen vorweggenommen hat, aber nie mit derselben Ursprünglichkeit und plastischen Kraft, nie auch mit derselben erhabenen Grossartigkeit, und dass die orientalische Schmuckkunst aus dem rein Dekorativen der Spätkunst durch neue geometrische und technisch bedingte Musterung einen neuen Reiz rein ornamentaler Gestaltung gerade des Vegetabilischen und Tierischen entwickelt hat, aber ohne die Umbildung des nur Dekorativen ins glaubhaft Lebendige

Marburger photo.

FIG. 17. AUTUN, KATHEDRALE, ÖSTLICHES KAPITELL
DES 4. SÜDLICHEN LANGHAUSPFEILERS
1. Viertel 12. Jahrhundert

und Dämonische, die wir in Frankreich neben den rein repräsentativen Darstellungen der Fassaden und Portale auch an jeder dekorativen Schöpfung finden.

Die Unerschöpflichkeit der Phantasie, die sich darin bewährt, die Unheimlichkeit und Gewalttätigkeit der Tiere durch Vervielfältigung von Haupt und Gliedern zu steigern, diese apokalyptische Tiermythik verbürgt uns, dass die Unheimlichkeit auch dort empfunden wurde, wo aus *dekorativen* Gründen ein Kopf zwei Leiber oder ein Leib zwei Köpfe erhalten hat. Aus einem jugendlichen, kindlichen Bewusstsein heraus, dem das Wunder — sei es in Form des Wunderbaren oder Verwunderlichen — des Glaubens liebstes Kind ist, erhöht sich auch das Dekorative ins Dämonische. Nicht in den zufälligen Quellen des Motives liegt die Brücke zum Verständnis, sondern in den Misch- und Missbildungen, die wir auch sonst, ohne dekorativen Zwang, ausgeführt finden. Wir denken an jene Menschen mit doppelten Leibern und Köpfen auf einem Beinpaar in Anzy-le-Duc (Fig. 14) und Vézelay oder an jenen doppelköpfigen Janus der Monatsdarstellungen, bei denen Hinweise auf lasterhaftes Leben von Gauklern und Seltsamkeiten mythischer Gestalten nahe beieinander liegen, oder an jenen Schattenfüssler, der mit einem riesenhaften Bein einem Schlangenmenschen ähnelt und mit übernatürlichen Kräften begabt ist: denn er läuft mit seinem einen Bein schneller als der Wind, und wenn er müde ist, setzt er sich in den Schatten seines eigenen Fusses, wie es ein Kapitell in St. Parize-le-Châtel zeigt (Fig. 15). Ein besonderes und immer wiederkehrendes Mittel, die Tiere zu übernatürlichen Wesen zu steigern und die Kraft wilder, vierfüssiger Bestien mit der raum- und zeitüberwindenden Fähigkeit der Vögel zu verbinden, ist die Ausstattung der Fabelwesen, der löwen-, greifen- oder ziegenartigen Chimären, mit Flügeln. Auch die Tiere, die durch ihre Gestalt dem Boden am meisten verhaftet sind, Eidechsen und zum Kriechen verurteilte Schlangen, erhalten Flügel und werden zu übernatürlichen Drachen. Mit den Flügeln konnte man den Himmel erobern. Den Vögeln gleichen, hiess sich über die Erde erheben und ins Jenseits enteilen können, denn die mythische Phantasie auch dieser Kunst denkt sich Himmel und Erde räumlich verbunden und räumlich real. Als Taube schwebt der Heilige Geist vom Himmel zur Erde herab. Durch Flügel werden aus den Menschen Engel — auch sie im Grunde Mischwesen von Vogel und Mensch — Sendboten des Himmels. Selbst Christus kann nur von Engeln gehalten oder emporgezogen zum Himmel auffahren. So zeigen es die meisten der Himmelfahrtsbilder. Das Streben des Menschen, durch die Lüfte sich im Flug zu erheben, ist nichts anderes als das Streben, Gott oder den Engeln gleich zu werden, und deshalb ein Zeichen des verdammenswertesten Hochmuts. Wer es unternimmt, wie Simon der Magier, ist ein Zauberer, ein Übermensch im Bunde mit dem Teufel; und wenn er, wie Ikarus, zu Boden stürzt, dann ist dies, wie bei Luzifer, ein göttliches Gericht, das ihn zu Boden schmettert, oder wie ein Sieg der olympischen Götter über die Titanen. Zwei Kapitelle in Autun stellen diesen Flug und Sturz des Zauberers vor den Augen der Apostel Petrus und Paulus dar, den Teufel im Hintergrund, der im Bunde mit ihm war und nun den Gestürzten als seine Beute empfängt (Fig. 16, 17). Der Stürzende selber wirkt wie ein Dämon mit den Flügeln an Armen und Beinen und dem tierisch verzerrten, weit aufgerissenen Mund. Petrus aber hält den riesigen Schlüssel wie eine Waffe und ein magisches Beschwörungszeichen steil empor. Sollte das nicht bedeuten, dass der Himmel dem Hochmütigen verschlossen ist? Ein anderes Bild gleichen Hochmutes ist das von Alexanders Greifenfahrt. Dieser fliegt nicht selbst, sondern spannt zwei Greifen vor seinen Wagen. Durch Köder, die er über sie hält, reizt er sie, immer höher zu fliegen in die Regionen des Himmels hinein, bis ihm ein

Vogel von menschlicher Gestalt begegnet und ihn drohend auffordert umzukehren. Auf der Erde sieht er eine im Kreis eingerollte Schlange, die ihm von dem Vogel als das Meer gedeutet wird, das die Erde umschliesst. So sieht man hier, wie der Engel, der den Himmel verteidigt, als Vogel empfunden wird, die sagenhafte Grösse aber des heidnischen Kaisers Alexander wiederum durch den Versuch, im Fliegen sich über die Erde zum Himmel zu erheben, zum Halbgott und Dämon gesteigert wird, und wie dies wiederum nur mit Hilfe mythischer Tiere, der Greifen, möglich wird. Eine alte Zeichnung der Kathedrale von Nîmes (Paris, Bibl. Nat. franç. 8648, um 1625, Fig. 18) verrät uns, wie der antike Fries-

Marburger photo.

FIG. 18. NÎMES, NOTRE–DAME, RELIEFS ÜBER DEM
PORTAL DER KATHEDRALE
ZEICHNUNG VON RULMANN, UM 1625

schmuck von gegenständigen Greifen der Darstellung zur Grunde liegt. Uns erscheint diese Geschichte der Vögel, die durch den Köder zum Fliegen und Transport verführt werden, wie eine lustige Fabel. Für das Verständnis aber ihrer Darstellung an den Kapitellen und Portalen der Kirche und ihrer strengen, monumentalen Form ist es nötig, an die Parallele zu dem Zauberer Simon und seinem grauenhaften Sturz zwischen dem Teufel und den Heiligen zu denken und zugleich an die mythisch-erhabene Vorstellung, mit der sich das naive Bewusstsein der Zeitgenossen einen Kaiser und Welteroberer und nun gar einen des grauen und heidnischen Altertums vorstellte. Es war wunderbar und aufregend genug, um daraus eine neue, dämonengefüllte Alexandersage im Stile dieser mittelalterlichen Mythologie zu machen. Die theologische Deutung aber des Bildes auf die Idee des Hochmutes steigerte nur den Ernst des Bildes. So ist denn mit diesen Bildern des Lasters zugleich immer eine übermenschliche, zauberische und höhere Wirklichkeit verbunden. Wir befinden uns im Bereich des Dämonischen.

Dies aber gibt uns die Gewähr, dass auch die Tierfabel nicht anders aufge-

fasst wurde, d.h. nicht als eine geistreiche Parodie menschlicher Verhältnisse
unter dem Vorwande einer Tiergeschichte, sondern umgekehrt, unter dem Vorwande moralischer Ausdeutung und allegorischen Hinweises auf menschliche
Verhältnisse, eine Steigerung des tierisch Unbewussten ins menschlich Böse und
Vernunftbegabte. Schon die Tatsache, dass diese Fabeln an heiligen Stätten
bis hin zu der bedeutungsvollsten eines Tympanons dargestellt wurden — in
Autun noch an einem Kapitell (Fig. 20), in Grézac an einem Fassadenfeld
(Fig. 19), in Bourges am Portal von St. Ursin —, verbürgt uns, dass diese Tiere
mit anderen Augen angesehen wurden als mit denen eines Satirikers, dem An-
spielung und Sinn die Hauptsache war. Feierlich symmetrisch wie in einer sa-
kralen Handlung stehen in Grézac die Tiere, Storch und Wolf, einmal neben der

Marburger photo.

FIG. 19. GRÉZAC, KIRCHE, RELIEF IM STREBEPFEILER
LINKS VOM WESTPORTAL
2. Viertel 12. Jahrhundert

flachen Schüssel, dann neben dem enghalsigen hohen Krug. Sie wachsen in
ihrer festen Form zu eindrucksvoller Grösse empor und gruppieren sich streng
wie ein Wappen an der Wand. Dass der Künstler realistisch schildern konnte,
zeigen die Gefässe. Dass er die Tiere so ins Erhabene steigerte, kann nur
den Sinn haben, dass die von der Deutung nahegelegten Eigenschaften der
Bosheit und Berechnung diese vernunftlosen Wesen in den Bereich menschlicher
Charaktere erheben, eine Erhöhung, die etwa der Flugfähigkeit der Vierfüssler
gleich zu werten ist. So wurden Fabeltiere mythische Verkörperungen des Un-
danks (der Wolf, dem der Kranich Knochen aus dem Rachen zieht, Fig. 20),
der Verstellung (der sich tot stellende Fuchs auf dem von Gänsen gezogenen
Leichenwagen), des Betruges (die Gelage von Kranich und Wolf, Fig. 19).

Ebenso sind der Leier spielende Esel, der Wolf in Mönchskutte, der lesen
lernt und den Anfangsbuchstaben A sofort unbewusst als Agnus (Lämmer-
beute) liest, nicht heitere Parodien auf den Unverstand der Törichten, die mit
kostbaren Funden nichts anzufangen wissen, wie der Hahn mit der Perle auf dem
Misthaufen, oder des Menschen mit unreinem Herzen, der bei äusserlich edlem
oder friedfertigem Aussehen seine Hintergedanken hat, sondern es sind Bilder

von Tieren, die durch das Menschentum nachahmende Verhalten ins Mythische gesteigert sind, nicht Vergleiche, nicht n u r Bilder, sondern Repräsentationen, Darstellungen von Wesen, deren Kräfte über das Natürliche hinauswachsen.

Bei den unheimlichen Fabelwesen, in denen sich die verschiedensten Tiernaturen mischen, erreicht man diese Erhöhung zu vernunftbegabten und absichtsvollen Geschöpfen dadurch, dass man ihnen einen Menschen beigibt, der das Tier nach seinem Willen lenkt, und dieser Wille ist böse durch und durch, auf das Verderben der Menschen gerichtet. In Autun sehen wir einen kleinen Menschen auf dem gigantischen Vogel; er fasst ihn beim Bart und bedroht ihn

Marburger photo.

FIG. 20. AUTUN, KATHEDRALE, MITTLERES WESTPORTAL
DER VORHALLE
1. VIERTEL 12. JAHRHUNDERT

mit seinem Schwert (Fig. 21). Ein Anderer sitzt mit Schwert und Schild auf einem greifenartigen Ungeheuer, ein anderer, auf einem nicht mehr erkennbaren Monstrum mit dem Leibe eines Stieres, reitet vor ihm her und scheint sich kämpfend gegen ihn zu wenden. Auf der Chimäre sass ein Mann mit einer Keule (Fig. 22). Alle sind nackt und schon dadurch der gewöhnlichen Menschendarstellung entrückt. In Vézelay werden diese Themen weitergesponnen mit einer herrlichen Kunst plastischer Rundung der Körper, schwungvoller Rhythmik der Bewegung und sorgfältigster Arbeit im Einzelnen. Faszinierenderes als diese Fabeltiere ist kaum je gebildet worden. Auf einem ungeheuren Greifendrachen sitzt ein Mensch, klein im Verhältnis zur Bestie, nackt, mit Spitzhelm (Fig. 23). Mit verrenkten Armen hält er hinter sich eine Kugel (zum Werfen?). Ihm begegnet in Gemeinschaft mit einer Schlange eine Kuh mit dem Oberkörper einer gekrönten Jungfrau und hält vor das dämonisch verzerrte Gesicht des Drachen auch eine Kugel (Fig. 24) — liegt hier dasselbe vor wie in dem Kapitell, wo ein Mann, begleitet von einem Tier, das halb Fisch, halb Heuschrecke ist, eine Riesenheuschrecke, vor einem Basilisken steht (auch dieser ist grösser als der Mensch), einer Missgeburt aus Hahn und Schlange, und ein Gefäss ihm vor die Augen hält (Fig. 25)? Hier ist nun die magische, übernatürliche Kraft dieser Fabeltiere deutlich gezeigt. Schon ihr Blick tötet und nur mit einem Glasgefäss, wie dem, das der Mensch in Händen hält, kann die totbringende Wirkung des Basiliskenblickes abgewendet werden. Der kleine Reiter aber auf dem Untier — dafür spricht die Nacktheit — ist selbst nur der böse Wille, die moralisch bewertbare Triebfeder, der Lenker und Leiter dieser tierischen, mit magischen Kräften begabten Gewalten. An einem anderen Kapitell, von wunderbarer Plastik der Formen, herrlich entfalteter Bewegung und rhythmischer Zusammenfügung aller Umrisse, ist denn auch der auf einem grossartigen Greifendrachen sitzende Mensch selbst nur Dämon, nackt, mit hervortretendem Rückgrat wie bei einem Tier und mit einem tierisch grossen, verzerrten Maul (Fig. 26). Mit einem Stab, den er wie eine Lanze hält, stösst er nach vorn, man weiss nicht, ob gegen den seitswärts stehenden Dämon oder auf ein beiden gemeinsames Ziel. Auch dieser scheint eine Schüssel zum Schutz gegen den magischen Blick des Tieres bereit zu halten. Alle diese nackten Reiter sind selber Dämonen. Durch sie erhalten die Tiere eine Seele, durch sie werden sie eine Person, durch sie aber vor allem werden sie zu dem Rang göttergleicher Wesen erhoben. Denn damit man solchen Wesen opfern kann, damit man durch Bitten oder Gebete, durch Zauberformeln oder Riten sie besänftigen oder schrecken kann, müssen sie wie Menschen das alles verstehen können. Deshalb bildeten ja auch die Alten ihre Tiergötter mit Menschenköpfen oder mit Menschenleibern. Zum Kultgegenstand wurden sie erst durch die Menschenwürde oder die Fähigkeit, in menschlicher Weise den Menschen Böses zu wollen.

Über diese dämonische, götterähnliche Bedeutung dieser Drachenreiter gibt die Darstellung des Goldenen Kalbes in Autun und Vézelay Auskunft (Fig. 27, 28). In Autun steht Moses vor dem Goldenen Kalb und beschwört es mit den Tafeln des Gesetzes, dahinter ein Dämon mit flammenden Haaren und fratzenhaftem Gesicht. In Vézelay aber reitet dieser Dämon auf dem Kalb, eine Missgestalt mit Vogelbrust und tierisch grossem Maul und verzerrten Zügen des halbmenschlichen Gesichtes. Das Goldene Kalb also ist ein Götze, d.h. aber nicht ein totes Bild, eine Wahnvorstellung irregeleiteter Menschen, sondern höchst lebendig, ein Gegengott, ein Feind, ein Gott des Lasters, der gegen die Gebote des guten Gottes ankämpft. Schon aus dem Kalb ist in der Darstellung ein höchst lebendiger, riesiger, brüllender Stier geworden. Seine dämonische Natur aber kommt erst ganz zum Ausdruck in den dämonischen Menschengestalten hinter und auf ihm: einem Dämon, der dem Stier aus dem Maule gefahren ist wie im Tode dem Menschen die Seele aus dem Munde.

Der Teufel aber ist selbst ein Halbtier. Durch ihn verstehen wir aber sofort die mythische Bedeutung aller der Tiermenschen, denen wir auf Schritt und Tritt an der Kirche begegnen. Meist sind es altbekannte Gestalten, die Natur-

FIG. 21. AUTUN, MUSÉE LAPIDAIRE,
KAPITELLE VON EINEM LANGHAUS-
PFEILER DER KATHEDRALE

1. Viertel 12. Jahrhundert

FIG. 22. AUTUN, MUSÉE LAPIDAIRE,
TÜRPFOSTENKAPITELL VOM
MITTLEREN WESTPORTAL
DER KATHEDRALE

1. Viertel 12. Jahrhundert

FIG. 23, 24. VÉZELAY, STE. MADELEINE, 1. SÜDL. LANGHAUSPFEILER, UM 1130

Marburger photo.

FIG. 25. VÉZELAY, STE. MADELEINE,
7. WANDVORLAGE IM NÖRDL.
SEITENSCHIFF, UM 1130

Marburger photo.

FIG. 26. VÉZELAY, STE. MADELEINE,
6. NÖRDL. LANGHAUSPFEILER,
UM 1130

Marburger photo.

FIG. 27. AUTUN, KATHEDRALE, SÜDL.
SEITENSCHIFF 6. PILASTER
1. Viertel 12. Jahrhundert

Marburger photo.

FIG. 28. VÉZELAY, STE. MADELEINE,
6. NÖRDL. LANGHAUSPFEILER,
UM 1130

götter antiker Mythologie. Aber nicht weil sie von der Antike überliefert sind, sind sie wieder da, sondern weil das neue mythische Bewusstsein sie erforderte und zu neuem Leben erweckte, sie um- und weiterbildete und ein dekorativ gleichgültig gewordenes Motiv zu neuer Kraft steigerte. Die antiken Halbgötter in Halbtiergestalt sinken zu höllischen Gestalten der christlichen Anschauung ab.

Sie treten ein in das Knäuel von Fabeltieren, die als Verderber der Menschen sich mit ihnen zu dicht beladenen Dekorationen verschlingen, wie in Aubeterre

Marburger photo.

FIG. 29. AUBETERRE, ST. JACQUES, WESTFASSADE, NÖRDL. BLENDARKADE

2. VIERTEL 12. JAHRHUNDERT

Marburger photo.

FIG. 30. ARLES, MUSÉE LAPIDAIRE

2. VIERTEL 12. JAHRHUNDERT

(Fig. 29). Wir finden den Centauren, dessen Bild sich als Symbol — als Symbol des Bösen zwar — zu mythischer Grösse erhebt. Neben dem Rosszentauren gibt es auch den Kuh- und Stiermenschen. Wir sahen ihn in Vézelay im Kampf mit dem Drachenreiter als gekröntes weibliches Wesen (Fig. 24), auf einem Kapitell in Arles männlich, geflügelt, mit breitem menschlichem Gesicht unter einer mitraartigen Kopfbedeckung, aber mit Ochsenohren, einem gefahrwitternden Tierblick und auf den Hinterbeinen aufgerichtet wie ein Mensch, die Vorder- beine wie Arme einem zweiten Tier auf den Rücken gelegt (Fig. 30). An einem anderen Kapitell in Arles stehen sich mit dem Rücken ein weiblicher und männ- licher Flügeldämon mit Stier- und Kuhleib gegenüber: der weibliche gekrönt, der männliche mit grossartig bärtigem Prophetenkopf — wie assyrische Gott- heiten (Fig. 31). Für den Dämon in weiblicher Gestalt bot sich das Bild der Sirene, das weibliche Halbtier mit Menschenkopf und Vogelleib. Das Mittelalter verstärkt die Bösartigkeit, indem es dem Vogelleib noch einen Drachenschwanz anhängt. In Toulouse noch etwas derb und grob (Fig. 32), wird dieses Fabel- wesen in Autun zu einem reizend bewegten dekorativen Gebilde, dem man den lockenden Gesang aus der Linienmelodie des Körpers abliest (Fig. 33).

Hellenistische Dekorationsmotive von Seepferdchen, Seeschlangen und Nerei- den und das lang geschwänzte Gebilde des Drachenvogels mochten zusammen-gewirkt haben zu der Vorstellung der Meersirene. Der Drachenschweif ist zum Fischleib geworden, auf dem nackt ein weiblicher Oberkörper mit Menschenkopf und -armen sitzt. Wir finden sie schon im 11. Jh. und zwar entsprechend der Erzählerfreude dieser Zeit in breit ausgesponnener, sagenhafter Situation. Sie hält in einer oder in beiden Händen einen Fisch, mit dem sie, wie Loreley mit ihrem Gesang, Fischer im Kahn herbeilockt und sie ins Verderben führt (Cunault,

FIG. 31. ARLES, MUSÉE LAPIDAIRE, ROMANISCHES KAPITELL
2. VIERTEL 12. JAHRHUNDERT

Fig. 34). Mit doppeltem Fischleib füllt sie in Arles eine Basenecke und bezaubert durch ein Gauklerkunststück mit zurückgebogenem Leib die Blicke der Zuschauer. Der Kopf mit den zu Boden fliessenden Haaren ist seltsam dämonisch.

Meist finden wir die Sirene als Glied eines Paares, die Sirene enteilend, hinter ihr eine männliche jugendliche Gestalt, die sie wie ein Wild verfolgt. So ist es in dem herrlichen Kapitell der Daurade in Toulouse, wo ein nackter Jüngling mit dem Speer auf die Fischsirene zielt (Fig. 35). Offenbar treten hier Lockung und Begierde (Jagd nach den Freuden der Welt) zu einem Bilde sich ergänzend zusammen. Es besagt wenig, ob wir den Jüngling als den sündigen Menschen oder selbst als Dämon, als mythisches Symbol eines Lasters auffassen. Berechtigt dazu sind wir durch die Tatsache, dass in Autun der Verfolger ein Satyr oder ein Faun ist. Dieser hübsche Jüngling mit dem Schild in der Hand hat Tierfüsse, der eine Fuss ist ein Huf, der andere eine Vogelkralle. Am Gürtel aber wachsen mähnenartige Haarbüsche wie bei den Zentauren dort, wo Tier- und Menschenleib zusammenstossen. Seine und der Sirene jugendliche Schönheit bestärken

FIG. 32. TOULOUSE, MUSÉE DES AUGUSTINS, KAPITELL
UNBEKANNTER HERKUNFT

1. VIERTEL 12. JAHRHUNDERT

FIG. 33. AUTUN, KATHEDRALE, SÜDL.
SEITENSCHIFF, 11. PILASTER

1. VIERTEL 12. JAHRHUNDERT

FIG. 34. CUNAULT, ABTEIKIRCHE,
KAPITELL AM NORDTURM

1. VIERTEL 12. JAHRHUNDERT

[443]

nur die Deutung auf die Laster der Lockung und Begierde. Das Abschreckende aber liegt in ihrer zauberischen, dämonischen Gestalt.

Auch an einem anderen schönen Kapitell der Daurade tritt der Faun als Jäger auf ein Menschenwild auf (Fig. 36). Hörner, Bocksohren, Bockshufe und der Ziegenbart ähneln sein Bild ganz dem des antiken Fauns an. Ein Schurz umgürtet seine Lenden. Über der Schulter hält er eine Axt, ein Mordinstrument. Mit der Linken aber, deren Finger auf die Gruppe vor ihm weist, scheint er den krokodilhaften Drachen auf die jugendliche Gestalt gehetzt zu haben, die sich verzweifelt gegen den Biss des Ungetüms zu wehren sucht. Wäre es eine weibliche Gestalt, wogegen Haare und Gewand nicht sprechen, dann hätten wir auch in diesem Faun den Frauenjäger. Eine mythische Gestalt ist sie jedenfalls, denn sie hat einen Gänsefuss. Ist die Gestalt ein Jüngling, dann bleibt für den Faun nur die allgemeine Bedeutung des Unheilbringers, der sich der Tiere als totbringender Werkzeuge bedient. Wenn ein solcher Faun einmal auch in hilfreiche Beziehung zu einem Heiligen tritt, wie in St. Paul de Varax, wo der faunus ficarius, der feigenfressende Faun, den Hl. Paul zum Einsiedler Antonius führt, so besagt das nicht mehr, als wenn zuweilen die wilden Tiere in den Bann des Heiligen gezogen werden. Ihre böse Grundnatur wird damit nicht aufgehoben. In Clermont-Ferrand ist der Satyr der Gegenspieler der Tugend. Die Mischung von Menschengestalt und Tier schlägt dort, wo diese Tiermenschen dem Heiligen dienen, besonders stark nach der Seite des Menschlichen, d.h. des Vernünftigen, moralisch Verantwortungsvollen aus. Im Allgemeinen aber ist hier das Böse im moralischen Sinne gemeint, und das Tierische in diesen Wesen ist nur ein Beweis der Wildheit und der Unmenschlichkeit, d.h. des über die Natur hinaus gehenden Unbekannten und Geheimnisvollen, des Dämonischen. Der Faun oder Satyr wird so zum Bilde des Teufels. Der Teufel erscheint in faunischer Gestalt. Das Maul mit den Tierzähnen öffnet sich zu einem Schlund, Hörner wachsen auf dem Kopfe, Raubvogelkralle und Bockshuf stehen nebeneinander, ein Schwanz wächst aus dem Rücken heraus. So sehen wir den Teufel neben dem stürzenden Simon Magus, die Zunge hängt ihm wie einem gierigen Hunde zum Maule heraus. Zu dem furchterregenden Mittel der tierischen Gestalt tritt noch die abscheuerregende Verzerrung der Fratze, eine dämonische Hässlichkeit wie bei den Götzen primitiver Völker. Flügel wachsen ihm wie den Engeln an den Schultern, denn auch er ist über Raum und Zeit erhaben und die Unterwelt ist, wie die des Himmels, *jenseits* der Erde, dem Himmel benachbart. Mit dieser Identifikation von Satyr und Teufel hat sich die Gottwerdung des Tierischen und der Fabelwesen vollendet. Aus der weltbeherrschenden Rolle des Teufels müssen wir auch die kultische Macht aller dieser Tiere und Mischwesen verstehen. Hinter dem Schiffe des von der Sirene berückten Fischers in Cunault steht ein Dämon. Die Sirene ist also im Bunde mit dem Teufel, ist selbst eine Teufelin. Solche weiblichen Teufel gab es auch sonst, in Angoulême die über den Flammen sich rasend gebärdende Frau mit dem Eberzahn im Munde und der Faunsmähne am Gürtel, in Arles die Frau, die in der Hölle auf dem Drachen reitet. Es ist die dualistische Vorstellung von

FIG. 35. TOULOUSE, MUSÉE DES AUGUSTINS, KREUZGANGSKAPITELL
AUS KLOSTER DAURADE

2. VIERTEL 12. JAHRHUNDERT

FIG. 36. TOULOUSE, MUSÉE DES AUGUSTINS, KAPITELL VOM
KAPITELSAALPORTAL DES KLOSTERS DAURADE

2. VIERTEL 12. JAHRHUNDERT

guten Göttern, die hier ganz unmittelbar wieder mythenbildend lebendig wird, und wie diese Zeit von dem Guten ein Bild in menschlicher Gestalt verlangte, so auch von dem Bösen. Würde und Erhabenheit und menschliche Formschönheit dort, Hässlichkeit, tierische Wildheit und übernatürliche Misch- und Missexistenz hier, das sind die Formen der Verbildlichung. Diese Halbtiere sind die Gegenheiligen, der Teufel, der Gegengott, der Antichrist, aber deshalb nicht weniger im Zentrum des religiösen Bewusstseins dieser Zeit als die Verkörperungen des Guten. Beide haben ihr Reich und beide kämpfen miteinander um die Seelen, ihr Reich damit zu füllen, die einen, sie des Glückes teilhaftig werden zu lassen, neben einem Höchsten zu sitzen, die anderen, um Objekte der Peinigung zu haben und sich an den Qualen der Unterworfenen zu weiden. Von diesem Kampf bildet einen Teil der Kampf der Heiligen mit dem Teufel in den Versuchungen und der Kampf Christi selber mit dem Teufel. Oft genügt zur Abwehr die Standhaftigkeit des sittlichen Willens, ausgedrückt durch die körperliche Standhaftigkeit, die unerschütterliche Haltung, z.B. des Hl. Antonius in Vézelay, auf den die tierischen Teufel mit Fäusten und Äxten losgehen. In einem anderen Kapitell in Vézelay versuchen Teufel den Gerechten aus dem Tempel zu zerren, in den er sich geflüchtet, indem sie mit grotesker Wut ihn von allen Seiten zausen und sich an ihn hängen und garnicht merken, dass ihre Anstrengungen sich selber aufheben. Das Ganze scheint eine Vision des Hl. Antonius zu sein, der fürbittend daneben steht. Oft bannt den Teufel die Heilige Schrift, auf die Christus, wie an einem Kapitell in Moissac, hinweist, oder die aufgeschlagen der Hl. Benedikt den Dämonen entgegenhält. Den Kampf um die Seele eines Menschen, der sich selbst dem Teufel ausgeliefert hat, schildert die Geschichte des Mönches Theophilus, der den Platz seines Bischofs begehrte und sich deshalb dem Teufel verschrieb. In Souillac sehen wir den Teufel ganz als Faun, mit Mähnenschurz, mit Huf und Krallen, mit Schwänzchen und einem phantastischen Kopf, der halb Vogel, halb Hund wohl das Scheusslichste darstellt, was die Phantasie der Zeit ersonnen hat. Er nimmt die Urkunde des Paktes entgegen, nimmt die Hände des Mönches in die seinen und nimmt so Besitz von ihm. Aber die Jungfrau Maria hat dem Teufel den Pakt gestohlen und kommt, von Engeln geführt, aus den Wolken herab und überreicht Theophilus das Schriftstück. Der Teufel hat keine Macht mehr über ihn.

Mit dem Teufel kämpft der Hl. Michael und kämpfen die Erzengel. Auch sie kämpfen zuweilen um die Seelen. Auf Kapitellen in Vézelay werden sie von ihnen in Schutz genommen und zum Himmel emporgetragen. Ein Kampf um die Seele ist auch die Seelenwägung. Beide Parteien suchen mit Herabdrücken die Wagschale auf ihrer Seite zum Sinken zu bringen, dadurch dass sie von ihrer eigenen Sippschaft einen hineinsetzen. Alles was in der Heiligen Schrift einmal Bild und Wort gewesen, wird jetzt wieder leibhaftige Gestalt und greifbare Gegenwart.

In ihrem Reich aber bedienen sich die Teufel der höllischen Tiere als Werkzeuge zum Quälen der Verdammten. Schon die Hölle selbst ist der Schlund eines ungeheuren Tieres, der Teufelsrachen. Schlangen, Kröten, Molche,

Marburger photo.

Marburger photo.

FIG. 37. MELLE, ST. HILAIRE, NORDPORTAL

1. HÄLFTE 12. JAHRHUNDERT

FIG. 38. MOISSAC, ST. PIERRE,
SÜDVORHALLE

2. VIERTEL 12. JAHRHUNDERT

Marburger photo.

Marburger photo.

FIG. 39.   AULNAY,
ST. PIERRE, APSIDE

1. HÄLFTE 12. JAHRHUNDERT

FIG. 40. MOISSAC, ST. PIERRE, KAPITELL IM
SÜDL. KREUZGANGSTRAKT, UM 1100

möglichst ekelhafte Tiere werden auf die Unglücklichen losgelassen (Autun). Mit solchen Schlangen wird auch der Leib der Luxuria, der Wollust, einer nackten weiblichen Gestalt, ausgestattet, der die Bestien an die Brüste und in den Schoss fahren. Ursprünglich ein Symbol der Terra, die Frau mit den Drachen an den Brüsten, die sie nährt, wird diese Gestalt jetzt höllischer und dämonischer, eine mythische Gestalt des Lasters. In Melle ist das alte Bild der Terra noch ziemlich rein erhalten, aber sicherlich als Laster umgedeutet (Fig. 37), in Moissac steht der Teufel schon daneben und weidet sich an den Qualen des Opfers (Fig. 38). Zuweilen, wie schon hier, ist nicht mehr deutlich, ob nicht diese Luxuria ähnlich der Sirene selbst ein Dämon ist, die Tiere ihre Attribute, der Teufel eine Art von Buhle und Verführer wie die Faune hinter den Sirenen. Ein anderes Laster, der Geiz, die Avaritia, ein Mann mit grossem Geldbeutel um den Hals, steht an einem Kapitell in Aulnay mit jedem Fuss in einem teuflischen Tierschlund, von den Seiten sperren Teufel, die tierischer als sonst gebildet sind, das Maul gegen ihn auf, den Kopf zu verschlingen (Fig. 39). Tier und Teufel sind hier eins, Herrscher und Bewohner der Unterwelt. Im Sinne der Kirche wird die Natur, das Tierische, dem Reich des Bösen zugewiesen, aber ganz im unchristlichen Sinne wird eine neue, übersinnliche und doch für wahr gehaltene, körperlich vorgestellte Dämonenwelt kultischen Bedürfnissen entgegengebracht. Ein Kapitell in Moissac (Fig. 40) lehrt uns, wie sehr Tier, d.h. phantastisches, wildes, magisches Tier, und Teufel eins sind. Ein Engel, der im Kampf über den Teufel gesiegt hat — man erinnert sich der Stelle der Apokalypse — führt ihn an einer Kette, um ihn im Abgrund zu verschliessen. Letzteres stellt auch ein Kapitell in Vézelay dar. In Moissac ist es ein ungeheuerlicher Drache, den der Engel so an der Kette abführt. Daneben aber stehen die Worte: serpens anticus qui est diabolus — die alte Schlange, welche der Teufel ist. Die göttergleiche Natur, das Dämonische des Tieres, ist durch diese Zuweisung an den Gott der Finsternis bewiesen. So ist denn dies Reich der Unterwelt, d.h. des Jenseits, zu Füssen der oberen Götter im Tympanon zu Beaulieu ganz gefüllt mit dämonischen Tieren (Fig. 41). Und zwar sind die Bewohner der Hölle: ein löwen- oder wolfsartiger Vierfüsser, vor ihm ein Greif mit Adlerkopf, zwischen ihnen ein Verdammter, grässlich zwischen den Beinen vom Löwenmaul gepackt, am Hals vom Greifenschwanz gewürgt, ihnen entgegengeführt vierfüssige Flügeldämonen mit Schlangenköpfen an den Schweifen. In der unteren Zone ein Bär, dann ein apokalyptisches Tier mit sieben Köpfen, davon zwei am Schwanze, und schliesslich das Ungeheuerlichste, ein Riesendrache mit menschlichem Kopf, am Schwanzende mit Drachenkopf, dessen gespaltene Zunge wie ein Pfeil hervorstösst, im Leibe zwei Öffnungen, aus denen zwei junge Teufel mit Hundsköpfen, menschlichen Armen und mit Schlangen als Waffen heraussteigen. Durch das Bild und die Beschreibung der Viper angeregt, ist hier etwas ganz Neues geschaffen: die ungeheuerlichste Häufung des Tierischen und die riesige, stärkste Furcht erregende Gestalt eines Drachen, die übernatürlichste mysteriöseste Mischung des Verschiedenartigen und die Krönung des Ganzen mit einem fast philosophenhaft vernünftigen bärtigen Männerkopf, der alle tierischen Kräfte in seinem Leibe

FIG. 41. BEAULIEU, ABTEIKIRCHE, SÜDLICHES LANGHAUSPORTAL
2. Viertel 12. Jahrhundert

Marburger photo.

FIG. 42. NEUILLY–EN–DONJON, KIRCHE, TYMPANON DES WESTPORTALS

[449]

herrscherlich verwaltet. In Anzy-le-Duc ritt noch ein Teufel, der die mit einer Kette gefesselten Verdammten hinter sich herzog, auf einem Riesendrachen auf den Höllenschlund in der Mitte des Türsturzes zu. Hier ist der Drache der Teufel selbst — serpens anticus.

Wieviel stärker aber das Bewusstsein des Volkes und der Künstler vom Dämonischen und Tiermythos erfüllt war als von den Bildern der Heiligen und der Menschwerdung Gottes, beweist das Tympanon von Neuilly-en-Donjon (Fig. 42). Hier baut sich das friedliche Bild der von den heiligen drei Königen verehrten Madonna mit Kind auf einem Sockel von zwei riesigen Höllendrachen auf, die mit der Wucht ihrer Leiber und ihrer zentralen Anordnung einen Entsetzen erregenden Anblick bieten und die liebliche Gruppe oben weit übertönen. Wie auf einer Brücke schreiten die Könige auf den Flügeln des einen Dämons zur Madonna hinüber. Statt der sanften Stimmen der Erlösung dröhnen die Posaunen des Jüngsten Gerichtes.

Aus dieser Nachbarschaft von Himmel und Hölle, Christ und Antichrist, Gott und Teufel bekommt die Abfolge von Tierarchivolten und solchen mit apokalyptischen Königen und Märtyrern in Aulnay, die Rahmung der Aposteltympana in Angoulême mit Tierarchivolten und ihre Fortsetzung nach unten in Jagdszenen einen neuen tieferen Sinn als nur den einer abwechslungsreichen Dekoration, und man versteht, warum in Dax neben einem Chorfenster dem Heiligen Grab auf der einen Seite, ein Feld mit Greifen auf der anderen entspricht. Es ist die Gegenüberstellung von Heiligem und Dämonischem, nicht die von Bild und Ornament. Sie stehen sich gleich in der Stärke ihrer Wirkung aufs Bewusstsein der Gläubigen; was hier Furcht erzeugt, erweckt dort Hoffnung. Nichts aber spricht wohl mehr dafür, und nichts beweist wohl wiederum mehr die Macht des Tieres in dieser Zeit, als dass die Stelle an den Kirchenportalen, die sonst dem Bilde Christi oder Maria oder einem Heiligen vorbehalten blieb, auch ganz allein von einem Tier, d.h. dem Dämon, gefüllt werden konnte, dem herrisch-siegreichen Greifen in Angoulême (Fig. 43), den in Ranken verwobenen Flügeldrachen an St. Etienne in Beauvais (Fig. 44), zwischen denen in der Ranke eine Königsbüste emporsteigt, und vor allem im Museum in Beauvais die Drachen, die in einen einzigen Kopf zusammengewachsen sind (Fig. 45), aber wiederum nicht zum spielerischen Ornament, sondern zum vielleibigen Dämon, wie der dreileibige Typhon der Antike. Der brüllende Kopf im Scheitel des Bogens verdichtet die tierische Masse, macht sie drohender, nicht dekorativer. Am Anfang des Raumes der Kirche, vor dem Eintritt, steht so das Bild des Teufels und des Tieres und verherrlicht dessen Gewalt. Die Kirche mochte wissen, dass auf die Gemüter solche Bilder stärker wirkten als die der Heiligen. Sie konnte gerade mit der Furcht vor diesen Dämonen die erlösenden Mächte preisen und die Sehnsucht nach der Zufluchtsstätte, der Kirche, dem Altar, stärken. Mit der geistigen Deutung auf das Moralisch-Böse konnte sie versuchen, den Glauben an die Wirklichkeit dieser im Bilde verkörperten Gestalten abzuschwächen und den religiösen Sinn von der Verehrung dieser Mächte, vom Tierkult, abzulenken. Nicht aber verhindern konnte sie, dass die Kunst diesen Gestalten opferte. Denn

Marburger photo.

FIG. 43. ANGOULÊME, MUSÉE ARCHÉOLOGIQUE, TYMPANON

1. HÄLFTE 12. JAHRHUNDERT

FIG. 44. BEAUVAIS, ST. ÉTIENNE, NORDPORTAL, TYMPANON UND ARCHIVOLTE

[451]

formenreicher, erfindungsvoller, plastisch bedeutsamer und dämonisch pak-
kender als diese Tierdämonen ist nichts in der romanischen Plastik dargestellt.
Diese Macht des Tieres über die Gemüter der Zeitgenossen und das Unchristliche
im Kult dieser Tiere hat der Hl. Bernhard von Clairvaux gefühlt, als er eine
neue Zeit, die Gotik, mit den Worten einleitete: " . . . was soll denn diese lächer-
liche Ungeheuerlichkeit, dieser garstige Prunk und diese prunkende Garstigkeit?
Diese unreinen Affen? Diese wilden Löwen? Diese monströsen Zentauren?
Diese Halbmenschen? Diese Tiger? Diese kämpfenden Männer? Der ins Horn
stossende Jäger? Du siehst unter einem Kopfe mehrere Körper und umgekehrt
auf einem Körper mehrere Köpfe; du siehst einen Vierfüssler in eine Schlange
auslaufen und einen Fisch mit dem Haupte eines Säugetieres; hier eine Bestie,
die vorn ein Ross und hinten eine Ziege ist, dort eine, die vorn Hörner und
hinten Pferdefüsse hat. So Vielerlei und Wunderbares bietet sich dar, dass es
vergnüglicher scheint, in dem Marmorbildwerk als im Buche zu lesen und
lieber den ganzen Tag hierüber, als über das Gesetz des Herrn zu grübeln. Bei
Gott! Habt Ihr vor diesen Albernheiten keine Scham, so habt wenigstens
Scheu vor den Kosten."

FIG. 45. BEAUVAIS, MUSEUM, TYMPANON AUS ST. GILLES

QUELQUES SURVIVANCES DE LA SCULPTURE ROMANE DANS L'ART FRANÇAIS

HENRI FOCILLON

LES STYLES ne naissent ni ne meurent d'un seul coup. Ils sont préparés par des expériences multiples, ils trouvent à un certain moment leur point de maturité et ce que l'on peut appeler une définition organique, enfin ils se défont, donnant lieu à des phénomènes en sens divers, dessèchement ou luxuriance déréglée. Cette courbe est bien sensible dans l'histoire de l'art du moyen-âge. Nous avons essayé d'en tracer le parcours pour l'art gothique et surtout pour l'art roman. Ce dernier commence par les recherches qui se développent au cours du XIᵉ siècle, où nous voyons surtout en France, mais aussi dans les pays méditerranéens et même en Grande Bretagne et en Irlande, se poursuivre dans des ateliers très divers des tentatives qui ont pour but d'accorder la sculpture monumentale à l'architecture, d'en définir l'emplacement dans la construction, de trouver une règle qui établisse l'harmonie de la forme sculptée et de la forme bâtie selon le cadre qu'offre cet emplacement même, de manière à constituer un tout homogène. Par là, dès qu'on peut la surprendre et la définir comme telle, la sculpture romane, quels que soient ses emprunts à la tradition carolingienne, s'en distingue de la manière la plus nette et crée en Occident un art nouveau. La fin du XIᵉ siècle apparait non comme la période à laquelle *commence* l'art roman, notion inexacte qui a peut-être pesé sur bien des controverses et qui les a déviées, mais comme un sommet, ou plutôt, si l'on veut bien adopter cette comparaison, comme le début d'un palier, inaugurant une seconde période. Il ne faut pas plus de cinquante années à cet art pour donner tout son fruit. La seconde moitié du XIIᵉ siècle le voit évoluer avec rapidité vers des données nouvelles, ce que nous avons appelé sa forme académique ou sa forme baroque, l'une caractérisée par l'application systématique de règles stylistiques qui, au cours de la période précédente, conservaient une sorte d'ardeur vivante et la possibilité presque indéfinie de s'enrichir de variations, l'autre par un désaccord fondamental entre ces variations et ces règles, par une profusion désordonnée ou plutôt par l'oubli des principes sur lesquels reposaient les convenances secrètes, les accords calculés avec soin qui donnent tant d'unité à l'art roman "classique." Ainsi, tout en faisant leur place légitime aux mutations, à la brusquerie créatrice des inventeurs, on ne saurait dire qu'il a éclaté soudain avec une vigueur explosive, et l'on ne peut pas dire non plus qu'il a disparu tout entier, d'un coup, pour faire place à l'art gothique.

C'est un bel objet d'étude que l'histoire de l'art roman après ce que nous appelons la période proprement romane. Le midi de la France et la Catalogne fourmillent d'exemples très nombreux des divers phénomènes auxquels nous venons de faire allusion, spécialement de cette production en série, de caractère industriel, qui se manifeste surtout, comme c'est le cas pour une série de chapiteaux du cloître de Sant Cugat del Vallès,[1] près de Barcelone, par la minceur et par la sécheresse, minceur des tiges ornementales, sécheresse des plans de feuillages, vivement découpés d'une arête tranchante. Il n'est pas moins curieux de voir s'infiltrer à l'intérieur des vieux cadres, dont le sens n'est plus très bien compris, les éléments d'une iconographie pittoresque toute gothique. De même que l'architecture des régions essentiellement "romanes" couvre de croisées d'ogive des masses qui ont encore la plénitude et la nudité de l'époque précédente et crée en quelque sorte une tonalité gothique tout étrangère aux pays du Nord, de même la sculpture monumentale concilie comme elle peut des données essentiellement contradictoires, tant l'imprégnation des formules traditionnelles reste puissante en présence d'une mode étrangère. Ce n'est là qu'une vue toute générale et superficielle sur un chapitre de l'histoire de l'art roman que développera sans nul doute M. Puig i Cadafalch dans son étude sur la sculpture romane en Catalogne, mais ses précédents travaux et ceux d'autres archéologues nous laissent apercevoir déjà tout l'intérêt de cette recherche.

Ce sont là les grandes lignes du développement historique d'un style. Mais il n'est pas moins curieux, et il est sans doute plus surprenant de voir surgir en pleine époque gothique et en terre gothique, c'est-à-dire dans les régions septentrionales de la France, des formes qui sont essentiellement romanes. Nous avons appelé l'attention à cet égard sur les gargouilles de nos églises. S'il est vrai, comme nous le pensons, que l'art roman repose avant tout sur un principe de métamorphose et que, pliant la forme vivante, non seulement à de vagues symétries décoratives, mais aux nécessités absolues de la structure architecturale et des fonctions de ses membres, il est amené à créer des monstres, où l'homme, la bête et la plante interviennent également dans le réseau de la composition, les gargouilles du XIIIe siècle et des époques suivantes appartiennent, pour la plupart, à l'ordre de ses créations. Leur fonction est bien définie: rejeter à distance des murs goutterots l'eau qui ruisselle des combles. Si l'artiste leur prête une forme vivante, il est nécessaire qu'il l'adapte rigoureusement à cette fonction même. Sans doute il est des cas où il n'a pas hésité à brandir horizontalement des figures identifiables, des êtres humains [2] ou des animaux dont il prit le modèle dans la nature: le plus souvent il inventa les monstres de ses gargouilles, combinant entre eux des éléments empruntés à la vie ou à la fiction, procédant comme le fit plus tard Léonard de Vinci, lorsqu'il composa par jeu son monstre imaginaire et vrai, sans autre but que d'ajouter une étrangeté de plus au répertoire des formes animées. Mais l'imagier gothique était conduit, comme le sculpteur roman, par une règle plus sévère, et, donnant à une fonction l'élégance d'une invention plastique, il adaptait et soudait les parties, non au gré de son

---

[1] Cf. J. Baltrusaitis, *Les Chapiteaux de Sant Cugat del Vallès* (Paris, 1931).

[2] Par exemple à l'abside de Saint-Urbain de Troyes, la figure humaine répandant l'eau d'un vase, véritable "statue" exécutée comme pour être posée verticalement sur un socle, puis fixée horizontalement au contre-fort pour remplir sa fonction de gargouille. Cf. Viollet le Duc *Dictionnaire d'architecture*, tome VI, p. 36, fig. 8. C'est vers la fin du XIIIe siècle que la figure humaine tend à remplacer les animaux. Cf. Viollet le Duc, *loc. cit.*, p. 25, fig. 7, gargouille d'une des chapelles du chœur de la cathédrale de Clermont.

caprice, mais pour répondre à un besoin déterminé. Il est vrai, comme Viollet le Duc l'a fait remarquer avec justesse, que le jet qui les unit est si nerveux, que les membres sont si bien liés les uns aux autres par des articulations et par des rapports apparemment si justes que ces êtres de fantaisie semblent appartenir à des espèces naturelles: ils paraissent, en tout cas, aptes à la vie physique, ce qui n'est pas vrai pour les monstres du XIIe siècle, enfantés non seulement par la règle d'une exacte conformité architecturale, mais, comme M. Baltrusaitis [3] l'a montré, par une dialectique ornementale. Ils n'en restent pas moins des monstres, définis par l'architecture. Ainsi, tandis que l'humanisme chrétien multipliait des représentations de l'homme et de la nature conformes aux données physiologiques, peut-être une pensée romane, réfugiée dans les parties hautes, continuait-elle à s'exercer là où elle répondait le mieux aux besoins. Elle avait, si l'on peut dire, un double support, le fonds inépuisable de l'imagination populaire et la fantaisie créatrice des maîtres. C'est ce que M. Mâle met admirablement en lumière: "Ces gargouilles qui resemblent aux vampires des cimetières, aux dragons vaincus par les vieux évêques, ont vécu dans les profondeurs de l'âme du peuple; elles sont sorties d'anciens contes d'hiver. Souvenirs d'ancêtres lointains, dernières images d'un monde disparu: le génie sombre et puissant du moyen-âge éclate ici." [4]

Cette tératologie présente d'ailleurs des aspects très divers. Elle ne se limite pas aux gargouilles. Si les gargouilles peuvent être interprétées, ainsi que nous venons de le faire, comme une nouvelle expérience, fraîche et vivante, sur l'adaptation des formes plastiques aux fonctions de l'architecture, il n'en est peut-être pas constamment de même pour d'autres catégories de monstres qui apparaissent plutôt comme des déchets durcis du passé roman, inaptes à une vie nouvelle. Ainsi se présentent à nous les reliefs qui décorent, à la cathédrale de Sens, les soubassements du portail central de la façade occidentale. Tandis que l'art des cathédrales nous montre, à Lyon par exemple, des bêtes authentiques étudiées avec un amical respect de la nature, le corbeau, le lapin, l'écureuil, l'escargot, sculptés "pour le plaisir de reproduire la nature vivante," l'artiste de Sens développe une zoologie et une géographie légendaires, conformes aux vieux textes où a puisé toute cette iconographie, de Pline à Solin, d'Honorius d'Autun et de Vincent de Beauvais aux *Loisirs Impériaux* de Gervais de Tilbury. Les étrangetés vraies y voisinent avec les étrangetés de la fiction. Au dessus d'un rang de rosaces géométriques, les reliefs de Sens (Fig. 1) sont disposés en deux étages qui obéissent aux retraits successifs de l'architecture du portail. Les reliefs de l'étage inférieur sont encadrés d'une épaisse bordure moulurée. Ceux qui les surmontent sont placés entre deux colonnes dont les chapiteaux portent un entablement. Là prennent place des figures symboliques assises, les Arts Libéraux, les Travaux des Mois, d'un relief généreux, et dont certaines, par la plastique et la couleur, ne sont pas sans évoquer certaines stèles romaines de la Gaule septentrionale. Dans le registre du dessous, à côté de l'éléphant, de

---

[3] *La Stylistique ornementale de la sculpture romane* (Paris, 1931).
[4] Emile Mâle, *L'Art religieux du XIIIe siècle en France* (cinquième édition, Paris, 1923), pp. 58 et suiv.

l'autruche et du chameau, voici le griffon, le sciapode (Fig. 2) et l'antique sirène.
Le monstre à jambe unique, brandie tout droit et retenue d'une main, tandisque
de l'autre il s'appuie contre le sol, s'ombrage sous son pied énorme. Nous n'avons
pas là seulement une iconographie romane, mais un "chiffre" roman, et tel
qu'il pourrait figurer, par exemple, sur un relief de Saint-Restitut. La rectitude
avec laquelle la jambe, puis le pied, à angle droit, suivent la direction de la
bordure d'encadrement illustre une des règles principales de la stylistique ro-

Photo. Archives photographiques

FIG. 1.   SENS, CATHÉDRALE, PORTAIL CENTRAL

mane. Certes nous ne trouvons pas toujours un conformisme aussi rigoureux
dans le reste de la série, mais il nous suffit que cette image, fixée une fois pour
toutes, ait survécu au naufrage de tout un art. Elle est là comme un débris et
comme un témoin, sans doute sauvée dans sa forme par la constance du contenu
iconographique.[5] Elle est incapable de se renouveler, comme jadis tous les
Protées de l'art roman, par le repli sans cesse noué et dénoué de ses membres.
Le temps de sa puissante vie inventive est passé. Elle apparait comme une de
ces figures que le sceau a frappées dans une matière molle, que les ans ont
durcie, et qui ne connaitront plus jamais les métamorphoses.

A Rouen, un siècle plus tard environ, le portail des Libraires et le portail de
la Calende nous mènent, sur des thèmes analogues, à d'autres pensées. Des
monstres encore y prennent place, non plus dans des cadres rectangulaires, mais

[5] Peut-être est-ce à un phénomène du même ordre que sont dues les figures symboliques des évangélistes (du moins les trois figures animales) sur le maître-autel de l'église d'Avioth dans la Meuse (début du
XIVe siècle).

dans des quatrefeuilles, monstres généralement exempts de symbolique chrétienne, tout de caprice, et, comme M.Mâle l'a montré, monstres gais. La vieille
inspiration romane qui fait jaillir de l'architecture et de l'ornement des combinaisons inédites et terribles, un monde de vision et de songe, a disparu pour
faire place à une veine de fabliau. Comme autrefois, les êtres sont composés de
parties hétérogènes, mais le secret qui présidait à leur agencement et qui l'im-
posait est perdu. Comme autrefois les corps se tordent, se contournent et se ren-

Photo. Archives photographiques

FIG. 2. SENS, CATHÉDRALE, LE SCIAPODE, DETAIL DE LA FIG. 1

versent, un principe d'éternelle mobilité semble animer les figures, mais si elles
se meuvent avec tant d'ardeur, c'est en vertu d'une impulsion qui leur est propre
et qui ne doit rien à une règle cachée. Sans doute la composition est heureuse-
ment adaptée au contour du quatrefeuille, elle le meuble bien, mais cet accord n'a
rien de systématique, il résulte d'un goût et d'une convenance harmonique, non
d'une règle. Ainsi se présentent à nous ces singuliers hybrides, le médecin urologiste, dont le corps finit en volatile, le centaure à capuchon qui a deux pieds de
cheval et deux pieds d'homme, la femme oiseau, l'homme chien et ce musicien,
coq par le bas, qui enseigne son art à un centaure. Ces éléments disparates s'ajust-
ent entre eux avec drôlerie, mais sans nécessité, et, tandisqu'une nécessité absolue
engendre l'absurde dans les monstres romans, c'est le pur caprice qui régit ces

monstres gothiques. Même dans ces créations extravagantes, l'étude de la nature
se fait jour, avec ce vif sentiment anecdotique et cette ingéniosité de détail qui
caractérisent la sculpture monumentale dès la fin du XIIIᵉ siècle et le début du
XIVᵉ, — la fiole de l'urologiste, les petites bottes du centaure, le capuchon dont il
est coiffé. On croit retrouver dans les reliefs du portail des Libraires des figurines
acrobatiques analogues à celles que nous avons maintes fois relevées dans la
sculpture romane, et dont on a de bons exemples dans le baladin de l'archivolte
de Vézelay, qui, faisant la roue, dessine avec son corps le contour même du
médaillon où il est exactement inscrit, ou encore dans ces Salomés poitevines et
saintongeaises qui, la tête renversée en arrière, laissent tomber leur chevelure
le long de l'arête de leur claveau. Mais les corps précipités tombent en vertu de
leur poids, et c'est l'effroi qui leur fait écarter les bras ou les jambes, non le
souci d'un chiffre bien adapté à l'architecture. Quelque différentes qu'elles
soient des monstres romans, les gargouilles en sont incontestablement plus près
que les grotesques de Rouen.

Encore ces derniers appartiennent-ils toujours à l'architecture, dans la
mesure où ils contribuent à la décorer avec harmonie, où ils sont incorporés à
la pierre et solidement isolés les uns des autres par le cadre des quatrefeuilles.
Mais il existe aussi toute une faune de monstres en liberté, dans les manuscrits à
vignettes marginales. Là encore nous sentons bien que le moyen-âge, même péné-
tré par son humanisme évangélique, même adouci au climat et aux proportions
d'une pensée tout humaine et naturelle, n'a jamais complètement renoncé à
l'obsession des métamorphoses. On dirait que l'homme est toujours aux prises
avec la bête, avec la plante, qu'il a peine à se libérer de ces étonnants adultères
de la forme, qu'il s'y complaît. Le musicien, monté sur une hampe horizontale
comme sur un perchoir, joue de son instrument et file son coup d'archet la tête
penchée: rien de plus juste comme mouvement. Il a des pattes de coq, une
queue emplumée prolongée par une sorte de rinceau qui fait boucle autour du
perchoir. Un ange guerrier tenant à deux mains une large épée jaillit du corps
d'un gros oiseau juché à l'extrémité d'une initiale. Des êtres indéfinissables faits
d'une feuille ornementale et d'un bec entr'ouvert font face à des humains bien
reconnaissables.[6] A propos de ces figurines monstrueuses ou grotesques, qui pul-
lulent dans les marges de certains psautiers et de certains bréviaires du XIIIᵉ
siècle, M. Mâle évoque l'imagination de Callot, et il a bien raison, car il y a,
chez le graveur lorrain (outre le trait de plume du calligraphe), une sorte de
survivance provinciale de cette vieille verve, à la fois terrible et comique. On
croit voir aussi s'agiter et s'essayer les commencements du monde étrange auquel
Jérôme Bosch, plus près du moyen-âge, conféra une vie surprenante, en y
ajoutant le délire de l'inanimé. Ne devons-nous pas surtout penser aux antécé-
dents de cette ménagerie qui nous paraît d'abord si bouffonne, et qui plonge,
par ses origines, dans un passé plus grave et plus mystérieux? L'alphabet zoo-
morphique des manuscrits mérovingiens, les oiseaux et les poissons encore entre-
coupés par les barrettes de métal cloisonnant les émaux qui leur servirent sans

---

[6] B. N. Ms. lat. 14284, cité par Mâle, *loc. cit.*, p. 59 et suiv.

doute de modèles, les lettrines ou les initiales, formées ou décorées de figures animales, des enlumineurs arméniens, les inextricables caprices des Irlandais et leurs entrelacs animaux peuvent être considérés comme les ancêtres lointains de ces figurines. Mais il se passe dans ce domaine un phénomène analogue à celui que nous avons constaté dans la sculpture monumentale et qui explique l'écart entre les monstres romans et les grotesque du portail des Libraires. Les alphabets zoomorphiques imposent la forme et le cadre de la lettre à l'image de la bête qui parait désormais née d'elle et pour elle; l'animal, oiseau ou poisson, est tout prêt à se plier aux exigences de la fonction calligraphique, il peut se dédoubler, se multiplier, devenir monstre, et toujours il est lettre, et toujours cette armature maintient et justifie ses caprices. Une logique profonde, mais qui dissimule son jeu avec soin et qui ne laisse jamais apercevoir son commencement ni sa fin, se cache dans les replis de l'entrelacs irlandais: dès que l'on en a saisi le fil, tout le système apparait dans sa cohérence et sa lisibilité. Ces initiales gigantesques où semblent fourmiller des mondes détruits ou les débris confondus d'une genèse chaotique, ces bandeaux où des rubans indéfiniment repliés laissent apercevoir des membres entrecroisés, des têtes, des cols passant les uns au dessus des autres dans un furieux élan immobile, toute cette invention de rêveurs, si attirante et si déconcertante pour la vue, est en réalité définie par quelques principes simples et rigoureux auxquels toujours elle reste fidèle. Mais les grotesques de nos illustrations marginales, survivants étriqués de ces expériences considérables, sont bien les exilés d'un monde disparu, ils ne tiennent à rien qu'aux fantaisies monotones de la liberté graphique.

Ce sont sans doute des différences analogues qui séparent les vieilles compositions ornementales de l'Asie antérieure, fertile répertoire de monstres, et les agréables inventions décoratives de l'art romain, stucs et peintures, leur descendance très transformée. L'art romain, puis l'art de la Renaissance, qui s'en inspire à cet égard, fabriquent leurs monstres selon d'autres lois. Dominés par un élégant naturalisme anthropocentrique, ils juxtaposent des élements hétérogènes, mais ils respectent la nature de chacun d'eux, sans les fondre dans une unité vivante. Une tête de femme, brillante de jeunesse, celle du dieu barbu qui mâche des feuillages, ces feuillages mêmes, le flexible rinceau qui les accompagne, les lampes suspendues par des chaînettes, les pattes nerveuses de la chimère, toutes les parties de cette faune et de cette flore bizarres dessinées avec une spirituelle sècheresse sur des fonds calmes et unis, ne s'accordent entre elles qu'en vertu d'une convenance optique et d'une harmonie de goût. Elles tendent à se libérer, ou plutôt, valant chacune par elle-même, elles sont indépendantes les unes des autres. Mais il n'y a pas lieu d'insister sur des phénomènes morphologiques qui n'intéressent pas directement notre recherche: nous les évoquons à titre de comparaison. Ce qui est sûr, c'est que la puissante vie des combinaisons préromanes et romanes, vie toute de raisonnement et de déduction, mais singulièrement féconde et violente dans ses effets, n'anime plus les figures les plus "romanes" de l'art gothique, exception faite pour les gargouilles, conditionnées par leur fonction.

Il y aurait intérêt à chercher comment se comporte l'art de la fin du moyen-
âge à l'égard de ce que nous appellerions volontiers la science perdue. Il n'est
pas dit que l'oubli le recouvre forcément de plus en plus avec les années, rendu
plus complet par les progrès de ce mouvement si complexe auquel on donne bien
improprement le nom de réalisme. L'étonnante luxuriance du décor ornemental, la multiplicité de ses flexions et de ses replis, toute la richesse des variations
animales et végétales sur le thème de la contre-courbe semblent nous y inviter
d'abord. L'art flamboyant contient plus d'un monstre dans son réseau. Selon
l'invariable loi de succession des styles, il fait succéder le délire du baroque à la
pureté de l'art rayonnant, et ce délire même donne libre cours à l'invention
fantastique, si bien qu'on est naturellement porté à penser à un réveil de l'imagination romane. Sous cette forme et dans ce sens, il en est bien ainsi: l'imagination comme faculté inventive des images aboutit ici et là à des figures qui ne sont
pas sans analogie entre elles. Il est même possible d'admettre, comme nous le
verrons plus loin, que, dans certains cas, le raisonnement formel est du même
ordre, la contrecourbe étant de même nature que le rinceau générateur du motif
en as de cœur, sur lequel ont été "montées" tant de compositions romanes. Sans
doute chaque époque dominée par l'ornement est-elle susceptible de présenter
des phénomènes identiques. Mais il ne faut pas oublier que la règle de l'art
ornemental roman est d'abord essentiellement architecturale, qu'elle a pour
principe l'accord avec les fonctions, et que la fin du moyen-âge voit au contraire
desserrer de plus en plus et finalement détruire les relations nécessaires entre
architecture et décoration. Les édifices deviennent en quelque sorte doubles.
Ils sont revêtus d'une chape extérieure, abondante en accessoires et en hors
d'œuvre. La vision du peintre a remplacé la logique du constructeur. Ces
réserves admises, nous pouvons analyser un ou deux faits curieux.

La façade de Saint Vulfran d'Abbeville est un des ensembles les plus caractéristiques de l'art flamboyant, qui, comme on le sait, en offre d'autres intéressants
exemples dans les églises tardives du Ponthieu. Elevée de 1488 à 1536, cette
façade montre côte à côte, au soir de l'époque gothique et en pleine Renaissance
(car, dans ces régions, nos divisions chronologiques sont encore plus flottantes
qu'ailleurs), des traces non équivoques de la résistance de notre vieux style
monumental, sans doute favorisée par ce que l'on est convenu d'appeler la "détente" de l'art français à la fin du XVe siècle, et, d'autre part, d'incontestables
apports italianisants.[7] Le parti est traditionnel: trois portails; dans les ébrase-
ments de chacun d'eux, ainsi que sur les contreforts qui les séparent, des statues
ou des groupes en ronde-bosse; des statuettes ou de petits groupes placés sous
des dais décorent également les cordons d'archivoltes. Au dessus de chaque
porte, un remplage flamboyant de soufflets et de mouchettes. Au trumeau du
portail central figurait, avant 1789, un Christ attendant son supplice, sous un
dais richement ouvragé qui occupe encore presque toute la hauteur du remplage.
Au portail de droite est toujours en place une Vierge de l'Assomption, soutenue

---

[7] La discrimination entre ces éléments a fait l'objet d'un excellent mémoire de M. Zanettacci, paru
dans le *Bulletin monumental*, 1937.

par deux anges musiciens, décorant le remplage même. C'est de la même manière que se trouve disposée, au portail de gauche (Fig. 3), la statue de saint Eustache entre le lion et le loup qui entrainent les deux enfants, — scène qui se retrouve, entre autres exemples, à la Trésorerie de Saint-Riquier.

Remarquons-le d'abord, cette composition est à demi tympan, à demi remplage. La partie supérieure, coupée verticalement par la figure du saint et par le dais sous lequel elle est placée, est constituée par la claire-voie, que par-

Photo. Archives photographiques

FIG. 3. ABBEVILLE, SAINT-VULFRAN, PORTAIL SAINT-EUSTACHE

courent les nerfs élégants du remplage. La partie inférieure est entièrement occupée par la sculpture, la représentation du fleuve au milieu duquel se passe la scène, le lion et le loup ravisseurs des deux enfants. Le saint est légèrement en hors œuvre, et ses pieds reposent sur une console au milieu du linteau. Mais ces deux parties ne restent pas étrangères l'une à l'autre. La composition sculptée n'est pas plaquée d'une manière indifférente contre la composition ornementale du remplage. Les mouchettes sont combinées de manière à former une sorte de double médaillon ovale, où se trouvent inscrits le buste et la tête du saint et qui les prolonge de part et d'autre, comme si la figure était pourvue de deux ailes, — ailes de verre nervées de pierre. Il se passe quelque chose d'analogue au tympan de droite, où la Vierge de l'Assomption, qui ne se développe pas d'ailleurs comme une composition et qui reste essentiellement une statue, est disposée avec harmonie dans un triangle curviligne, au milieu des vastes lobes de la rose flamboyante formée par les mouchettes qui s'épanouissent autour d'elle. Nous sommes bien éloignés de voir dans ces agencements habiles un souvenir, même lointain, des procédés du XIe et du XIIe siècles. Il convient de noter qu'il y a là un intéressant accord du décor architectonique et du décor figuré, qui diffère moins, en son principe, de la composition romane des tympans que le système des registres superposés, pratiqué au XIIIe et au XIVe siècles.

Mais il y a plus. Saint Eustache debout entre le lion et le loup qui "passent" à droite et à gauche, reproduit un très ancien schéma roman, qui, né du motif en as de cœur, a donné les innombrables variations thématiques de la sirène-poisson. On dira que c'est là une pure rencontre, et c'est fort possible, encore que les remarques suggérées plus haut par le rapport du remplage et des figures nous amènent à considérer que le bonheur de cette composition ne saurait être dû tout entier au seul hasard. D'autre part le style et l'exécution des parties, prises en elles-mêmes, sont bien de leur temps. Le saint Eustache a l'élégance et le nerf d'une jolie figurine de bois, et son hanchement léger semble préluder à quelque mouvement de danse. Les animaux n'ont apparemment rien des monstres du passé, ils sont traités avec un évident souci de la vérité du détail, et le riche déploiement des ombres du fond, sur lequel ressortent en clair les volumes, a surtout une valeur picturale. L'enfant ravi par le lion est un agréable nu de la Renaissance. Il n'en reste pas moins que le chiffre de la composition est un chiffre roman, très bien adapté au cadre de l'architecture. La silhouette du lion, la tête retournée en arrière, la queue passant entre les pattes de derrière pour former sur la cuisse une sorte de boucle et terminée par une touffe ornementale, évoque le souvenir du félin asiatique qui poursuit, sur tant de vieux chapiteaux, sa course éternelle.

Pour expliquer la rigueur de cette symétrie et la singularité de l'analogie avec l'art roman, il est loisible d'alléguer une nécessité iconographique. Les deux animaux, les deux enfants emportés par eux ne devaient-ils pas être naturellement répartis de chaque côté du saint, figure principale? Et l'artiste n'était-il pas amené par cette répartition même à l'exactitude de la correspondance entre les éléments de la composition? Mais cette dernière pouvait aussi bien être tout autre, à une époque où était si forte la vogue du détail pittoresque et de l'inspiration anecdotique, et nous ne nous expliquons pas aisément que les bêtes adossées de Bourg-Argental, de Luz, de Maguelonne, de Neuilly en Donjon et même de Moissac, pour citer quelques tympans fameux de l'époque romane, se retrouvent à l'extrême fin du moyen âge, à la porte Saint-Eustache de Saint-Vulfran d'Abbeville, loin du terroir roman et de toute source directe d'inspiration.[8]

Ce n'est pas seulement l'art monumental qui, à la fin du moyen-âge, pré-

[8] Dans une étude complète de ces survivances, il y aurait lieu de ne pas négliger la petite sculpture. Telle "Miséricorde" de Saint-Martin-aux-Bois (Oise) est équilibrée comme un chapiteau roman historié; les stalles des Ponts-de-Cé (Maine et Loire) montrent des figures courtes sous arcade (Jonas, la Sibylle Hellespontique) qui évoquent, par la composition et par les proportions l'art des frises, des linteaux et des antependia romans, etc.

sente de remarquables analogies avec des formes très anciennes de la sculpture en pierre et les grandes compositions qui décoraient les portails des églises. Nous avons eu déjà l'occasion de faire remarquer qu'un certain nombre de compositions peintes au XVᵉ siècle par des artistes du Nord, étaient ordonnées comme des tympans.[9] Leur cadre est rectangulaire, mais les personnages sont répartis et groupés selon des principes analogues à ceux qu'oublièrent les maîtres gothiques et qui étaient familiers à leurs prédécesseurs. Avec ces artistes, que l'on pourrait appeler provisoirement, sous réserve d'une certaine impropriété, "les peintres de tympans," nous sommes très loin de la miniature, nous nous retrouvons en face d'un ordre, d'une subordination et d'un enchainement. On peut penser que les grandes tapisseries décoratives et les toiles peintes ne sont pas étrangères à la renaissance d'un style monumental en peinture, par exemple dans l'art de Rogier Van der Weyden. Peintres et hautlissiers travaillaient ensemble et les cartons de l'Apocalypse d'Angers, dessinés par Jean de Bruges, ne constituent sans doute pas un exemple unique. On se rappelle d'ailleurs tout ce qui sépare, au point de vue de l'iconographie et du style, cette rêverie étrange, une des dernières grandes pages inspirées par la vision de Saint Jean avant Albert Durer, et les vieilles apocalypses languedociennes. Dans l'étude de ce mouvement, il ne faut pas non plus négliger la collaboration des imagiers et des peintres pour la polychromie des statues et des reliefs et, dans un milieu comme Tournai par exemple, la longue tradition du travail de la pierre. Mais la forme sculptée, depuis le slutérisme, offrait des partis et des modèles qui ne sont pas gothiques, à proprement parler, et romans moins encore. Il reste difficile d'expliquer l'art des "peintres de tympans." Et pourtant, c'est un fait. Le rétable du *Jugement dernier*, de Van der Weyden, conservé à l'Hospice de Beaune, nous offre, dans sa partie centrale, une composition très fortement organisée, à la manière d'un tympan. En bas, au registre inférieur ou, si l'on veut, au linteau, la résurrection des morts, comme à Autun. Elle est départagée par l'ange de la pesée des âmes. Au-dessus, le Christ juge, encadré avec symétrie par la Vierge et par des saints en prière. Le même maître nous offre, dans la fameuse *Descente de Croix* de l'Escurial, une autre matière à des remarques analogues. La composition est inscrite dans un cadre rectangulaire dont la bordure supérieure s'interrompt pour ménager une saillie carrée, dans laquelle prennent place la tête de Joseph d'Arimathie et l'image de la croix, — comme l'archivolte intérieure de la *Pentecôte* de Vézelay s'interrompt pour laisser passer la tête du Christ. De part et d'autre du corps du Crucifié, les Saintes Femmes et les Apôtres, progressivement penchés, dessinent un hémicycle, comme la distribution des figures dans un tympan. L'influence de la statuaire ne se marque pas seulement à la beauté d'une composition organique, composition qui, transportée dans la pierre, pourrait figurer avec autorité sous les archivoltes d'un portail: elle n'est pas moins sensible à la puissante sobriété du modelé. Nous sommes à égale distance des effets dramatiques et pittoresques de Sluter et de l'exigeante enquête analytique de Van Eyck, cet extraordinaire cartographe d'îlots humains. Les figures de

⁹ *Les Mouvements artistiques dans la civilisation occidentale du moyen-âge* (Paris, 1934), pp. 651 et suiv.

Van der Weyden conservent toujours leur plénitude, leur simplicité dense, leur poids de pierre. Unité remarquable dans la pensée et dans les moyens, et qui se rattache à une tradition bien antérieure.

On peut faire des remarques du même genre à propos du *Couronnement de la Vierge* de Villeneuve-lès-Avignon peint par Enguerrand Charonton en 1453 (Fig. 4). Nous sommes à peu près au terme de l'évolution d'un thème iconographique qui, comme le Jugement Dernier, a longtemps décoré les portails de nos églises

Photo. Giraudon

FIG. 4. ENGUERRAND CHARONTON, LE COURONNEMENT DE LA VIERGE

et auquel l'art gothique a donné des expressions variées et pleines de grandeur. Elles représentent le Christ et la Vierge, couronnée par un ange ou par son Fils, siégeant côte à côte avec majesté. Le *Couronnement* de Charonton obéit à d'autres principes, il est combiné dans ses parties essentielles comme ces fleurs enigmatiques, largement épanouies, riches en replis, faites de figures humaines et de figures monstrueuses, dont l'art du XIIe siècle a laissé tant d'exemples. Au-dessus d'un linteau animé d'une foule de petits personnages qui, sur un fond de paysage d'une aérienne pureté, se pressent de part et d'autre du Christ en croix, le Père et le Fils, vis à vis l'un de l'autre, unis par la colombe du Saint-Esprit, tiennent la couronne chacun d'une main et la posent sur la tête de la Vierge, de face, un peu au-dessous d'eux. Des groupes d'élus, d'anges et de séraphins forment une sorte de couronne autour du motif central. La hiérarchie des proportions progresse des figures du linteau à ces dernières et, de ces dernières, à celles de la Vierge, du Père et du Fils, que cette différence d'échelle fait paraître colossales et qui constituent une indivisible Trinité. Il n'est pas possible d'isoler l'un des membres de ce groupe mystérieux, unis entre eux par le vaste déploiement de leurs manteaux qui se rejoignent et se prolongent les uns les autres, de manière à composer une de ces images synthétiques où la vie individuelle des êtres, apparemment respectée, mais aimantée par une force secrète, tend à se fondre dans un tout plus vaste. Le mouvement ornemental des draperies assure et définit l'équilibre de cette triple figure. Si l'on compare le *Couronnement* de Villeneuve-lès-Avignon à deux œuvres contemporaines, le *Couronnement de la Vierge* et la *Trinité dans sa gloire* des *Heures d'Etienne chevalier*, on se rendra mieux compte de l'originalité profonde de Charonton et de la tradition qu'elle représente. Les figures de Fouquet sont nettement séparées et distinctes. Chacune d'elles vit pour son propre compte et appartient à un univers où l'identité personnelle n'admet plus de se plier à des échanges et à des fusions. Et pourtant, à l'extrémité de cette longue procession d'élus, sous des archivoltes vivantes faites de séraphins ailés, la scène de l'Intronisation apparait bien comme une sorte de tympan au-dessus d'un portail par lequel pénètrent les rangs pressés des fidèles. Il est vrai qu'elle en occupe la place, mais elle est un petit tableau et non un tympan. Le fait est d'autant plus remarquable que Fouquet est assurément, à d'autres égards, en particulier dans sa conception de la figure humaine prise en soi, l'héritier direct des expériences séculaires de la sculpture française.[10] Charonton va plus loin: dans sa composition du *Couronnement*, il semble ressusciter un ordre oublié.

Comment interpréter ces survivances ou ces réveils? Sont-ils le fait d'une inspiration consciente, révèlent-ils l'étude volontaire d'un modèle, ou bien est-ce à travers les générations une de ces rencontres naturelles chez les artistes d'une même race, soumis à une mystique analogue, dans le cadre d'une même iconographie? Ce qui est sûr, c'est que les grandes inventions ne périssent pas d'un seul coup et qu'une fois leur temps passé, il n'est pas dit qu'elles entrent dans la région des formes mortes. Même quand le style et la mode ont changé, après bien des années, il est possible qu'elles renaissent à la lumière, qu'elles acquièrent une vitalité nouvelle. Jusqu'à présent, nous nous trouvons en présence de cas peu nombreux. Il ne saurait être question d'un courant ou d'un mouvement. Mais une enquête plus étendue nous ferait peut-être connaitre d'autres exemples de ces curieuses récurrences. Elles ne sauraient paraitre hasardeuses et problématiques aux observateurs attentifs de la forme. Un style n'est pas une collection de données inertes, mais un ordre cohérent de mesures et de rapports. Comme nous le rappelions au début de notre étude, l'équilibre de ces rapports se cherche par voie d'expériences, trouve son aplomb et sa stabilité, puis se défait

---

[10] Cf. notre article sur "Le Style monumental dans l'œuvre de Jean Fouquet," *Gazette des Beaux-Arts*, janvier 1936.

par oubli des règles qui l'ont assuré. Mais cette défection et cet abandon n'excluent pas la possibilité d'une résurrection plus ou moins spontanée, surtout aux époques où la multiplicité des recherches et le renouvellement des valeurs autorisent, comme au XVe siècle, des retours, non au passé immédiat, mais à un passé plus lointain.

AN ENAMELED RELIQUARY FROM CHAMPAGNAT

MARVIN CHAUNCEY ROSS

THE medieval archaeologists of the nineteenth century accepted without question the theory that all the champlevé enamels of a recognized type dating from the Middle Ages were made in the town of Limoges in France.[1] Recently there has entered some doubt into the minds of scholars whether all of these enamels were actually made in Limoges. Otto von Falke[2] proved, for instance, that a chasse in Berlin is in reality a German imitation of the Limoges work and not French at all, while the Metropolitan Museum possesses another example of the same sort.[3] The article by von Falke has naturally confirmed scholars in the belief that these medieval enamels need to be scrutinized more closely before they can be called Limoges work in a wholesale way merely for the reason that we know from documents that the place[4] was famous for its enamels even so early as the third quarter of the twelfth century.

Several other writers claim that a number of enamels which relate closely together may be Spanish in origin rather than from Limoges, as they have been described at other times. The most important of these are the altar frontal and the several panels on an ivory box, both in the Provincial Museum at Burgos, and the panels from a book cover divided between the Museo de Osma in Madrid and the Cluny Museum in Paris.[5] The strongest argument hitherto for a Spanish origin for these enamels is that none exist today in the region around Limoges, although many Limoges enamels of various classes can be seen still in the churches there. On the other hand, two of the enamels are known to be from the abbey of Santo Domingo de Silos near Burgos in Spain, and a third is in a Spanish museum.

The author[6] of the little catalogue of the Burgos Museum, taking his ma-

---

[1] Rupin, *L'Œuvre de Limoges* (Paris, 1893–1894).

[2] "Aus der Fritzlarer Goldschmiedeschule des XII. Jhs.," *Pantheon*, IV (1929), 551.

[3] "Ein Emailbild der Fritzlarer Werkstatt," *Pantheon*, XII (1933), 278.

[4] Abbé Arbellot, *Bulletin de la Société Arch. et Hist. du Limousin* (1888), p. 89.

[5] Bibliography: O. Luciano Serrano, *Real Monasterio de Sto. Domingo de Silos* (Burgos), p. 161. A. K. Porter, *Romanesque Sculpture of the Pilgrimage Roads* (Boston, 1923); see index. Dom Roulin, "Orfèvrerie et émaillerie d'Espagne," *Rev. Art Chrét.* (1903), pp. 19 ff. Roulin, *Le Trésor de Silos*. F. and R. Azner, *Sto. Domingo de Silos*. J. Perez de Urbel, *Claustro de Silos* (Burgos, 1930), p. 296. G. G. King, "The Triumph of the Cross," *Art Bull.* (1929), p. 317. L. Guibert, *Les Émaux à l'exposition de 1900* (ext. *Bull. Soc. Archéol. et Hist. du Limousin*, Limoges, 1900). R. Tyler, *Spain* (New York, 1909), p. 173. Dieulafoy, *La Sculpture polychrome d'Espagne*, p. 49. Roulin, "Plaque Émaillé d'un coffret de Silos," *Bulletin de la Société scientifique de la Corrèze* (1898), p. 251. J. Ferrandis, *Marfiles españoles* (Barcelona, 1928), p. 84. Rupin, *L'Œuvre de Limoges*; see index. *La Collection Spitzer, L'orfèvrerie religieuse* (text by L. Palustre, p. 96), Pl. III. Huici and Juaristi, *El Sanctuario de San Miguel in Excelsis* (Barcelona, 1929). W. L. Hildburgh, "On a Copper Processional Cross," *Metropolitan Museum Studies*, III (1930–1931), p. 238. E. de Leguina, *Esmaltes españoles* (Madrid, 1909). V. Juaristi, *Esmaltes* (Barcelona, 1933), p. 177 ff. W. F. Stohlman, "Quantity Production of Limoges Champlevé Enamels," *Art Bull.* (1935), p. 394, n. 6. Cf. also "Le Devant d'autel emaillé d'Orense," *Gazette des Beaux-Arts* (1933) p. 272.

[6] Matias Martinez Burgos, *Museo Arqueologico Provincial de Burgos* (Burgos, 1929), p. 71.

terial chiefly from an article by Artinano in *Arte Español*,[7] wrote that there was certainly an atelier for making enamels at Silos or in the region, a statement backed by no documentary or other evidence and quite unacceptable in so far as our present knowledge stands. His next statement is that the Mozarabic ivory casket in his museum was repaired with panels in enamel, thus proving the enamels to be Spanish. This is no argument for local workmanship, for the enamels fit only roughly the places where the ivory panels are missing, while one strip may even be a missing fragment from the enameled altar frontal in the same museum. Churches and museums are filled with reliquaries which have been made up in comparatively recent times from several individual injured or broken ones, notably the little Limoges chasse in the Museum at Châteauroux.[8] The reference to this ivory box in an earlier inventory of the abbey has no mention of the enameled panels, thus making this argument of little weight except to prove that the ivory box and the enamels were once in the same place, a fact already accepted. Then the Spaniards argue that there are Arabic elements in the decoration of the altar frontal from Silos, but against this argument it can be pointed out that Arabic decorative motifs, Kufic writing notably, spread pretty much all over France [9] and occur frequently in the enamels still found in the churches about Limoges. Lastly, the suggestion is put forward that the figure of Sto. Domingo on the box of Burgos is proof of local origin, since he is a saint peculiar to the region. This seems to me to prove nothing more than that the panel was a special order from some atelier and might have been made as easily at Limoges as at Silos, the two being on the Pilgrimage Road and accessible to one another, while Sto. Domingo's name would have been as familiar at Limoges as was that of St. Martial, the great saint of the Limousin, at Silos.[10]

Against the argument that these enamels are Spanish and not French — because until now none were known in France in the churches for which they were originally made, while, on the other hand, two out of the three in Spain came from the abbey at Silos — can be brought a dismembered reliquary now in the Metropolitan Museum of Art. The Museum has six panels which when united formed the usual tomb-shaped reliquary current in the twelfth century. On these are represented Christ between Mary Magdalen and St. Martial (Fig. 2). Above them is the hand of God between two censing angels (Fig. 1). The gabled panels (Figs. 3 and 4) for the ends have represented on them two apostles (Peter and Paul), while on the pieces from the back are the four symbols of the Evangelists and two arabesques (Figs. 5 and 6). These enamels, first published by Molinier in 1891, were exhibited by Sigismond Bardac at the Exposition Universelle in Paris in 1900. They were acquired by Georges Hoentschel, whose collection later was bought by Mr. J. P. Morgan, Sr. Today they form an important part of the Morgan Collection at the Metropolitan Museum of Art.

---

[7] "Esmaltes Españoles," in vol. IV.

[8] J. J. Marquet de Vasselot, *Les Émaux limousins à fond vermiculé* (ext. *Revue Archéologique*, 1905 and 1906).

[9] *Id.*, "Les Influences orientales," in A. Michel, *Histoire de l'art*, II, pt. 2, pp. 882 ff.

[10] Magister Robertus, a French sculptor, worked at Silos (Justo Perez de Urbel, *El Claustro de Sto. Domingo de Silos*, p. 210).

FIGS. 1–6. PANELS OF A DISMEMBERED RELIQUARY
METROPOLITAN MUSEUM, NEW YORK

While I was studying in Limoges some years ago, my friend M. Albert Lacrocq [11] pointed out to me the existence of a number of notebooks in the Archives Provinciales which had been kept by A. Bosvieux, archivist at Guéret in the mid-nineteenth century, while he journeyed about the Limousin on a mule to study the monuments of the region. Under Champagnat (Creuse) he jotted down a detailed description of a chasse which fits exactly the dismembered reliquary now in New York. Bosvieux's note (Fig. 7) reads as follows:

Très beau reliquaire du XIVe en dos d'âne cuivre uni sans guillochures sur lequel sont incrustés à la face 3 personnages a mi-corps: Dieu le Père bénissant de la droite, la main gauche sur le boule du monde; à sa droite Ste. Marie MARIA; à sa gauche MARCIALIS. Dieu entre l'Alpha et l'Omega. Sur la toiture la main bénissante, entre 2 anges à genoux qui l'encensent.

Toutes les 5 figures sont en émail blanc, le nimbe bleu clair, la tunique de dessous verte, le manteau bleu foncé, le tout rehaussé de 99 ornements en émail rouge. La Ste. Vierge tient, de la gauche, une palme et de la droite un coeur, en émail rouge.

Sur le panneau du pignon St. Martial bénissant — mêmes émaux, dans les mêmes conditions.

Revers — Des arabesques très délicates en émail bleu très foncé, s'épanouissant en rinceau et feuillages verts et bleus, entre 2 bêtes de l'apocalypse, tenant les pieds sur le livre. L'une a des pattes de griffon, l'autre des pieds de bouc, des cornes et une queue rouge. Cette partie est placée au bas sur le pan droit. Sur la toiture arabesque à peu près semblable entre l'ange à genoux et l'aigle . . . émaux vert, bleu clair, bleu foncé (rouge très peu par petites parties); figure de l'ange blanche; blanc et rouge celles des bêtes (*1)." [12]

This description fits exactly the fragments of the chasse now in the Metropolitan Museum, except for a few minor mistakes due to a lack of knowledge that is quite understandable in the writings of a French provincial archaeologist of the time of Bosvieux. The most striking instance of this mistaken judgment is that the enamels are of the twelfth century, not the fourteenth century. The figure of Mary is not the Mother of God holding a heart, but more likely Mary Magdalen with the jar of ointment, who appears again with St. Martial on a painted altar frontal of the late fifteenth century from Spain, now in the Cloisters, New York.[13] Christ rather than God the Father is carrying a book, not a globe, while the two figures on the gabled ends are not repetitions of the St. Martial on the front but are the familiar SS. Peter and Paul, who always figure together on later reliquaries in this same manner. Lastly, the four beasts of the Apocalypse on the back are the symbols of the Evangelists found so frequently in medieval art. These mistakes are all due to ignorance and do not change Bosvieux's description of the chasse. The colors he noted exactly, and the names he copied just as they are inscribed on the chasse. Since the enamels only entered into commerce late in the nineteenth century, while Bosvieux had seen them earlier, the conclusion

---

[11] I am indebted also to M. Lacrocq for the photograph of the notebook.

[12] Carnet 13, pp. 78–80. One may gauge the accuracy of Bosvieux by comparing his description of the St. Peter formerly at Alleyrat (Carnet 25, pp. 18–20) with the original now in the Musée Debouché at Limoges.

[13] *The Cloisters, a Brief Guide* (New York, 1931), p. 25.

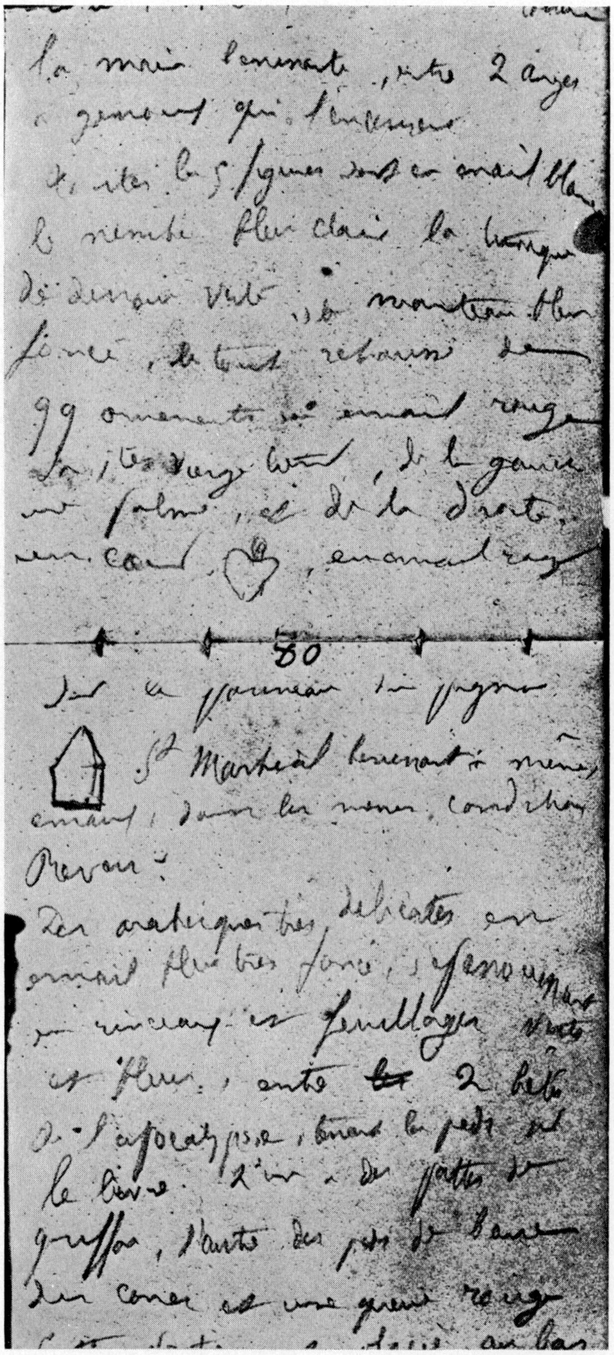

A. Laerocq

FIG. 7. DETAIL OF BOSVIEUX'S NOTEBOOK

must be that the chasse Bosvieux saw at Champagnat in the Limousin is the
dismembered one now in New York.

This chasse [14] belongs to the group of enamels already referred to, the two
most important of which are at Burgos, so that the strongest argument put forth
by the Spaniards for proving these enamels to be Spanish in origin is destroyed
now that it is demonstrated that the New York enamels belonging to the same
group came from a church not far from Limoges. As mentioned above, Limoges
was famed for making enamels as early as the third quarter of the twelfth century, according to existing documents, whereas no documents tell us that enamels
were ever made at Silos.   The presence of St. Martial, the apostle to the Limousin,[15] on the New York plaque points to Limoges, although this cannot be taken
as infallible proof.   But the strongest argument for a Limousin origin is in the
iconographical scene on the front of the chasse with Christ in Majesty between
Mary Magdalen and St. Martial below, and the two censing angels on either
side of the Hand of God above.   Minus the hand and with St. Benedict replacing
the Magdalen, this scene is repeated in a manuscript [16] now in the Bibliothèque
Nationale, but originally from the monastery of St.-Martial (Fig. 8).   The manuscript is certainly French and doubtless was illuminated at St.-Martial.   The
iconography of the scene in the manuscript is the same almost exactly as that
on the two plaques which formed the front of the Champagnat reliquary.   This
close relationship between the enamels and the manuscript points clearly again
to Limoges as the place where the enamels were made.   The *Maiestas* in this
manuscript has another detail which brings it in even closer contact with the
whole group of enamels under discussion.   The drapery about the knee of Christ
is caught in a shield-like effect.[17]   This detail was repeated endlessly in the Limoges
enamels of the thirteenth century, but is unknown to me in Spanish art.   More
important still, it occurs on the book cover in the Cluny Museum (Fig. 9), the
companion piece to the Crucifixion in the Museo de Osma.   The comparison between the Cluny enamel and the famous manuscript [18] from the Cathedral at
Limoges, also now in the Bibliothèque Nationale (Fig. 10) is more striking still.
This twelfth-century manuscript suggests strongly the Cluny enamel in other
ways.   The heads of the bull and the lion at the lower corners and the eagle's
head in the right corner seem almost to have been drawn after the Cluny book

[14] Cf. Huici and Juaristi, *El Santuario de San Miguel in Excelsis.*

[15] It might also be noted that St. Martial holds a book and has the attitude of blessing usually reserved
for apostles in the early Middle Ages. St. Martial's being in this position recalls the belief held in the Limousin from the early eleventh century that St. Martial was sent out to apostolize this part of France by St.
Peter (Abbé Arbellot, *Sur l'apostolat de St. Martial*). A famous statue of the saint, now lost, was made in the
late tenth century by the monk Josbert. A medieval description of this reads as follows: "iconem sancti
Martialis apostoli fecit, sedentem super altare et manu destra populam benedicentem, sinistra librum tenen-
tem Evangeli" (Duplès-Agier, *Chroniques de St.-Martial*, p. 43). The description fits very closely the saint as
depicted in the enamel. This strengthens considerably the theory of a Limousin origin for the enamels.

[16] A. Leroux, E. Molinier, and E. Thomas, *Documents historiques sur la Marche et le Limousin* (Limoges,
1883). MS. Lat. 5, fol. 243.

[17] The Metropolitan Museum possesses a later example of this. Cf. W. F. Stohlman, *Assembling Marks
on Limoges Enamels* (ext. *Art Bull.*, 1934) Figs. 7 and 4.

[18] MS. Lat. 9, fol. 438. See Leroquais, *Les Sacramentaires et les missels manuscrits* (Paris, 1924), Pl. xxxiv
and vol. i, p. 213.

FIG. 8. PARIS, BIBLIOTHÈQUE NATIONALE, LAT. 5, FOL. 243

FIG. 9. PARIS, CLUNY MUSEUM, BOOK COVER

Archives photo.

[474]

FIG. 10. PARIS, BIBLIOTHÈQUE NATIONALE, LAT. 9, FOL. 438

cover, while the same detail of drapery over the knee is repeated once again. The manuscript further shows other influences of metal-work, such as the rectangular designs on the drapery copied after such gem-studded plaques as those to be seen on the Virgin of Salamanca. Thus the enamels in the Metropolitan Museum relate closely with manuscripts from Limoges, which are without any doubt whatsoever French in origin.

The enamels and manuscripts are so closely connected that they must be approximately of the same period. The manuscripts are of about the mid-twelfth century, a date which would suit the enamels admirably, judging from what we know concerning the history of enamel work in the Limousin. The earliest ones [19] are those on the portable altar at Conques of the first decade of the twelfth cen-

Courtesy of the Walters Art Gallery

FIG. 11.   MARTYR SAINT
WALTERS ART GALLERY, BALTIMORE

tury, which are direct imitations of cloisonné enameling. A plaque with the representation of a martyr saint (Fig. 11), now in the Walters Art Gallery,[20] illustrates the technique admirably, the design being cut from one panel which is soldered to another, thus giving much the same effect as the more laborious and costly cloisonné type of enameling. The next step as seen on the Conques, Roda de Isabena, and Bellac (near Limoges) boxes is almost entirely champlevé, although the artists had not yet learned the complete range of colors as found on the several enamels discussed in this article. These last illustrate the mastery of the technique on the part of the enamelers and are among the finest champlevé enamels ever produced. In color and design they seem to me to be superior even to the greatest work from the Mosan region, as represented by the work of Godefroid de Claire, who made about 1140 the chef-reliquaire of St. Alexander, now in the Brussels Museum.[21] Later the Limoges products tended to become mere shop-work made in quantities, but in these earlier instances the enamelers proved

[19] For discussion in detail see "El Relicario de Roda de Isabena" (Pub. in *Bull. de la Facultad de la Universidad de Zaragoza*, 1933).

[20] No. 44. 152.

[21] Frauberger and von Falke, *Deutsche Schmelzarbeiten des Mittelalters* (Frankfurt, 1904), Pl. 69.

themselves true artists with an aesthetic appreciation of color, design, and fine craftsmanship.

Thus, although the large number of enamels ascribed to Limoges by such writers as Rupin can no longer be accepted as such without further study, these enamels now in Burgos, Paris, Madrid, and New York do withstand the criticism aimed at them. One of them comes from the Limousin itself, while iconographical details connect them with the illuminations in manuscripts from Limoges and technically they fit in with the development of enameling in the region, such as it is known to us. From the work of the enamelers who produced these early pieces were to arise several of the ateliers which in the later twelfth and thirteenth centuries were so prolific at Limoges.

REINTEGRATION OF A BOOK OF HOURS EXECUTED IN THE WORKSHOP OF THE "MAÎTRE DES GRANDES HEURES DE ROHAN"

ERWIN PANOFSKY

I. The Manuscript

THE illuminated manuscripts which can be grouped around the Grandes Heures de Rohan (Paris, Bibl. Nat., MS. lat. 9471, datable around 1425) are equally remarkable for their style and for their peculiar iconography. They were first lined up by Paul Durrieu [1] and were thoroughly dealt with in an excellent article by Adelheid Heimann, who not only increased the material by several new attributions but also succeeded in solving the main problems of location, date, stylistic sources, and iconographical content.[2]

No attention has been paid, however, to the fact that one of the more important Books of Hours belonging to the Rohan group [3] is so incomplete that it is practically only half a manuscript. This is the Book of Hours, Paris, Bibl. de l'Arsenal 647, a Horae for Troyes use which, as it is, contains only 121 folios.[4] It is composed of the following elements (in Latin, if not otherwise indicated):

Fol. 1–12^v. Calendar (in French).

Fol. 13–18. Passages from the Gospels. (Two pages, containing the passage from St. Luke and the picture of this Evangelist, are missing.)

Fol. 18^v–76^v. The Hours of the Virgin.

Fol. 77–98^v. The Seven Penitential Psalms and the Litanies.

Fol. 99–106^v. The Hours of the Cross.

Fol. 107–115^v. The Hours of the Holy Ghost and some prayers. (Between fol. 106 and fol. 107 one page is missing, the back of which must have shown

---

[1] *Revue de l'art ancien et moderne*, XXXII (1912), p. 81 ss. and 161 ss.

[2] *Städeljahrbuch*, VII–VIII (1932), p. 1 ss. After this a drawing by the main master of Paris, lat. 9471, was published and very instructively discussed by Millard Meiss, *Gazette des Beaux-Arts*, LXXVII (1935), p. 65 ss.; recently an unconvincing attempt has been made to ascribe the work of the definitely non-French Master of Heiligenkreuz to the Rohan Master (G. Ring, "Primitifs français," *Gazette des Beaux-Arts*, LXXXV, 1938, p. 149 ss.). The iconographical originality of the Rohan workshop has been emphasized by all previous writers. One of the most striking examples is a representation of the Trinity which is assimilated to the "apocalyptic" Madonna emerging in half-length from behind a crescent and foiled by the sun: Book of Hours, Paris, Bibl. Ste. Geneviève, MS. 1278, fol. 21^v (our figures 15 and 7).

[3] Dr. Meiss has brought to my attention two further manuscripts of the Rohan workshop: a Book of Hours in the Victoria and Albert Museum, London, and the Bible Historiale, Brussels, Bibl. Royale 9004 (containing only one illuminated page, fol. 1), of which he did not feel quite sure on the basis of a photograph. Upon inspection of the original, it can be stated that this page was certainly executed in the Rohan workshop, but is rather heavily repainted, particularly in the Creation of the Animals (Fig. 12). Some related miniatures may also be found, I think, in the Bible Historiale, Paris, Arsenal 5058, fol. 403–420. The miniature of Moses on Mount Sinai is particularly suggestive.

[4] Henri Martin, *Catalogue général des manuscrits des bibliothèques publiques de France, Bibl. de l'Arsenal*, I (1885), p. 487. Cf. Durrieu, l.c., p. 172 and Fig. 20; Heimann, l.c., p. 11 and Fig. 11. The description in Martin's *Catalogue* is somewhat inaccurate and has been corrected in the text of this article.

the Pentecost miniature and the words "Domine labia mea aperies. Et os meum"; as it is, the Hours of the Holy Ghost begin abruptly with "annunciabit laudem tuam.")

Fol. 116–121ᵛ. The Fifteen Joys of the Virgin (in French) which are also incomplete at the beginning (one page missing, as can be concluded from the text).

Although the elements of a Book of Hours — subject as they were to the personal wishes of a private owner and to the special inclinations of individual workshops and artists — vary to such an extent that, according to the greatest expert in this field, hardly two specimens of exactly the same composition can be found,[5] there are certain rules and conventions which permit us to decide whether a given manuscript is a complete or an incomplete representative of its type. According to these rules we are entitled to expect that a Horae as sumptuous as Arsenal 647 should contain at least the Suffrages, the two great prayers to the Virgin, "Obsecro te" and "O Intemerata," the Vigils of the Dead, which are never omitted from any more developed Book of Hours, let alone a Horae produced in the Rohan workshop,[6] and the "Sept Requêtes à Notre Seigneur," which are intrinsically connected with the "Quinze Joies de Notre-Dame."[7]

In point of fact, Mr. Robert Garrett in Baltimore, Md., owns a Book of Hours which turns out to be nothing but the other half of the manuscript Arsenal 647.[8] In the recent *Census of Mediaeval and Renaissance Manuscripts in the United States and Canada* by Seymour de Ricci and W. J. Wilson this manuscript is described as "Horae, ca. 1420, written in France. Modern velvet." and is identified with "a manuscript in the John Boykett Jarman sale (London, 13. June 1864, No. 41), bought by Boone, then in an old leather binding, rebacked."[9] No more is known about the Baltimore manuscript (henceforth to be referred to as "B"). But the fact that it originally formed one Book of Hours with the Arsenal manuscript (henceforth to be referred to as "A") is easily demonstrated by the following proofs:

1. *Composition.* The 105 folios of B contain only such elements as are conspicuously absent from A, namely:

fol. 1–5, "Obsecro te."

fol. 5–9, "O Intemerata."

fol. 9–11ᵛ, "Concede mihi, misericors deus."

fol. 12–19ᵛ, the Suffrages.

fol. 20–56ᵛ, the Offices of the Passion.

---

[5] Abbé V. Leroquais, *Les Livres d'heures manuscrits de la Bibliothèque Nationale* (1927), I, vii.

[6] Cf. Heimann, l.c., p. 4; Leroquais, l.c., p. iv, where the "Office des Morts" is called one of the "éléments essentiels du Livre d'Heures."

[7] As to these technicalities cf. Leroquais, l.c., Introduction.

[8] The thanks of the writer are due to Mr. Garrett and M. le Conservateur de la Bibliothèque de l'Arsenal for their kind permission to reproduce the miniatures of the two manuscripts, and to his colleagues A. M. Friend, Jr., Donald D. Egbert, and Mrs. Grace Hollis for much help and several valuable suggestions.

[9] *Census*, I (1935), p. 873, no. 48.

fol. 57–60^v, the "Sept Requêtes à Notre Seigneur" (in French).

fol. 61–105^v, the Vigils of the Dead.

2. *Identical size.* The dimensions of B are 215 × 160 mm. as against 220 × 164 mm. in A, and this slight difference is accounted for by the fact that B has been cut down somewhat more ruthlessly than A, so that even the catchwords, placed as they are near the lower margin of the pages, are sometimes sadly mutilated (e.g., on fol. 57^v and 97^v).

3. *Identical border-ornament* (see illustrations).

4. *Identical script* (15 lines per page).

5. *Identical organization of the miniature-pages.* All of these, excepting, of course, the Calendar, exhibit a peculiar compositional scheme. A central picture provided with a semicircular top is flanked by one smaller miniature on either side, in such a way, however, that the base-line of this "triptych" does not always form one horizontal line, but is more often than not broken up into two or even three levels, while a fourth miniature, separated from the main one by three lines of text and generally an ornament, is placed at the bottom of the page.[10]

Moreover, the original connection between the two manuscripts can be established by the following observation: B is composed of thirteen gatherings. Twelve of these are regular "Quaternios" of eight pages each. Only the eighth gathering consists of nine pages, because fol. 57, that is the beginning of the "Sept Requêtes," has been inserted (Fig. 5). On the other hand, the "Quinze Joies de Notre-Dame" in A occupy only six pages (fol. 116–121, which is the last page of A) and are incomplete at the beginning. As the "Sept Requêtes" almost invariably *follow* the "Quinze Joies" the inference is that B, fol. 57, originally followed A, fol. 121. When the whole manuscript was divided this page, bearing as it did the beginning of the "Sept Requêtes," was obviously cut out of A and added to B before fol. 58, so as to be united with the rest of the "Sept Requêtes," while the other half of the sheet (originally placed before A, fol. 116) was thrown away. This, then, accounts for the fact that the "Quinze Joies de Notre-Dame" (A, fol. 116–121) are incomplete *at the beginning*, as can be made clear by the following diagram:

A, FOL. 116–121   B, FOL. 57–65
("Quinze Joies")   ("Sept Requêtes" and beginning
                                        of the Vigils of the Dead)

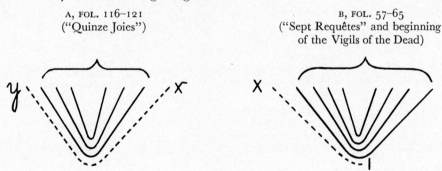

x is the first page of the "Sept Requêtes," originally following A, fol. 121, now forming B, fol. 57

y is the first page of the "Quinze Joies," originally preceding A, fol. 116, now missing.

---

[10] This arrangement is very similar to that seen in three pages in the Book of Hours, Chantilly,

In addition to proving beyond doubt the connection between A and B, this observation shows that the elements of B were *rearranged* after the division was made. Originally, the irregular gathering B, fol. 57–65, must have followed the page A, fol. 121; that is to say, it must have stood at the beginning of the part now forming B. Now, as the last six gatherings of B (fol. 57–105), containing nothing but the "Sept Requêtes," immediately followed by the Vigils of the Dead, form one coherent unit, while the first seven gatherings of B (fol. 1–56) form another coherent unit — which is proved partly by the context, partly by catchwords,[11] partly by both —, we must conclude that the sequence of these two units has been reversed: what now seems to be the second part of B (fol. 57–105) originally preceded what now seems to be its first part (fol. 1–56).

The reasons for this rearrangement — which, incidentally, explains the fact that the pages B, fol. 1 and 57, having had to suffer a great deal from the whole procedure, are in less good condition than the others [12] — are rather obvious. For B, fol. 105^v (end of the Vigils of the Dead, ending with "Requiescant in pace. Amen.") happens to have only eleven written lines, followed by an ornament and an empty space, and therefore conveys the impression of finality, while fol. 56^v (end of the Hours of the Passion) happens to be a regular fifteen-line page, which would have made a far less plausible ending of a book. This permits the further conjecture that the original manuscript may have ended with some special prayers, without illustrations, or with a number of empty pages for private entries.[13]

In contrast with the Garrett part of our Horae the Arsenal part has not been subject to a general rearrangement, but it shows a greater number of lacunae, as has been pointed out in the above description. Thus the whole Book of Hours [14] may be reconstructed as follows:

1. Calendar (in French): A, fol. 1–12^v.
2. Passages from the Gospels (St. Luke-section missing): A, fol. 13–18.
3. The Hours of the Virgin: A, fol. 18^v–76^v.
4. The Seven Penitential Psalms and the Litanies: A, fol. 77–98^v.
5. The Hours of the Cross: A, fol. 99–106^v.

Mus. Condé, MS. lat. 1171, rightly ascribed to the Rohan workshop by Heimann, l.c., p. 60 and Fig. 41 (cf. J. Meurgey, *Les Principaux Manuscrits à peintures du Musée Condé à Chantilly, Publ. de la Soc. Franç. de Réprod. de Manuscrits à Peintures*, 1930, nr. 29, p. 58, Pl. xxxviii), with the difference, however, that in the Chantilly manuscript the base-line of the triptych forms always an unbroken horizontal, and that the top of the central frame is a little more complicated, ⌐⌐⌐ instead of ⌒. It would seem that the Chantilly scheme is due to a subsequent systematization of that employed in the Arsenal-Garrett Hours, which also seems to have influenced a manuscript from the Bedford workshop preserved in the Petit Palais (see V. Leroquais, *Les Trésors des bibliothèques de France*, iii (1930), p. 95 ss.

[11] Catchwords can be seen on fol. 8^v, 16^v, 24^v, 73^v, 89^v, 97^v.

[12] Folio 1 is heavily repainted, fol. 57 somewhat rubbed and disfigured by a fold in the middle.

[13] Of the Books of Hours listed by Leroquais only one, Paris, Bibl. Nat., MS. lat. 1396 (Leroquais, l.c., 1, 227), ends with the Hours of the Passion. In the Garrett manuscript the last page is followed by an empty Quaternio of modern origin.

[14] In A, the passages from the Gospels (now six pages) formed originally one Quaternio; similarly the "Fifteen Joys of the Virgin" (now six pages, with one page lost, and one page inserted into B), while the Hours of the Holy Ghost occupied originally ten pages (now nine). The Calendar consists of one gathering of twelve pages, and the section fol. 19–106 still consists of eleven continuous Quaternios.

6. The Hours of the Holy Ghost (one page missing at the beginning): A, fol. 107–115ᵛ.

7. The Fifteen Joys of the Virgin (one page missing at the beginning): A, fol. 116–121ᵛ.

8. The "Sept Requêtes à Notre Seigneur": B, fol. 57–60ᵛ.

9. The Vigils of the Dead: B, fol. 61–105ᵛ.

10. "Obsecro te": B, fol. 1–5.

11. "O intemerata": B, fol. 5–9.

12. "Concede michi, misericors deus": B, fol. 9–11ᵛ.

13. The Suffrages: B, fol. 12–19ᵛ.

14. The Offices of the Passion: B, fol. 20–56ᵛ.

15. Special Prayers(?).

The separation of A and B and the rearrangement of B must have taken place well before the Garrett part was sold in 1864 and subsequently provided with its modern English velvet binding, for the Arsenal part still has an eighteenth-century binding and the foliation of the Garrett part shows a definite eighteenth-century character. It seems therefore safe to assume that the original manuscript, which in 1688 was part of the legacy of D. Matthieu Picquet, was divided some time before that sale in which the Marquis d'Argenson (who died in 1787, after having sold his library to the Comte d'Artois in 1785) acquired the Arsenal portion for seventy-two livres.[15]

II. THE ILLUSTRATIVE CYCLE

Setting aside the twenty-four Calendar illustrations (A, fol. 1–12ᵛ) which show the customary representations of the zodiacal signs and the Occupations of the Months,[16] as well as a small half-length Madonna in the initial of the "O intemerata" (B, fol. 5), the Book of Hours thus reintegrated contains now twenty-four illuminated pages, each exhibiting the above-mentioned combination of one large miniature in the center and three smaller ones around it.

This decorative scheme was to put a heavy strain on the iconographical imagination of the illustrator. He might have chosen to fill the three minor spaces with typological parallels after the fashion of the Biblia Pauperum or the Speculum Humanae Salvationis, or to use them for the illustration of an independent iconographic cycle, as is the case with two other manuscripts of our group, namely the Grandes Heures de Rohan, Paris, Bibl. Nat., MS. lat. 9471, where

[15] Cf. H. Martin, l.c., and Larousse's *Dictionnaire*, s.v. "Argenson."

[16] The only interesting feature in the Calendar illustrations is the substitution of a Unicorn for the zodiacal Capricorn on fol. 12ᵛ (December). This substitution, which shows that the Unicorn had become a kind of obsession with the late-medieval mind, is, however, not unique: it occurs, e.g., in the Morgan manuscripts, M. 280 (Augsburg, about 1260), fol. 12ᵛ, M. 358 (Luxembourg?, about 1440), fol. 12ᵛ, and M. 511 (Italy, 14th century); in a provincial Book of Hours (Troyes?) of around 1400 in the Art Museum of Princeton University; and in a Book of Hours for Troyes use of around 1400 (Paris, Bibl. Nat., MS. lat. 924, fol. 12ᵛ). It is thus possible that the substitution of the Unicorn for the Capricorn had a symbolical significance in connection with the fact that December is the month of Christmas, and that the Unicorn was traditionally interpreted as a symbol of Christ.

469 smaller miniatures form a rather complete "Bible Moralisée,"[17] and the Horae, Cambridge, Fitzwilliam No. 62, where the smaller spaces are devoted to a coherent illustration of the Apocalypse and the three "Pélerinages" by Guillaume de Deguileville.[18] But he endeavored, instead, to keep the content of the smaller miniatures in close contact with that of the main picture without having recourse to typological parallels,[19] and in doing so was bound to run into certain difficulties.

In the case of the Evangelists' portraits he could not think of anything better than to repeat their symbol in each of the three smaller spaces.[20] In the other cases his method varies according to circumstances. Sometimes (Fig. 5) he distributed the elements of one Biblical scene over all the four pictures (for instance, A, fol. 47, 51[v]; B, fol. 30, 40[v], 57). Sometimes (Fig. 2) he used the three smaller spaces for what may be called "variations" on the leading theme shown in the central picture (for instance, A fol. 29[v], 41), and sometimes (Figs. 6, 7, 10), finally, for what may be compared to "marginal glosses," that is, for the representation of subjects connected with the central scene either historically (as is the case with the majority of the miniature pages), or symbolically (as is the case, e.g., with B, fol. 1, 53, 63).

Thus the iconography of the Arsenal-Garrett Hours, especially of the Garrett part, offers some points of very real interest and justifies a brief enumeration of the ninety-six miniatures, which will be listed according to their original sequence.

A, FOL. 13. (Passages from the Gospels.)

Main picture: St. Matthew.

In each of the three smaller compartments there appears an angel with a scroll.

A, FOL. 15. (Passages from the Gospels.)

Main picture: St. Mark.[21]

In each of the three smaller compartments there appears a lion with a scroll.

A, FOL. 16[v]. (Passages from the Gospels.)

Main picture: St. John.

---

[17] Cf. A. Heimann, l.c., pp. 5 and 27 ss. Furthermore, A. de Laborde, *La Bible moralisée illustrée* (1911 ss.), text, p. 117 ss., plates, vol. IV, 768–781.   [18] Cf. Heimann, l.c., pp. 5 and 57 ss.

[19] Similar illustrative principles can of course be observed in the three pages in the Horae Chantilly, MS. 1171 which were mentioned above (p. 482). They mark the beginnings of the Heures de la Vierge, the Penitential Psalms (ill. in Meurgey, l.c., Pl. xxxviii) and the Vigils of the Dead (ill. in A. Heimann, l.c., Fig. 41). The first of these pages shows the Annunciation in the main miniature, while a group of mother and child can be seen in each of the lateral pictures (according to Meurgey, the Virgin with the Infant Jesus and St. Elizabeth with the little St. John, but more probably the Madonna represented twice), and the Virgin alone appears in the bottom picture. The main miniature of the second page shows God the Father; He blesses David, who appears in the left miniature, as he throws the stone and with a sword threatens Goliath, who is seen breaking down in the right picture, while the bottom picture shows David playing the lyre. (In Meurgey's text the figures of David and Goliath are, curiously enough, described as "deux paysans.") The third page exhibits a funeral procession in the main miniature, a gravedigger in the left miniature, two gravediggers making graves for four corpses in the right miniature, and a nude corpse lying by a half-opened coffin in the bottom-picture.

[20] Cf. A. Heimann, l.c., p. 13, Fig. 11 (St. Mark).

[21] Illustrated in A. Heimann, l.c., p. 13, Fig. 11.

In each of the three smaller compartments there appears an eagle with a scroll.

A, FOL. 18ᵛ. (Heures de la Vierge, Matines): "matitinas" (*sic!*). (Fig. 1.)

Main picture: The Annunciation, "ecclesiastical type."

Left picture: The Annunciation, "exterior type." [22]

Right picture: The Annunciation without architectural setting, the angel flying downward.

Bottom picture: the Virgin at the loom.

A, FOL. 29ᵛ. (Heures de la Vierge, Laudes.)

Main picture: St. Elizabeth kneeling before the Virgin Mary.

Left picture: St. Elizabeth and the Virgin Mary, shaking hands.

Right picture: St. Elizabeth and the Virgin Mary, embracing.

Bottom picture: St. Elizabeth and the Virgin Mary, standing apart under a heavenly glory.

A, FOL. 41. (Heures de la Vierge, Prime.) (Fig. 2.)

Main picture: Nativity. The scene is staged in an enclosure partly sheltered by a tall shed, the Virgin Mary adoring the Infant, who is seated on the ground, while God the Father sends down the Dove. Within the enclosure there are two boxes and the two animals, whereas St. Joseph and an angel lean over the wicker fence to participate in the adoration.

Left picture: The Virgin Mary alone, adoring the Infant in a shed. The Infant is seen lying on the ground.

Right picture: The Virgin adoring the Infant in a shed. The Infant stands on a couch and longingly reaches out for her, while two adoring angels lean over the wicker fence and the Dove approaches from a glory.

Bottom picture: The Virgin adoring the Infant, who sits on the ground. Outside of the shed two adoring angels, God the Father sending down the Dove. [23]

A, FOL. 47. (Heures de la Vierge, Tierce.): "Ad terciam de beata Maria Uirgine psalmus."

Main picture: The Annunciation to the Shepherds.

In each of the three smaller compartments there appears one more shepherd.

A, FOL. 51ᵛ. (Heures de la Vierge, Sexte.)

Main picture: Adoration of the Magi, the Virgin enthroned. In each of the three smaller compartments there appears one Magus on horseback, looking at the star.

A, FOL. 56. (Heures de la Vierge, None.)

Main picture: The Presentation of Christ, the kneeling Virgin supported by an angel.

---

[22] As to the various types of the Annunciation cf. E. Panofsky, *Art Bulletin*, XVII (1935), p. 433 ss., and, more circumstantially, D. Robb, *ibid.*, XVIII (1936), p. 480 ss.

[23] The absence of St. Joseph from the three "variations," which is unusual in French art at this period, was noted by Bella Martens, *Meister Francke* (1928), text-vol., p. 250, n. 256. Cf., however, E. Panofsky, *Conrad von Soest and Meister Francke in the Light of Some Illuminated Manuscripts in American Collections* (in print).

Left picture: The Virgin Mary kneeling on the ground. She prays with her arms crossed before her breast, a book lying on the ground.

Right picture: The Virgin Mary praying as before, but her hands are joined in an adoring gesture; an angel kneeling behind her joins in her prayer.

Bottom picture: Two kneeling women offering birds (one a goose, the other a basketful of pigeons); two kneeling men offering lambs.

A, FOL. 61. (Heures de la Vierge, Vêpres.): [24] "Ad uesperas de beata uirgine." (Fig. 3.)

Main picture: Flight into Egypt.

Left picture: Two elderly beggars, man and woman, the man holding a cup in his right hand.

Right picture: A man harvesting corn.

Bottom picture: Four richly attired riders.

The unfortunate couple in the left picture seems to represent the cripples miraculously healed by the Infant Jesus according to Pseudo-Matthew, cap. 31,[25] while the harvester apparently alludes to the miraculous cornfield growing up from the seeds sown by the Divine Child according to Pseudo-Matthew, cap. 34.[26] The riders in the bottom picture either belong to the retinue of the Egyptian prince Affrodisius (Pseudo-Matthew, cap. 24), or, more probably, to the henchmen of Herod. In the Grandes Heures de Rohan, fol. 99, both the harvesting man and the swaggering riders are included in the picture of the Flight into Egypt itself.[27]

A, FOL. 67[v]. (Heures de la Vierge, Complies.): "Ad completorium psalmus."

Main picture: The Coronation of the Virgin.

Left picture: Two angels, one holding a scroll, the other pointing at the main scene.

Right picture: Two angels praying.

Bottom picture: Four angels, holding a book.

A, FOL. 77. (Penitential Psalms.). Very much damaged. (Fig. 4.)

Main picture: God the Father enthroned. He holds with His left hand the transversal beam of a crucifix, which is placed in front, but to one side of Him, and the stem of which is supported by four little cherubs. His glance is fixed on the head of the crucified Christ and His right arm is raised with an emphatic gesture of blessing. Although the Dove has been omitted the composition is derived from such representations of the Trinity as found in the Heures du Maréchel de Boucicaut (fol. 118[v]), or in a Horae in the Walters Art Gallery at Baltimore whose miniatures are stylistically connected with the Bedford group but draw heavily from the Boucicaut tradition (MS. 287, fol. 125).

[24] Illustrated in Durrieu, l.c., p. 181, Fig. 20.

[25] Cf. M. R. James, *Burlington Magazine*, XLII (1923), p. 32 ss., concerning a series of English fourteenth-century tiles with scenes from the infancy of Christ and MS. Bodl., Selden supra 38 (likewise English, fourteenth century). In the latter the healing of the cripples is represented on fol. 19.

[26] Cf. *Burl. Mag.*, l.c., p. 35, Fig. C, 1. In Bodl., Selden supra 38, the scene is represented on fol. 22.

[27] Illustrated in Durrieu, l.c., Fig. 16. The Flight into Egypt in the Horae Paris, Bibl. Nat. MS. lat. 1161, fol. 87, shows the harvester and the Massacre of the Innocents in the background.

Left picture: God the Father, dividing light from darkness.

Right picture: God the Father measuring the universe with a compass.[28]

Bottom picture: God the Father creating Eve.

A, FOL. 99. (Beginning of the Hours of the Cross.) [29]

Main picture: The Crucifixion (Christ between St. John and the Virgin Mary).

Left picture: One of the Thieves.

Right picture: The other Thief.

Bottom picture: The resurrected Adam, wrapped in a white shroud, emerging from a coffin placed before the three empty crosses.

B, FOL. 57. (Requêtes à Notre Seigneur.) (Fig. 5.)

Main picture: A special version of the Last Judgment which was particularly in favor with the Rohan workshop (cf. A. Heimann, Fig. 18). This version is characterized by the absence of the Virgin Mary and St. John the Baptist, and by the fact that Christ, who is seated on a rainbow supported by two angels and rests His feet on the globe, appears as a synthesis between the white-headed "First and Last" from Apoc. I, 14 and the "Man of Sorrows": He wears the crown of thorns and beneath His gorgeous mantle displays His nude body girded with a loincloth.[30] At the bottom of the picture there can be seen three Resurrected.

Left picture: One Resurrected.

Right picture: Three Resurrected.

Bottom picture: Three Resurrected.

B, FOL. 63. (Vigils of the Dead.)

Main picture: The dead man lies by his open coffin on a shroud placed on the floor of a vaulted room. He is surrounded by his mourning family and praying "Pleureurs." A metal crucifix is seen on a sideboard. (Fig. 6.)

Left picture: Christ at the Cross.

Right picture: Three standing corpses, set out against a starred blackish background.

Bottom picture: Three riders in a landscape, one of them pointing in the direction of the corpses.

When "read" together, the right and bottom miniatures constitute a representation of the Legend of the Three Living and the Three Dead,[31] the appear-

---

[28] Cf. our Fig. 5 and innumerable other Bibles Historiales which were obviously the source of the three smaller miniatures on this page. As to the significance of the compass motive, cf. E. Panofsky and F. Saxl, *Dürers Kupferstich "Melencolia I"* (1923), 67.

[29] On fol. 98ᵛ: "Sequitur de sancta cruce ad matutinas psalmus."

[30] As to this version of the Last Judgment, cf. Heimann, l.c., p. 46; also E. Panofsky, "Imago Pietatis," *Festschrift für M. I. Friedländer* (1927), p. 296 ss., and "Conrad von Soest and Meister Francke in the Light of Some Manuscripts in American Collections" (in print).

[31] Cf. A. Heimann, l.c., p. 56. Our miniature is the only complete representation of this legend in the manuscripts executed in the Rohan workshop, Paris, Bibl. Nat., MS. lat. 13262, fol. 121, showing in the same connection only the three skeletons, but not the three Living. The representation of the two groups in separate pictures is not unnatural in view of the dialogical character of the original conception and occurs much earlier than in the one instance adduced by A. Heimann: see Paris, Bibl. Nat., MS. fr. 378, fol. 1, illustrated (with erroneous inscription) in R. van Marle, *Iconographie de l'art profane*, vol. II (1932),

ance of which in connection with the main scene needs no explanation. The Crucifixion in the left miniature signifies the redemption of the soul of the dead man through the sacrifice of Christ, and its combination with the main scene may be compared to the two last illustrations of the "Ars Moriendi," where the crucifixion scene appears as a vision at the bed of the "Agonizans," to visualize firstly the victory of the "Inspiratio bona" over the Last Temptation (that of Avarice), secondly the Ultimate Triumph of the celestial powers.[32]   The text referring to the victory over Avarice contains the following passage: "Memento etiam paupertatis Christi in cruce per te pendentis," and the text referring to the Final Triumph mentions the "virtus passionis," as well as the custom of showing the dying person a crucifix.[33]

B, FOL. 1.   (Obsecro te.). Heavily repainted. (Fig. 7.)

Main picture: The Virgin on the crescent, which is supported by two angels.

Left picture: The Virgin alone, reading in a prayer book.

Right picture: The Virgin turning round from her *prie-dieu* and looking with some surprise at the Infant sitting on the floor, while a glory appears in the right upper corner of the picture.

Bottom picture: The Virgin, having dropped her book, receives the Infant, who runs into her arms.

The three small miniatures may be called a cinematographic and somewhat playful analysis of the Annunciation scene as shown in those numerous representations of the fourteenth and fifteenth centuries in which the Infant Jesus is proleptically included.[34]

B, FOL. 20.   (Heures de la Passion, Matines.) (Fig. 8.)

Main picture: The Betrayal.

Left picture: St. Peter, ruefully kneeling before the Cock.

Right picture: St. Peter and the Maid-Servant.

Bottom picture: A nimbed youth hurrying away from a man who grasps a cloak relinquished on the ground.

The last scene is of special interest as a unique representation of the much-discussed passage, Mark XIV, 51–52,[35] which relates that, when Christ was captured, a youth followed him "amictus syndone super nudum, et tenuerunt eum. At ille relicta syndone nudus profugit ab eis." Even literal illustrations of this passage are not too frequent,[36] but in no other representation hitherto published

---

Fig. 419, and Brit. Mus., Arundel 83, II, fol. 127, ill. in R. Freyhan, *Burl. Mag.*, LIV (1929), 328. MS. fr. 378 (around 1300) contains another version of the legend of the Three Living and the Three Dead (fol. 7ᵛ, entitled "C'est des trois mors & des trois vis"), which is also illustrated by two separate miniatures; but these are of an altogether different type in that they hint at the relationship between the sexes: one of them showing a nun between two skeletons, the other a skeleton between two worldly ladies (our Fig. 13).

[32] Cf. Lionel Cust, *The Master E. S. and the Ars Moriendi* (1897), ill. 29, 35, 58, 60, text pp. 59 and 61.

[33] Cf. also Paris, Bibl. Nat., MS. lat. 1156 A, fol. 114 (title miniature of the Vigils of the Dead), which shows two skeletons in a grave, a Franciscan reading prayers, two crosses in the background landscape, a Prophet (probably Ezekiel) pointing, and Christ proffering a monstrance with the Crucifixion, while God the Father and the Dove appear in the sky (our Fig. 14).

[34] Cf. A. Heimann, l.c., p. 42 ss., and D. Robb, l.c., p. 523 ss.

[35] This was pointed out to the writer by Prof. A. M. Friend, Jr.

[36] I quote, rather at random: Codex Aureus Escurialensis, fol. 81, ill. in W. Cook, "The earliest painted

does the youth appear with a halo and in the formal attire of an Apostle. Now the enigmatical youth referred to by St. Mark has always asked for identification, all the more so because a great many of the Greek manuscripts have νεανίσκος εἶς instead of νεανίσκος τις. By recent commentators he is often identified with the Evangelist himself; earlier authorities, however, suggest either a resident of the house where the Lord had eaten the Passover, or St. James, the brother of the Lord, or, finally, St. John the Evangelist. And as the last identification, championed as it was by St. Ambrose, Chrysostom, and Bede,[37] enjoyed the greatest popularity, the nimbed figure in our miniature would seem to be the youthful St. John, identified with the fleeing youth according to St. Mark, XIV, 51–52; in this case the incident, bearing witness to the temporary weakness of one of the Disciples, would be a most appropriate parallel to the St. Peter scenes.

B, FOL. 30. (Heures de la Passion, Laudes.)

Main picture: The Agony in the Garden, Christ accompanied by SS. Peter, James, and John; the Jews already climbing over the fence, which is unusual at this early date (later on, cf. e.g. H. Multscher, Berlin). Generally, e.g. in the Horae Paris, Bibl. Nat. lat. 1161, fol. 142, the soldiers are only shown approaching from the background.

Left picture: Three other Disciples.

Right picture: Three other Disciples.

Bottom picture: Three other Disciples.

The fact that this page follows the page with the Betrayal, instead of preceding it, must be due to an error of the illuminator, as the sequence of the first four gatherings (fol. 1–32) has not been disturbed (witness the catchwords on fol. 8ᵛ, 16ᵛ, 24, and the conspicuously initialed [38] "Incipit," "Domine, labia mea aperies" on fol. 20).

B. FOL. 34ᵛ. (Heures de la Passion, Prime.)

Main picture: Christ before Pilate.

Left picture: The Mocking of Christ.

Right picture: Christ before the High Priest.

Bottom picture: Christ before Herod, receiving the slap in His face.

B, FOL. 37ᵛ. (Heures de la Passion, Tierce.): "Ad terciam."

Main picture: Flagellation of Christ.

Left picture: Christ before Pilate again (after having been sent back to him by Herod).

Right picture: Christ dragged away by a henchman.

Bottom picture: Christ before Herod again, stripped of His clothes by two henchmen.

B, FOL. 40ᵛ. (Heures de la Passion, Sexte.): "Ad VI. psalmus."

---

panels of Catalonia, V," *Art Bulletin*, x (1927), Fig. 52; one of the Monreale mosaics (D. Gravina, *Monreale*, 1859, Pl. 18 B); Hamilton Psalter, Berlin, Kupferstichkabinett, MS. 78 A. 5, fol. 76; Bible Moralisée, Laborde, l.c., vol. III, Pl. 524; a lost composition by Correggio (the Parma replica ill. in G. Gronau, *Correggio*, Klassiker der Kunst, 1907, p. 143).

[37] Cf. Herny Barclay Swete, *The Gospel According to St. Mark* (3rd. ed., 1927), p. 354.

[38] The initial shows a woman crouching in prayer.

Main picture: The bearing of the Cross.

Left picture: The first Thief carrying his cross.

Right picture: One of the horsemen.

Bottom picture: The second Thief carrying his cross.[39]

B, FOL. 44ᵛ. (Heures de la Passion, None.)

Main picture: Crucifixion.

Left picture: Nailing to the Cross.

Right picture: Two Roman soldiers.

Bottom picture: Four Roman Riders.

B, FOL. 49. (Heures de la Passion, Vêpres.): "Ad uesperas." (Fig. 9.)

Main picture: Descent from the Cross, the Magdalen embracing it.

Left picture: The Virgin Mary and Maria Salomae, sadly approaching the Mount of Calvary.

Right picture: The Virgin Mary swooning in the arms of St. John.

Bottom picture: *Pietà* group,[40] accompanied by St. John and Maria Salomae.

In the Book of Hours, Bibl. Ste. Geneviève, MS. 1278, fol. 45 (our Fig. 11) we find a miniature in which the Descent from the Cross and the *Pietà* as appearing in the Garett Hours are united in one picture, which combination, with the body of Christ appearing twice in the same composition, seems to be less logical than that in the Garrett Hours. As to the group of the Virgin swooning in the arms of St. John — later on an outstanding feature of Roger van der Weyden's Crucifixions, but here conceived as an *Andachtsbild* even more isolated than is the case in the famous miniature in the Grandes Heures de Rohan — cf. A. Heimann, l.c., p. 18, Fig. 16, and particularly p. 46 ss., with many parallel instances, mostly of German origin.[41]

B, FOL. 53. (Heures de la Passion, Complies.) (Fig. 10.)

Main picture: Lamentation of Christ.

Left picture: The Virgin Mary and St. Joseph kneeling in prayer on a piece of lawn.

Right picture: Joseph of Arimathea, negotiating with Pilate.

Bottom picture: Three soldiers, representing the watch asked for by the Jews and instated by Pilate (Matthew, XXVII, 64 ss, and Mark, XV, 44 ss).

The scene depicted in the left miniature may be called a Nativity minus the Infant. In so far as it is a Nativity, it forms a pathetic contrast with the Lamentation, and yet foreshadows it by absence of the Child. The peculiar interrelationship can be accounted for by numerous texts in which a melancholy comparison is drawn between the death and the infancy of Christ — texts which

[39] As to the types of the two Thieves, cf. the Bearing of the Cross in the Grandes Heures de Rohan, Paris, Bibl. Nat., MS. lat. 9471, fol. 17, where Christ Himself is shown in a similar posture and is also clad with a loin-cloth only.

[40] The expression *Pietà* is here used as an equivalent of the German *Vesperbild*, denoting a compositionally isolated figure of the Virgin Mary with the dead body of Christ on her knees.

[41] The Descent from the Cross in Bibl. Ste. Geneviève, MS. 1278 ill. in A. Heimann, l.c., p. 5, Fig. 5. For the motif of the swooning Virgin cf. also a miniature in the Ghent missal of 1366, The Hague, Mus. Meermanno-Westreenianum 10, A. 14, ill. in A. W. Byvanck, *Les Principaux Manuscrits à peintures de la Bibl. Royale des Pays-Bas et du Musée Meermanno-Westreenianum à la Haye* (1924), Pl. XLV.

also throw light on the fact that the earliest known instances of the *Vesperbild Pietàs* show a diminutive child-like Christ (Fig. 17) and seem indeed to result from a synthesis of the Madonna type with the type of the mourning mothers seen in many representations of the Slaughter of the Innocents.[42] "O my son," the Virgin Mary says in one of these texts, "on this bosom of mine thou hast often slept the sleep of childhood, now thou sleepest thereon the sleep of death." [43] She revels in the memories of His birth and infancy,[44] and often even accuses the Angel Gabriel of having announced to her an ineffable bliss which was to turn into ineffable sorrow.[45] It is entirely in harmony with these lines of thought when the Church interprets the *corporale* (that is, the cloth spread over the altar for the Host, or a fragment of it, to rest upon) both as a symbol of the winding-sheet that covered the Saviour in His grave, and of the swaddling cloth in which the new-born Babe was wrapped.[46]

[42] Cf. E. Panofsky, "Imago Pietatis," *Festschrift für M. I. Friedländer* (1927), p. 266, and H. Swarzenski, *Zeitschrift für Kunstgeschichte*, IV (1935), p. 141 ss. My friend Dr. Meiss calls my attention to the fact that the *Pietà* in the Grandes Heures de Rohan, fol. 41 (A. Heimann, l.c., p. 50 ss., Fig. 32, our fig. 18) is very similar to one of the mourning mothers in the Bible Moralisée, Paris, Bibl. Nat., MS. fr. 9561, fol. 138 (our Fig. 16), which, as was already observed by Emile Mâle, was thoroughly exploited by the Rohan workshop (cf. A. Heimann, l.c., p. 22 and 27 ss). As to the re-transformation of the *Pietà* with the child-like body of Christ into a Madonna with a corpse-like Infant, cf. A. Heimann, l.c., p. 52, Fig. 34. Cf. also H. Schrade, *Ikonographie d. Christl. Kunst*, I, *Die Auferstehung Christi* (1932), p. 365.

[43] Symeon Metaphrastes, quoted by G. Millet, *Recherches sur l'iconographie de l'Evangile*, Bibl. de l'Ecole des Chartes, no. 109 (1916), p. 490. A similar text (from George of Nicomedia) quoted *ibid*. As to the later sources cf., for instance, a passage from St. Bernardine of Siena, quoted by Domvikar Dolfen, "Das Vesperbild des Domes zu Osnabrück," *Jahresbericht des Diözesanmuseums Osnabrück* (1930): "When the body of the dead Saviour reposed in the lap of the Virgin she sensed again the infant that had rested on her bosom in Bethlehem." Dolfen feels that passages like this one are too late to afford an explanation for the diminutive size of Christ in *Pietà* groups of the beginning of the fourteenth century, but overlooks the existence of sources as early as Simeon Metaphrastes. Needless to say, these sources could give rise to the *Pietà* composition only under the spell of a specific religious impulse which, at about the same time, generated many other *Andachtsbilder* because it was strong enough to bridge the distance between written word and preëxistent visual types, vz., in our case, the Madonna with the Infant Jesus on the one hand, the Mourning Mothers seen in representations of the Massacre of the Innocents on the other. It is also interesting to note that in a Latin poem contemporaneous with the earliest *Pietàs*, the "Vita Beatae Virginis Mariae rhythmica," the dead body of Christ is referred to as *corpusculum*: "Sic filii corpusculo mater incumbebat, Amplectus illud, et ab hoc avelli vix valebat" (ed. Vögtlin, *Bibliothek d. Literar. Vereins*, Stuttgart, vol. 180, 1888, p. 197, l. 5976; quoted, but without reference to the expression "corpusculum," by W. Pinder, "Die dichterische Wurzel der Pietà," *Repertorium für Kunstwissenschaft*, XLII, 1920, p. 154).

[44] Cf., for instance, one of the earliest German *Marienklagen* (F. J. Mone, *Schauspiele des Mittelalters*, I, 1846, p. 217, l. 17): "Si gedahte, wie er ir was geben" (she remembered how He was given to her), or a passage from the "Sermo Angelicus" by St. Bridget of Sweden, XVII, quoted by Dolfen, l.c.

[45] Cf. E. Wechssler, *Die Romanischen Marienklagen* (1893), p. 8.

[46] Cf. Yrjö Hirn, *The Sacred Shrine* (1912), p. 80.

FIG. 1. PARIS, BIBLIOTHÈQUE DE
L'ARSENAL, MS. 647, FOL. 18ᵛ

FIG. 2. PARIS, BIBLIOTHÈQUE DE
L'ARSENAL, MS. 647, FOL. 41

FIG. 3. PARIS, BIBLIOTHÈQUE DE
L'ARSENAL, MS. 647, FOL. 61

FIG. 4. PARIS, BIBLIOTHÈQUE DE
L'ARSENAL, MS. 647, FOL. 77

FIG. 5. BALTIMORE, MR. ROBERT GARRETT,
HORAE, CENSUS 48, FOL. 57

FIG. 6. BALTIMORE, MR. ROBERT GARRETT,
HORAE, CENSUS 48, FOL. 63

FIG. 7. BALTIMORE, MR. ROBERT GARRETT,
HORAE, CENSUS 48, FOL. 1

FIG. 8. BALTIMORE, MR. ROBERT GARRETT,
HORAE, CENSUS 48, FOL. 20

FIG. 9. BALTIMORE, MR. ROBERT GARRETT, HORAE, CENSUS 48, FOL. 49

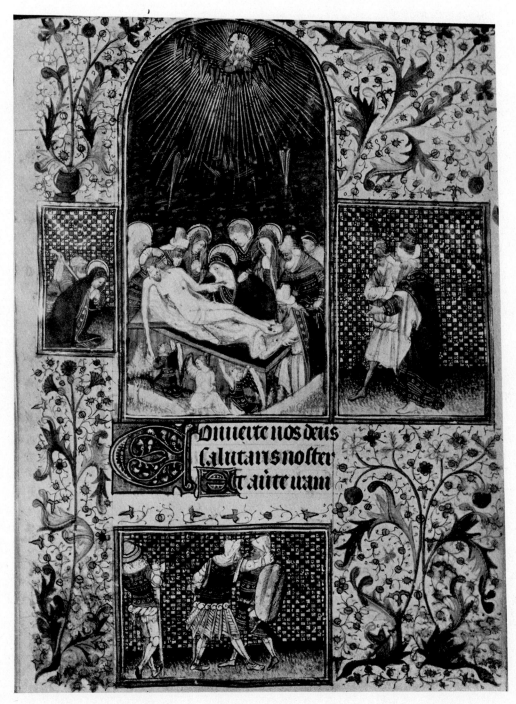

FIG. 10. BALTIMORE, MR. ROBERT GARRETT, HORAE, CENSUS 48, FOL. 53

FIG. 11. PARIS, BIBLIOTHÈQUE STE. GENEVIÈVE, MS. 1278, FOL. 45

FIG. 12. BRUSSELS, BIBLIOTHÈQUE ROYALE, MS. 9004, FOL. 1

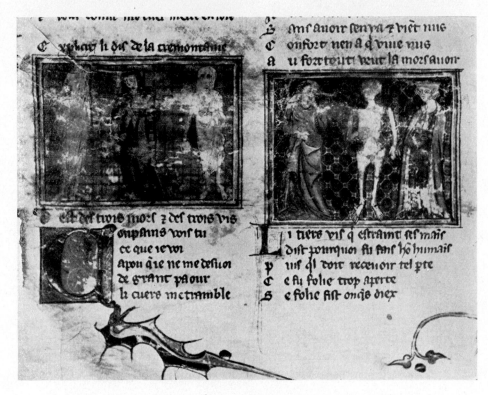

FIG. 13. PARIS, BIBLIOTHÈQUE NATIONALE, MS. FR. 378, FOL. 7ᵛ

FIG. 14. PARIS, BIBLIOTHÈQUE NATIONALE, MS. LAT. 1156 A, FOL. 114

FIG. 15. PARIS, BIBLIOTHÈQUE
STE. GENEVIÈVE, MS. 1278, FOL. 21ᵛ

FIG. 16. PARIS, BIBLIOTHÈQUE
NATIONALE, MS. FR. 9561, FOL. 138 (Detail)

FIG. 17. MIDDLE-RHENISH PIETÀ
GROUP (c. 1300)
GERMAN PRIVATE COLLECTION

FIG. 18. PARIS, BIBLIOTHÈQUE
NATIONALE, MS. LAT.
9471, FOL. 41

VI. MEDIEVAL ART IN GERMANY AND SWITZERLAND

DIE STELLUNG DER WESTTÜRME DES NAUMBURGER DOMES

PAUL FRANKL

ES WAR im Mittelalter die Regel, bei zweitürmigen Westfassaden dreischiffiger Kirchen die Türme so vor die Seitenschiffe zu stellen, dass ihre West-Ost-Achse (mehr oder weniger genau) mit der Achse der Seitenschiffe zusammenfiel. In Naumburg dagegen sind die Türme derart nach seitwärts verschoben, dass ihre Mittellinien auf die äusseren Seitenschiffmauern treffen. Diese Turmstellung dürfte ungemein selten nachzuweisen sein. Ich kenne sie nur noch in den Domen von Cefalù und Monreale in Sizilien. Da in der Literatur allgemein angenommen wird, dass in Naumburg ursprünglich (statt des gotischen Westchors) zwischen den Türmen eine Westvorhalle beabsichtigt oder begonnen war, wird die Ähnlichkeit noch grösser. Es kommt hinzu, dass Naumburg anfänglich als Flachdeckbasilika gedacht war und eine Rekonstruktion dieses Entwurfs die Ähnlichkeit mit Cefalù so schlagend macht, dass man sich fragen muss, ob Naumburg von Cefalù durch tatsächliche Beziehungen abhängig ist. Um es gleich zu sagen: solche Beziehungen sind nicht nachweisbar, im Gegenteil: man ist in Naumburg selbständig durch besondere örtliche Umstände zu einer ähnlichen Anlage wie in Cefalù gekommen, ohne dass die beim Entwurf Beteiligten eine Kenntnis der sizilianischen Bauten gehabt haben müssen. Ist also der Ertrag dieser Untersuchung in der einen Richtung negativ, so in der anderen, wie ich glaube, positiv: wenn es glückt, die Gründe der Turmstellung in Naumburg zu erkennen.

I. DIE REKONSTRUKTION DES FLACHDECK-ENTWURFS VON NAUMBURG

Am Naumburger Dom steigt auf der Westseite des *Nordquerarms* dicht neben der anstossenden Seitenschiffmauer eine Lisene hoch, die knapp über der Trauflinie des Seitenschiffs aufhört. Eine neue Lisene setzt etwas höher daneben, zur Mittelachse des Querarms verschoben, an und steigt bis zum Rundbogenfries (Fig. 1). Bergner[1] schloss daraus, dass in diesem Nordquerarm eine Flachdecke beabsichtigt war, die für die Fensterausteilung freie Hand gelassen hätte. Erst der Entschluss zur Wölbung zwang dazu, hier die Fenster nach der Mitte zu rücken, also auch die Lisene zu verlegen.

Dieser überzeugende Nachweis eines älteren Entwurfs hat alle später erschienenen Untersuchungen der Baugeschichte des Naumburger Doms beeinflusst, aber es fehlt bisher der Versuch einer zeichnerischen Rekonstruktion. Um ihn durchzuführen (Fig. 6–10), muss man in Gedanken alle "späteren" Zutaten wegstreichen und dann den so erhaltenen Stumpf ergänzen.[2] Wegzustreichen ist

[1] Heinrich Bergner, *Beschreibende Darstellung der älteren Bau- und Kunstdenkmäler der Stadt Naumburg* (Halle a.S., 1903), S. 48.

[2] Fast alle Voraussetzungen dafür beobachtete bereits Selmar Lüttich, *Dritter Beitrag zur Baugeschichte*

— grob gesprochen — alles, was mit der Wölbung zusammenhängt, ferner die Oberteile der vier Türme, der Westchor von 1249 und der Ostchor von etwa 1320. Es bleiben die Wände der Ostteile und der Seitenschiffe bis zu gewisser Höhe, die Westtürme bis auf die noch genauer zu besprechenden Ergänzungen und die ersten (östlichen) quadratischen Pfeiler des Mittelschiffs, die auf die Vierungspfeiler folgen.

Ergänzen lässt sich dieser Torso zunächst ohne Schwierigkeit durch die einstige (vorhanden gewesene) *Hauptapsis*. Sie schliesst an das Chorrechteck genau über der erhaltenen Apsis der Krypta an.

Symmetrisch zu der bereits erwähnten Lisene des Nordarms steigt auch am Südarm eine Lisene hoch, bricht ab, und wird durch eine in die Mittel- achse gerückte neue Lisene fortgesetzt, oder, besser gesagt, ersetzt. Also auch der Südarm sollte eine Flachdecke erhalten, mithin vermutlich auch die Vierung. Flachgedeckt sollte also das ganze *Querhaus* werden. Die Vierung war gewiss ausgeschieden, also durch Rundbogengurten gegen die vier Nachbarräume abgetrennt. Die Vierungspfeiler sind deshalb vermutlich anfangs als Kreuz- pfeiler entworfen worden.

Ob der *Chorarm* gewölbt werden sollte, ist ungewiss. Man kann die Anlage der Osttürme als Gewölbewiderlager deuten. Die jetzigen Vorlagen und Dienste am Chorbogen (die nicht nachträglich vorgesetzt scheinen), könnten sehr wohl auch bei der Absicht einer Flachdecke des Chores errichtet worden sein. Wahr- scheinlicher aber ist die Annahme, dass sie im ersten *Entwurf* fehlten. Ich zeichne deshalb in der Vierung Kreuzpfeiler.

Im *Langhaus* ist das östliche Doppeljoch ziemlich eindeutig in derjenigen Form erhalten, wie sie der Flachdeck-entwurf vorsah. Die quadratischen Pfeiler lassen einen minor chorus, wie er in der Hirsauer Bauschule heimisch war, erraten, d.h. das östliche Joch gehörte liturgisch noch zum Chorbereich, das folgende zur Gemeindekirche. Über der Deckplatte des Pfeilers steigt eine Lisene bis zur Sohlbanklinie der Fenster; das durchgezogene Gesimse — jetzt das Kämpfergesimse der Gewölbe — verkröpft sich über der Lisene. Es ist anzunehmen, dass das Gesimse ebenso wie die Lisene vom Meister des Flachdeck- entwurfs ausgeführt wurde. Dass dieser Meister hier bis zur Höhe der Decke gelangte, sieht man aussen auf der Westwand des Südarms aus der Verzahnung, die vom Hauptgesimse zum Seitenschiffdach herabsteigt und sich bis zur abge- brochenen Lisene (neben der Seitenschiffmündung) fortsetzt.

Die quadratischen *Pfeiler* sind mit Eckdiensten ausgestattet. Auf den Kapi- tälen dieser Eckdienste finden sich am südlichen Pfeiler skizzenhaft vorgeritzte, unausgeführt gebliebene dekorative Plastiken; es sind deutliche Beweise, dass diese Meisselarbeit erst "après la pose" ausgeführt werden sollte; sie verweist auf einen älteren Meister, als den der übrigen Kapitälornamentik von Naum-

---

des Naumburger Doms u. der anliegenden Baulichkeiten (Naumburg, 1904). Leider hat Lüttich keine Zeichnung seiner Rekonstruktionsvorstellung gegeben und gemeint, seine übertrieben genauen Massangaben reichten aus. Er gibt stellenweise Messungen bis auf Millimeter, aber sein Text ist unübersichtlich und ermüdend; vermutlich haben ihn die meisten, die sich mit Naumburg abgaben, nicht zu Ende gelesen.

FIG. 1. NAUMBURGER DOM.   ECKE DES NORDQUERARMS UND DES LANGHAUSES

burg. Der Wechsel des Architekten hatte wohl auch den des Steinmetzen, der
die Schmuckteile zu bearbeiten begonnen hatte, zur Folge.

Von diesen Pfeilern des minor chorus steigen die je beiden *Arkadenbogen* auf
(Fig. 2). Die erhalten gebliebenen Bogenanfänge ergeben in ihrer Fortsetzung
Halbkreise. (Bergner, S. 48.) Da auch die Gurtbogen, die von diesem Pfeiler
aus die Seitenschiffe in Joche zerlegen, anders ansetzen, als nachher der Wölbungsmeister sie brauchen konnte, ergaben sich auch hier Knickungen, die stets
das Kopfschütteln der Architekturkritiker erregt haben. Es ist durchaus möglich,
dass schon der Flachdeckmeister im Seitenschiff gratige Kreuzgewölbe oder
wenigstens jochtrennende Gurtbogen (vielleicht nur an dieser Stelle zur Abgrenzung des minor chorus) beabsichtigte, aber zwingend ist diese Annahme nicht.
Ich rekonstruiere daher Flachdecken für die Seitenschiffe. Für die übrigen
Stützen des Langhauses kann man sowohl Pfeiler als Säulen annehmen. Ich
rekonstruiere *Säulen*, entsprechend den Hirsauer Vorbildern. Die Zahl der
Joche war dieselbe wie jetzt. Das ergibt sich aus den Lisenenansätzen, die auf
der Aussenwand des nördlichen Seitenschiffes stehen geblieben sind. Hier
erkennt man auch, wie hoch die Mauer über den Boden gediehen war, als man
zur Wölbung überging. (Fig. 1.) Der Wölbungsmeister begann auf dieser Seite
einen Kreuzgang anzulegen, auf dessen mehrfache, in der Literatur besprochene
Eigenheiten ich nicht einzugehen habe, da ich mich auf den Flachdeck-Entwurf beschränken will. Aber mit den Gewölbeausteilungen des Kreuzganges
waren die Lisenen nicht mehr vereinbar.

Bei der zeichnerischen Rekonstruktion der Lisenen und ihrer wohl mit zu
ergänzenden Rundbogenfriese rücken die Fenster beträchtlich tiefer als sie
jetzt liegen. Ihre jetzige auffallend hohe Lage ergab sich aus dem Zwang, sie
über den First des Kreuzgangpultdachs zu rücken.

Die sich aufdrängende Frage, ob auch im Obergaden Lisenen beabsichtigt
waren, bejahe ich, weil im Dachraum des nördlichen Seitenschiffes ein Lisenen-
ansatz vorhanden ist, der vermutlich sich über dem Dach fortsetzen sollte. Er
liegt an der Grenze zwischen dem vierten und fünften Seitenschiffjoch (von
Westen her gezählt). Jetzt mündet auf ihn die Strebemauer des Wölbmeisters,
und der Durchgangsbogen der Strebemauer stützt sich auf die "Wandlisene,"
— nur stimmen hier auffallender Weise die Masse nicht zusammen: Stütze und
Bogen sind gegeneinander verschoben. Eben deshalb meine ich, dass die Stütze
schon ausgeführt war, ehe jemand an Strebewerk denken konnte. Neben dieser
Stelle trennt eine schon von Bergner beobachtete Baunaht das östliche Doppeljoch vom folgenden. Dieses östliche Doppeljoch (mit dem quadratischen Pfeiler
innen) stammt teilweise vom Flachdeckmeister,[3] mithin wohl auch die Lisene

---

[3] Da die spitzen Arkadenbogen vom Wölbmeister herrühren, kann man gewiss auch annehmen, dass
der Flachdeckmeister über den Bogenanfänger des Arkadenbogens gar nicht hinauskam. Aber "technisch"
ist durchaus möglich, dass die innere Lisene und entsprechend der Wandteil über den anderen Pfeilern
dieses Doppeljoches schon vom Flachdeckmeister hochgeführt waren. Man könnte erwägen, ob mit diesem
Einbau der Spitzbogenarkade sich die sonderbaren (spitzen) Entlastungsbogen erklären lassen, die sicher
auch erst vom Wölbmeister angeordnet wurden. (Die halbkreisförmigen Entlastungsbogen, deren Scheitel
in den Pultdachräumen der Seitenschiffe sichtbar sind, liegen höher und haben grössere Spannweite.)

im Dachraum. Ich rekonstruire danach Lisenen im Obergaden aussen an den Grenzen der Doppeljoche.

Für die Rekonstruktion des Langhauses ist die *Höhenlage* der Flachdecke durch die Höhe des jetzigen Hauptgesimses ziemlich genau bestimmt, sie ergibt sich ausserdem durch Eintragung des gleichseitigen Dreiecks über der gesamten

Staatliche Bildstelle, Berlin

FIG. 2. NAUMBURGER DOM. QUADRATISCHER
PFEILER IM LANGHAUS, VON
NORDOSTEN GESEHEN

lichten Breite für das Hauptschiff, und zugleich für die Seitenschiffe. Die Fenster des Seitenschiffes waren wenigstens im östlichen Joch etwas anders gedacht, was daraus hervorgeht, dass aussen die erste (östliche) Lisene des nördlichen Seitenschiffes, die bis zum Gesimse durchgeführt ist, das Fenster etwas überschneidet. Ich rekonstruiere deshalb in diesem Joch der Seitenschiffe nur *ein* Fenster.

Für den Flachdeckmeister ist charakteristisch, dass er meist den *Halbkreis-bogen* anwandte. Im Ostchorarm ist innen das nördliche (linke) Portal, das zur

Turmtreppe führt, rundbogig, das südliche dagegen spitzbogig. Die Kapitäl-ornamentik ist für die stilistische Scheidung der Architekturteile selbst nicht verbindlich, da — wie gesagt — die Gewohnheit, "après la pose" die Ausmeis-selung durchzuführen, in Naumburg vielfach überzeugend belegbar ist. So sind auch an den Kapitälen der späteren Mittelschiffpfeiler die plastischen Dekora-tionen unfertig geblieben.

Man kann aber, auch abgesehen von der erst nachträglich ausgeführten Kapitälornamentik, nicht sicher sagen, dass der ältere Meister niemals den Spitzbogen zuliess. Umgekehrt hat ja auch der Wölbungsmeister bei den Fenstern des Langhauses an der Halbkreisform festgehalten, obwohl er für die Langhaus-Arkaden, für das Hauptportal am Südarm und die Gurtbogen der Gewölbe den Spitzbogen einführte.

Im Westen schloss der Flachdeck-entwurf mit den auseinandergerückten Westtürmen (Fig. 3) und der dazwischen liegenden *Vorhalle*, die Bergner eben-falls schon angenommen hat (S. 55): "Der Zwischenraum (sc. der Westtürme) von 16.60 m würde eine stattliche Vorhalle nach Art einiger Kölner oder der Speirer zulassen. Gewiss stammt auch diese Disposition vom Udonischen Bau." Ob letzteres gar so gewiss sei, ist noch zu überlegen. Vorläufig handelt es sich um die Frage, wie diese Vorhalle ausgesehen hat oder aussehen sollte. Dass sie begonnen worden ist, geht nach allgemeiner Überzeugung aus den Abbruch-spuren der östlichen Vorhallenwand hervor, die man in den Zwischengängen je zwischen Turm und Westchor sieht. Da Bergner sich als erster mit der Frage befasste, ist es das Gerechteste, ihn hier wörtlich zu zitieren. Er sagt im An-schluss an den oben abgedruckten Satz: "Denn weder der romanische Meister, noch der Gotiker des Westchors haben sich in die weiten Verhältnisse zu finden gewusst. Der erstere hat die Innenmauern der Türme durch eine Quermauer verbunden, deren Abbruchspuren gleich neben den Eingängen sichtbar sind, der zweite hat dunkle Gänge liegen lassen, welche zwischen Chor und Türmen zu den westlichen Spindeltreppen führen. Dass die Mauer des Nordturmes nach Osten schmäler wird, bleibt auch damit unerklärt. Hierzu kommt die vielbe-sprochene, aber nie erklärte Erscheinung, dass an den inneren Westecken zwei Lisenen ohne Verband selbst im Sockel neben einander hochsteigen, die ur-sprüngliche innere nur bis zum Ende des zweiten Geschosses am roh gearbeiteten Mauerwerk kenntlich, wo sie in einer Schräge an die äussere anfällt. Da das innere Mauerwerk davon garnicht berührt wird, vielmehr die äussere Lisene ganz richtig die Ecke des Turmes bezeichnet, so ist die Annahme hinfällig, als seien die Türme schmäler geplant gewesen. Es muss vielmehr zur Zeit der Grundlegung die Absicht bestanden haben, in der Flucht der inneren Turm-mauern nach Westen weiter zu bauen. Wir haben uns also an Stelle der Lisene eine herausstehende Verzahnung zu denken, welche vielleicht erst beim Beginn des Chorbaues abgehauen, mit Quadern verblendet und mit dem durchgehen-den Sockel versehen wurde, wie er den Westchor umzieht."

Von einer solchen Verzahnung ist nichts nachgewiesen. Aber aus statischen und aesthetischen Gründen ist es sehr wahrscheinlich, dass die beabsichtigte

FIG. 3. NAUMBURGER DOM. NORDWESTTURM
VON WESTEN GESEHEN

Vorhalle — im Entwurf — ein wenig vor die Westflucht der Türme vorgezogen war. Nur dann wird die äussere Lisene (Fig. 3) — "äussere" von der Mittelachse des Domes her gesehen — verständlich.[4] Unter Zurückstellung der genauen Untersuchung dieser Baufuge kann die Vorhalle rekonstruiert werden. Wahrscheinlich sollte sie unten durch drei Halbkreisbogen auf Pfeilern gegen den Freiraum sich öffnen und darüber eine Westempore erhalten, die sich nach innen gegen das Mittelschiff öffnete und in ihrer Westwand Fenster hatte. Von dieser Westempore sagt Memminger, der Bauleiter der Domrestaurierung von 1890: "Ein Zwillingskapitäl von Säulen dieser Sängerbühne wurde 1874 im Fussboden des Westchors gefunden."[5] Wie man beweisen will, dass dieses Kapitäl aus der Westempore stammt, ist mir unbekannt. Ebenso unbewiesen ist Memmingers Satz (l.c., Seite 7): "Den westlichen Kirchengiebel sollte eine grosse. . . . Fensterrose zieren, während zur Belichtung der Sängerbühne über der Vorhalle und für diese selbst mehrere kleine Doppelfenster — wie sie der Sängersaal der Wartburg hat — vorgesehen waren und wie sie die Obergeschosse der Osttürme haben." Aber er scheint sich auf eine Überlieferung zu stützen und darum mögen seine an sich nicht unwahrscheinlichen Angaben für die Rekonstruktion Verwendung finden. Die Absicht der Ausführung einer Westempore ergibt sich aus der Vorhallenhöhe von 9.65 m (gemessen von der Oberkante des Sockelgesimses aus). Wenigstens reicht bis zu dieser Höhe das alte Quaderwerk der Westtürme. Übrigens dürfte Memmingers Ausdruck Sängerbühne irrig sein, denn vermutlich dienten die Westemporen dem Adel.

Wer eine Westempore annimmt, muss auch eine Treppe zu ihr annehmen. Memminger dachte sich zwei Wendeltreppen in den "dunklen Gängen" (l.c. Seite 6) östlich gegenüber den jetzt vorhandenen gotischen. Er vergass, wie es scheint, dass diese "dunklen Gänge" erst bei der Anlage des Westchors entstanden, als man keine Westempore mehr zu versorgen hatte. Die jetzigen Wendeltreppen führen ausser zu der Triforiengalerie der Stifterfiguren und den seitlichen Emporen des ersten Chorjochs (in denen jetzt die Orgelprospekte stehen) zu den Obergeschossen der Türme, deren mit Halbkreis gedeckte Türen romanisch sind. Auch die Bestimmung der Turmräume als Kapellen stammt aus romanischer Zeit, sie haben Apsiden mit Altären auf der Ostseite. Also muss anfänglich mindestens *eine* Treppe in das Obergeschoss geführt haben. Schon Lüttich hat für dieselbe Stelle wie Memminger romanische Wendeltreppen angenommen und wenigstens rechnerisch nachgewiesen, dass sie an dieser Stelle gerade noch Platz hätten. Aber diese Rekonstruktion ist unwahrscheinlich, da die Treppen in den hinteren Ecken der Vorhalle schlechtes Licht gehabt hätten. — Auf der Suche nach der Lage der Treppe geriet ich auch auf die im westlichen Joch des südlichen Seitenschiffes gelegene Öffnung, deren Schwelle etwa 4.80 m über dem Fussboden des Schiffes liegt (Fig. 4). Diese Türe ist jetzt mit Brettern verschlossen. Sie führt in die Lehrerbibliothek des Gymnasiums und ist dort als Wandnische sichtbar und zur Einstellung eines

---

[4] Bergner nennt umgekehrt diese Lisene die "innere," er rechnet von der Turmachse her.
[5] K. Memminger, *800 Jahre Baugeschichte des Naumburger Domes* (Naumburg, 1920), S. 5 und 6.

FIG. 4. NAUMBURGER DOM. ERSTES WESTLICHES JOCH
DES SÜDLICHEN SEITENSCHIFFES

Bücherregals ausgenutzt. Mündlicher Überlieferung nach ging von hier eine
Holztreppe in das Schiff hinab. Aber ich vermute, dass diese Türe erst im 18.
Jahrhundert eingebrochen wurde, als man die hölzernen Emporen einzog, die
1874 wieder entfernt wurden.[6]

Als Zugang zum Obergeschoss des Südturmes und somit auch zur Westempore ist vielmehr die Türe zu betrachten, die — in gleicher Flucht mit den
anderen Turmtüren — jetzt aus einem Klassenzimmer des Gymnasiums herein
führt. Die Tatsache, dass der Rundbogen der Türe auf der Innenseite grösser
ist und auf der Aussenseite konzentrisch kleiner, ergibt nach dem Turminneren
eine andere Kopfhöhe, weshalb die Vermutung ausgesprochen wurde, dass hier
Stufen mündeten (Fritz Haesler). Spuren eines einstigen Treppenhauses sind
weder an dieser Südseite des Turmes weiter unten in der Durchfahrt, noch oben
im und über dem Dach zu sehen. Die alte Aufnahme Fig. 5 zeigt die Ecklisenen
(die auch im Kreuzgang sichtbar sind) in sehr brüchigem Zustand. Bergner
sah darin mit Recht die Einwirkung eines Brandes. Aber auch das Abschluss-
gesimse mit den übereck gestellten Konsolen hat diese durch Hitze entstehenden
rundlichen Verbildungen; 1890 wurden diese die Aussenansicht schädigen-
den Steine ersetzt, aber man sieht die Brandspuren heute noch im Seitenschiffdach in der unterhalb anschliessenden Mauerpartie. Der Brand muss also
erst in einer Zeit diese Ecke ergriffen haben, als die gesuchte romanische Treppe
längst durch die Wendeltreppen des Westchors überflüssig geworden war.
Vielleicht sind hier die Spuren des grossen Brandes von 1532 wiederzuerkennen.
Dass die Treppe nie begonnen worden sei, ist unwahrscheinlich; denn gewiss
wurden schon in der Zeit vor der Anlage des gotischen Westchors die Turm-
obergeschosse benutzt. Man könnte auch auf den Gedanken kommen, dass die
Treppe abseits in der südlichen Klausur lag und man durch deren Obergeschoss
hindurch die südliche Zugangstür des Turmobergeschosses erreichte, — wie
heute. Aber die südliche Klausur muss mehrere Jahre später entstanden sein
als die Westtürme, also bleibt nur die Anlage einer Treppe, die zu dieser Türe der
Südwand des Südwestturmes führte, übrig.

Ich trage die Türe in die Zeichnung in ihrer ungefähren Höhenlage ein.
(Es ist zu wünschen, dass Lüttichs genaue Aufnahmen ergänzt, oder, falls die
Ergänzungen bereits amtlich vorliegen, veröffentlicht werden.) Ein Treppen-
haus anzugliedern, kann ich mich nicht entschliessen, weil keinerlei Abbruch-
spuren auf der Südwand des Südwestturmes zu finden sind. Die Treppe dort
zu ergänzen, wo dies Lüttich vorschlug, ist deshalb so verlockend, weil die Abbruchspur (der Vorhallenrückwand) mancherlei Ergänzung gestattet.

Es ist ungewiss, wie der Meister des Flachdeck-entwurfs sich die obere Fortsetzung der Türme dachte. Alle, die sich bisher zu der Frage äusserten, nehmen
an, dass die ersten beiden Achteckgeschosse der Osttürme auf ihn zurückgehen.
Ich zeichne sie — soweit dies ohne genaue Bauaufnahmen möglich ist — ein.

---

[6] Vgl. Memminger, l.c., Seite 23: "Im nördlichen Querschiff gelangte man vermittels einer Holztreppe
zum Orgel- und Sängerchor." Dies muss ein zweiter Zugang gewesen sein, falls Memminger sich nicht
verschrieb und statt Querschiff Seitenschiff meinte.

FIG. 5. NAUMBURGER DOM. ANSICHT VON DER SÜDKLAUSUR HER. AUFNAHME
VOR DER RENOVIERUNG UND DER TURMERGÄNZUNG VON 1890

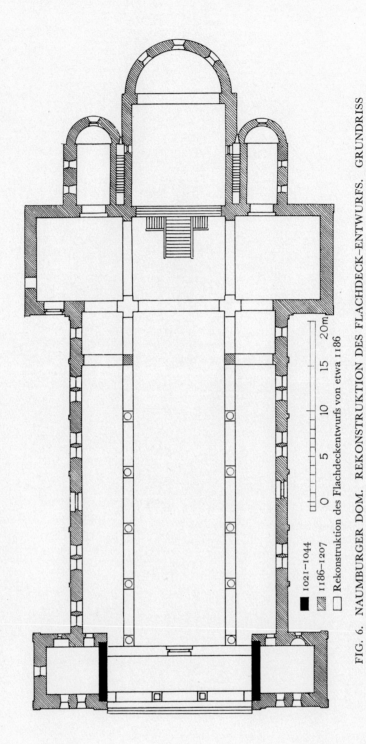

FIG. 6. NAUMBURGER DOM. REKONSTRUKTION DES FLACHDECK–ENTWURFS. GRUNDRISS

■ 1021–1044
▨ 1186–1207
□ Rekonstruktion des Flachdeckentwurfs von etwa 1186

0   5   10   15   20m

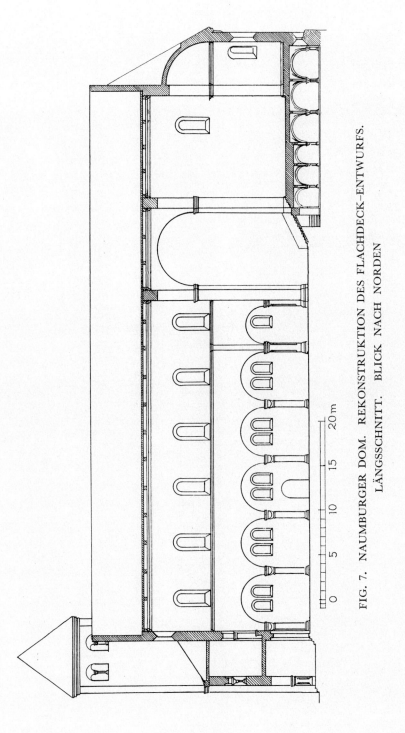

FIG. 7. NAUMBURGER DOM. REKONSTRUKTION DES FLACHDECK-ENTWURFS.
LÄNGSSCHNITT. BLICK NACH NORDEN

0   5   10   15   20 m

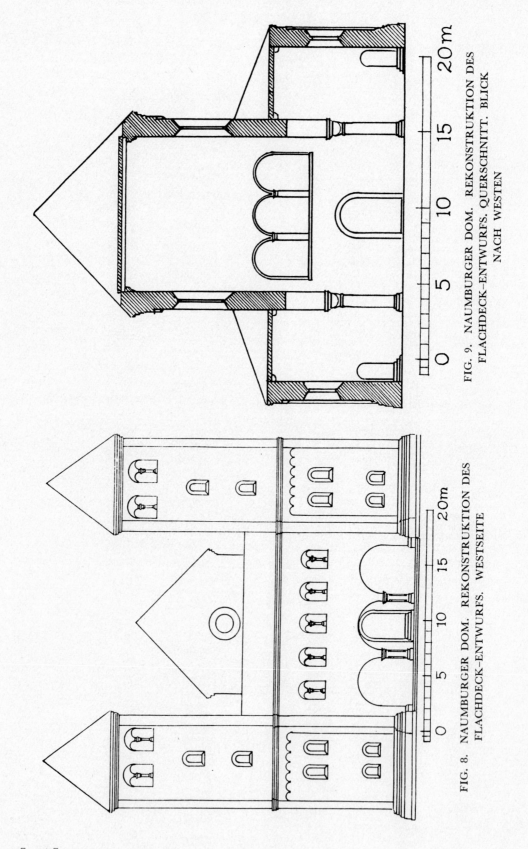

FIG. 9. NAUMBURGER DOM. REKONSTRUKTION DES FLACHDECK-ENTWURFS. QUERSCHNITT. BLICK NACH WESTEN

FIG. 8. NAUMBURGER DOM. REKONSTRUKTION DES FLACHDECK-ENTWURFS. WESTSEITE

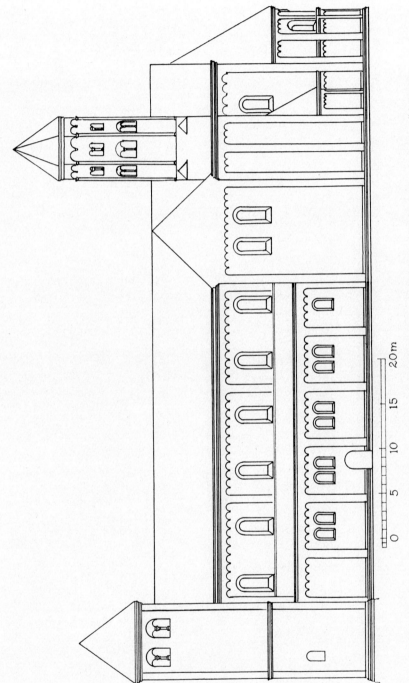

FIG. 10. NAUMBURGER DOM. REKONSTRUKTION DES FLACHDECK-ENTWURFS. SÜDSEITE

Die Westtürme sind vielleicht auch niedriger beabsichtigt gewesen, als sie später ausgeführt wurden. Den Nordwestturm setzte — von der Höhe von 9.65 m über Sockelkante — der Westchormeister auf. Er zog ein Gesimse in der Höhe seines Chorgesimses durch und führte das darauf folgende Achteckgeschoss mit seinen achteckigen Ecktürmchen auf. Wie seine Fortsetzung geplant war (anstelle der jetzigen aus dem 14. oder 15. Jahrhundert), gibt der Südturm, den Memminger 1874 entwarf und Werner nach 1890 ausführte, ungefähr richtig an. Für die Rekonstruktion der romanischen Turmendigungen hat man freie Hand. Meine Skizze ist ganz allgemein gehalten und unverbindlich. Nur, *dass* Türme beabsichtigt waren, ist festzuhalten. Dies dürfte aus der Stärke der Mauern mit Sicherheit zu folgern sein.

Für die Rekonstruktion der Krypta ist die jetzige Vorkrypta, die erst der Wölbmeister mitsamt der Vorziehung des Westchors in die Vierung und mitsamt dem Ostlettner anlegte, wegzustreichen. Die Spuren der einstigen Treppen zur Krypta sind erhalten. Bergner hat den Krypteneingang (S. 25 seines Buches) rekonstruiert. Die Mittelkrypta ist aus einem älteren Bauzustand in den Neubau übernommen worden.

Mit diesen Überlegungen ist die Flachdeckanlage in der Hauptsache so zu rekonstruieren, wie dies in den Fig. 6 bis 10 dargestellt ist.

II. Cefalù und Monreale

Cefalù (Fig. 11 bis 13) ist ziemlich aus einem Guss.[7] Unfertig blieb im Ostteil das Abschlussgesims. Die Obergeschosse der Westtürme sind in gotischer Zeit erneut, die Kreuzrippen-Gewölbe der Vorhalle sind vielleicht spätere Zutat und ihre Säulen sind im 15. Jahrhundert von Ambrogio da Como erneut. Die Datierung der zurückliegenden Teile der Westfassade soll durch eine Bauinschrift, die Johannes Panictera als Architekten nennt, für das Jahr 1240 gesichert sein.[8] Es ist nicht ganz klar, wie der Anteil dieses Meisters an der Westfassade genau abzugrenzen ist. Rippengewölbe in der Vorhalle wären an sich für eine normännische Arbeit von 1130 nichts Unmögliches, aber ich habe, als ich Cefalù vor Jahren sah, nicht auf ihre Form, vor allem ihre Rippenprofile geachtet. Die Rippengewölbe des Chores von Cefalù sind durch die mit ihnen verbundenen Mosaiken, die inschriftlich 1148 datiert sind, als Werke der Erbauungszeit festgelegt.

Der Hauptbestand des Domes von *Monreale* stammt von der Gründung durch Wilhelm II. von Sizilien im Jahre 1172. Eine Weihe fand schon 1176, dann nochmals 1182 statt, letztere durch Papst Lucius III. Auch Monreale ist ein sehr einheitlicher Bau. Nur die jetzige Loggia und die Vorhalle sind späte Zutaten. Die Vorhalle wurde erst im 18. Jahrhundert gebaut.[9] Der ursprüng-

---

[7] Ausführliche zeichnerische Aufnahmen und die historischen Nachrichten findet man bei Serradifalco (Domenico lo Faso Pietrasanta Duca di Serradifalco), *Del Duomo di Monreale e di altre chiese siculo-normane* (Palermo, 1838), Seite 29, Taf. XVIII–XXII.

[8] Rosario Salvo di Pietraganzili, *Cefalù* (Palermo, 1888), S. 125.

[9] Enrico Mauceri, *Monreale* (Milano, ohne Jahr — um 1930).

liche Zustand der Westfront ist unklar. Lello bildet in seinem Buch ein altes Siegel des Domes ab, das die Westfront darstellt.[10] Die Türme sind in ihrer West-flucht durch eine Mauer, die sich gegen die Türme nicht absetzt, nahtlos ver-bunden. Eine Mitteltüre führt in die geschlossene Vorhalle, und zwei obere kleine Fenster beweisen, dass der Zeichner des Siegels über der Vorhalle eine Westempore annahm. In der Mitte zwischen den Türmen erscheint eine grosse Kuppel, die nur als Vierungskuppel zu deuten ist. Wieviel an dieser Zeichnung vom ersten Zustand Kunde gibt, wieviel an ihr Phantasie oder Wunschbild ist, lässt sich kaum entscheiden. Meines Wissens hat die Vierungskuppel nie bestan-den. Ist dies der Fall, dann ist die Glaubwürdigkeit des Siegels auch für die übrigen Bauteile sehr herabgesetzt. Es ist also die Annahme, dass auch Mon-reale von Anfang an eine offene Westvorhalle hatte, nicht ohne Weiteres durch das Siegel zu widerlegen.

Monreale hat auf der Nordseite eine Loggia; sie spannt sich zwischen den Nordquerarm und den Turm der Fassade grundsätzlich ebenso wie in Naum-burg der beabsichtigte Flügel der Nordklausur sich gespannt hätte. Aber diese im ersten Augenblick verblüffende Ähnlichkeit zerfällt, sobald man hört, dass diese Loggia kein Kreuzgangflügel ist und erst um 1550 entstand (ausgeführt von den Söhnen des Antonello Gagini).

Was Naumburg mit Cefalù und Monreale gemein hat, lässt sich auf eine kurze Formel bringen. Alle drei Dome sind dreischiffige, ungewölbte Säulen-Basiliken mit Querhaus, Hauptchor, zwei Nebenchören, auseinandergerückten Westtürmen und dazwischen liegender Vorhalle.

Diese Gemeinsamkeiten erfahren eine Abschwächung, sobald man betont, dass die Säulen für Naumburg nur Hypothese sind und dass der negative Aus-druck "ungewölbt" in das Positive gewendet in Naumburg Flachdecke bedeutet, in den sizilianischen Bauten aber offenen Dachstuhl.

Hiermit sind die Unterschiede bekanntlich nicht erschöpft. Naumburg hat Osttürme, die in Cefalù und Monreale fehlen. In Monreale sind die Mauerstär-ken in den Nebenchören denen der Westtürme gleich, hier könnte man also die Absicht von Osttürmen verteidigen; ebenso sind die Mauerstärken von Cefalù ausreichend, um Osttürme zu errichten. Aber man kann dennoch nicht die Osttürme, weil sie möglich sind, in die Reihe der gemeinsamen Merkmale einschmuggeln. Cefalù hat eine rechteckige Vierung. Cefalù und Monreale haben keine Krypta, im Mittelschiff Spitzbogenarkaden (während Naumburg Rundbogenarkaden bekommen sollte), durchwegs andere Proportionen als Naumburg, Mosaiken, die einen unvergleichbar anderen Stimmungston erzeu-gen, aussen Blendzwerggalerien, sich kreuzende Rundbogenreihen, auf den Rundbogen Zickzackornament und schliesslich die südlich flachen Dächer. Cefalù hat ausserdem im Querschiff echt normännische Laufgänge innerhalb der Mauerstärke. Es ist in der Gesamtwirkung das "Ganze" so völlig anders als in Naumburg, dass die Gemeinsamkeiten für den lebendigen Anblick überhaupt

---

[10] Luigi Lello, *Historia della chiesa di Monreale* (Roma, 1596), S. 140 (nicht paginiert, gleich im Anfang des Anhangs).

nicht mitsprechen. Und so hat auch gewiss noch niemand in Cefalù und Monreale an Naumburg und niemand in Naumburg an Cefalù und Monreale
gedacht.

Immerhin sind beide sizilianischen Bauten für ihre südliche Gegend sehr
nordisch. Zimmermann hat auf den nordischen Einschlag nachdrücklich hingewiesen.[11] Er zählt als nordische Merkmale auf: die Rundbogenfriese, die
Zwerggalerie, die gezackten Bogen und die mit dem Kirchengebäude unmittelbar
verbundenen Türme, setzt aber hinzu: "Die Türme sind vor die Ecken des
Gebäudes getreten und hängen fast wie zufällig unmittelbar mit der Baumasse
zusammen. Man merkt aus dieser mehr nur andeutenden Verbindung deutlich
heraus, dass man bisher gewohnt war, die Türme frei neben der Kirche zu
sehen." Und Naumburg? muss man gegenüber dieser Deutung fragen. Aber
Zimmermann will nur das Nordische beider Bauten herausheben und hat damit
allerdings Recht. Noch energischer hat Hasak das Normännische betont, das
diese Normannenbauten in Sizilien mit englischen Bauten des 12. Jahrhunderts
verbindet;[12] er hält sich vor allem an die Gemeinsamkeiten der Schmuckformen,
verweist auf die gekreuzten Bogen (Christ church in Hants und das Kapitel-
haus in Bristol, aus denen er auch die Einführung der Spitzbogen ableitet).
Dies alles zugegeben, hätte Naumburg auch als Flachdeckbau nordischer gewirkt
als die "nordischen" Dome in Sizilien, die eben doch sehr viel Südliches und
Östliches in sich aufnahmen.

Aber da nun einmal gerade in der Stellung der Westtürme von Cefalù und
Monreale etwas Nordisches steckt, könnte man geneigter werden, eine unmittelbare Beeinflussung anzunehmen, wobei nur die Abhängigkeit des sächsischen
Baus von den normännischen Bauten in Sizilien in Frage käme, da sie unbedingt
älter sind — mindestens ist Cefalù, das 1130 begonnen wurde, wesentlich früher
als der Naumburger Flachdeck-entwurf, der bestenfalls, d.h. wenn man ihn sehr
früh — mit Bergner in die Zeit Udos II. (1161-1186) — datieren wollte, ein
Zeitgenosse des Doms von Monreale würde.

Für eine solche Abhängigkeit lässt sich keinerlei historische Überlieferung
beibringen. Nirgends bietet die Kirchengeschichte eine Berührung des Bistums
Naumburg mit Sizilien. Vermutlich war mancher Bischof vor oder nach seinem
Amtsantritt in Italien und im gelobten Land, sicher wissen wir, dass Bischof
Udo II (1161-1186) im Jahre 1162 in Pavia und Turin war, 1174 in Roveredo,
1179 in Rom, dass Bischof Berthold II (1186-1206) am 3. Janur 1197 seine Wal-
fahrt nach Palästina antrat und um Jakobi (25. Juli?) 1198 heimkam,[13] gewiss
ist mancher Architekt, besonders wenn er zugleich Geistlicher war, weit herum-
gekommen und auch die Laienarchitekten zogen die grossen Strassen der Wal-
fahrten, die Kingsley Porter als Verbindungsnetz der Kunstgeographie entdeckte,
aber das ergibt für Naumburg nur vage Vermutungen. Andererseits ist die

[11] Max Georg Zimmermann, *Sizilien* (Leipzig, 1905), Bd. II, S. 74.
[12] Hasak, *Die normännische Baukunst* (Die Denkmalpflege: Berlin, 1915), Bd. XVII. Ergänzende Beispiele findet man bei Francis Bond, *An Introduction to English Church Architecture* (Oxford, 1913), in Band 1
passim.
[13] C. P. Lepsius, *Geschichte der Bischöfe des Hochstifts Naumburg* (Naumburg, 1846).

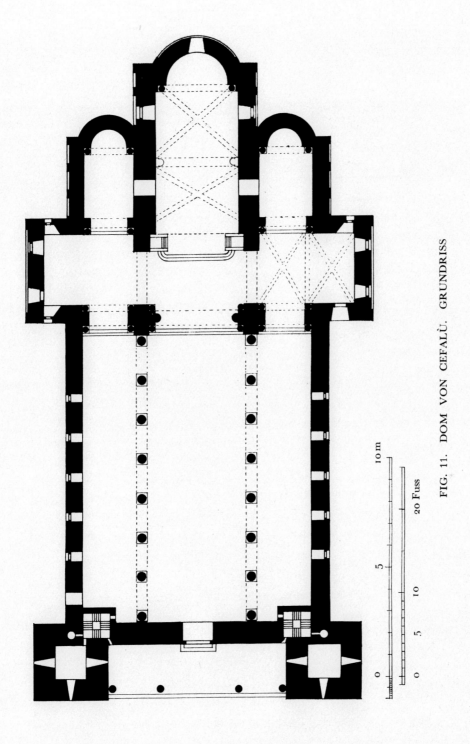

FIG. 11. DOM VON CEFALÙ. GRUNDRISS

FIG. 12. DOM VON CEFALÙ. WESTANSICHT

FIG. 13. DOM VON CEFALÙ. NORDANSICHT

schriftliche Überlieferung so lückenhaft, dass jeder Kunsthistoriker ein Recht hat, sich auf die Sprache der Steine zu berufen; und Alois Riegl hat den Grundsatz ausgesprochen, in der Kunst werde nichts zweimal erfunden, d.h. wenn es wiederkehrt, dann ist es als abhängig von der ersten Erfindung anzusehen.

Hinter der Frage, ob Naumburg von Cefalù (und Monreale) abhängig sei, steht also eine sehr umfassende methodische Frage grundsätzlicher Art.

III. Die Erklärung der Vertikalfugen in den Naumburger Westtürmen

Die sonderbare Fuge, die schon am Erdboden beginnt und den ganzen Sockel vertikal durchschneidet, steigt bis 9.65 m über Oberkante des Sockelgesimses gemessen hoch. Das ist die Höhe der ursprünglich beabsichtigten Vorhalle mitsamt ihrem Obergeschoss. Bis hierhin haben die Türme auf den freiliegenden Aussenseiten einheitliches Quaderwerk, das sich deutlich von dem des (gotischen) Zwischenstücks unterscheidet (als "Zwischenstücke" bezeichne ich die Teile zwischen den Westtürmen und dem gotischen Westchor). Bereits Bergner und Lüttich, die ihre Forschungen gemeinsam anstellten, waren sich klar darüber, dass die Fuge nicht — wie man erwarten möchte — an der *äusseren* Turmecke liegt, sondern an der *inneren*, d.h. an der Ecke des Innenraums. Die Messung ergibt einwandfrei, dass die Fortsetzung der Fuge diese innere Raumecke der Turmkapellen trifft, dass also — wenn die Fuge wirklich durchgeht — die "vierte" Turmwand (das ist die nächst dem Westchor von Osten nach Westen streichende) von den drei anderen abgeschnitten würde. Und, *dass* die Fuge wirklich durchgeht, ist im Nordwestturm im Obergeschoss feststellbar: sowohl an der Südwestecke, wie an der Südostecke. Bergner hat in seiner Grundrisszeichnung (l.c., S. 32) diese Wand von den drei übrigen Turmwänden nicht durch andere Schraffur abgetrennt und sich überhaupt nicht ausführlicher dazu geäussert, als in der oben S. 508 zitierten Stelle enthalten ist. Lüttich sagt: "Es scheint, als ob der Meister hier zunächst die an den Innenraum der Kirche stossenden Wände errichtete und erst nach einiger Zeit die anderen Wände hinzufügte." (l.c., Seite 50.)

Ohne Kenntnis der Schriften von Bergner und Lüttich kam ich 1922 auf Grund der Fuge zu der Überzeugung, dass die "vierte" Turmwand zeitlich die erste sein müsse und garnicht als Turmwand gemeint war, sondern als äussere Seitenwand der Vorhalle. Diese These, die ich nicht geheim hielt, hat Giesau von mir übernommen und veröffentlicht.[14] Aber seine eigene Schlussfolgerung, "dass der Plan der Erbauung der beiden Westtürme von Anfang an verbunden war mit dem Plan der Errichtung eines Westchors" dürfte sich kaum aufrecht erhalten lassen. Die drei äusseren Turmwände stehen untereinander im Verband, die Ostwand steht mit der im rechten Winkel anstossenden Seitenschiffwand im Verband, deren Oberteil die Ansatzstücke der beabsichtigten Nordklausur enthält. Diese Ansatzstücke (Konsolen und Schildrippe) finden sich ebenso an der Turmostwand. Also müsste der Westchor schon zugleich

---

[14] Hermann Giesau, *Der Dom zu Naumburg* (Magdeburg, 1927), Deutsche Bauten, Bd. IX, S. 57.

mit dem Übergang zum Wölbausbau beschlossen worden sein. Für Giesau ist diese Annahme halbwegs möglich, weil er den Baubeginn, sogar des Flachdeckbaus, auf 1220 heruntersetzt.

Auch Lüttichs Satz ist nicht ganz annehmbar. Nach ihm müsste die westliche Abschlusswand des Seitenschiffs mit der Seitenwand der Vorhalle (der jetzigen "vierten" Turmwand) im Verband stehen. Dies ist nicht der Fall. Vielmehr ist die westliche Abschlusswand des Seitenschiffs von Anfang an als östliche Turmwand gemeint und steht mit der anstossenden nördlichen in Verband.

Man muss also in der Tat anerkennen, dass die beiden Seitenwände der Westvorhalle durch Fugen vollständig von den Türmen losgelöst sind. Sie haben eine geringere Mauerdicke als die Turmwände, was man nur dann verständlich und entschuldbar findet, wenn sie älter als die Türme und nicht als Turmwände gedacht sind. Nur bei dieser Zeitfolge wird auch die auf der Westseite sogar durch den Sockel durchgehende Fuge erklärbar. Eine abgearbeitete Verzahnung zu erfinden (Bergner), ist überflüssig.

Eine Fortsetzung der Vorhallenseitenwand nach Westen, wie sie Bergner erwog, führte zu der Frage, ob Fundamente dafür gelegt worden sind. Lüttich hat zwar nicht nachgegraben (was das Einfachere gewesen wäre), aber er hat durch Bohrungen feststellen lassen, dass Fundamente nicht vorhanden sind. (l.c., Seite 42.)

An dieser Stelle A (in der schematischen Skizze Fig. 14) stösst an der Fuge zweierlei Quaderwerk zusammen. Am Nordwestturm hängt das Mauerwerk links der Fuge (nördlich) mit dem romanischen der Turmseiten bis zur Seitenschiffmauer zusammen, während das Mauerwerk der Lisene rechts der Fuge (südlich) mit dem Zwischenstück und dieses wieder mit dem gotischen Westchor in regelrechtem Verband steht. Also auch die rechts der Fuge aufgehende Lisene stammt vom gotischen Meister. Von ihm stammt auch die Wendeltreppe bis auf die oberste Fortsetzung, die aus unbestimmbarer späterer Zeit herrührt (aber nicht erst aus der Renovierungsperiode des 19. Jahrhunderts). Die westliche (gotische) Eingangstüre zur Wendeltreppe hat geraden Sturz, weil die Treppendrehung einem Spitzbogen nicht Platz bot. Dagegen sind die nach innen führende Türe und ebenso die schmalen Fenster des Zwischenstücks spitzbogig bis auf das oberste, kreisförmige Fenster. Die Treppe hat anfangs weniger hoch geführt, weil zwischen Turm und Westchor ein Freiraum blieb. Daher setzt sich das Kranzgesims des Westchors jetzt unter Dach fort. Es ist nur dort, wo die Wendeltreppe fortgesetzt wurde, die Deckplatte abgenommen worden, weil sie den Raum zu sehr verengt hätte. Man steht, hier oben angelangt, auf dem spitzbogigen Tonnengewölbe, das den Emporenraum deckt, der jetzt die Orgelpfeifen enthält; das Zwischenstück ist also nur im Erdgeschoss ein "dunkler Gang" (jetzt künstlich beleuchtet), in seinem Obergeschoss aber zum Innenraum des Westchors gezogen. Dort oben auf dem von Nord nach Süd streichenden Gewölbescheitel sieht man auf dem anderen (östlichen) Ast des Tonnengewölbes drei Stufen, die vielleicht nur als Auflager des Daches dienten, das im ersten Zustand als Satteldach zwischen Turm und Westchor, entsprechend dem Gewölbe, mit First von Nord nach Süd zu denken ist.

Das Westende A der Wand A D wird durch die Wendeltreppe verdeckt, also just die Stelle, die wir für die Rekonstruktion der Vorhalle kennen möchten.

Im Punkt B steht die Wand B C selbstverständlich mit der Wand A B im Verband. Sie ist Bestandteil des gotischen Westchors.

Im Punkt C stösst die Wand im Osten an die Rückseite des letzten romanischen Langhauspfeilers. Dies hat Lüttich schon erkannt und Bergner anerkannt und in seinem Grundriss durch die Schraffur eingetragen. Der Langhauspfeiler in C hat, wie nach Osten, so auch Vorlage und Dienst nach Süden zu. Der untere Teil ist auf der Südseite vom gotischen Lettner verdeckt, aber die Abgrenzung ist hier nicht fraglich. Strittig scheint dagegen die Zugehörigkeit des Wandstückes C D. Die Türe, die hier vom Seitenschiff in das Zwischenstück führt, ist nach Proportion, Profilierung und Spitzbogen gotisch. Es wäre an sich denkbar, dass die Wand ebenfalls gotisch ist und nur der Pfeiler in der Ecke C selbst romanisch (vom Wölbmeister). Diese Meinung hatte Lüttich. Er machte sich zwar klar, dass die Fortsetzung dieser Wand über das Seitenschiffdach hinaus von aussen her sichtbar ist, meinte aber, das Quaderwerk dieser Stelle sei gotisch. Alles, was ich bisher ausführte, gilt bis auf geringe Unterschiede [15] symmetrisch auch für den Südturm und das südliche Zwischenstück. Auf der Ostwand dieses südlichen Zwischenstücks sieht man aussen vom Südhof her ein rundbogiges Fenster (Fig. 5). Lüttich meinte, dies Fenster habe der gotische Meister angelegt und zur Anpassung an die Turmfenster rundbogig gemacht. Aber das ist ein Irrtum. Die Wand C′ D′ steht (analog der Wand C D) mit der anschliessenden Turmwand D′ F′ im Verband. Erst höher oben, wo die Wand viel später fortgesetzt wurde, um die Lücke zwischen Turm und Chor zu schliessen,[16] werden die Höhen der Steinschichten anders (vgl. den alten Zustand Fig. 5). Man kann im Pultdach des südlichen Seitenschiffes sich überzeugen, dass hier keine Fuge das Zwischenstück vom Turm trennt.[17] Eine Türe führt vom Pultdach in den Emporenraum des Zwischenstücks (wo jetzt die Orgelpfeifen auch auf der Südseite untergebracht sind). Man sieht die nämliche Türe von der Orgelempore her, allerdings hoch über deren Fussboden und darüber jenes rundbogige Fenster, das in letzter Zeit mit Holz verschlossen worden ist, weil es die Geistlichen, wenn sie sich am Altar stehend nach Osten wandten, blendete. Die Stücke CD und C′D′ sind also ebenso wie die ohne Unterbrechung ansetzenden Stücke

[15] Die obere Ergänzung der Wendeltreppe der Südseite, die von etwa 1890 stammt, ist innen und aussen etwas anders. Auf dem Tonnengewölbe des südlichen Zwischenstücks ist der östliche Teil durch Bretter zugedeckt, daher weiss ich nicht, ob auch hier Stufen liegen. In der südlichen Orgelempore sieht man von innen (vom Westchor) her ziemlich hoch in der Schildwand einen (durch Verputzen) undeutlichen Mauerabsatz, der vermutlich der alten Höhe der Wand A′ D′ entspricht.

[16] Diese hochgeführte Wand überschneidet jetzt den Rundbogenfries der Südaussenseite des Obergadens, — was längst bekannt ist.

[17] Im Pultdach sieht man einen Wandrücksprung von 22 cm genau an der Innenkante der Seitenschiffmauer, was man durch Messung feststellen kann. Der Rücksprung ist ebenso im Seitenschiff selbst durch Messung von Lüttich festgestellt worden. Diese Stelle ist aber nicht die Turmecke! Auf der entsprechenden Seite des Nordturms fehlt der Rücksprung sowohl im Raum des nördlichen Seitenschiffdaches, wie auf dem über das Dach aufsteigenden Mauerteil.

DF und D'F' romanisch, auch das Fenster des Zwischenstücks ist romanisch, muss aber ursprünglich für die Vorhalle bestimmt gewesen sein. Aber nicht für die Vorhalle des Flachdeckmeisters, denn die Rückwand dieser Vorhalle lag weiter westlich in den Punkten d und d'. Dies beweist, dass noch der Wölbmeister mit einer Vorhalle rechnete. Obwohl mir keine genauen Höhenmasse zur Verfügung stehen, glaube ich sicher zu erkennen, dass dieses — jetzt zwecklose — Fenster seiner Höhenlage nach dem Raum im Pultdach der Westvorhalle entspricht; es sollte also diesen von Osten her ausgibig erhellen.

Die Abbruchspur im Punkt d (Fig. 14) zeigt, dass die abgebrochene Vorhallenrückwand mit ihrer östlichen Seite die westliche Seite der Wand C D berührt hätte, ausserdem lässt sie erkennen, dass die romanische Mauer A D (die mit der Vorhallenrückwand d d' in Verband stand) noch ein Stück hinter der östlichen Flucht der Vorhallenrückwand nach Osten weiter ging (Fig. 15). Wie weit sie ging, lässt sich ohne Eingriff in das Mauerwerk nicht genau entscheiden. Aber sie geht nicht bis zur Innenwandfläche des Seitenschiffs durch, hört also in der Mauer C D auf.

Ebenso muss das westliche Ende A der romanischen Mauer A D unsicher bleiben. Die Mauer geht hier über den Eckpunkt des Turminnenraumes hinaus nach Westen weiter, erscheint aber nicht mit ihrer Flanke an der Westseite, da hier die gotische Lisene des Westchormeisters vorgesetzt ist. Sie endet also innerhalb jener Strecke, die der Mauerdicke der Turmwand A G entspricht, und zwar etwa in der Mitte dieser Mauerdicke von A G. Der romanische Teil der Mauer zwischen den Punkten A und D hat nicht gleichmässige Stärke, die Mauer wird nach Osten zu keilförmig dünner, wofür ich keine Erklärung finde. Die entsprechende Mauer der Südseite zwischen A' und D' dagegen ist von gleichbleibender Stärke. Mit diesem Rundgang von A über B C D d nach A zurück ist die Zusammengehörigkeit wie die Nichtzusammengehörigkeit der einzelnen Mauerstücke geklärt; entsprechend die der Südseite.

Nach Ablösung des gotischen Mauerwerks und desjenigen romanischen, das mit den Mauern A D und A' D' nicht im Verband steht (Fig. 15), bleiben drei Mauern übrig, die untereinander im Verband standen. Die Fuge ist dadurch erklärt, dass man beim Bau der Westtürme diese drei Mauern vorfand und wieder verwenden wollte.

Da die Westtürme zum Entwurf des Flachdeckmeister gehören, müssen die drei Mauern, die ich kurz "Vorhallenmauern" nennen will, damals schon vorhanden gewesen sein, und da sie erhalten wurden, obwohl ein so grosser Bau durch Abreissen und Wiederaufrichten der Mauern kaum beträchtlich wäre verzögert worden, muss dafür ein liturgischer Grund mitgesprochen haben. (Man hat allerdings nachher die Verbindungsmauer d d' doch noch abgebrochen.) Die Hauptfrage, die sich nunmehr einstellt, ist die nach dem Alter und der ursprünglichen Bedeutung der drei Vorhallenmauern.

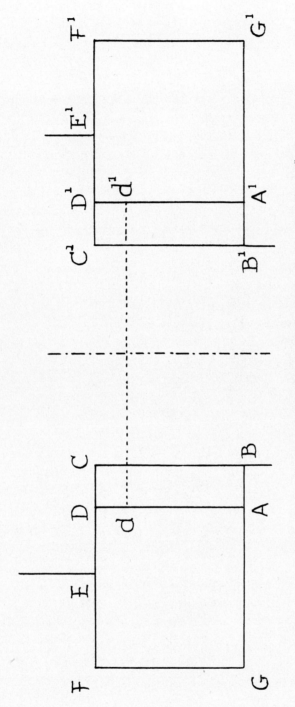

FIG. 14. NAUMBURGER DOM. GRUNDRISS-SCHEMA DER WESTTÜRME

IV. Die ältere Baugeschichte des Naumburger Domes

"Bei den Erneuerungsarbeiten 1874–78 sind die Fundamente einer älteren Bischofskirche aufgegraben worden, welche verhältnismässig bescheidene Ausdehnung hatte." (Bergner, l.c., 20.) Es sind dies die Reste des aufgehenden Mauerwerks der einstigen Seitenschiffmauern und der Querarme. Bergner hat eine Rekonstruktion dieses ersten Domes von Naumburg gezeichnet und als Daten festgelegt: Gründung 1021, Erhebung zur Kathedrale 1028 (bei der Verlegung des Bischofssitzes von Zeitz nach Naumburg), Weihe 1044. Unsicher ist in

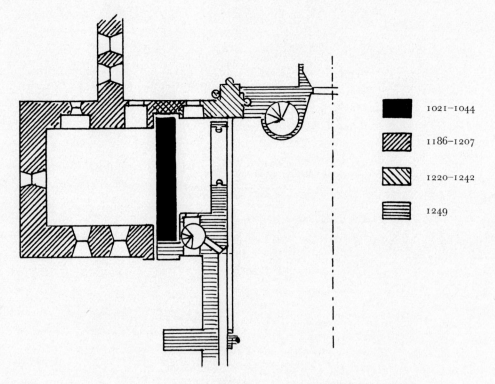

FIG. 15. NAUMBURGER DOM. GRUNDRISS DES NORDWESTTURMS UND DER
"ZWISCHENSTÜCKE"

Bergners Rekonstruktion vor allem die Westvorhalle (mit zwei Westtürmen?), die er nur geringfügig über die Seitenschiffmauern vorspringen lässt. Die Gesamtbreite des Langhauses betrug 16 m. Von diesem Bau sind nach Bergner in der heutigen Mittelkrypta noch die an den Seitenwänden entlanglaufenden, steinernen, bankartigen oder sockelartigen Gebilde von 37 cm Breite und 40 cm Höhe sichtbar; es sind die zu Tage tretenden Reste der einstigen Kryptawände.

Aus einer *zweiten* Bauperiode stammt diese heutige Mittelkrypta. Bergner sagt: dem Bischof Udo I (1124–1148) wird "freilich ohne urkundliche Belege, der Neubau des Domes, von dem noch die mittlere Krypta erhalten ist, zugeschrieben" (l.c., Seite 9.) Die Chorweihe von 1144 bezog er auf den Bau, zu dem die Krypta gehörte; Udo habe 1125 sofort mit Regierungsbeginn den Neubau mit Errichtung der Krypta begonnen (l.c., Seite 26.) und um 1130 ihn durch den Bau von Chor und Vierung fortgesetzt. Danach wäre die Mittelkrypta 1125–1130 zu datieren. Giesau dagegen — um nur den letzten Bearbeiter zu nennen — verlegt sie in das dritte Viertel, oder auch in das letzte Drittel des zwölften Jahrhunderts,[18] ohne diese Spanne von 50 Jahren näher zu begründen. Sein sonst empfehlenswertes Buch ist als Führer für Laien gedacht und bietet nicht Raum für ausführlichere Untersuchungen. Ich möchte mich zwar hier, wo es für den Gedankengang auf die genaue Datierung der Mittelkrypta nicht ankommt, in dieser schwierigen Frage nicht festlegen, muss aber bekennen, dass mir gegen Bergners Datierung wenig Durchschlagendes einwendbar scheint. Als Beispiele der Ornamentik von Kapitälen sei etwa auf die der Krypta von Maria Laach verwiesen, die stilistisch der gleichen Stufe wie die der Naumburger Mittelkrypta angehören, und nach der Bauanalyse von Schippers eine längere Zeit (vielleicht seit 1110 "avant la pose") bereit lagen und um 1130 nach der Baupause eingesetzt wurden. Man kann auch auf die Kapitäle des Langhauses in Maria Laach sich berufen, die zwischen 1140 und 1156 entstanden.[19]

Naumburg bietet bequeme Gelegenheit, die Entwicklungstendenz von der romanischen zur gotischen dekorativen Plastik sich klar zu machen. Die Palmettenblätter der Kapitäle der Mittelkrypta liegen in einer Reliefschicht von gleichbleibender Stärke; die der Vorkrypta und noch mehr die der Ostkrypta haben eine Reliefschicht von nach oben zunehmender Stärke, die Blätter liegen am Säulenhals an, biegen sich allmählich vor und entfernen sich vom kelchförmigen oder kelchwürfelförmigen Kapitälkern. Das Blattwerk des Westchors geht darin noch unvergleichlich weiter, der Kelchkern des Kapitäls ist konkav, die äussere Hüllfläche der Blattbüschel konvex, und jedes einzelne Blatt bekommt die Freiheit der Bewegung nach allen drei Raumdimensionen. Diese hochgotische Stufe, die aus Reims stammt, gibt den Hintergrund für den Vergleich der Kapitäle in der Mittelkrypta mit denen in der Ostkrypta. Sie sind noch hochaltertümlich streng in der Festhaltung der Reliefstärke, sie sind, gemessen an der zunehmenden Elastizität und Naturähnlichkeit, noch sehr starr (kristallomorph) und "naturfern," d.h. der Natur von Pflanzen fern; sie geben die "Idee" des Blattes und nicht wie im gotischen Westchor die individuelle Wirklichkeit bestimmter, botanisch benennbarer Pflanzen, aber auch nicht die zwar immer noch ideenhafte Blattform wie die Kapitäle der Ostkrypta, die immerhin schon das lebensvolle Wachstum der Blätter zur Anschauung bringt. Diese Hauptstufen der Entwicklung erlauben auch feinere Unterstufen zu unterscheiden. Die zweite Hälfte des 12. Jahrhunderts bringt meist eine Auflösung der Reliefkonstanz und die Zunahme der Relieftiefe mit entsprechendem Auskosten der Tiefenschatten, was in einem vermutlich frühen Beispiel in Schwarzrheindorf 1151 sich beobachten lässt. Aus diesen Überlegungen

---

[18] L.c., S. 106, unter der Abbildung steht: 3. Viertel, dagegen S. 49 letzte Zeile: letztes Drittel.
[19] Adalbert Schippers, *Das Laacher Münster* (Köln, 1927), S. 21 u. 22.

heraus halte ich die Entstehung auch der Kapitäle, also der ganzen Mittelkrypta, in der Zeit vor 1150, genauer um 1130 für durchaus möglich.

Die *dritte* Bauperiode ist die des Flachdeck-entwurfs. Lüttich und Bergner verlegen sie in die Zeit Udo II 1161–1186 (in dieselbe Zeit etwa, in der Giesau die Mittelkrypta entstanden denkt). Giesau dagegen erst in die Zeit des Bischof Engelhardt (1207–1242), der aber kaum vor 1220 den Bau begonnen habe. Eine zeitliche Trennung des Flachdeckbaus vom Entschluss, zur Wölbung überzugehen, finde ich bei Giesau nicht. Man kann aber die dritte Bauperiode bis zu einem gewissen Grade von der vierten her abgrenzen.

Diese *vierte* Bauperiode, die Zeit des Wölbmeisters, dürfte um 1220 beginnen. Alles was als rheinisch und teilweise als westfälisch erkannt worden ist, gehört in diese Zeit: also die begonnene Nordklausur, die südliche Vorhalle zugleich mit der Verlegung des Hauptportals von der Westvorhalle, für die ein Haupteingang wohl gedacht war, in den Südquerarm, die Wölbung des Ostchors und fortschreitend nach Westen die Aufführung und Wölbung der anderen Joche, soweit nicht schon der gotische Meister (im letzten Mittelschiffjoch) eingriff. Diese grösstenteils geklärten Fragen des Fortschreitens der Bauausführung von Osten nach Westen brauchen hier nicht verfolgt zu werden. Lüttich hat die Grenzen, wie weit der Flachdeckmeister kam, mit ungewöhnlichem Eifer gesucht, mit Scharfblick wohl auch gefunden, worüber zu referieren oder was gar zu kritisieren ich mich enthalte.[20] Der Wölbbau wurde nach Engelhardts Tod, aber noch in seinem Todesjahr 1242 geweiht.[21] Er war damals fertig bis auf das Gewölbe des westlichen Mittelschiffjochs; die Westtürme erreichten die Höhe der Vorhalle (9.65 m über Sockeloberkante), die Vorhalle blieb unausgeführt. Für den Baubetrieb war dies selbstverständlich, weil man die Westseite erst schliessen konnte, wenn das letzte Joch fertig gewölbt war. Man brauchte einen Zugang für Gerüstmaterial usw.

Wenn der Meister des Wölbbaus erst um 1220 den Bau übernahm und Engelhardt, durch die politische Lage behindert, kaum vorher an eine Bautätigkeit denken konnte (Giesau), muss der Beginn des Flachdeckbaus mindestens in die Zeit seines Vorgängers Berthold II verlegt werden. Und wenn er bis zu seiner erzwungenen Resignation bereits sehr weit gediehen war, und die letzte Regierungszeit durch das Zerwürfnis mit dem Papst für den Baufortgang vielleicht ebenfalls ungünstig war, muss der Baubeginn mindestens auf die Anfangsjahre der Regierung Berthold II angesetzt werden, also seit 1186. Weiter zurückzugehen sehe ich keinen Grund. Im Gegenteil. Wenn der Bau unter Udo II, 1161–1186 (Bergners und Lüttichs Annahme) wäre begonnen worden, müsste er so lange unterbrochen gewesen sein, dass man wie bei manchem anderen mittelalterlichen Bau durch die Korrosion der ungeschützt dem Wetter preisgegebenen Steinlagen die erreichte Höhe viel leichter sehen würde, als es der Fall ist.

[20] Lüttich unterscheidet drei Bauperioden (abgesehen vom Gründungsbau und der Mittelkrypta): der Flachdeckbau vollzieht sich, soweit er kam, unter Udo II 1161–1186 und den Wölbbau zerlegt er in zwei Phasen, die eine unter Berthold 1186–1206, die andere unter Engelhardt 1207–1242.

[21] Walter Greischel, *Die sächsisch-thüringischen Lettner des 13. Jahrhunderts* (Magdeburg, 1914), Anmerkung 1 auf Seite 81. Der Weihbischof weihte den Bau am 29. Juni 1242.

Die Baupause von etwa 1207 bis etwa 1220 war zu kurz, um die Grenze des Flachdeckbaus durch Verwitterung einzuzeichnen.

Eine gewisse Unterstützung, sich die Zwischenzeit vom Bau der Mittelkrypta und der dazugehörigen Ostteile unter Udo I (der als Gründer des Neubaus gilt) bis zu Berthold II vorzustellen, gibt die Nachricht, dass Udos I. Nachfolger: Bischof Wichmann (1150–1154), der nachmalige Erzbischof von Magdeburg, einen Zoll vom Naumburger Markt und einen Zins von 30 Solidi zur Erhaltung der Domdächer stiftete. Daraus darf man schliessen, dass alte, ausbesserungsbedürftige Domdächer vorhanden waren.   Und wenn die Annahme, dass Udo I die Ostteile gerade neu errichtet hatte, stimmt, können das nur die Dächer des Langhauses und der Westteile des alten Doms gewesen sein; dies war aber immer noch der Gründungsbau, den wir nach den Ausgrabungen von 1874 in den Hauptzügen kennen.

Und nun schliesst sich mir der Gedankengang.   Die drei "Vorhallenmauern" sind älter als der Flachdeckbau, älter als 1186.   Im Westen stand damals noch der Westteil des Gründungsbaus von 1021 bis 1044.   Also gehören die drei Vorhallenmauern zu diesem Gründungsbau.   Da aber das Langhaus, falls die Ausgrabungsbefunde zuverlässig sind, schon viel weiter östlich endete, können die Vorhallenmauern nur zu einem westlich vor der Kirche liegenden Bau gehört haben; und dies kann wohl nur ein *Atrium* gewesen sein (Fig. 16).

Die Entfernung von Fuge zu Fuge, also die Breite der Westvorhalle mitsamt ihren Mauern beträgt 18,50 m.   Die Breite des ausgegrabenen Langhauses beträgt mitsamt den Mauerstärken 16 m.   Man mag es rekonstruierende Phantasie nennen, oder (wohlwollender) eine Arbeitshypothese für eine Nachgrabung, wenn ich ein solches Atrium an die von Bergner gezeichnete Rekonstruktion ansetze.   Es will mir eine bessere Erklärung der drei Vorhallenwände nicht gelingen.

Angesichts aber einer solchen Hypothese wird man sich fragen, ob in diesem Atrium etwa die Taufkapelle lag.   Dies ist zu verneinen.   Die Erdgeschosskapelle des Nordturms hiess zwar Johanniskapelle, aber sie war dem Evangelisten geweiht, nicht dem Täufer.   Letzterer hatte einen Altar an der Ostseite des nördlichen Kreuzarmes und dieser Altar ist heute noch vorhanden.[22]   Die zwei von den drei Vorhallenwänden, die für die Türme übernommen wurden, reichen in das Obergeschoss hinauf.   Dagegen ist die dritte Vorhallenwand, nach der Abbruchstelle zu urteilen, nur 4.27 m (über Domfussboden) hoch gewesen. Deshalb kann man sich die seitlichen Flügel des Atriums mit Obergeschossräumen ausgestattet denken (wobei wieder die Frage nach einer Treppe dringlich wird).   Ich gehe deshalb noch einen letzten Schritt weiter und spreche die — ganz hypothetische — Vermutung aus, dass hier die Wohnräume der Kleriker lagen.   Eine Urkunde von 1244 — also nach der Weihe des Domes (1242) und in einer Zeit, da das letzte Mittelschiffjoch noch ungewölbt war — sagt: "Dekan und Kanoniker sollen für ihre Prozessionen nach dem Chor und aus dem Chor, weil ja ein Kloster gegenwärtig nicht vorhanden ist (quia claustrum in praesens

---

[22] Selmar Lüttich im Dritten Beitrag (von 1904), S. 22.

non extat) an einem anderen, hierfür geeigneten Ort an Festtagen zusammen-
kommen, bis es gelingt, das Kloster wieder herzustellen (quousque claustrum
reparari contingat)." [23] Das Wort reparare klingt ja mehr danach, dass eine
vorhandene und nur damals unbrauchbare Klausur ausgebaut werden sollte;
aber die erste Wendung "dass zur Zeit ein Kloster nicht existiert," ist umso
bestimmter. Für die Datierung der spätromanischen Teile des Südkreuzgangs
käme danach die Zeitspanne von 1244 bis zum Beginn des Westchors 1249 in
Frage, da hier noch die Hand des spätromanischen Wölbmeisters deutlich erkenn-
bar ist. Besonders in dieser Vorhalle spricht die Freude an geknickten Rippen für
ihn. Giesau sagt mit Recht, dass zur Zeit der Errichtung des Hauptportals am
Südarm des Querschiffs (um 1220) an eine Südvorhalle noch nicht gedacht war,
da es sich als unmittelbar in den Freiraum öffnend darbietet. Wenn aber die
Südklausur 1242 noch fehlte, das Projekt der Nordklausur längst war fallen
gelassen worden, — wie lange waren die Kleriker ohne Wohnung? Denkt man
sich das Atrium als eine westlich vorgelegte Klausur, dann konnte es während
der Errichtung des neuen Domes sehr lange weiterbestehen. Es ist bekannt, dass
die Mauern des Neubaus um den alten Dom herum hochgeführt wurden. Erst
ganz am Ende dieser Bauführung, also gegen 1242, musste das Atrium fallen,
da es die Stelle des letzten Jochs einnahm.

Meine zeichnerische Auftragung dieses Atriums unter Benutzung der drei
erhaltenen Wände ist zwar an sich willkürlich, aber wenn man ihr einige Wahr-
scheinlichkeit zubilligt, dann darf man als liturgischen Grund für die Ausdehnung des Neubaus bis zum Westende des Atriums annehmen, dass in ihm ausser
Wohnungen auch geweihte Räume lagen, die man nicht profanieren wollte.
Bei diesem Streben musste der entwerfende Architekt — schon der Meister des
Flachdeck-entwurfs — darauf stossen, dass man die Wände des Atriums teilweise
für den Neubau verwerten könne.

Behielt man aber diese Mauern bei, dann ist die Verschiebung der Türme
in Naumburg durch die örtlichen Verhältnisse erklärt, und wir brauchen nicht
anzunehmen, dass die Dome von Cefalù und Monreale dabei Pate gestanden
haben. "In der Kunst wird nichts zweimal erfunden," lehrte Riegl. Man
müsste den Satz — so richtig er für die Methode ist — einschränkend abändern:
in der Kunst wird nichts zweimal aus gleichen Motiven erfunden. Was den
normännischen Meister von Cefalù bewog, die Türme nach aussen zu schieben,
wissen wir nicht. Dass sich darin die südliche Gewohnheit verrate, Türme un-
verbunden neben die Kirche zu stellen (Zimmermann), ist eine bedenkliche
Unterschiebung einer Halbheit. Sicher ist die allgemeine Tendenz des romanischen Stiles, jeden Bauteil von seinem Nachbarn durch einspringende Winkel
additiv zu trennen, bei dieser Turmstellung, gegenüber der sonst üblichen, nur
noch gesteigert. Mögen also die Motive in Naumburg andere gewesen sein als
in Cefalù, im tiefsten Grunde lag die Auseinanderrückung der Westtürme in den
Prinzipien des gemeinsamen romanischen Stiles beschlossen und konnte bei
besonderen, aber unter einander verschiedenen Voraussetzungen aus dem
Bereich des nur Möglichen in die Wirklichkeit treten.

[23] Selmar Lüttich im Zweiten Beitrag (von 1902), S. 31.

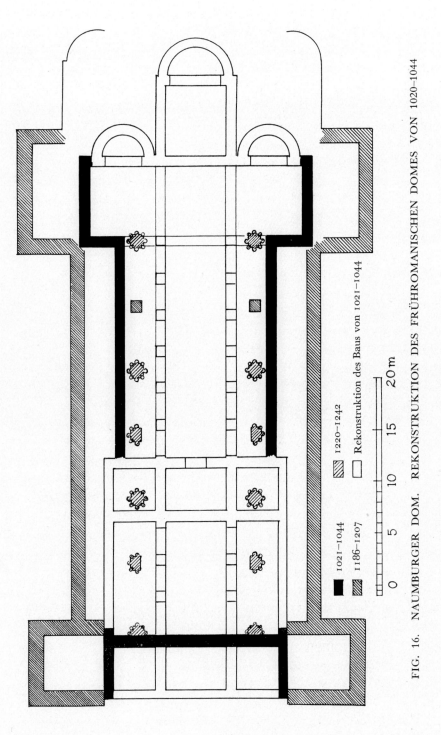

0   5   10   15   20 m

FIG. 16. NAUMBURGER DOM. REKONSTRUKTION DES FRÜHROMANISCHEN DOMES VON 1020–1044

Nachtrag

Dieser Aufsatz war im Dezember 1935 abgeschlossen; es sind zwei Ergänzungen inzwischen nötig geworden.

Erstens erfuhr ich von einem weiteren Kirchenbau mit auseinandergerückten Türmen. Hans Reinhardt hat in einem von mir übersehenen Aufsatz: "Die Ausgrabungen der ersten Anlage des Klosters Allerheiligen in Schaffhausen" (im *Jahrbuch für Kunstgeschichte*, Leipzig, 1928, S. 33) den ersten Bau von Schaffhausen, der 1050 gegründet wurde, rekonstruiert. Tatsächlich sind hier die beiden Türme der Westfassade etwas nach aussen verschoben. Der Grund dafür liegt aber diesmal vielleicht in der Kleinheit der Masse; das Mittelschiff hat etwa 6m Breite und bei normaler Stellung der Türme wäre die Vorhalle dann sehr schmal geworden, der Mittelturm, den Reinhardt über der Westempore annimmt — etwa wie in Mauersmünster — wäre sehr klein geraten oder er hätte mit den Seitentürmen sich schwer vertragen. Reinhardt spricht die Vermutung aus, dass der sehr reiche Plan "so gut wie sicher" in Schaffhausen fertig übernommen wurde. "Es ist sehr wohl möglich, dass wir nichts anderes als eine verkleinerte Replik eines oberrheinischen Domes vor uns haben" (S. 41). Allerdings scheint mir nicht notwendig, dass dies im Masstab grössere Vorbild seinerseits die auseinandergerückten Türme gehabt haben müsse. Reinhardt ist seither nochmals auf das Thema zurückgekommen: Das erste Münster zu Schaffhausen und die Frage der Doppelturmfassade am Oberrhein (*Anzeiger für Schweizerische Altertumskunde*, Zürich, Band XXXVII, 1935, S. 241 ff.).

Der zweite Nachtrag ergibt sich durch den inzwischen erschienenen Aufsatz von Werner Hirschfeld: "Die Erneuerung der Baldachinreihe im Westchor des Naumburger Domes" (im *Jahrbuch der Denkmalpflege in der Provinz Sachsen und Anhalt*, Burg, 1935, S. 48). Im zweiten Teil dieses Artikels: "Die Baugeschichte des Westchors," der eine zweite selbständige Abhandlung bildet, veröffentlicht Hirschfeld seine Entdeckung eines Kellerraumes unter der Elisabeth-Kapelle, d.h. unter dem Erdgeschoss des Nordwestturmes. Der Baubefund bestätigt, dass das ganze Fundament der Mauer des Zwischenstücks (in meiner Bezeichnung der Mauer A D) älter ist als die Mauerfundamente der drei anderen Seiten des Turmes. Hirschfeld fogert, dass dies Fundament zu einem älteren Bau gehört haben muss. Für mich ist dieser Fund und Befund eine willkommene Bestätigung. Aber Hirschfeld hält trotzdem die über diesem Fundament hochgehende Mauer für gleichzeitig mit den drei anderen Turmmauern des Erdgeschosses, also für beträchtlich jünger. Wie man dies angesichts der durchgehenden trennenden Fugen glauben kann, ist mir unverständlich. Übrigens sagt Hirschfeld von dem Bau, zu dem das Fundament der Mauer A D gehörte: "Über seine Gestalt, ob Westvorhalle, Westtürme, Westwerk oder Atrium wird sich wohl nie etwas Genaueres ermitteln lassen." Der jüngste Aufsatz von Reinhardt lässt diese Resignation nicht ganz gerechtfertigt erscheinen; ich glaube danach, dass der erste Bau von Naumburg von 1021 kaum Westtürme hatte und ein Atrium immer noch das Wahrscheinlichste ist.

Die übrigen Beobachtungen Hirschfelds scheinen mir einwandfrei; sein Versuch, einen unausgeführten Westchorentwurf relativ kurze Zeit vor dem nachher wirklich ausgeführten zu rekonstruieren, ist mindestens sehr bestechend. Er ist als eine Kopie des Bamberger Ostchors gedacht und würde in die Jahre kurz nach der Weihe des Bamberger Domes, d.h. nach 1237, anzusetzen sein, da der Naumburger Bischof Engelbert 1237 Zeuge der Domweihe in Bamberg gewesen ist. Erst nach dem Tode Engelberts 1242 und nach dem Interregnum von 1242–1245 und spät nach dem Regierungsantritt von Bischof Dietrich, wäre dieser Entwurf fallen gelassen und durch den jetzigen gotischen Westchor ersetzt worden (Hirschfeld, S. 69). Diese interessante Rekonstruktion eines unausgeführten Planes von etwa 1240 berührt — mag sie nun richtig oder falsch sein — nicht meine Rekonstruktion des alten Zustandes von 1021 und die Begründung der Turmstellung in Naumburg.

München, im September 1938

UNTERSUCHUNGEN ZUM STIL DER BASELER GALLUSPFORTE

OTTO HOMBURGER

ARTHUR KINGSLEY PORTER hat in seinem monumentalen Werke "Romanesque Sculpture of the Pilgrimage Roads" eine verschwenderische Fülle von Werken der romanischen Plastik aus Frankreich, Italien und dem nördlichen Spanien vor uns ausgebreitet. Aber bedauerlicherweise sind die Fäden, an denen die Wanderung der Motive und der Stile verfolgt wird, nicht über die Grenzen der angeführten Länder hinaus gespannt worden, obwohl sich der Autor mehrfach als Kenner auch der Denkmäler des deutschen Sprachgebietes ausgewiesen hat und obwohl er sich dessen bewusst war, dass Strömungen, die ausgingen von den Hauptstationen auf den westeuropäischen Pilgerstrassen, wie Arles und Toulouse, und von Santiago de Compostela, dem Ziel der Wanderungen, auch über den Jura in das Gebiet des Oberrheines getragen worden sind.

Auf die Abhängigkeit der Apostelfiguren in Chur von der Portalskulptur an St. Trophîme in Arles ist mehrfach hingewiesen worden.[1] Nach der Mitte des 12. Jahrhunderts haben Bildhauer und Steinmetzen, die aus dem nordkatalonischen Kreis der Nachbarorte Vich und Ripoll ausgewandert sind, an dem plastischen Schmuck des Züricher Grossmünsters entscheidend mitgewirkt.[2] Dem 1928 von mir hierfür zusammengestellten Beweismaterial sind als wichtige Glieder die aus dem Dom zu Vich stammenden Reliefs anzufügen, die Porter in seiner "Romanische Plastik in Spanien" veröffentlicht hat.[3] Eine nicht viel später im Elsass arbeitende Schule, der wir den Schmuck des ehemaligen Kreuzganges zu Eschau,[4] eines Kapitelles aus St. Marx im Colmarer Museum[5] und des Adelochussarkophages zu St. Thomas in Strassburg verdanken,[6] die in ihren weiteren

---

[1] Arthur Lindner, "Die Basler Galluspforte und andere romanische Bildwerke der Schweiz," *Studien zur Deutschen Kunstgeschichte*, XVII (1899), S. 84 ff.; Richard Hamann, *Deutsche und Französische Kunst im Mittelalter*, I (1922), S. 25–27, Abb. 51 u. 52. Hamann vertritt die Ansicht, dass die südfranzösischen Einflüsse auf dem Weg über die Lombardei in die Schweiz eingemündet seien. — Vgl. ferner: E. Poeschel im *Anzeiger für Schweizerische Altertumskunde*, N. F. 32 (1930), S. 174–175 u. S. 185.

[2] Otto Homburger, "Studien über die romanische Plastik und Bauornamentik am Grossmünster zu Zürich," *Oberrheinische Kunst*, III (1928), S. 5–18.

[3] *Burlington Magazine*, LII (1928), S. 121, Taf. V D. *Romanische Plastik in Spanien*, I (1928), S. 7, Taf. 56–58. Puig y Cadafalch, *Butlletí dels Museus d'Art de Barcelona*, Novembre 1933, S. 330–334 (dankenswerte Mitteilung von M. Lavedan). (Das Stück mit der Darstellung von Philippus, Judas und Bartholomeus ist 1932 in das Victoria und Albert Museum gelangt.)

[4] Hausmann-Leitschuh-Seyboth, *Elsässische Kunstdenkmäler* (1900), Taf. 66; zuletzt eingehend behandelt von Robert Forrer in "Cahiers d'Archéologie et d'Histoire d'Alsace," *Anzeiger für Elsäss. Altertumskunde*, XVIII–XXI (1930), S. 198–211.

[5] F. X. Kraus, *Kunst und Altertum in Elsass-Lothringen*, II (1884), S. 340–341. Marburger Phot. 26202–26206.

[6] Hausmann-Leitschuh-Seyboth, a.a.O., Taf. 78. Robert Forrer, a.a.O., S. 211, Fig. 120–121. Marburger Phot. 25847–25855. s. auch Anm. 7.

ABB. 1. BASEL, MÜNSTER, DIE GALLUSPFORTE

Auswirkungen an der Fassade von Andlau zu verfolgen ist,[7] zeigt Zusammenhänge mit den frühromanischen Richtungen der Languedoc, und auch die antikisierende Strömung, die in den viel besprochenen Vincentius- und Aposteltafeln des Münsters zu Basel sich auswirkt, hat — wie ich das demnächst zu belegen hoffe — ihren Weg das Rhonetal hinauf sich gebahnt.[8]

Weniger deutlich offenbaren sich an einem anderen, nicht minder umstrittenen Denkmal des Baseler Münsters die Zusammenhänge mit den damals politisch wie kulturell führenden Gegenden des heute französischen Südwestens, der Provence und der Languedoc; gemeint ist das feingliederige, überaus reichgeschmückte Portal, durch das der Weg in das nördliche, einst dem Hl. Gallus geweihte Querschiff des Münsters führt, die sogenannte "*Galluspforte*" (Abb. 1).

Es mag befremden, dass dieses Werk, losgelöst aus dem logischen wie organischen Zusammenhang, der Tor und Kirchenbau verbindet, hier besprochen werden soll, und mehr noch, dass die beabsichtigte Untersuchung von vorn herein unter das Zeichen bestimmter Abhängigkeiten gestellt wird, zumal doch oft genug voreiliges Bestreben, Beziehungen zwischen räumlich getrennten Werken festzustellen, davon abgehalten hat, das beiden Wesentliche zu erkennen und zur Grundlage weiterer Folgerungen zu machen. Beiden Einwänden mag durch die *eine* Tatsache begegnet werden, dass die Galluspforte — abgesehen davon, dass sie in die fertige Querschiffwand nachträglich eingelassen worden ist [9] — im Stil der Figuren wie der Ornamentik vereinzelt dasteht, während die künstlerische Ausschmückung des Langhauses sowohl, wie die andersartige des Chores, eng zusammenhängen mit je einer Gruppe benachbarter Bauten des oberrheinischen Gebietes: An dem Langhaus des Baseler Münsters haben offenbar die gleichen Steinmetzen gearbeitet, von denen der Kreuzgang des Grossmünsters in Zürich [10] und die romanischen Teile der Collégiale zu Neuchâtel [11] ausgeschmückt worden sind. Der Stil der überaus prächtigen Bauornamentik und der Plastik des Chores dagegen kehrt wieder an der Stiftskirche von St. Ursanne [12] und an dem romanischen Chor des Freiburger Münsters [13] und

---

[7] Forrer, a.a.O., XXII–XXIII (1931–32), S. 53–79, "Les Frises historiées de l'église romane d'Andlau." Marburger Phot. 26102–26173.

[8] A. Lindner, a.a.O., S. 96–116, Taf. VIII, IX. Hermann Beenken, *Romanische Skulptur in Deutschland* (1924), S. 252–255. Einzelaufnahmen von B. Wolf.

[9] Karl Stehlin in *Baugeschichte des Basler Münsters*, herausgegeben vom Basler Münsterbauverein (1895), S. 32–33.

[10] S. Vögelin in *Mitteilungen der antiquarischen Gesellschaft Zürich*, 1 (1840), mit Stichen nach Zeichnungen von Hegi. Konrad Escher, Die beiden Züricher Münster (Die Schweiz im deutschen Geistesleben, 10), 1928, S. 31–34, Taf. 24–26. Hans Wiesmann, "Die Baugeschichte des Chorherrn-Stiftsgebäudes in Zürich," *Züricher Monatschronik*, II (1933), S. 89–97. s. das Nachwort!

[11] M. F. Du Bois de Montperreux, "Les Monuments de Neuchâtel" in *Mitt. der Antiquar. Gesellschaft in Zürich*, V (1852), Taf. XII–XXIII. Alfred Lombard, *L'Eglise collégiale de Neuchâtel* (1932), insbes. Fig. 51, 57d.

[12] Albert Naef in *Kunstdenkmäler der Schweiz*, Neue Folge, III (1903). Hans Reinhardt, *Das Basler Münster, die spätromanische Bauperiode* (1926), S. 85–87. Phot. B. Wolf.

[13] *Freiburger Münsterblätter*, II, 1906 (Fr. Panzer, "Der romanische Bilderfries," etc. . . ., mit Abb. nach verschiedenen Werken der Gruppe) und ebenda III, 1907, S. 45–65 (Karl Schuster, "Der romanische Teil des Freiburger Münsters"). Jan. Fastenau, "Romanische Bauornamentik in Süddeutschland," *Studien zur Deutschen Kunstgeschichte*, CLXXXVIII (1916), S. 52, 54–56, 60. Reinhardt, a.a.O. (1926), S. 89–90. Hans Jantzen, "Das Münster zu Freiburg" (*Deutsche Bauten*, 15), 1929, S. 6–12, 68–69.

ist darüber hinaus einzureihen in einen weiten Kreis spätromanischer Arbeiten,
die am Mittel- und Niederrhein wie in den von hier abhängigen, weiter östlich
gelegenen Landstrichen reich vertreten sind und dieser letzten Phase deutsch-
romanischer Baukunst ihr Gepräge gegeben haben.[14]

Die Galluspforte ist mehrfach eingehend behandelt worden, so von Arthur
Lindner und von Hans Reinhardt,[15] dem derzeitig besten Kenner seines hei-

ABB. 2.   BASEL, GALLUSPFORTE, TEIL

matlichen Münsters; zahlreiche Kunstgelehrte haben sich im Zusammenhang
grösserer Aufgabenkreise zu dem problematischen Werk geäussert.[16] Wir ver-
zichten auf eine Beschreibung des Aufbaues und der Bildinhalte, auch auf die

[14] Wesentliche Beispiele: Worms, Westchor des Domes; Limburg a.d.L., Westfassade; Andernach;
Bonn, Münster; Köln, Westchor von St. Georg; Naumburg, Langhaus.

[15] Arthur Lindner, a.a.O., S. 15–41. Reinhardt, a.a.O. (1926), S. 9–22. Ders., "Das Münster zu
Basel" (*Deutsche Bauten* 13), 1928, S. 23, Abb. 70–75. Masstäbliche Aufnahme in: *Das Münster zu Basel,
Tafeln zur Baugeschichte des Basler Münsters* (1895), Taf. XIII.

[16] Voege, *Repertorium*, XXV, S. 412, Anm. 11. Burkhard Meier, "Die romanischen Portale in Sachsen,"
Beiheft zur *Zeitschrift für Geschichte der Architektur* (1911), S. 23 ff. (auch Dissertation Halle, 1911). Hans

Frage nach der Persönlichkeit des vorgeführten Stifters, indem wir auf die Ausführungen bei Lindner, Reinhardt und Panofsky verweisen, und heben nur hervor, dass als Gegenstand des bildlichen Schmuckes das Jüngste Gericht — nach Matthäus, Kapitel 25 — ausgewählt worden ist. Dass hierbei auch die Klugen und Törichten Jungfrauen wiedergegeben wurden, lässt an die nordfranzösischen Portalzyklen denken, wo — mit weitem Vorsprung vor allem folgenden — in St. Denis diese Parabel mit dem Gerichtsbild verbunden ist.[17] Wenn in Basel — entgegen aller französischen Gepflogenheit — dies Thema in dem wagerechten Türsturz zu Worte kommt, wo die Jungfrauen zu beiden Seiten des Hauses und des davor erscheinenden Bräutigams aufgereiht sind,[18] so werden wir an Darstellungen in dem damals mehrfach illustrierten "Speculum Virginum" erinnert,[19] ohne dass ein Zusammenhang behauptet werden soll (Abb. 1 und 2).

Einem bestimmten Portaltypus lässt sich das Denkmal nicht einordnen. Es seien vielmehr drei Eigentümlichkeiten hervorgehoben, die in gleicher Weise in die Augen fallen und Anlass zu weiteren kunsthistorischen Erörterungen geben. (1) Die Pforte ist ein Portal mit dreifach abgestuftem Gewände, dessen Rücksprünge durch die Säulen und die sie bekrönenden Kapitele ausgefüllt werden. (2) Auf beiden Seiten des Gewändes sind je zwei Evangelistenfiguren, die Schriftbänder halten, in diagonaler Richtung so aufgestellt, dass sie die für sie entfernte Pfostenkante ersetzen. (Um sie sichtbar zu machen, treten die sehr schlanken Säulen ungewöhnlich weit vor das Gewände.) (3) Die rundbogig abgeschlossene Tür wird eingefasst durch einen rechteckigen, noch näher zu behandelnden Aufbau, der im Zusammenhang mit der aufgelockerten Vorderschicht der Säulen Richard Hamann veranlasst hat, von einem Triumphbogenportal zu sprechen. Schon Burkhard Meier hat darauf hingewiesen, dass der Typus des dreifach abgestuften Säulenportals in Italien nur ganz vereinzelt vorkommt. Ausserordentlich häufig begegnet er dagegen im südlichen Frankreich und im nördlichen Spanien, und durch die Wanderung katalonischer Bauleute ist wohl sein erstes Auftreten im Oberrheingebiet zu erklären, wo wir ihm an der Nordseite des Grossmünsters zu Zürich begegnen.[20] Dieses, das Hauptportal des Baues, ist breit, massig und weit in die Mauer eingetieft, wenn auch die Säulen schlanker gebildet sind, als die Gegenstücke an zwei führenden, so oft miteinander in Beziehung gebrachten Bauten des Südwestens, der Porte Miègeville an St. Sernin zu Toulouse[21] und der Puerta de las Platerias zu

Christ, *Zeitschrift für Geschichte der Architektur*, VI (1913), S. 125–137. Konrad Escher, "Die Bildwerke des Basler Münsters im Lichte der neuesten Forschungen," *Anzeiger für schweizerische Altertumskunde*, XII (1920), S. 120–133, 192–206. Albert Rieder in *Basler Zeitschrift für Geschichte und Altertumskunde*, 22 (1924), S. 183. s. ferner das Nachwort.

[17] Marcel Aubert, *Die gotische Plastik Frankreichs, 1140–1225* (1929), Taf. 1.

[18] Abb. bei Beenken, a.a.O., Fig. 128. Reinhardt, a.a.O. (1926), Fig. 7. Reinhardt, a.a.O. (1928), S. 72.

[19] Walther Lehman, "Die Parabel von den klugen und törichten Jungfrauen" (Freiburger Dissertation, 1916), S. 22, 23, 43 ff. Arthur Watson, "The Speculum Virginum . . . ," *Speculum*, III (1928), S. 445–469.

[20] Konrad Escher, a.a.O. (1928), S. 26 ff., Taf. 11–13. O. Homburger, a.a.O., insbes. S. 10–11, Abb. 1.

[21] In das Gewände sind hier auf jeder Seite nur zwei Säulen eingefügt. Lit.: A. Auriol und R. Rey,

Santiago de Compostela (1103).[22] Zeitlich mag die Züricher Pforte, die die
Skulpturen der Fassade von Ripoll voraussetzt, mehrere Dezennien nachfolgen.
Die schmuckhafte, schlankere, in ihren Teilen gelockerte Basler Tür kann —
zumal bei den sonstigen Verschiedenheiten — unabhängig davon in einem
wesentlich späteren Zeitpunkt entstanden sein; inzwischen hat man auch in den

ABB. 3. BASEL, GALLUSPFORTE, GEWÄNDE

Gebieten zu beiden Seiten der Pyrenäen begonnen, die Säulen schraubenartig
auszukehlen und zu kannelieren, wie das zu Basel geschehen ist.[23]

Betrachten wir nun die Paare von schmalen, eng nebeneinander sich aufrich-
tenden Evangelistenfiguren (Abb. 3, 4), so stellt sich zunächst die Erinnerung
an die in Figuren aufgelösten Gewändeportale ein, wie sie in Nordfrankreich

St. Sernin de Toulouse (1930), S. 108 ff. Ernst H. Buschbeck, Der Portico della gloria von Santiago de Compostela
(1919), S. 25–26, Abb. 27–30. Paul Deschamps, Die romanische Plastik Frankreichs (1930), Taf. 9. Marburger
Phot. 32478–32504.

[22] Ernst H. Buschbeck, a.a.O., S. 36 ff., Abb. 32. A. Kingsley Porter, Romanesque Sculpture of the Pilgrimage Roads (1923), S. 211, Taf. 674–691. Ders., Romanische Plastik in Spanien, I (1928), S. 67, Taf. 59–62.

[23] Puig i Cadafalch, L'Arquitectura Romanica a Catalunya, III (1918), Fig. 1094, 1099, 1100, 1104, 1105.
Ebenso häufig sind die Wulste im Bogengewände schraubenartig gedreht. Fig. 1108, 1109, 1111.

durch eine glänzende, mit der Westfassade von Chartres beginnende und bis zur reifen Gotik fortgeführte Reihe vertreten sind.   Aber in all diesen Fällen sind die überaus schlanken Gestalten vor Säulen gestellt, mit denen sie gleichsam zu *einem* Wesen verwachsen sind.   Dass dagegen die Heiligenfiguren, in einer Front ausgerichtet, im Gewände an Stelle der Pfeilerecken treten, indem sie sich

ABB. 4.   BASEL, GALLUSPFORTE, GEWÄNDE

deren Volumen einfügen, dafür kann nur *ein* analoger Fall aufgezeigt werden, das Portal, das einst an der Kathedrale St. Etienne zu Toulouse Kapitelsaal und Kreuzgang verband.[24]   Die Statuen, Kapitelle und Kämpferbruchstücke des

---

[24] Lange Zeit hat der Kreuzgang den Vornehmen der Stadt und den Würdenträgern des Kapitels als Begräbnisstätte gedient, s. R. Rey, *La Cathédrale de Toulouse, Petites Monographies des grands édifices de la France*, 45 (1929).   Zur kunstgeschichtlichen Stellung der Skulpturen vgl. W. Vöge, *Die Anfänge des monumentalen Stiles im Mittelalter* (1894), S. 69–79, Abb. 20–23.   Ernst H. Buschbeck, a.a.O., S. 31–33, Abb. 40–42.   A. Kingsley Porter, *Romanesque Sculpture of the Pilgrimage Roads* (1923), S. 150 ff., Taf. 434–449.   Ders., *Romanische Plastik in Spanien* (1928), *passim*.   Paul Deschamps, a.a.o. (1930), S. 30, Taf. 25 (Die hier abgebildete Rekonstruktion lehrt, dass das Portal breiter und schwerer war als die Galluspforte, dass das Verhältniss der ornamentierten Kämpferzone zu dem simaartigen Aufsatz der Anordnung in Basel ungefähr entsprochen hat).   Marburger Phot. 32686–32741.

1813 zerstörten Denkmals sind im Museum zu Toulouse aufbewahrt und neuer-
dings nach einer in der dortigen Bibliothek erhaltenen Zeichnung wieder zusam-
mengesetzt worden (Abb. 5).[25] Nur die mittleren Paare auf jeder der beiden
Seiten kommen für unsere Gegenüberstellung in Betracht (Abb. 6–8).

Und nun drängt sich die Frage auf: Lassen sich auch in formaler Hinsicht
Vergleiche ziehen zwischen den Toulousaner Figuren, die um 1130–1150 entstanden sein mögen, und ihren Gegenstücken am Basler Münster?

Die stilistische Untersuchung der vier Evangelisten in Basel mit den zu ihren
Häuptern angebrachten, überraschend lebendig gebildeten Symbolen, wird

Kunstgesch. Seminar Marburg

ABB. 5. TOULOUSE, MUSEUM, PORTAL IM EHEMALIGEN KREUZGANG
VON ST. ÉTIENNE, REKONSTRUKTION

erschwert dadurch, dass aus irgendwelchen Gründen Teile überarbeitet worden
sind; so scheidet der Kopf des Johannes (Abb. 3), an dem nur die nach vorn
fallenden und leicht eingerollten Haarsträhnen noch einiges von dem alten
Zustand erkennen lassen, für die Untersuchung aus. An dem Lukas (Abb. 4)
sind Teile des Gesichtes verändert, dagegen sind die perrückenartig aufgesetzte
"Haarhaube" und der lang ausgezogene Bart, dessen schrägschraffierte Strähnen nach aussen sich einrollen, zu verwerten.

Trotzdem die Gestalten in der Art, wie sie nebeneinander aufgereiht sind, wie
ihre als Stoffmassen fühlbaren, von enggelegten Strähnen durchfurchten Gewänder fallen, an französische Portalplastik des späteren 12. Jahrhunderts erinnern,
so sind sie doch dem Gesamteindruck nach der hochromanischen Stilstufe

---

[25] Aufgenommen vom Marburger Seminar, Nr. 32686.

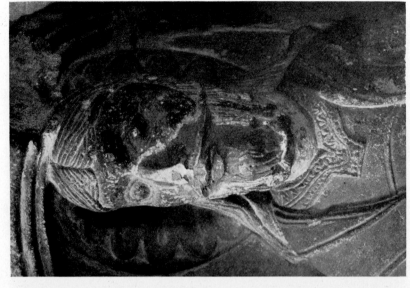

ABB. 8. TOULOUSE, MUSEUM, PORTAL VON
ST. ÉTIENNE, KOPF DES ANDREAS

ABB. 7. TOULOUSE, MUSEUM, PORTAL VON
ST. ÉTIENNE, KOPF DES THOMAS

ABB. 6. TOULOUSE, MUSEUM, PORTAL
VON ST. ÉTIENNE, THOMAS
UND ANDREAS

einzuordnen. In die harte, fleischlose Oberfläche des zum vorgestülpten Mund hin sich verjüngenden Schädels sind die metallisch scharf geformten Gesichtsteile flach eingetragen. Die Linienrhythmik des Romanischen belebt ebenso die durch gesträhnte Wulste mannigfach geschichteten Teile von Haupthaar und Bart, wie die Stofflagen des Gewandes, dessen Säume, von Borten reich verziert, an den Rändern sich zu wellen- oder trichterförmigen Bildungen ineinanderschieben.

In einer von romanischen Bewegungsenergieen vorgeschriebenen Kurve überschneidet bei Lukas der Mantel den Leib, während an der Brust und den unteren Teilen des Gewandes flach übereinander geschichtete Stofflagen durch nach unten ausschwingende Parallelen begrenzt werden, ganz im Sinne romanischer Abstraktion (Abb. 4). In ängstlich primitiver Weise werden die so entstehenden Flächen durch senkrechte Strichlagen schraffiert, eine Vorliebe für "Belebung," die ähnlich bei einem künstlerisch sehr hochstehenden Torso des Historischen Museums zu Basel,[26] auf einem Relief des ehemaligen Fraumünster-Kreuzganges zu Zürich, wie in gleichzeitigen Buchmalereien der Schule von Engelberg begegnet.[27]

Betrachten wir demgegenüber zwei von den Aposteln des Kreuzgangsportales von St. Etienne, — es sind die beiden Figuren des Thomas und Andreas (Abb. 6), die ehedem durch die stolze Künstlerinschrift des Gilabertus gezeichnet waren, — so finden wir ähnliche Motive der Bewegung und des Stehens, aber die Haltung ist ungezwungen und natürlicher; ein eben noch fühlbares Auswiegen, ein lässiges Nachgeben und Drehen widerspricht der archaischen Frontalität der Basler Evangelisten, die hierin einigen der Pfostenfiguren im Kreuzgang von Arles näherstehen.[28] Gegenüber der steinharten, unstofflichen Oberfläche in Basel scheinen die Köpfe des Gilabertus von organischem Leben durchblutet zu sein (Abb. 7, 8). Die Augen sind natürlich und weich eingebettet in die sich rundenden Wangenflächen. Aber trotz dieser Verschiedenheiten, die vielleicht

[26] Hist. Museum, 1931/109, Höhe 45 cm. (Ich verdanke der Liebenswürdigkeit der Museumsdirektion eine Aufnahme des schönen Stückes.) Ebenda Nr. 1906/3584, ein weiterer Torso einer Gewandfigur, deren Mantelsaum feinfühlig von einer Palmettenborte eingefasst ist. Auch hier ist eine gewisse Verwandtschaft mit St. Etienne-Toulouse nicht zu verkennen. Beide Werke, ebenso wie ein Bogenstück Nr. 1906/3682, lassen darauf schliessen, dass im 12. Jh. noch weitere, den Schöpfern der Galluspforte zum Teil überlegene Bildhauer in Basel tätig waren.

[27] Bibliothek Kloster Engelberg, Cod. 14, s. Durrer im *Anzeiger für schweizerische Altertumskunde*, N. F. III (1901), Fig. 76. Ders. in *Kunstdenkmäler des Kantons Unterwalden* (1899–1928), Taf. 7.

[28] Man vergleiche die Figuren des Trophimus und des Stephanus an den beiden Eckpfeilern des Nordflügels (Porter, *Romanesque Sculpture of the Pilgrimage Roads*, 1923, Taf. 1345–1346, 1354, 1356). Wenn auch demgegenüber die freiere und stofflichere Art der Haar- und Gewandbehandlung an der Fassade zu Arles einer viel mehr stilisierten Darstellung der metallisch harten Gesichter und der strähnigen Gewänder Platz gemacht hat, so ist doch noch ein weiter Schritt zu den linear begrenzten, gleichmässig geriefelten Draperien in Basel. Die von Deckblättern eingehüllten, antikisierenden Ranken unterscheiden sich grundsätzlich von der Basler Ornamentik. In diesem Zusammenhang sei noch auf ein anderes Denkmal der Provence hingewiesen, auf das mit der Skulptur von St. Gilles nahe verwandte Portal von St. Barnard zu Romans. Hier nehmen in dem dreifach abgestuften Gewände je zwei eingestellte Säulen zwischen sich einen Pfeiler, an dem auffallender Weise *zwei* senkrechte Kanten durch Rücken an Rücken aufgestellte Figuren ersetzt sind; die beiden nach vorn schauenden Gestalten vertreten völlig den Platz unserer Toulousaner Heiligen. Marburger Phot. 43839. A. Kingsley Porter, *Romanesque Sculpture of the Pilgrimage Roads* (1923), Taf. 1334–1336.

grundsätzliche Gegensätze zwischen französischer und deutscher (wie italienischer) Romanik wiederspiegeln, bestehen im Gegenständlichen, in der Schichtung und Stilisierung von Haupt- und Barthaar, in der Vorliebe für reichgestickte Borten, in der Bewegung der in Basel so viel müder verlaufenden Gewandsäume doch so viele Analogieen, dass wir glauben möchten, der in Basel tätige Bildhauer hat das Toulousaner Portal gekannt. Das kunstvolle konzentrische Linien-

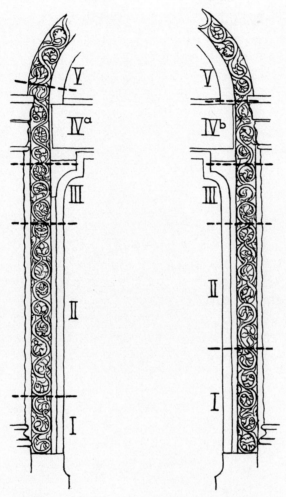

ABB. 9.   BASEL, GALLUSPFORTE RANKE

spiel, mit dem die überaus fein geschichteten Stofflagen des Gilabertus überzogen sind, hat der Basler freilich entweder — wie bei den Tympanonfiguren — vergröbert oder stattdessen durch die senkrechte Riefelung der Draperien eine den Gesetzen der Schwere gehorchende Stofflichkeit vorgetäuscht, die zeigt, dass er hier Fortschrittliches reduziert, im Sinne seiner romanischen Formauffassung.[29]

Man hat mehrfach versucht, in den übereck angebrachten und über ein völlig andersartiges Gewände verteilten, zu "Puppen verkümmerten" Figürchen der

---

[29] Man denke an Statuen in der Art der Portalplastik von Senlis (ca. 1170–1180). Marcel Aubert, a.a.O., S. 75 ff., Taf. 55–56. Marburger Phot. 36611–36615.

Domportale zu Verona [30] und Ferrara [31] Vorbilder der Basler Evangelisten zu sehen; diese Herleitung von Italien, die schon von Lindner abgewiesen worden ist, erscheint mir ebensowenig zwingend, wie die Ansicht, dass man in der Ranke, die den inneren Rand der Galluspforte umzieht (Abb. 1), einen Abkömmling ähnlich verlaufender, aber in Stil und Motiv verschiedenartiger Bordüren an italienischen Portalen [32] erblicken dürfe.

Es liegt nahe zu fragen, ob diese in Flachrelief modellierte, wellenförmig verlaufende Stielranke der Ornamentik des Langhauses oder der des Chores — die auf einigen Emporenkapitellen wiederkehrt — ihrem Formcharakter nach anzuschliessen ist. Und dabei stellt sich heraus, dass sie selbst durchaus nicht einheitliches Gepräge trägt, sondern dass mindestens vier, wahrscheinlich fünf Stilarten als Repräsentanten von ebenso vielen "Händen" zu scheiden sind (Abb. 9). Da auf den einzelnen Steinblöcken jeweils nur *eine* Richtung vertreten ist, hat es den Anschein, als ob von vornherein die Arbeit auf die verschiedenen Bildhauer verteilt worden sei. Mit der am Oberrhein im letzten Drittel des 12. Jahrhunderts heimischen Art der Blattbehandlung scheint *der* Steinmetz am ehesten vertraut zu sein, der die Ranke in ihrem bogenförmigen Verlauf gemeisselt hat (Abb. 2), nur die erste Einrollung, unten links, gehört noch dem Vorgänger an. All diesen reich variierenden, aus Arazeenformen,[33] Trauben, geschlossenen und gespaltenen Palmetten zusammengefügten Blüten ist eigentümlich, dass die Blätter durchwegs tief eingeschnitten und die so entstehenden Lappen entweder löffelförmig ausgekerbt oder dazu noch von einer Mittelrippe längs durchzogen sind; letztere Art ist der Chorornamentik eigen, während die einfach ausgeschälten Blattpalmetten das immer wiederkehrende ornamentale Einzelmotiv der Gruppe Grossmünsterkreuzgang-Baseler Langhaus bilden.

Ueberraschend und neuartig in dieser Gegend wirken die vielfach zusammengesetzten Blüten. Sie hier eingeführt zu haben, ist das Verdienst des Meisters, der die Mittelteile der senkrechten Rahmen geschmückt hat und schon durch die Verwendung des Bohrers bei der Konturierung seines üppigen Blattwerkes sich als ein im Süden Geschulter ausweist. (Hand II, Abb. 3, 4, 10.) Eine ausserordentlich schöpferische, ornamentale Phantasie lässt in erstaunlicher Mannigfaltigkeit aus breitlappigen, gleichsam durch Treibarbeit geriefelten Blattbüscheln üppige Blütenbildungen entstehen, denen, bald greifbarer, bald mehr oder weniger entfernt, die Arazeenform zugrunde gelegen hat. Diese massiven Blüten, die mitunter wie von einem Luftzug geschüttelt und durcheinander gewirbelt werden (Abb. 10), stehen in augenfälligem Gegensatz zu den vorher besprochenen Bildungen, wo ein Lappen zum andern zugefügt erscheint, wo

---

[30] C. Martin, *L'Art roman en Italie*, II, Taf. 76–78. Hamann, a.a.O., Abb. 107. A. Kingsley Porter, *Lombard Architecture* (1915), Taf. 217.

[31] C. Martin, a.a.O., I, Taf. 70–72. Hamann, a.a.O., Abb. 103–104. A. Kingsley Porter, a.a.O. (1915), Taf. 89.

[32] Modena, Hauptportal und Porta dei Principi. C. Martin, a.a.O., I, Taf. 45–47. G. Bertoni, *Atlante storico artistico del duomo di Modena* (1921), Taf. 4–7, u. Taf. 23.

[33] E. Jacobsthal, "Araceenformen in der Flora des Ornaments," *Festschrift der Technischen Hochschule, Berlin* (1884).

ABB. 10, 11, 12.   BASEL, MÜNSTER, EINZELHEITEN VON DER GALLUSPFORTE

man einen Blattstiel nach dem anderen von der Palmette abzupfen möchte (Abb. 2, 11). Dieses "additive" Blattgebilde ist genetisch das ältere, als Vertreter der hochromanischen Ornamentik, während die grosslappige, vielfach gefaltete aber unteilbare Blüte im letzten Drittel des 12. und am Anfang des 13. Jahrhunderts in der Buchmalerei — und zwar zunächst in der englischen — phantastisch reiche und üppige Formen angenommen hat.[34] Es wäre zu untersuchen, ob sich unter den spätantiken Denkmälerresten irgendwelche Stücke auffinden lassen, die als Vorbilder für die mit dem Bohrer gearbeiteten Gewächse angesehen werden können.[35]

Sehr viel gezähmter und sachlich klarer, wenn nicht trockener, wirken die Palmetten eines weiteren Bildhauers (Abb. 9, iva), der links vom Fries der Klugen Jungfrauen Rankenwindungen modelliert hat (Abb. 2); auch hier erhalten wir den Eindruck, dass nicht (wie unmittelbar darüber) einzelne schmale Lappen eingeschnitten und ausgehöhlt sind, sondern dass ein breitlappiges Gebilde in enggelegte, metallisch scharfgeformte und ganz bestimmt abgestufte Riefeln gepresst worden sei. Und etwas von dieser Oberflächenbehandlung ist wohl auch übergegangen in die Modellierung der Gewänder. Sicher gehört in die gleiche Gruppe der ornamentale Schmuck der Pfosten, auf denen die Evangelisten aufgestellt worden sind und eine Anzahl von Kapitellen im Laufgang des nördlichen Querschiffs, auf die wir später zurückkommen werden.

Es sei noch hingewiesen auf zwei weitere Arten der Rankenstilisierung: einmal die Teile (Abb. 9, iii; Abb. 3, 4), die nach oben die Arbeit des Antikisierenden fortsetzen und sich auszeichnen durch die sehr präzise Formgebung der dem Ende zu gespaltenen Ranke und durch die klare Silhouette, mit der das sparsame Blattwerk sich vom Grunde abhebt, im Gegensatz zur dichten Füllung im Werk von II. Nahe verwandt damit sind die Windungen am Fuss der Ranke (Abb. 9, 1; Abb. 11): hier lösen sich von den rückwärts ausgesandten Rankenschösslingen weich und rhythmisch geschwungene, in schmale Lappen gespaltene Halbpalmetten und Trauben ab, auf der rechten Seite ist von dem gleichen Meister — wohl in Anlehnung an antike Akanthusranken — zweimal der Versuch gemacht worden, eine Rosette in Vorderansicht zu zeichnen.

Mit diesen Ausführungen, die eine Beschreibung nicht ersetzen sollen, ist nur in Umrissen der Charakter der verschiedenen Rankenteile wiedergegeben worden; mögen die Hinweise dazu anregen, in dem Gebiet der romanischen

[34] Es ist reizvoll zu beobachten, wie sich dieser Wechsel von hochromanischer zu spätromanischer (= frühgotischer) Ornamentik, dem ein völliger Umschwung in der Auffassung des Stofflichen entspricht, mitunter im gleichen Denkmal vollzieht. So begegnen beide Stilstufen in der dreibändigen Bibel der Kathedrale von Winchester (Phot. Victoria & Albert Museum), um 1170–1180, wie in dem um 1198 geschriebenen Evangelistar des Speyerer Doms (Karlsruhe, Landesbibliothek, Publikation Hiersemann mit Einleitungen von Preisendanz und Homburger, 1930).

[35] Eine gewisse Verwandtschaft (insbes. mit Teil ii, iii, und iva der Basler Ranke) zeigen die Bruchstücke eines spätantiken Frieses, die jetzt teils im Museum St. Pierre zu Vienne und im Museum zu Lyon aufbewahrt werden, teils in St. Maurice zu Vienne, anschliessend an einen romanischen Tierkreisfries, im nördlichen Seitenschiff eingemauert sind (Marburger Phot. 36808). Kopiert worden sind im 12. Jahrhundert Teile des Frieses an dem Kämpfer des Portales zu Romans, Marburger Phot. 43844 (Abbildungen der Stücke im Museum von Vienne: Marburger Phot. 44994 und bei E. Rey, *Monuments de Vienne*, 1821).

Bauornamentik wie der Buchmalerei nach Analogien zu suchen. Noch weniger ist es die Aufgabe dieses Aufsatzes, die an der Galluspforte auftretende Ornamentik in allen Einzelheiten durchzusprechen; vieles, wie die Friese, die über die Kapitellzone hinziehen oder die einzelnen Tabernakel trennen (Abb. 3, 4, 12), ist entnommen dem Motivenschatz der oberrheinisch-schweizerischen Romanik, deren Wesen und Herkunft im Zusammenhang untersucht werden muss. Die reichen Blattgebilde, die die Kämpfer und — wie schon gesagt — die Sockel des Gewändes schmücken, sind weitere Zeugnisse des Stiles, der uns in der grossen Ranke begegnet ist (Abb. 9, IV). Zu dem mannigfaltigen, dreisträhnigen Bandgeflecht, das die rechteckig eingerahmten Wangenstücke der Geschosse überzieht (Abb. 3), ist zu sagen, dass es sich hier um ein im späteren 12. Jahrhundert häufig zu beobachtendes Zurückgreifen auf weitverbreitete Motive der Karolingerzeit handelt. Als Beispiele seien die Kaminplatten im Kaiserpalast zu Gelnhausen angeführt.[36]

Eine eingehendere Betrachtung gebührt von unserem Blickpunkte aus den sechs Säulenkapitellen im Gewände (Abb. 12). Das innerste Paar vertritt einen Typus, der im Süden und Westen Europas häufig wiederkehrt und eine weit zurückreichende Geschichte hat.[37] Es ist das Zwillingstier mit *einem* Kopf, der die vier oberen Ecken des Kapitells betont, während die acht Leiber sich paarweise auf die vier Seiten des Kapitells verteilen; es sind jedesmal zwei gegenständig angeordnete, mit dem Körper aufgerichtete Löwen, deren äussere nach oben ausgestreckte Tatzen sich in Scheitelhöhe der Köpfe berühren, während die inneren Pranken auf einen menschlichen Kopf aufgesetzt sind. Das merkwürdige Auftauchen dieser Kopfmaske aus der leeren Fläche heraus wird verständlich,[38] wenn wir zwei andere Kapitelle dieses Typus zum Vergleiche heranziehen: eines, das in dem um 1100 erbauten Kreuzgange zu Moissac [39] (nahe bei Toulouse) ein Säulenpaar bekrönt, und ein zweites, rund hundert Jahre jüngeres vom Portal zu St. Ursanne, also aus dem Umkreis der Basler Chorwerkstatt.[40] In beiden Fällen wird mit dem Kopf der Oberkörper sichtbar und in St. Ursanne zugleich das Paar der Hände, die sich festklammern an dem Schaftring des Kapitells, während die hier auf den Hinterpfoten voll aufgerichteten Raubtiere sich aufstützen auf den von ihnen — als den Vertretern des Bösen — bedrängten Menschen.

Nach aussen folgt ein Paar von Kapitellen, deren Kern umstellt ist von vier Vögeln. Es sind nicht die schweren, eulenartigen Tiere mit breiten flächenfüllenden Flügeln, die in Basel im Langhaus, ausserdem in Petershausen, unter den Resten des Fraumünsterkreuzganges in Zürich und in Neuchâtel [41] begegnen,

---

[36] Ferdinand Luthmer, *Romanische Ornamente und Baudenkmäler* (1896), Taf. XVII. *Bau- und Kunstdenkmäler im Regierungsbezirk Kassel*, I, Gelnhausen, Taf. 33. Marburger Phot. 9376, 9717–9719.

[37] Rich. Bernheimer, *Romanische Tierplastik* (1931), S. 100, Taf. XV.

[38] Ein Kapitell mit gleichem Motiv im Inneren des Basler Langhauses. Phot. Wolf 53.

[39] Marburger Phot. 30869. Deschamps, a.a.O., S. 22–25.

[40] Abb. Freiburger Münsterblätter, II, S. 26, Fig. 44. Phot. B. Wolf, Basel. Bei einem Kapitell der Freiburger Nikolauskapelle (ebenda Fig. 45) ist der Oberkörper schon verkümmert.

[41] Basel: Reinhardt, *Das Basler Münster, die spätromanische Bauperiode* (1926), Abb. 6; Petershausen: Hecht, *Romanischer Kirchenbau des Bodenseegebietes*, I (1928), Taf. 166–167; Zürich: Fraumünster, *Mitteil-*

und deren Auftreten geradezu eine Strasse lombardischer Steinmetzen von Oberitalien bis nach Sachsen bezeichnet,[42] sondern sie sind langbeinig schlank und elastisch, und die Leiber wölben sich nach vorn. Auch hierfür finden sich Vorläufer in Toulouse,[43] Zeitgenossen in St. Ursanne,[44] und ähnlich schlanke, wenn auch strenger frontal aufgefasste Vogelbildungen kennen wir von Ripoll, Elne (Kreuzgänge) und dem damit zusammenhängenden Grossmünsterportal.[45] Wo in Basel der Kapitellkörper zwischen den Vögeln sichtbar wird (und auffallender Weise auch hinter oder anstelle eines herausgebrochenen Tieres), ist die Fläche als Mauerwerk mit bogenförmig geschlossenen Fensteröffnungen behandelt; das sorgfältige Quaderwerk lässt sich mit ähnlichem auf Kapitellen von St. Pierre des Cuisines [46] in Toulouse vergleichen. Von dem dritten Kapitellpaar ist nur das rechte erhalten, im linken Gewände ist später ein gotisches Stück eingesetzt worden; das romanische Original zeigt die Gesamtform des Würfelkapitells, das im Gegensatz zu der typischen Blockhaftigkeit durchbrochen ist und in einer tieferen Schicht kleine Bogenstellungen erkennen lässt, während die vordere Ebene aufgelöst ist in geperlte Ranken, die sich in zwei nebeneinander angeordnete Höhenlagen paarweise an der Ecke begegnen, um nach unten prachtvoll geschwungene Arazeenblüten, beziehungsweise zweifach eingerollte Arabesken zu entsenden; während deren Blattsubstanz ganz nach Art der gleichsam getriebenen, in sich zusammenhängenden Blattlappen charakterisiert ist, steigen von den unteren vier Ecken, die Arabesken einrahmend, Palmetten auf, die durch Parallelkerbung modelliert sind.

Wir kommen schliesslich auf den rechteckig rahmenden *Aufbau* zu sprechen, der dem Portal eine Sonderstellung verleiht. Er wird nach oben wagerecht abgeschlossen durch einen ornamentalen Fries (Abb. 13), der in drei hintereinander ansteigenden Schichten zunächst eine Reihe von bogenartig verbundenen Palmetten zeigt; die Blattlappen, von denen der mittelste auch nach unten zwischen den Bogenbändern sichtbar wird, sind von einer Mittelrippe durchzogen, eine Horizontalleiste ist wie ein Band davorgespannt: "Auf Lucke" zu diesen Palmetten sind mehr oder weniger antikisierende, verschiedenartig gerandete Akanthusblätter aufgereiht, und nach oben schliesst ein Pfeifenfries das Band ab. Unmittelbar darunter sind links und rechts Gruppen von Auferstehenden verteilt, die zum Lebendigsten und Reizvollsten am Portal gehören, die aber in diesem Zusammenhang nicht weiter erörtert werden sollen.

Zu beiden Seiten wird die Türöffnung eingerahmt durch breite Pfeiler, die aus einem Sockel und fünf übereinander angeordneten Geschossen aufgebaut

---

ungen der Antiquarischen Gesellschaft, XXV (1901), Heft 2, Taf. 11; Neuchâtel: ebenda V (1852), Taf. 15/1; A. Lombard, a.a.O., Fig. 51 a, b.

[42] *Monatshefte für Kunstwissenschaft*, III (1910), Abb. 11, 12, 13 (Adolph Goldschmidt).

[43] Marburger Phot. 32582, nackter Mann mit Vögeln, St. Sernin, südliches Querschiff, Westempore.

[44] Abb. Freiburger Münsterblätter, II, S. 18, Fig. 28. Phot. Wolf.

[45] Homburger, a.a.O., Taf. 8/1, Taf. 10/2. Deschamps, a.a.O., Taf. 88. Puig i Cadafalch, a.a.O., Abb. 447 u. 1021. Marburger Phot.: Zürich 4654, 4655; Elne 39148; Ripoll 55146.

[46] Gleichfalls dreifach abgestuftes Säulenportal. Phot. Archives d'art et d'histoire, 85830; Marburger Phot. 53286–53291, insbes. 53288.

sind; unterhalb des Kämpfergesimses begegnen in je drei von ihnen reliefartige
Darstellungen der Taten der Barmherzigkeit,[47] ein Stoff, der ebenso wie die
Parabel von den Klugen und Törichten Jungfrauen dem 25. Kapitel Matthäi
entnommen ist.[48] Darüber stehen unter höheren, halbkreisförmig geschlossenen
Tabernakeln die beiden Johannes, ganz oben knieen Engel, die in der einen Hand
ein Blütenszepter halten, mit der anderen das Horn ansetzen, um zum Gericht
aufzurufen. Man hat als Vorbild für die Anordnung des Ganzen auf die "Porte
noire" zu Besançon,[49] der kirchlichen Metropole des Bistums Basel, verwiesen,

ABB. 13.   BASEL, GALLUSPFORTE, ORNAMENTALER FRIES

und so einleuchtend diese Hypothese ist, so reizvoll ist es sich zu vergegen-
wärtigen, in welcher Weise der mittelalterliche Baumeister das antike Denkmal,
das viele Einzelszenen durch Hauptakzente gegliedert wiedergibt, ins Klein-
teilige umgesetzt hat.

Nun ist durch alte Stiche und Zeichnungen überliefert, dass das Portal der
1832 abgebrochenen Klosterkirche Petershausen bei Konstanz, das zwischen
1173 und 1180 errichtet wurde, gleichfalls eingerahmt war von halbkreisförmig
abgeschlossenen Reliefs, auf denen entsprechend die Taten der Barmherzigkeit
wiedergegeben waren.[50] Aber dieses Tor der Petershausener Kirche berührt
sich noch in einem zweiten wichtigen Punkte mit der Baseler Pforte. Auch hier
standen hinter locker vorgestellten Säulen, die die Gewänderücksprünge ausfüll-
ten, menschliche Figuren, allerdings nur eine auf jeder Seite [51] (Abb. 14), wie
das bald darauf an dem — in manchem — von Basel abhängigen Südostportal
der Stiftskirche zu Neuchâtel wiederholt worden ist.[52] Dargestellt sind zwei Titu-

[47] Auch hier hat rohe Ueberarbeitung der Köpfe den Eindruck verfälscht. Rein erhalten sind nur
die beiden zu oberst angebrachten Reliefs (Speisung u. Krankenpflege).

[48] Ueber die verschiedenen Wiederholungen des Zyklus hat zuletzt Fritz Geiges, *Der mittelalterliche
Fensterschmuck des Freiburger Münsters* (1931), S. 16, gehandelt (Gleichzeitig als Jahrgang 56–58 der Zeitschrift *Schauinsland* erschienen).

[49] Abb. bei Emile Espérandieu, *Basreliefs . . . de la Gaule Romaine*, VII (1918), S. 5–28.

[50] Homburger, "Materialien zur Baugeschichte der zweiten Kirche von Petershausen," *Oberrheinische
Kunst*, II (1927), S. 161–164, Taf. 76–79. Jos. Hecht, a.a.O. (1928), S. 241 ff., Taf. 161–162, 167–168.

[51] Abb. Hecht, a.a.O., Taf. 169 u. 170.

[52] *Mitteilg. der Antiquarischen Gesellschaft*, V (1852), Taf. 18–20. A. Lindner, a.a.O., S. 54–63, mit Abb.
A. Lombard, a.a.O., Fig. 37.

larheilige der Klosterkirche, Bischof Gebhard und Papst Gregor, die ebenso wie das Tympanon mit der Darstellung der Himmelfahrt noch erhalten sind und im Landesmuseum zu Karlsruhe aufbewahrt werden. Aus diesen zweifachen

Phot. Fritz Schmidt, Karlsruhe

ABB. 14. KARLSRUHE, LANDESMUSEUM, STATUEN VOM
PORTAL DER EHEM. KIRCHE ZU PETERSHAUSEN

Beziehungen zwischen den beiden, den Querverlauf des Oberrheines abriegelnden Kirchen, ist auf Abhängigkeit des Petershausener Portales von dem zeitlich nicht festgelegten Baseler geschlossen worden, eine Annahme, die bei jedem, der die Skulpturen der beiden Werke vorurteilsfrei vergleicht, auf Bedenken stossen muss. Der Verfasser behält sich vor, den Stil der Petershausener Plastik im Zusammenhang mit verwandten Werken in Zürich (Fraumünster) und Schaffhausen zu behandeln; es müssen deshalb hier einige das Resultat vorwegnehmende Andeutungen genügen. Verglichen mit dem Formcharakter der Baseler Skulpturen, denen man anmerkt, dass ein Einheimischer, der vielerlei zu Gesicht bekommen hat, Erinnerungen an zeitlich entferntere Vorbilder vermischt mit Eindrücken von gleichzeitiger westlicher Kunst, tragen die Petershausener Statuen rein das Gepräge der hochromanischen Kunst; man beachte die Sachlichkeit und Präzision, mit der die einzelnen Teile des Ornates charak-

ABB. 15. RELIEF AM
PETERSHAUSENER PORTAL

ABB. 16. BASEL, GALLUSPFORTE,
RELIEF

terisiert und formal gegeneinander abgesetzt sind, den plastischen Reichtum in der Lagerung der Gewändsäume, die Grösse der Formauffassung, die sich in den Heiligenköpfen ausspricht. An den Kaseln liegen die Stoffbahnen wie geplättet auf, so dass ihr Rand durch scharfe, mit erlesenem Gefühl für Rhythmus geführte Linien bezeichnet wird. Und wenn auch die Taten der Barmherzigkeit nur in missverstandenen Stichen erhalten sind, so gewinnen wir doch vom Stil der Szenen ein bestimmtes Bild, das durch Vergleich mit noch erhaltenen Figuren des Grossmünsterkreuzganges,[53] vor allem aber mit einer Gruppe italienischer Werke,[54] ein festes, kaum trügendes Gepräge erhält. Und so mag es denn erlaubt sein, etwa die Szene der Krankenpflege an beiden Portalen zu vergleichen (Abb. 15, 16). Wie unbeholfen und schlecht proportioniert wirken die Figuren des Baseler Werkes, wie schwerfällig und müde verlaufen die Säume des schematisch geriefelten Bettuches. Es wäre trotzdem verfehlt oder zum mindesten gewagt, aus dieser Verteilung der Wertakzente zu folgern, dass das Baseler Portal zeitlich

---

[53] Der "Steinmetz" ist, worauf mich Kantonsbaumeister Wiesmann hingewiesen hat, Originalstück, möglicherweise ist es auch der Hornbläser, was noch zu untersuchen wäre (Abb. *Mitteilungen* a.a.O., I, Taf. 14–15). Vgl. das Nachwort.

[54] Trude Krautheimer-Hess, "Die figurale Plastik der Ostlombardei von 1100–1178," in *Marburger Jahrbuch für Kunstwissenschaft*, IV (1928), S. 284 ff.: D. Der Reduktionsstil (vgl. bes. Abb. 66–67).

dem festdatierten Petershausener Werk gefolgt sein muss, zumal das Programm bei letzterem den einheitlichen Charakter der Galluspforte (Jüngstes Gericht) vermissen lässt. Wenn also, von hier aus gesehen, die Datierung des Baseler Portales nicht eindeutig festgelegt werden kann, so ergibt die weiter oben vorgenommene Untersuchung der Ornamentik doch wenigstens *eine* Handhabe, das zeitliche Verhältniss des Tores zum Bau, dem es ja offenbar nachträglich eingefügt worden ist, zu bestimmen. Es begegnet nämlich an den Kapitellen [55]

ABB. 17, 18.   BASEL, MÜNSTER, KAPITELLE AM OBERGESCHOSS DES QUERSCHIFFS

einer Bogenstellung, die am Laufgang des nördlichen Querschiffs — also an der Wand über dem Gallustor — vorgeblendet ist, ein Stil des Blattwerks, der enge Verwandtschaft zeigt mit der Ranke des Portals und darauf schliessen lässt, dass diese Stücke von der gleichen Gruppe von Steinmetzen gemeisselt worden sind, die jene ausgeführt haben. In enger Anlehnung an die Bohrertechnik des "Südfranzosen" (II) wird bei dem 1. und 4. Kapitell der Nordseite (Abb. 17, 18) der Konturierung der buschigen, stark unterschnittenen Blätter nachgeholfen durch kleine Eintiefungen; letzteres (Abb. 18) vertritt den Stil IV b der Ranke, und entsprechend finden wir im Laufgang der südlichen Querschiffwand 2 Kapitelle (3. und 4. von Westen), die den Kämpferstücken der Johannestabernakel nahestehen. Es ergibt sich daraus, dass die Galluspforte errichtet worden ist ungefähr zu gleicher Zeit, als man am oberen Geschoss des Querschiffs arbeitete,[56] also *gegen oder um die Wende* des 12. Jahrhunderts. Ob das Tor schon

---

[55] Ausser auf (neuere) Wolf'sche Aufnahmen sei auf eine Abb. bei F. Luthmer, a.a.O., II, Taf. 30, unten links, hingewiesen.

[56] Herrn Kantonsbaumeister Wiesmann in Zürich, verdanke ich den Hinweis, dass mehrere Steinmetzzeichen zugleich am Chor und an der Galluspforte des Basler Münsters begegnen.

Für die Abbildungen von Skulpturen des Baseler Münsters dienten Aufnahmen von Bernhard Wolf, Basel (Freie Strasse 4), als Vorlage, s. *Katalog der Basler Münsterphotographien* von Bernhard Wolf, mit begleitendem Text herausgegeben von Konrad Escher (Basel, 1918). Seitdem hat Herr Wolf, allen Wünschen von Forschern in liberalster Weise entgegenkommend, noch zahlreiche Einzelheiten aufgenommen.

damals an seinen jetzigen Platz versetzt worden ist oder später erst, in der Zeit, als die gotische Fassade erbaut wurde, entzieht sich unserer Entscheidung.

NACHWORT

Da der vorliegende Aufsatz schon 1936 abgeschlossen war, konnten die seitdem veröffentlichten Arbeiten, darunter das gedankenreiche und tiefschürfende Buch von Maurice Moullet, *Die Galluspforte des Basler Münsters* (Holbein Verlag, Basel, 1938), nicht mehr berücksichtigt werden. Ueber das "Grossmünster" in Zürich sind wichtige Untersuchungen erschienen von Hans Wiesmann und Hans Hoffmann in den *Mitteilungen der Antiquarischen Gesellschaft*, XXIII (Zürich, 1937–38), ferner hat Joseph Gantner in seiner *Kunstgeschichte der Schweiz*, I (1936), und in einem Aufsatz: "Die Galluspforte am Basler Münster," *Basler Zeitschrift für Geschichte und Altertumskunde*, 36 (1937), zu den hier behandelten Problemen sich geäussert.

GERMAN LATE GOTHIC SCULPTURE IN THE GARDNER MUSEUM, BOSTON

CHARLES L. KUHN

GERMAN sculpture of the Late Gothic period has been very much neglected by American collectors. From the end of the nineteenth century until the World War it was comparatively easy to obtain, but our collectors, trained in the more formal canons of Italian and French art, failed to see the emotional power and decorative quality of the German works. Indeed, the Germans themselves have appreciated this phase of their national art only in relatively recent times. Most of the examples of German sculpture in American collections are of little importance, having been purchased to satisfy a romantic desire for "quaintness" or antiquity.[1] When forming her collection at the end of the nineteenth century, Mrs. Isabella Stewart Gardner, following this romantic impulse, assembled a large number of German statues which have no interest aside from that of being "of the period." Her innate good taste, however, manifested itself in this as in other fields, and several of the German works now in the Gardner Museum are of considerable interest. To treat them chronologically is to make a survey of many of the important phases of the development of the Late Gothic style.

For an illustration of the earliest style of the fifteenth century, we must turn to a work that is North Italian rather than German, — the enthroned Madonna and Child (height, 18¾ inches) which was produced under German influence (Fig. 1). The swinging drapery which ends in calligraphic curves is characteristic of the so-called *weiche Stil* which flourished in Germany about 1420 to 1440. The poorly articulated fingers, the generalized modeling of the nude child, and the rather sullen and lifeless face of the Virgin indicate that the author was not German. In general spirit, the figure resembles the carved tympanum of the portal of the Campo San Zaccaria at Venice of the early fifteenth century.[2] The lively position of the child seems to indicate that the work was part of an Adoration of the Magi.

The tender calligraphic style disappeared from Germany about the middle of the century and was supplanted by a more vigorous angular one, which was introduced from Burgundy and the Netherlands. This phase of German sculpture, which finds its best expression in the works of Nikolaus Gerhaert and Hans

---

[1] In spite of this, however, there are many notable works in the country. In the Metropolitan Museum alone are such significant pieces as the monumental figure of St. James from the thirteenth century; the charming fourteenth-century Visitation group; the early fifteenth-century Austrian Annunciation; the Madonna and St. George from later in the century; two busts of the school of Nikolaus Gerhaert; and many others.

[2] L. Planiscig, *Venezianische Bildhauer der Renaissance* (Vienna, 1921), p. 24, Fig. 20.

FIG. 1. MADONNA AND CHILD ENTHRONED, NORTH ITALIAN
(*c.* 1420–1440)

Multscher, is not represented in the Gardner Museum, but the so-called Trinity Altar, which dates from the eighties of the fifteenth century, reflects much that is to be found in the work of the earlier generation. It consists of a group of figures gathered together from various parts of a single altar and placed in a *schrein* (height, 60 inches; width, 50½ inches) for which they were not originally intended. The *schrein* is of soft wood and is decorated with tracery that is characteristic of South German work at the end of the fifteenth century, whereas the figures are of oak and are carved in a style that is some twenty years earlier (Fig. 2). In the center of the group is a representation of two members of the Trinity — God the Father supporting the figure of Jesus. At the left stands St. Catherine holding a book and a spoke of her wheel, while at her feet crouches a small figure of Maximin clutching a fragment of the wheel. At the right is a bishop-saint.

There are many elements in the style of the group that point to Swabia. The fierce solemnity of the Christ with his twisted, rope-like crown of thorns recalls the famous Man of Sorrows by Hans Multscher of the Cathedral of Ulm. The diadem of the Lord, in outline and proportion, resembles the crown of the figure of Charlemagne by Multscher from the Ulm town hall. These works by Multscher are many years earlier than the Boston figures, but they give a clue to their provenance.

More pertinent analogies can be found in Swabia in the second half of the fifteenth century. The luxuriant and stylized hair and beard of the Lord have their counterpart in the stone figure of Solomon on the *Sakramentshaus* in the church of St. Michael at Hall;[3] in the Bust of David in the Deutsches Museum, Berlin (no. 2222), which is given to the school of Jörg Syrlin the Elder and is dated about 1470;[4] and in the God the Father from the Altar of 1483 in the Schlosskirche of Wernigerode.[5]

Many other comparisons are to be found in the sculpture of Ulm and of Syrlin and his circle. The St. Catherine with her slender proportions, sharp features, and small puckered mouth resembles the female saints in a drawing in Stuttgart which Schuette links with the name of Syrlin and regards as a sketch for a proposed high altar for the Cathedral of Ulm.[6] Similar characteristics appear in the figure of the Virgin in the drawing of the Coronation belonging to the same project.[7] In this latter drawing, the open work of the diadem resembles the crown on the statue of the Lord. The pointed features and small mouth of the St. Catherine appear frequently in the Ulm choir-stall carvings by the elder Syrlin — for example, the so-called Portrait of the Artist's Wife,

[3] Marie Schuette, *Der Schwäbische Schnitzaltar, Studien zur Deutschen Kunstgeschichte*, vol. XCI (Strassburg, 1907), Pl. 24. Professor Wilhelm Koehler first called my attention to the Swabian character of the Trinity Altar.

[4] Theodor Demmler, *Die Bildwerke des Deutschen Museums*, vol. III (Berlin and Leipzig, 1930), pp. 200–201.

[5] *Das Schwäbische Museum* (1925), p. 188, Fig. 2.

[6] Schuette, *op. cit.*, Pl. 65.

[7] *Ibid.*, Pl. 66.

FIG. 2. ALTAR OF THE TRINITY, SWABIAN (*c.* 1480)

the Phrygian Sibyl, the Delphic Sibyl, and the Cumaean Sibyl.[8]   In the Syrlin Self-Portrait and the Ptolomey, the heavy jowls, high cheekbones, and vertical depressions in the flesh of the cheeks resemble the face of the bishop-saint.[9]

Many points in common with works of the school of Syrlin at the end of the century are also found. Although more primitive, harder in modeling, and more stylized, the fierce, austere figure of the Lord is very like the Jesse of the *Dreisitz* at Blaubeuren by Jörg Syrlin the Younger and like the bust of Sigiboto from the choir stalls of the same church.[10]   The figure of Maximin at the feet of St. Catherine has strong analogies with the bust on the choir stalls of Ennetach of the early sixteenth century. The overhanging nose, strongly modeled nostrils, high cheekbones, and strong line of the eyebrows appear in both.[11]

We have seen similarities between the Trinity Altar and Swabian sculpture ranging in date from the second quarter of the fifteenth to the opening years of the sixteenth century. The work is closest to the products of the Syrlin atelier. It is rather more stylized than the works of Jörg Syrlin the Elder but less advanced than the style of his son. It therefore must be a Swabian work and probably of the school of Ulm.

Almost contemporary with the Trinity Altar but far from the main stream of German sculpture is the small figure of a man (height, $40\frac{1}{2}$ inches) on a prancing horse (Fig. 3). Stylistically, the work is related to a long series of South German St. Martins which range in date from 1430 to 1500. The facial type and the treatment of the hair resemble the relief of St. Martin of about 1480 in the Stiftskirche of Aschaffenburg.[12] The St. Martin on the epitaph of Ortwin Lupold and his mother in the cloister of the same church, which is dated after 1483, is strikingly like the Boston work, even to the curious short ears of the horse.[13] The rather childish treatment of the animal in strict profile with the foreleg raised appears in such provincial works as the St. Martin of about 1480 in the church at Stephling[14] and the crude stone relief of about 1480–1490 on the church at Grossostheim.[15] These comparisons indicate that the figure is a provincial Southern German work of about 1480 to 1490.

The small round cap and long sleeves reveal that the figure is a huntsman, for they are details of costume that appear frequently in falconing scenes in illuminated manuscripts of the second half of the fifteenth century. The long sleeves were part of the fashionable dress earlier in the century but lingered on

[8] Julius Baum, *Ulmer Kunst* (Stuttgart and Leipzig, 1911), pp. 89–93.

[9] *Ibid.*, pp. 89–95.

[10] Julius Baum, *Kloster Blaubeuren* (Augsburg, 1926), pp. 25, 39.

[11] Erich Grill, *Jörg Syrlin d. Ä.*, *Studien zur Deutschen Kunstgeschichte*, vol. CXXI (Strassburg, 1910), Pl. XII, Fig. 17.

[12] *Die Kunstdenkmäler des Königreichs Bayern, Regierungsbezirk Unterfranken und Aschaffenburg*, vol. XIX (Munich, 1918), p. 48, Fig. 22.

[13] *Ibid.*, pp. 142, 144, Fig. 108.

[14] *Die Kunstdenkmäler von Bayern, Niederbayern*, vol. XX, *Bezirksamt Bogen* (Munich, 1929), pp. 410, 412, Fig. 262.

[15] *Die Kunstdenkmäler von Bayern, Unterfranken*, vol. XXIV, *Bezirksamt Aschaffenburg* (Munich, 1927), pp. 24, 25, Fig. 13.

FIG. 3. ST. HUBERT, SOUTH GERMAN (*c.* 1480–1490)

for a considerable time in hunting costumes and were used to wrap around the wrist as a protection against the talons of a falcon. Since the man is surely a hunter, the artist designed the work as a representation of St. Hubert. The left hand of the figure is making a gesture, presumably toward the stag, and the right hand originally held a weapon, probably a cross-bow. An unmounted St. Hubert, similarly arranged, formed part of an altar of about 1480 in the Stiftskirche at Aschaffenburg.[16]

One of the loveliest manifestations of the German Late Gothic is to be found in the sculpture of the region of the Upper Rhine. This school began as a result of Flemish influence introduced by the engraver, Master E. S., and the sculptor, Nikolaus Gerhaert, but rapidly developed a character of its own. A delicate femininity, a restless mannerism that is almost rococo, is to be found in the Dangolsheim Madonna, the altar of Lautenbach, and the high altar of the church at Nördlingen — works which are among the masterpieces of this school.

In the Gardner Museum is a figure of St. Elizabeth (height, 47 inches) which, in style and quality, is among the best of the Upper Rhenish products (Fig. 4). Her widow's veil is wrapped closely about her head, and she holds a loaf of bread in her right hand. The wine pitcher which was once held in her left hand has disappeared. The costume and attributes resemble the St. Elizabeth of the high altar in the Church of St. James at Rothenburg on the Tauber.[17] The position of the Boston figure, with one leg bent and the other straight, the voluminous drapery falling in long angular folds, the line of the mantle drawn diagonally across the body and held by the left arm, the slender attenuated fingers carefully articulated, and the sharply modeled features all indicate that the work belongs to the Upper Rhine School.

The saint is closely related to the little linden-wood St. Barbara in the Berlin museum (no. 2240)[18] and with the Madonna of the Lautenbach altar[19] which were executed in the eighties of the fifteenth century. The style is slightly more advanced, however, the face more subtle in its expression, and the feeling for form beneath the drapery more pronounced, indicating that the work is about ten years later.

Not very much later in date than the St. Elizabeth but having none of her mannered charm is the tall gaunt figure of St. George (height, $58\frac{1}{2}$ inches). The armor of the saint (Fig. 5), from which the gilding has almost entirely disappeared, is of the type in fashion in the last quarter of the fifteenth century. The St. George of about 1500 in the museum at Sigmaringen is clad in very similar armor.[20] The tassets, fastened to the underside of the taces without visible

---

[16] *Die Kunstdenkmäler des Königreichs Bayern, Regierungsbezirk Unterfranken und Aschaffenburg*, vol. XIX (Munich, 1918), p. 59, Fig. 29.

[17] W. Pinder, *Die Deutsche Plastik vom ausgehenden Mittelalter bis zum Ende der Renaissance* (Potsdam, 1929), vol. II, p. 338, Fig. 317.

[18] Demmler, *op. cit.*, pp. 144–146.

[19] Otto Schmidt, *Oberrheinische Plastik im ausgehenden Mittelalter* (Freiburg i. B., 1924), Pl. 49.

[20] *Staedel-Jahrbuch*, vols. III–IV (1924) p. 74, Pl. XXXI.

FIG. 4. ST. ELIZABETH, UPPER RHINE (*c.* 1490)

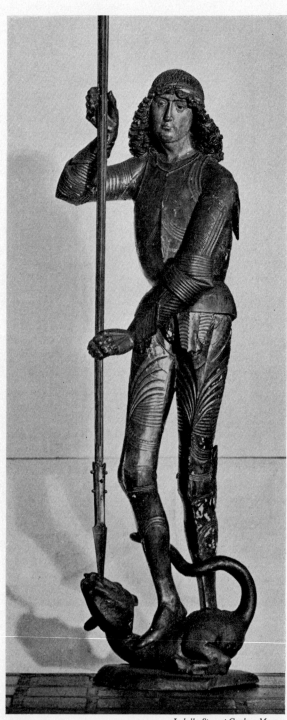

FIG. 5. ST. GEORGE, TYROLESE (*c.* 1490–1500)

FIG. 6. ST. CHRISTOPHER AND ST. GEORGE, TYROLESE (*c.* 1500)

buckles, differ from the Sigmaringen figure but are similar to the treatment in
a Tyrolese painting of St. Christopher and St. George in the Elderkin Collection
at Princeton (Fig. 6). The many points of similarity between the Boston figure
and the painting, as well as with other works of the Tyrol school, indicate that
the statue was executed in that district.

The period that saw the dawn of the Renaissance and Reformation — the
late fifteenth and early sixteenth centuries — was an age of great individuals
in Germany. Luther, Melanchthon, Hans Sachs, Maximilian I, Dürer, Cranach,
Grünewald, Altdorfer all belong to these years; and among the sculptors we
find such great names as Pieter Vischer, Tilmann Riemenschneider, Veit Stoss,
and Adam Kraft. The sculpture of these years still clung to the Late Gothic
style with its vigorous dynamic pictorialism. At times it created tremendous
crescendos of tumultuous chaotic movement and indistinct form, as though in
conscious protest against the clear, static, plastic style of the Italian Renaissance.

To this period belongs the small linden-wood figure of St. Jerome (height,
$24\frac{1}{2}$ inches) which is of the Lower Franconian School and related to the work of
Tilmann Riemenschneider (Fig. 7). Comparing the face with that of the St.
Luke from the Münnerstadt altar now in Berlin, we find the same detailed rendering of physiognomy, the same wrinkles beneath the eyes, the same sunken cheeks
and high cheekbones, the same thin mouth and small pointed chin. A similar
treatment of facial detail appears in the St. Kilian of the Neumünster at Würzburg and the St. Matthew in the Deutsches Museum in Berlin.[21]

The work lacks the sharpness and the careful articulation of Riemenschneider
himself, who never would have rendered the fingers as monotonously as those of
the right hand. The face is rather too positive in feeling and lacks the dreamy
subjectivity of the master. Moreover, the drapery is too simple and the figure too
frontal and static in pose to be a creation of Riemenschneider himself.

The Late Gothic style in Germany became such a perfect expression of the
national temperament that in many districts it took on the character of a folk
art. This was particularly true in Bavaria, where it lived on in one form or another until almost the end of the eighteenth century. During the course of the
sixteenth century it became somewhat subdued by classicism but burst forth
again with its characteristic illogical exuberance in the baroque and rococo.

The very spirited group of St. Martin and the Beggar (height, 49 inches),
which is a Bavarian work of about 1520 (Fig. 8), was executed at a time when
classicism was first making itself felt in southern Germany but, aside from the
sixteenth-century costume, there is little suggestion of the Renaissance in the
work. The lively figure style and restless mannered drapery are typically Late
Gothic.

A number of Bavarian examples are closely related to this work, the most
striking being the St. Martin from Freising, now in the Bavarian National Mu-

[21] Justus Bier, *Tilmann Riemenschneider* (Würzburg, 1925–1930), Pls. 28, 118, 119, 131.

FIG. 7. ST. JEROME, LOWER FRANCONIAN
(*c.* 1510)

FIG. 8. ST. MARTIN AND THE BEGGAR, FRANCONIAN (*c.* 1520)

seum at Munich,[22] and the group from the altar in the chapel of the palace of Reichersbeuern near Tölz.[23] The figure style and facial type of the Boston work slightly resemble those of the Munich Christophorus Master.

The Altar of the Holy Kinship, which was executed a few years later than the St. Martin, has somewhat more Renaissance influence, as is seen in the ample proportions and the relatively broad handling of the drapery (Fig. 9). In the

Isabella Stewart Gardner Museum

FIG. 9. ALTAR OF THE HOLY KINSHIP, SAXON (*c.* 1520)

schrein (height, 61 inches; width, 41½ inches) is the conventional arrangement of the Holy Kinship, while on the interior of the wings (width, 20½ inches) are high-relief carvings of St. Barbara, St. Dorothea, St. Catherine, and an unidentified female saint. The exterior of the wings is painted with poorly preserved figures of a bishop-saint, St. Martin, St. George, and St. Roch. The polychromy of the interior is somewhat repainted.

The feminine types, with their high rounded brows and small doll-like features, are almost identical with those found in a Thuringian or Saxon altar of about 1510 to 1520 in the Deutsches Museum at Berlin (no. 7711).[24] Even

[22] *Cicerone*, vol. IV (1912), pp. 379–380, Fig. 4.

[23] Richard Hoffmann, *Bayerische Altarbaukunst* (Munich, 1923), no. 80, pp. 77, 270–271.

[24] Demmler, *op. cit.*, pp. 293–294.

FIG. 10. ST. FLORIAN, SOUTH GERMAN (*c.* 1525)

the hard slender figures of saints painted on the exterior of the Berlin altar resemble the paintings of the Boston work. The figure style of the latter is slightly more advanced, the proportions more ample, indicating that it must be somewhat later in date.

The Late Gothic traits that still linger in the Holy Kinship altar are almost completely absent in the St. Florian, a South German work (Fig. 10). The figure (height, 62 inches) is encased in so-called Maximilian armor which was covered with tin foil, now completely hidden by a dirty brown coat of paint. The fully developed ridges on the breast plate, the blunt shoes, and the long jointed taces that cover the legs almost to the knees are typical of armor of about 1525.[25] The armor and the pose of the figure are very similar to those of a Bavarian St. Florian of about 1525, formerly in dealers' hands.[26]

Many elements in the style of the figure indicate that its author deliberately attempted to work in a Renaissance style. The simple plastic mass differs completely from the pictorial aims of the Late Gothic. The frontal position, with one leg bent and the other straight, is in imitation of the antique. The curious helmet that resembles a guardsman's headgear of the nineteenth century is a naïve effort at an archaeological reconstruction of Roman armor. When we find the German artist thus consciously imitating a foreign style, we know that the wonderful spontaneity of the Late Gothic is dead.

[25] I am indebted to Mr. Stephen V. Grancsay for many of the comments on the armor of the figures of St. George and St. Florian.

[26] *Münchener Jahrbuch der Bildenden Kunst*, vol. II (1907), p. 79, Fig. 15.

VII. MEDIEVAL ART IN SCANDINAVIA AND THE BRITISH ISLES

THE SCULPTURED STONES OF WALES

R. A. S. MACALISTER

THE ancient monumental stones with incised or sculptured ornament to be seen in the Principality of Wales present certain anomalous features which it is not easy to explain. The standard of artistic attainment is, on the whole, low — sometimes quite remarkably so: and at first sight we are tempted to look upon these relics as late degradations of the school of design to which they belong. But some of them bear inscriptions which, if their purport has been rightly apprehended, would oblige us to assign to them a date earlier, even by some centuries, than the chief sculptured stones of Ireland, and almost as early as the earliest crosses of Northumbria. They therefore seem to belong rather to the upward stage in the development of this type of art, which, however, never succeeded in attaining perfection within the Principality. Only a few of them adventure any attempt at figure sculpture: in the great majority the decoration is of the ordinary "Celtic" types, interlacements, key patterns, and so forth. And even these are often badly and clumsily set out.

There are three groups: slabs with incised ornament, slabs with incised crosses, and standing crosses. Of the first, which is naturally the smallest of the three, by far the most remarkable is the stone from Llywell, B.,[1] now in the British Museum (Fig. 1).

This stone has been utilized for monumental purposes more than once. On one face it bears a single cup-mark, which presumably comes down from prehistoric antiquity. On the same face there is an Roman inscription, commemorating one *Macu-Treni of Salicidunum*, wherever this place may have been: the epitaph is echoed in Ogham letters on the edge of the stone. On the opposite face there is a group of devices which look more like a specimen of Red Indian picture-writing than anything else. Presumably it is Christian in purport, as crosses are included in the complex. Its arrangement in panels reminds us of the figured panels of standing crosses in Ireland, which Professor Kingsley Porter worked so hard to elucidate. In the panels there appear human figures, serpents (?), ships (?), and waves of water (?), but (as these few words show) a query has to be affixed to every statement that may be made about them. Various attempts, all obviously unsuccessful, have been made to interpret these crude figures: they are really too rudimentary to tell their story. Before them we feel like a man who has never learned shorthand, confronted with a page of stenographic curves and strokes. Possibly they have reference to the biography of the

---

[1] This and similar initials throughout the present paper stand for the names of the counties of Wales:

A.	Anglesey	Cn.	Carnarvon	Mg.	Montgomery
B.	Brecon	D.	Denbigh	Mr.	Merioneth
Cd.	Cardigan	F.	Flint	P.	Pembroke
Cm.	Carmarthen	G.	Glamorgan	R.	Radnor.

man to whose memory the stone was appropriated; and without the knowledge
of his personality, which is nowhere available, we have no clue to their explanation. He was certainly not the citizen of Salicidunum mentioned on the other
side of the stone; for it is clear that these barbaric figures are not contemporary
with the inscriptions, and have nothing to do with them. When the stone is set
up so as to show the inscriptions, and to place them in the normal direction of
reading, the device is partly buried in the ground, and is turned upside down:
and vice versa.

The other stones with incised ornament need not detain us. A zigzag between two lines appears above the inscription on the *Culidori* stone at Llangaffo,
A. (Fig. 2); and there is a slight ornamental development of the geometrical
device of a square with its diagonals, on inscribed stones at Devynock, B. (Fig. 3),
and Tregaron, Cd. (Fig. 4) — the latter is now in the National Museum of
Wales. But for the greater part the incised decoration takes the form of crosses
in one shape or another; and this leads us to our second group.

As in Ireland, so in Wales, there is a considerable number of rude memorial
stones inscribed with plain or slightly ornamental crosses. Many of these bear
no other device: others have an inscription in addition to the cross. But it is not
always certain, in such cases, that the cross is contemporary with the inscription; there are indeed some stones of which it is quite certain that the cross is a
later addition. Such are the inscribed stones at Egremont, Cm., Clydai, P., and
Silian, Cd., upon which plain crosses have been cut, partly defacing the lettering of the inscription; and the Llywell stone, already mentioned, where a
similar plain cross is awkwardly inserted between the words of the Roman inscription, and can hardly have been put there by its author.

This being so, we cannot always with assurance use the inscriptions, so far
as they are datable, as guides to a chronology of the types of the crosses. We
have indeed hardly any indications upon which to found any such chronology.
In a device so simple as a cross, its form may depend upon the competence of
the artist, as much as upon the year or the century in which he worked: and the
way in which the design is carried out shows only too clearly that, in the majority
of cases, the artist's competence was of a very low order.

Perfectly plain crosses, consisting of two strokes and nothing else, are not
common, though they are not unknown. The crosses on both faces of the Llywell stone are examples of this most rudimentary of forms. As a rule, however,
some effort is made to add interest to the device. The simplest and commonest
way is to make the four branches terminate outward in expansions, usually
triangular or semicircular; more rarely circular (Fig. 5). As an illustration may
be cited the cross cut on the top of the *Bodvoc* stone from Margam Mountain, G.,
now in the lapidary museum at Margam Abbey. The cross on the *Artbeu* stone
in the Church of Merthyr Tydfil, G., shows the same scheme, varied. There is
here a plain Latin cross, the top of which is broken off; a circle is drawn round
the center, and the remaining arms run through semicircles or triangles (Fig. 6).

The stem and arms of a cross may be formed of two parallel lines (not of single strokes) diverging, or otherwise ornamentally treated, at their outer ends. In such cases the lines may cross one another at the center, or one pair of strokes may be stopped to allow the other pair to pass through, or both pairs may be stopped, leaving the crossing open. These varieties are represented diagrammatically in Figures 7–9: specimens will be found at Llanfihangel Cwmdu, B., Llangors, B., and Margam, G., respectively.

Crosses with bifid ends appear at Caldey Island, P. (Fig. 10), and a cross potent, a rare form in Wales, at Margam (Fig. 11). The stem and arms are fantastically shaped on a slab at Llangwyryfon, Cd. (Fig. 12).

Next in order comes the elaboration of the cross by the addition to the corners of pellets (Trawsmawr, Cm., Fig. 13), of a triangle of pellets (Pen y Mynydd, B., Fig. 14 — the top of this device is now broken off), or crosslets (Bryngwyn, R., Fig. 15). Here may also be mentioned stones bearing the Alpha-Omega in the corners. There are two of these, both in Brecon. The first (Fig. 34), from Cildu, near Llanwrtyd Wells, now in Brecon Museum, has the Greek letters in the upper quarters of the cross. The second, of which the relevant part is shown in Fig. 35, is a stone at Llanddetty, covered with extremely crude ornament and a difficult inscription. Here there is an *Alpha* in each of the upper corners, and an *Omega* in each of the lower corners: it takes a few minutes to recognize those devices, and it is quite evident that the artist of the cross copied them without having the faintest idea of their meaning.

The last three stones show a cross surrounded with a circle, or what is meant for a circle. Of this form there is a long series of varieties, too numerous to catalogue here. Almost every specimen has some individuality of its own. But they may be grouped primarily into two divisions, Greek crosses and Latin crosses: in the former the entire cross is within the circle, in the latter the stem projects downward outside the circle. Of the former we may mention the Clydai, P., stone (Fig. 16), in which the cross is *pattée* (formed of four segments of circles "addorsed" in pairs); the Bridell, P., stone (Fig. 17), on which it assumes almost (but not quite) a quatrefoil form; and the curious example at Llandyssilio, P. (Fig. 18), in which the center and the four arms are defined by five circles. Ornamental varieties, introducing fret and interlacing devices, meet us in the stones from Pen Arthur, P., now preserved in St. David's Cathedral (Figs. 21, 22).

Of the Latin type we may mention an ingenious example at Llanfrynach, B. (Fig. 23), in which the stem, carried downward, is transformed into the stem of another cross in relief by cutting away the background; and a stone (half of it broken away) at Llanllyr, Cd. (Fig. 24), bearing a cross in which the stem is forked below and ends in two spirals. A similar device appears at Llanddewi Brefi, Cd., but in this case there is no circle.

One of the Margam stones shows a strange anomaly (Fig. 19). This bears a plain Latin cross in a circle; near the bottom of the stem it is crossed by a segment of a circle, concavity upwards (resembling the flukes of an anchor). If the concavity were downward (as on a stone at Southill in Cornwall) this curve

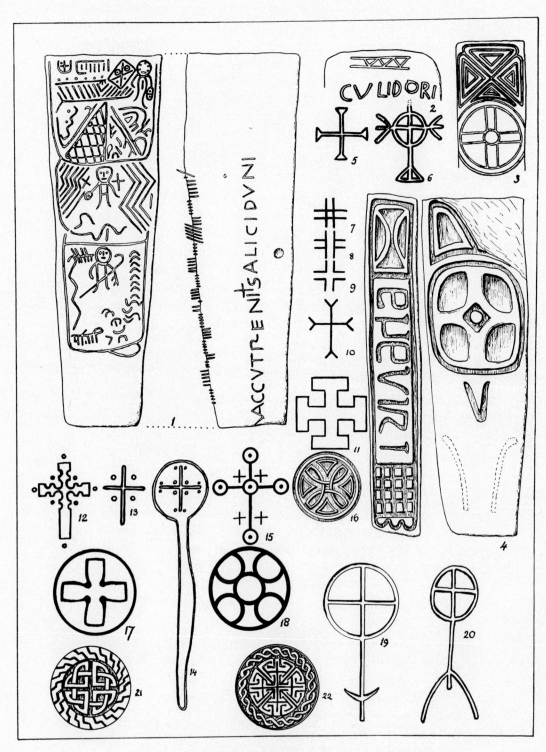

ORNAMENT ON SCULPTURED STONES OF WALES

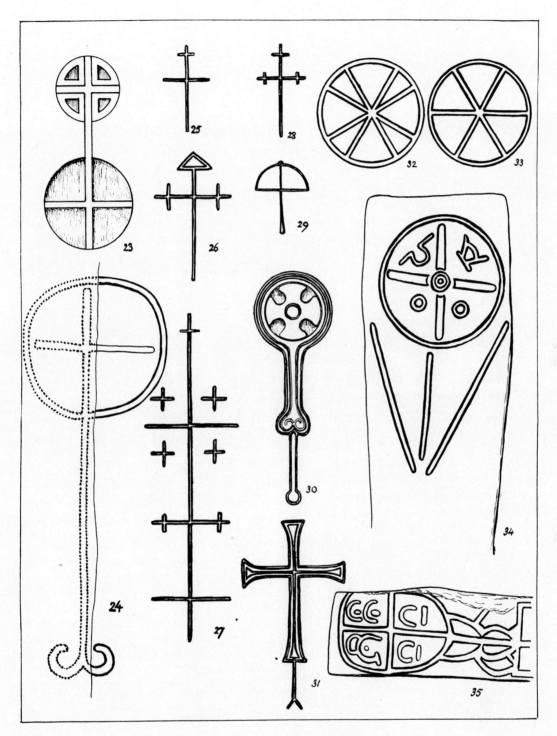

ORNAMENT ON SCULPTURED STONES OF WALES

would certainly be meant as a suggestion of the Calvary-hill on which the cross was set: the reversed curve is most probably an artistic variation, by some one who had forgotten the original meaning of the device. It is correctly rendered on a stone from Tre Hywel, P. (Fig. 20).

Crosslets on the arms of the cross are rare, and not found, in any example, on all four arms. At Llanddewi Brefi (Fig. 25), in one stone, the top is crossletted; three arms were crossletted in a cross on a stone, now destroyed, at Llangyndeyrn, Cm. (Fig. 28); while at Capel Colman, P. (Fig. 26), the side arms are thus treated, but the top terminates in a triangle, the base of which, exceptionally, is turned toward the center of the cross and not away from it. More elaborate crossletting is to be seen on the stone at Llanfihangel Ioreth, Cm. (Fig. 27).

A well-known stone from Llandeilo Fawr, Cm., now in the Carmarthen Museum, bears a device resembling an arrow in a bow (Fig. 29). Obviously this is not the artist's intention, however, for the point of the arrow, not the butt, is held against the string of the bow. We must treat it as a cross in which the circular segments in the lower quarters have been suppressed.

There is an interesting series of Latin crosses, derived from processional crosses; in these the head forms a complete cross-device below which an extension projects, evidently representing the staff upon which the cross was carried. Good examples of this are to be seen on some of the numerous slabs at St. Dogmael's, P. (Fig. 30). There is another, and a simpler, example, at Llangynnor, Cm. (Fig. 31). The Pen y Mynydd stone, already quoted (Fig. 14), shows a cross, with ornamental pellets, inside a circular disc. This is mounted on a stem (the curvature of which is probably due to the artist's incompetence), and the stem ends in a point — suggesting something that would be thrust in the ground. The legend of how one of St. Patrick's catechumens was wounded accidentally in the foot by the saint's crozier during the ceremony of baptism shows that these objects were sometimes very sharply pointed.

The most remarkable of the cross-slabs is a group confined to southwestern Glamorganshire, evidently the products of a single artist or of his school. From the numerous examples of the type in Margam Abbey, this may be called the "Margam type." The cross is a cross *pattée* — of the kind commonly but erroneously called "the Maltese Cross" — inside a circle. In crosses of this kind the four arms are of equal length, and triangular in shape. These arms in the "Margam type" are not solid, but merely outlined, so that the cross assumes the shape of a wheel with eight radiating spokes; and it would appear that the artist came to look upon it as a wheel, for the spokes sometimes do not, as they ought to do, group naturally into pairs, and they are not invariably eight in number. (See the diagrams, Figs. 32, 33.)

The sculptured crosses were studied, from the point of view of the construction of their ornament, by the late J. Romilly Allen, in an elaborate paper in *Archaeologia Cambrensis* (1899, p. 1). It is hardly necessary to retrace the ground which he there covered; but some points omitted by him may here be noted.

In the history of the development of standing crosses in Ireland, among the earliest — certainly the rudest — are those which consist of a slab of stone with two semicircular nicks cut in each of the edges. These nicks separate the arm from the sides of the cross, but the arm does not project beyond the sides. The next step in the evolution is to deepen the nicks and to shave off some inches from the surface of the edges above and below them, thus making the arm project slightly. In Ireland this rudimentary form of cross is found only in the regions which must always have been the most backward, such as the western islands; and the cross thus fashioned has seldom any ornamentation upon its surface. It is therefore surprising to find in an important ecclesiastical center like Llanbadarn, near Aberystwyth, Cd., and in a cross of some artistic pretensions, this crude device of formation followed. The word "pretensions," it must be said, is appropriate; for the artistry of the sculpture is actually of a very degraded quality.[2] It has one large figure in one of the panels, but nothing to indicate whom it is intended to represent; two panels of grotesque animal figures; and another panel containing the crudest extant representation of a scene, not infrequently found on sculptured crosses, which Professor Kingsley Porter was the first to identify as Jacob wrestling with the Angel. The rest of the stone is covered with key pattern and interlacements, of no artistic merit whatsoever.

In Romilly Allen's paper, above quoted, eighty-four stones in Wales are enumerated as bearing "Celtic" ornament. Since he wrote, a few more have been discovered; the total may now be in the neighborhood of ninety. But on the other hand Allen's list must be slightly reduced. For example, he counts separately four fragments which were found during the restoration of the church of Llanddewi-aber-Arth, Cd., and which are now preserved inside the building. It is certain that these fragments all belonged to one monument, which must have been well above the ordinary Welsh average in both artistic and epigraphic interest.

The stones enumerated by Allen [3] are classified by him under the following heads:

Unshaped cross-slabs	5
Rectangular cross-slabs	14
Complete erect crosses	21
Cross-shafts still erect	13
Fragments of cross-shafts	9
Cross-bases	3
Recumbent coped stones	3
Miscellaneous fragments	9

but this requires some correction. The "unshaped cross-slabs" includes the Llanwnnws, Cd., stone, which, though broken, is not of a haphazard shape;

---

[2] This can be seen very clearly in the best available illustration, *Archaeologia Cambrensis*, 1897, facing p. 152.

[3] Seven stones in his list are for some reason omitted from this classification, which thus contains only 77 items.

and one unrecorded example at Margam should be included. The Neuadd Siarman, B., and Llanarthney, Cm., stones, included as "complete erect crosses" are slabs rather than crosses; the "Coychurch No. 2" stone (G.), having been broken by the fall of the church tower, and having lost some of the fragments, must unfortunately be removed from the list of "complete erect crosses"; and the Llanddewi-aber-Arth fragments, which should be together under the heading "fragments of cross-shafts" are scattered under the heads "recumbent coped stones" and "miscellaneous." A "corpus" of these stones, to supersede the incomplete and inartistic work of Westwood (already nearly sixty years old) is much needed. When the Royal Commission on Ancient Monuments in Wales and Monmouthshire has finished its labors, then will be the time to begin this and a number of similar synthetic works on the antiquities of the Principality.

Figure-subjects are found on the following monuments (in addition to the Llanbadarn Cross, already mentioned):

Llandough, G. On all four sides the base of the cross has figures, the significance of which is unknown. On the north and south faces are busts, the southern one apparently wearing a crown; on the eastern face is a row of five busts, one of them crowned, and three bearing crosses; and on the southern face is a horseman, drawn with a very low seat upon his horse, and with the leg extended forward, after the manner of horseman figures represented in some of the illuminated manuscripts. The upper part of the monument is decorated exclusively with simple interlacing patterns. The architectural character of the cross, with heavy corner bowtells to the stem, is unique.

Margam, G. (*Conbelin* cross). Two figures, possibly (but doubtfully) the Virgin Mary and St. John, one on each side of the central cross. This cross must have been broken at some early time, for it was found necessary to discard the lower part of the base, and to fashion a new tenon at the bottom end of the upper part. The base has a number of animal figures resembling the groups of animals on the base of the cross of Kells in Ireland.

Mynydd Gelli Onen, G. A very crude figure of the Crucifixion, with the figure apparently robed in a tunic bordered with geometrical ornament. (Westwood puts difficulties in the way of finding this monument by calling the place "Mount Gellyonen" and saying that it is not far from "Llandewick" near "Pontadawr" railway station. There are no such places on the map: they should be "Llangiwg" and "Pontardawe" respectively.

Gnoll, G. now in the Museum of Swansea Institution. A figure with a kilt and with hands upraised, but probably meant for a crucified figure,[4] though there is no indication of the cross.

Llangan, Cm. A crucifix figure with the sponge- and spear-bearer at the sides: the only example in Wales of this usual Celtic grouping.

---

[4] It may also be an *Orans*.

Llandefaelog Fach, B. A warrior in a tunic reaching to his knees, and carrying a spear (?) and a dagger. On a slab, otherwise decorated with a cross and interlacements, and with an unfinished inscription, *Briamail flou.* . . .

Llanhamlach, B. A slab bearing a cross and very crude geometrical ornament. Beneath the arms of the cross and two figures, male and female, at first sight apparently clothed in tunics, but really nude (Adam and Eve). There is an imperfect inscription in Latin, to the effect that "Moridic raised the stone," which commemorates a certain "(N.N. son) of Iohannes." The designs upon the stone are of the crudest and rudest style of art.

Llanfrynach, B. Much the same may be said about the stone in the neighboring Church of Llanfrynach, which commemorates one "Ioh(ann)is," perhaps the father of the owner of the Llamhamlach memorial. Along with badly executed interlacing ornament it has a figure with hands upraised, resembling that on the Gnoll stone, and presumably to be interpreted in a like manner.

St. David's, P. A broken slab bearing an ornate cross covered with interlacement, and a figure of a seraph with six wings, of which three are shown, disposed in accordance with the vision of Isaiah.

Meifod, Mg. Cross *pattée* in a circle, with crucified figure. Remainder of stone covered with a cross, interlacements, etc.

Penmon, A. A cross showing in its ornament close affinity with the carvings of the Isle of Man and of Ireland. A figure-scene similar to that on the Kells Cross, interpreted by Professor Kingsley Porter as the Temptation of St. Anthony. Another apparently representing David and his sheep.

Maen Achwyfan F., *Disert* F. On these two miserable specimens of degraded art there are small figures, but nothing to indicate what, if anything, the sculptor intended by them.

The ornamental devices have been so fully analyzed by Romilly Allen, in the paper quoted above, that there is little to add to what he has said on this part of the subject — or to his conclusion, that the North Wales stones show indications of Mercian and Scandinavian influence, and those of South Wales are cognate with some of the crosses in Cornwall and Devon, and with Carolingian manuscripts. We may further remind ourselves of the evident combination of Irish and Manx influence just where we should expect it, on the Penmon Cross.

But Allen has hardly, if at all, touched on the subject of chronology. It was said, earlier in the present article, that we cannot always assume that a rude cross and an inscription which happen to come together upon a stone are necessarily contemporary; but in the case of more elaborate monuments we are justified in seeking for light upon the date of the stones from the inscriptions which they bear, and from any historical names which they may contain. The following is a chronological list of all the identifications which can be reasonably made, and gives us a certain chronological framework into which the rest of the monuments have to be fitted.

CENTURY	PLACE	PERSON
VI.	Llanfallteg, Cm.	Voteporix, King of Dyfed
	Llansadwrn, A.	St. Sadwrn Farchog
VII.	Llangadwaladr, A.	Cadfan, King of Gwynedd
VIII.	Llantwit Major, G.	Samson, abbot (two stones) [5]
	Margam, G.	Peter and Ilci, mentioned in Book of Llandaf
IX.	Llanfynydd, Cm.	Iudon, son of Meredydd, King of Dyfed
	Carew, P.	Meredydd, King of Dyfed, and his son Regin
	Nevern, P.	Eugan, son of Meredydd, King of Dyfed
	Valle Crucis, D.	Eliseg's monument, erected by Concenn, King of Powys
	Llandough, G.	Irbic, a person mentioned in Book of Llandaf
	Llantwit Major, G.	Howel ap Rhys, King of Glywysing
XI.	Partrishow, B.	Font dated to time of Cenhillyn, *ca.* 1060 A.D.
XII.	Llanfihangel y Traethau, Mr.	Monument dated to time of Owein Gwynydd
XIII.	Pentre Foelas, D.	Stone bearing the name of Llywelyn ap Iorwerth and dated 1233
XIV.	Newcastle Bridgend, B.	Monument of Ricardus, vicar 1265–1305

Of these, certainly the most important is the group of crosses at Carew, Nevern, and Llanfynydd — the last-named now in the National Museum. These three monuments are certainly not only contemporary, but are the work of one hand: an unskilful hand, it must be confessed, for his attempts at interlacing devices are singularly amateurish! His inscriptions also are difficult to read, at least in the first two of these monuments. But they certainly contain the names of Meredydd (spelled *Margiteut*) and *Eiudon* (not so obviously *Regin*, but that is the only interpretation of the end of the Carew inscription which will make sense). The Nevern stone gives us the name *Hauen*, which might pass as a phonetic rendering of *Owein*, the later form of Eugan. This is the "snag" in the identification, for at so early a date this name should still retain its *g*. But it is next to impossible to discard the identification. Here are three crosses, obviously commemorating closely related persons of outstanding importance. Here are four names, every one of which occurs in the royal family of the region where the stones are found: and the similarity of these stones to one of the Abbot Samson stones at Llantwit, which again is quite clearly a work of the same designer, dates these monuments to the beginning of the ninth century — the date of the family in question. So far from philology correcting the identification, it is not too much to say that the

---

[5] End of eighth or beginning of ninth century.

identification corrects philology, and shows that although the *g* might have been retained in literary spelling as a fossil of speech (like the *l* in the English word *would*) it had already dropped out of popular pronunciation and might be omitted when a person of small literary attainments wrote the name phonetically. This group of four stones gives us a fixed chronological point in the history of Celtic art, and they must be reckoned with in all future studies of its development.

SOME EXAMPLES OF VIKING FIGURE REPRESENTATION IN SCANDINAVIA AND THE BRITISH ISLES*

ESTHER ISABEL SEAVER

LEGEND and history have so long described the Vikings as conquerors and destroyers only that it has become the custom of archaeologists and art historians alike to assume that these northmen must have been without either innate artistic ability or interest. The result has been that when objects of real originality or aesthetic merit have appeared either in Scandinavia itself or in the Viking colonies in the British Isles, Swedish and Norwegian scholars, with characteristic modesty concerning the creative powers of their barbarian ancestors, have all too frequently attributed whatever good these objects possessed to foreign influences if not execution. To a slightly lesser degree the same prejudices have governed Scandinavian philologists in formulating their theories regarding the spread of the great body of heroic legends among the various peoples of the north.[1] However, as has been pointed out before,[2] this assumption that these Vikings were without artistic imagination is especially widespread in connection with figure representation, for recently Scandinavian ornament of the pre-Romanesque period has fared better at the hands of critics, due perhaps to its more obvious relationship to the ornament of the British Isles and the continent.[3]

The purpose of this paper is threefold: first, to define briefly the distinguishing characteristics of figure representation as practiced by Swedes, Norwegians, and Danes in the various parts of Scandinavia prior to the period of the great Viking migrations of the ninth and tenth centuries which resulted in the establishment of colonies in distant regions;[4] second, to show how this style was modified during the Viking period in the several localities within the larger geographical divisions of "Atlantic North" and "Baltic North";[5] and last, to suggest how this style was not to be supplanted by the more cosmopolitan "Pilgrimage" one until it had left its imprint upon the earlier Romanesque in those regions where it had previously held sway.

---

* This article is an outgrowth of a more detailed study of "The Sigurd Saga in Art," which was done as a doctoral dissertation under the guidance of my teacher, the late A. Kingsley Porter.

[1] Sophus Bugge, *Home of the Eddic Poems* (London, 1899), translated by W. H. Schofield.

[2] Seaver, "Figured Sculptures on the Isle of Man," *Johnny Roosval den 29 Augusti 1921. AMICO AMICI*, pp. 109–116.

[3] Brøndsted, *Early English Ornament* (London, 1924); Nils Åberg, *Forhistorisk nordisk ornamentik* (Stockholm, 1925).

[4] T. D. Kendrick, *The Vikings* (London, 1930), for a general account of the migrations as well as the settlements.

[5] Johnny Roosval, *Romansk Konst* (Stockholm, 1930). Roosval divides Europe geographically into territories based upon pilgrimage routes and the artistic styles that prevailed; to the "Baltic North" belongs Sweden, to the "Atlantic North" Norway.

That Scandinavian pictorial artists have always had a strong feeling for design and a tendency to reduce the human figure to a two-dimensional quantity is a thesis that might be substantiated for periods other than those dealt with here. This lack of interest in three-dimensional form is further demonstrated by the fact that from the period before the middle of the eleventh century, or the period before Christian artists from England and France had changed the native style, there does not remain a single piece of monumental sculpture in the round; nor is there any attempt on the part of artists working in relief to simulate the plastic. The sagas which frequently refer to the other arts make no mention of such sculptures.

Although these Vikings apparently had little use for sculpture in the round, they took great delight in a good story — carved or woven as well as written or sung. Figures in relief were either completely subordinated to a decorative formula, as on the Oseberg wagon (Fig. 5), or they were scattered over the entire surface of the panel in a disorderly fashion (Fig. 8). In the latter scheme several episodes were included in a single compartment. A few exceptions to these generalizations will be noted later.

During this pre-Romanesque period the chief mediums employed for figure representations were precious and base metals, wood, stone, and textiles. Of the first three there are many examples; of textiles there are a few actually dated in the ninth century, and several executed later after earlier prototypes. Since the stone reliefs in all these regions often show that the craftsmen were more familiar with the technique of wood carving than that of stone cutting (Figs. 9 and 10), it would seem reasonable to conclude that wood, which was plentiful, must have been the favorite material. When we consider how perishable it is, we realize what a small proportion of the whole production has probably survived.

Of the interest in figure portrayal during the migration period (*c.* 400–*c.* 700) there is ample testimony in the large number of metal objects, such as the helmet from Vendel, the Torslunda bronze reliefs, and the many gold bracteates. These last are thin flat plaques of gold with figures and ornament in repoussé. They vary in diameter from one to three inches, usually, though there are a few slightly wider ones. Most of them are decorated with a head or figure in the center, which in the larger ones is framed by a series of concentric moldings. Often these were worn as personal adornments and strung together as necklaces. It is generally agreed that the latest of these can hardly be after *c.* 700, which marked the end of the great gold age for the Scandinavian peninsula. There can be little doubt that the portrait heads which appear on some of these were done after Roman coins (Fig. 1); but the full-length figures used on others can hardly be regarded as of Roman derivation (Figs. 2 and 3). These suggest eastern models rather than western Mediterranean ones because of their stubby proportions, sprightly actions, and contour lines such as the Scythians used in the drawing of men and animals. Then, too, their heads are thrown back and drawn in profile, while the bodies are directly frontal, and their features bear more resemblance to those of animals than of men. In any case, whatever the ultimate source for these stylistic qualities may be — and I venture the hypothesis that the region will be east and not west — what is most important for our purposes is that on these little objects is formulated the style of figure representation that may be termed Viking.[5a]

The question as to the subjects shown on some of the more elaborate of these objects (Figs. 2 and 3) has been answered most satisfactorily by Worsaae, who

Stockholm Historical Museum

FIG. 1. GOLD BRACTEATE.
PORTRAIT HEAD

Oslo Historical Museum

FIG. 2. GOLD BRACTEATE.
SIGURD BURNING HIS THUMB

Copenhagen Historical Museum

FIG. 3. GOLD BRACTEATE.
SIGURD LISTENING TO THE BIRDS

Copenhagen Historical Museum

FIG. 4. GOLD BRACTEATE.
GUNNAR IN SERPENTS' DEN

interprets these as Sigurd understanding the talk of the birds by virtue of having tasted the dragon's heart.[6]

On the well-known wagon of the Oseberg ship,[7] dating from the first half of the ninth century, are two figure groups which are injected into otherwise completely ornamental compositions. This would imply that they must be there for some narrative purpose. On one side a man and woman on foot approach a rider. The woman appears to be trying to prevent her husband from attacking the approaching visitor with the weapon which he holds in his upraised right hand. This calls to mind the legend of Gudrun protecting her brother Gunnar from her husband, Atli. The drawing is very similar to that described in connection with the bracteates. On the end of the wagon (Fig. 5) is the carving of a man surrounded by serpents. This presents even stronger proof of the con-

[5a] Since the writing of this article an important work by J. Baum, *La Sculpture figurale en Europe à l'époque merovingienne* (Paris, 1937), has appeared. In this the whole matter of migration figure style is discussed.

[6] J. J. A. Worsaae, "Om forestillingerne paa guldbracteaterne," *Aarboger for nordisk Oldkyndighet* (Copenhagen, 1870).

[7] Brögger, Falk, and Schetelig, *Osebergfundet* (Christiania [Oslo], 1920), vol. III, Pls. IV–VI.

tinuity of style in figure representation from the earlier period to the Viking, as a comparison of it with a bracteate (Fig. 4) shows. The subject of this relief has been called both Laocoön and Gunnar in the serpents' den.[8] The latter seems the more likely interpretation.

Concurrently on the Isle of Gotland stone cutters were continuing to enrich the figure repertory of the so-called "pictured stones," and also increased their height at this time from three or four feet to nine or ten. These pictorial reliefs are particularly significant because they are the most pretentious stone sculptures extant from the Viking period in Scandinavia. If the subjects are ever identified, they may throw light on the development of literary as well as artistic motives.

Oslo University Museum

FIG. 5. WAGON FROM OSEBERG SHIP. GUNNAR IN SERPENTS' DEN

In shape these slabs are high and narrow, sloping slightly toward the top, and they are crowned by somewhat wider semicircular heads, the surfaces of which are treated more or less like tympana (Figs. 6–8). Professor Lindquist[9] divides all these stones into three groups, and of these we shall have concern with his second and third groups only, the former of which is to be dated to the end of the eighth and the beginning of the ninth century, the latter to the end of the tenth and the beginning of the eleventh century. Both of these classes are marked by a somewhat formal treatment of their semicircular tops and by a complete covering of the remaining surfaces with human figures and boats.

In the second or ninth-century group Professor Lindquist places the slabs from Stenkyrka and Lärbro (Figs. 6 and 7) and suggests that the finest work was done at this time rather than early in the eleventh century, the date formerly given to this group. As ninth-century works they are rather surprising in Scandinavia, for not only are the figures more stylized and taller than the simple chubby ones that occur on other contemporary works such as we have

[8] Just Bing, "Laokoongruppen paa Osebergvognen," *Kunst og Kultur* (Oslo, 1921).

[9] Sune Lindquist, "Gotlands Bildstenar," *Rig* (1933), the publication of the Föreningen för svenska Kulturhistoria, pp. 97–117.

seen, but they are also placed neatly in superimposed registers. This formality of arrangement is further emphasized by the fact that the backgrounds were originally painted in bright contrasting colors, which brought out the piquant silhouettes even more vividly. There are no similar compositions in contemporary Scandinavia, though the shape of the stones is one that goes back to the

Stockholm Historical Museum

FIG. 6. PICTURED STONE FROM LÄRBRO,
ISLE OF GOTLAND, BUNGE MUSEUM

fourth century. On the other hand, certain Scottish stones of the tenth century offer slight similarities in figure style and arrangement.[10] The iconography of one of these has been discussed by Andreas Lindblom.[11]

The third group includes two of the most interesting examples, the Tjängvide[12] and the large Ardre (Fig. 8). Both of these are covered with figures in the mi-

[10] Joseph Anderson, *Early Christian Monuments of Scotland*, pt. III, pp. 148 ff., for illustrations of stones of Class II, the figures of which resemble the above.

[11] Andreas Lindblom, *Medeltida Vävnäder och Broderier i Sverige* (Stockholm, 1928), vol. I, p. 17.

[12] Johnny Roosval, *Swedish Art* (Princeton, 1932), p. 1, Fig. 4.

gration and early Viking style. The common prototypes that may have served for these and the Manx crosses have been dealt with elsewhere.[13] Professor Lindquist regards these as decadent works based upon the nobler art of Stenkyrka and Lärbro. In the chaotic disposition of their figures, the concentration upon narrative, and the poverty of ornamental invention, these sculptures have little

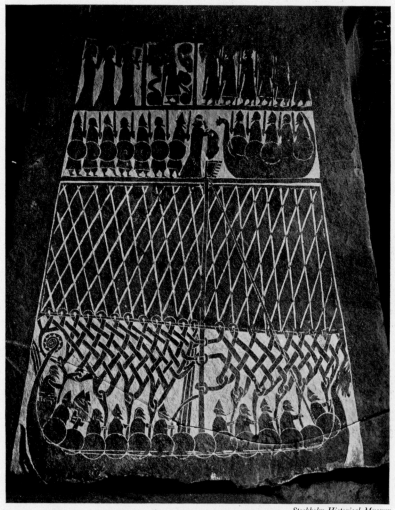

Stockholm Historical Museum

FIG. 7.   PICTURED STONE FROM STENKYRKA
VISBY, GOTLAND'S FORNSAL

in common with other eleventh-century work in Gotland or Uppland. However, the question of the dating of these two groups has little bearing on the matter of the spread of the Viking style abroad, since the stone cutters in both regions probably patterned their works after similar models in metal and other minor arts.

During the tenth century the chief center of Viking artistic activity shifted from Norway and Sweden to the British Isles, where so many Viking colonies

[13] Seaver, *op. cit.*

FIG. 8. PICTURED STONE FROM ARDRE

had been established. The localities which are richest in remains of this habitation are the Isle of Man, the Hebrides, and parts of Northumbria. Of the more than hundred Manx crosses [14] a dozen at least are unquestionably of Scandinavian workmanship. In these it is interesting to see two trends brought together, that of the Norwegian wood-working technique and ornament and that of the peculiar Vendel, Tuna, or Gotland figure style. This combination is happily illustrated on the slate slab at Kirk Andreas (Fig. 9), on one side of which Sigurd is portrayed standing before the fire roasting the dragon's heart, on the other Loki bound or Gunnar in the serpents' den. Both of these stocky figures are almost lost in the elaborate ornament, which is an early specimen of the Jellinge style. A second example of the blending of the Gotland figure and Norse wood manners is to be seen on the cross at Kirk Michael on which is cut Hyndla with her staff and below her a quadruped that may possibly have been intended to represent Sigurd's horse Grani (Fig. 10). Thorwald's Cross at Kirk Andreas (Fig. 11) offers a surprising variation upon the figure theme with its depiction of the nude Odin in conflict with the Fenris-Wolf. This slab is also noteworthy because of the uncommon restraint in composition and the simplification of the ornamental framework.

In the little museum on the Isle of Iona there exists a fragment of more than usual interest, a rubbing of which was published by the late W. G. Collingwood.[15] One whole side is taken up with ornament, while the lower half of the other has a boat filled with small men, who are quite like those of the Manx crosses described. Although no similar scene appears on any of the extant Manx sculptures, the fact that the figures present stylistic affinities to Manx ones and that the material is slate, which is not native to Iona but which was the favorite medium of the Manx carvers, would tend to support the hypothesis that this Iona stone represents another phase of Manx art.

Another English work that is reminiscent of the discursive manner of the large Ardre stone is the Northumbrian cross at Halton (Fig. 12). In the lowest panel on one side a smith is seated before his anvil and surrounded by various tools, not to mention a beheaded figure at the top. This is probably a depiction of the smith Regin in the act of forging Sigurd's sword and Regin's later beheading by Sigurd. Above this is shown a man standing in front of a fire and putting his thumb into his mouth, a favorite Sigurd episode with the illustrators. This is only one of a large group of crosses in Northumbria and adjacent counties from about the year 1000 or earlier on which reflections of the Viking habitation appear.[16]

Before returning to a brief survey of the later Viking style in Norway and

---

[14] M. P. C. Kermode, *Manx Crosses* (London, 1907), for classification and dating of these crosses.

[15] W. G. Collingwood, "Viking Cross at Iona," *Saga Book of Viking Club* (1903), vol. III, pp. 304–306.
The writer visited Iona in 1932 and attempted to photograph the stone without success. However, the rubbing here published by Collingwood gives a remarkably accurate impression whether or not the interpretation of the subject as Sigurd is convincing.

[16] W. G. Collingwood, *Northumbrian Crosses of the Pre-Norman Age* (London, 1927), pp. 120–136, for discussion and illustrations of these Viking monuments.

FIG. 9.   CROSS FROM KIRK ANDREAS,
ISLE OF MAN.   SIGURD ROASTING THE
DRAGON'S HEART

FIG. 10.   CROSS FROM KIRK MICHAEL,
ISLE OF MAN.   HYNDLA WITH STAFF

FIG. 11.   CROSS OF KIRK ANDREAS,
ISLE OF MAN.   ODIN AND THE
FENRIS–WOLF

FIG. 12.   HALTON CROSS.   SMITH REGIN
AND   SIGURD   ROASTING   THE
DRAGON'S HEART

Sweden mention should be made of the way in which this Norse or Danish style, as it is termed by Prior and Gardner,[17] left its stamp upon much of the architectural sculpture of Christian England. It may be significant that from about 1000 A.D. to 1150 A.D. there was a great vogue for the dragon-killing saints, and for Michael in particular, as subjects for tympanum decorations. Frequently these were executed in a style very like that of various Scandinavian or Anglo-Scandinavian monuments of a slightly earlier date. This coincidence of the persistence of both pagan subject and method of representation is another evidence of the strong foothold that the Vikings gained in the British Isles.

In the tympanum of Southwell Minster[18] (c. 1000) we feel the Nordic style more in the two clearly defined planes and in the ornament surrounding the figure of St. Michael, which is so like that on the cross at Kirk Andreas (Fig. 9), than we do in the figure of the saint, which has a slightly plastic quality that, despite its crudeness of execution, calls to mind earlier Anglian work. A second portal of about the same date is that at Ault Hucknall (Fig. 13), on the lintel of which is St. Michael fighting the dragon. There is no display of ornament here, but the figure of Michael is drawn in profile with the same disregard for features that is characteristic of the Manx crosses. The Pitsford tympanum, done about the middle of the twelfth century (Fig. 14), reflects the Viking background in the vigorous carving of saint and dragon in two sharply defined planes, though in the lower part of the figure of Michael there is an overtone of something more truly sculptural. The rope border and beaded ornament of the dragon's tail have their counterparts at Halton. To facilitate action St. Michael has put his wings to one side!

The capitals in the crypt of Canterbury cathedral[19] afford examples of the influence of the Viking style in the south of England, and in technique and subject matter offer many parallels to the works just discussed.

In the parish churches near Hereford are many instances of the combination of Celtic and Norse fancy in the treatment of figures and ornament alike and the apotheosis of this manner is illustrated in the well-known sculptures at Kilpeck executed about 1140.[20] It would seem that the sculptor of these corbels must have had some wooden heads such as the one from the Oseberg ship (Fig. 17) in mind when he did those wild-faced creatures. May we not find an echo of the strangely garbed and elongated portal figures of Kilpeck in the Luxury of Master Byzantios on Väte church in Gotland (Fig. 15)?

On the early Norman portal of Lincoln cathedral, done about 1140, and which in its medallion arrangement may have influenced the Norwegian sculptors of the wooden portals, there is an unusual handling of the innermost jamb (Fig. 16). From the top to the bottom of this are placed masklike heads, the stylized beards of which are extended so that they bend around the column in much the same way as the beaks of birds bend around the voussoirs of the portals

---

[17] Prior and Gardner, *Mediaeval Figure Sculpture in England* (Cambridge, 1912), pp. 127–131, 152–162.
[18] *Ibid.*, p. 129, Fig. 108.
[19] *Ibid.*, p. 164, Fig. 142.   [20] *Ibid.*, pp. 166–170.

FIG. 13. PORTAL OF AULT HUCKNALL, DERBY. ST. MICHAEL
KILLING THE DRAGON

W. A. Call

FIG. 14. TYMPANUM OF PITSFORD, NORTHAMPTONSHIRE. ST. MICHAEL
FIGHTING THE DRAGON

of Iffley and Kilpeck. Subject and feeling of wood remind us once more of objects
like the Oseberg carved posts (Fig. 17).

The eleventh century in Norway and Sweden witnessed the coming of the
first Christian missionaries, who significantly enough, were English. It is not
strange then that the Anglo-Norse style described above was the first one used
on Christian monuments, nor is it surprising that pagan gods and heroes very
grudgingly gave their places to Christian saints and martyrs on the newly built
and decorated churches. In fact, never before had the stone cutters and weav-
ers of Sweden been so prolific in their illustrations of the feats of the old Norse
gods and heroes as they were during the first half of the eleventh century.

Among heroes Sigurd held an enviable position, and there are literally dozens
of stones from the provinces of Uppland and Södermanland alone upon which
subjects connected with him appear.[21] The best known of these and the one
which may very likely have served as a model for many of the others is the Ramsund rock (Fig. 19). The low relief of the contemporary and earlier stones of
Gotland has been replaced here by incised lines that were originally colored.
Three dragons constitute the improvised frame within which several successive
events of the drama take place. One of these beasts serves the secondary purpose
of being the dragon Fafnir, which Sigurd is in the act of stabbing from below.
The other events of Sigurd burning his thumb, the beheading of Regin, and the
horse Grani with the pack of treasure on his back are all to be seen within. Mention might be made in passing of the similarities in proportion between these
figures and those on the Stenkyrka and Lärbro stones (Figs. 6 and 7). A second
stone, much simpler in design and cruder in execution, is that from the parish of
Aspö in Södermanland (Fig. 20) on which we may have a representation of Gunnar in the serpents' den, though the absence of the harp at so late a date makes
such an identification doubtful.

The elaborate ornament of the Jellinge style [22] left its imprint upon four small
stones from Ardre in Gotland where the figures are practically lost in the interlacing framework. Another monument in which ornament and figure work are
combined is the baptismal font from Norums church in Bohuslän (Fig. 21), on
one side of which is portrayed Gunnar in the serpents' den playing the *rotta*, the
northern version of the harp, with his feet.

A craft to which no reference has been made thus far and one in which the
Scandinavians have always taken great delight and shown great accomplishment is that of wrought iron. In the twelfth century they designed elaborate
figure and ornamental schemes in this medium for the decoration of doors and
chests. Two centers of this art were Vestergötland, where the architecture and
sculpture show the strong influence of contemporary English work, and the
neighboring Östergötland. The door of Versås [23] (Fig. 22) is signed by Asmund

[21] Henrik Schuck, "Sigurd Ristningar," *Nordisk Tidskrift* (Stockholm, 1903).

[22] See Brøndsted, *op. cit.*, pp. 270–304, for discussion of this ornament. For illustrations, see Francis
Beckett, *Danmarks Konst* (Copenhagen, 1924), vol. I, pp. 25–26. For illustrations of the small Ardre stones,
see Lindquist, *op. cit.*, p. 102.

[23] Axel Romdahl, "Röglösadörren," *Fornvännen* (1914), pp. 231–245. A series of these doors is dis-

FIG. 15. PORTAL OF VÄTE CHURCH,
ISLE OF GOTLAND. LUXURY

S. Smith

FIG. 16. NORMAN PORTAL, LINCOLN
CATHEDRAL

Oslo University Museum

FIG. 17. HEAD OF POST FROM
OSEBERG SHIP

FIG. 18. DOOR OF STILLINGFLEET
CHURCH

FIG. 19. INCISED STONE FROM RAMSUND, SÖDERMANLAND
EPISODES FROM SIGURD SAGA

FIG. 20. INCISED STONE FROM ASPÖ, SÖDERMANLAND. GUNNAR IN SERPENTS' DEN

and is arresting in the way in which it combines the old figure drawing with the new symmetrical framework, the elements of which are the old ribbons and interlaces. The dragon-killer who occupies the top panel is more closely related to the figures of Man and Gotland than to those of Lombardy. The figures which appear in the four arches below very likely represent from left to right God, Adam, Eve, and the devil with a serpent, as identified by Romdahl. This

Stockholm Historical Museum

FIG. 21. BAPTISMAL FONT FROM NORUMS CHURCH,
BOHUSLÄN. GUNNAR IN SERPENTS' DEN

door was probably executed during the first half of the twelfth century. Another door which may be considered as belonging to the middle of the century is that of Ekeby (Figs. 23, 24) in Uppland, on which various birds and animals appear amidst much decoration. In the upper register are a man and woman coming toward each other, in the lower a man, who holds in his right hand a string-like object that may be a snake, in his left a horn. Who these people may be or what they are doing it is difficult to say, but that their proportions and drawing are one more echo of the pagan background there can be little doubt.

Not unlike these doors is a very simple one on the parish church at Stilling-fleet in England, the wrought iron of which must have suffered considerable damage (Fig. 18). Figures of men and boats are scattered over its surface.

---

cussed here, and the author considers them to be copies of doors in Novgorod, which were in their turn based upon those of San Zeno in Verona. So far as the figures are concerned close parallels are to be found in native works such as those here illustrated.

In Swedish Romanesque stone sculpture the interplay of influences between England and Vestergötland is aptly illustrated in the work of Master Othelric,[24] who was active between 1140 and 1170 and who signed the tympanum of Skalf-

Stockholm Historical Museum

FIG. 22. DOOR OF VERSÅS CHURCH,
VESTERGÖTLAND

vum. The baptismal font in Norra Härene church (Fig. 25) is indicative of the way in which the more barbaric Anglo-Norse style of Romanesque with its two-plane relief and incised lines was adopted by native workers in Vestergötland. It is hardly necessary to point out similarities between such works as this and the capitals of Canterbury crypt.

[24] Ernest Fischer, *Vestergötlands Kyrkliga Konst under Medeltiden* (Uppsala, 1920), gives a full account of English influence in architecture and sculpture. For Master Othelric see pp. 83–88.

FIG. 23. DOOR OF EKEBY CHURCH,
UPPLAND

FIG. 24. DETAIL OF FIG. 23

Stockholm Historical Museum

FIG. 25. BAPTISMAL FONT IN NORTH HÄRENE CHURCH,
VESTERGÖTLAND. MASTER OTHELRIC

[605]

While such a variety of figure sculpture was being produced in Sweden during the first half of the eleventh century, little or none was being made in Norway. To the middle of that century, however, belongs what is perhaps the most beautiful piece of ornament of the period in Scandinavia, the wooden portal of Urnes church.[25] That unique Scandinavian architectural phenomenon, the stave church, which is no less remarkable for its decoration than for its structure, was evolved in the eleventh century and reached the peak of its development during

Oslo, Bygdö Museum

FIG. 26.   BENCH FROM HITTERDAL CHURCH, TELEMARKEN.
GUNNAR IN SERPENTS' DEN

the twelfth.[26]   Not only were the portals and capitals sculptured, but the contemporary furniture, of both ecclesiastical and secular origin, came in for its share of embellishment.   It is in these wooden objects that we can best trace the transition from the Viking style to that of the fully developed Romanesque in Norway.

In the church from Gol now set up at Bygdö, the outdoor museum near Oslo, there is a wedding bench which came originally from the wooden church of Hitterdal in Telemarken (Fig. 26).   The back is divided into two panels, an upper and a lower.   The center of the former is occupied by a small short figure in a frontal position who plays a *rotta* with his feet because his hands are bound.

[25] Roosval, *Swedish Art*, Pl. 8.

[26] L. Dietrichson, *De Norske Stavkyrkor* (Christiania, 1892), is still the chief work on these churches.   For more recent theories on the development of the architectural forms as well as for the dates and stylistic sources of the ornament the work of Gerda Boethius, *Hallar, Templar, och Stavkyrkor* (Stockholm, 1931), is invaluable.

This is Gunnar in his familiar pose. The rest of the panel is filled with the serpents, which are arranged to form a ribbon-like ornament similar to that of certain of the Manx crosses and the large Ardre stone. In the lower panel the central portion is taken up by two lions cut in very high relief of the two-plane

Oslo University Museum

FIG. 27.   PORTAL FROM LARDAL CHURCH
EPISODES FROM SIGURD SAGA

variety. Their bodies are decorated with ornament, and the incised technique and expressions recall the Lincoln and Oseberg subjects. At the right is a serpent the body of which is contorted into a most decorative interlace; at the left, however, are the very different motifs of a palmette and a rinceau. The fact that these are incised into the lower plane and that they are entirely out of keeping with the rest of the bench has suggested to me the possibility that we have here evidence that a later artist considered this style very old-fashioned and started to re-carve the bench in the new mode. A similar palmette appears in a diminutive scale on the vertical bannister at the extreme right. The original ornament and figure suggest that this can hardly be later than the second half of the eleventh century.

In the portal from Lardal (Fig. 27) in Telemarken is exemplified a combination of the old figure representation (in the scenes of Regin before his anvil and

Oslo, Bygdö Museum

FIG. 28.   ALMS–BOX

Sigurd killing the dragon) and the new medallion framework. In each panel there is only one event portrayed, while the interstices between the medallions and the spaces above them are filled with palmettes and rinceaux as they are on the portals of Lincoln and Ely. Even the animals have acquired foliated tails like those at Pitsford. Since Norway was Christianized by English missionaries it is credible that portals such as those at Ely and Lincoln could have served as models for these Norwegian artists, and that what there is of French feeling in their work probably came via England.

The alms-box discovered by the writer in the museum at Bygdö [27] is quite a

[27] The undecorated side of this was exposed to view and it was only accidentally that the sculptured side, which was turned to the wall, was noticed.

remarkable object, made up as it is of two very early fragments of wood carving (Fig. 28). The partially covered vertical panels, which are the earlier, probably formed part of a portal. On these are two animals, which have their closest parallels at Vaage, dated by Gerda Boethius [28] between 1060 and 1100. Those

Oslo University Museum

FIG. 29. PORTAL FROM HYLLESTAD CHURCH
EPISODES FROM SIGURD SAGA

on our alms-box appear to be slightly later. The horizontally placed panel, which partly covers the vertical ones, has a rinceau ornament at the top, and at the bottom a figure of a man half in profile who is kneeling in the act of killing a dragon. Undoubtedly this was the main panel of a chair like that from Hitterdal.[29] The modeling of the man's body, as well as the ornament, indicates that

[28] Boethius, *op. cit.*, p. 131, for illustration.
[29] Lindblom, *op. cit.*, p. 20, for illustration of one side of this.

this is to be classified as a somewhat cruder version of the new Romanesque style of Hyllestad rather than as a development of the older Viking manner.

The superbly designed and finely executed portal from Hyllestad (Fig. 29) from the third quarter of the twelfth century brings us rather suddenly from vigorous, if often barbaric, figure compositions to one of the masterpieces of wood carving done in the "Pilgrimage" style of France and Spain.[30]   Line which had been used formerly only for the purpose of defining areas or accenting contours is here directed to convey the beauties of plastic form with a sensitiveness worthy of a manuscript illuminator.   But even in this cosmopolitan Norse artist the love of all-over pattern is not quite dead, for in the left panel, on which are represented Sigurd roasting the dragon's heart and Sigurd killing Regin, the medallion treatment has been abandoned for the old continuous method in which the figures are subordinated to the profusion of ornament furnished by the bending trunk and branches of the tree.

[30] This parallelism has been pointed out by William Anderson, "Internationalismen i Konsten under 1100 talet," *Tidskrift för Konstvetenskap* (Stockholm, 1926).

THE CANON TABLES OF THE BOOK OF KELLS

A. M. FRIEND, JR.

IN THE conclusion of his discussion of the Book of Kells, J. A. Bruun says, "And we hope to show in a following article, in which the characteristics of the Carlovingian Art are to be considered, that there exist, in fact, between the non-Celtic elements of the decoration shown in the *Book of Kells* and the art dialect just alluded to, such affinities as will hardly leave room for doubt that the Celtic manuscript was produced under the influence of that early *renaissance* which commenced in the Frankish Empire under the reign of Charlemagne."[1] Bruun never wrote the second section of his book in which the promised demonstration was to have taken place, nor has his acute observation stimulated others to attempt a comparison of the affinities alluded to. The object of this paper is to leave as little "room for doubt" as possible that Bruun was in the main quite right and to prove that the Book of Kells owes many of its peculiarities to the fact that it is, indeed, based on a lost gospel manuscript of Continental origin which had already left its imprint on the manuscripts of one of the schools of the Carolingian Renaissance.

To judge from Bruun's description of the Book of Kells, the chief of the non-Celtic elements which led him to his interesting conclusion were the foliaceous motifs of ornament which occur with relative profusion throughout this manuscript. These leaf ornaments are extremely rare in Celtic illumination. The Lindisfarne Gospels, rich as it is in ornamental motifs, is entirely devoid of plant and vegetable ornament.[2] In all the rest of the Celtic manuscripts the only vegetable ornamentation I know is in the Book of Durrow, fol. III[r],[3] where little pointed trefoils sprout out unexpectedly from the geometric spirals and interlace, making the page unique in this manuscript.

It is not, however, the mere presence of leaf ornaments in the Book of Kells, but the manner of their use which challenges comparison with Carolingian and Continental decoration. On foll. 2[r] (Pl. III), 4[r] (Pl. VII), and 8[r][4] can be seen Celtic versions of the classical rinceau with its tendrils, leaves, and grapes. In the first instance this non-Celtic motif occurs as the decoration of an arch over the canon tables [4a] just as in the Soissons Gospels of the Carolingian Ada School (Pl. XIX). Indeed, the Book of Kells in this point surpasses the Carolingian manuscript. It is closer to classical prototypes in that the vines spring out of vases and

---

[1] *An Enquiry into the Art of the Illuminated Manuscripts of the Middle Ages: Part I. Celtic Illuminated Manuscripts* (Edinburgh, 1897), p. 81.

[2] Eric George Millar, *The Lindisfarne Gospels* (London, 1923), p. 23.

[3] H. Zimmermann, *Die vorkarolingischen Miniaturen* (Berlin, 1916), Taf. 163b.

[4] *Ibid.*, Taf. 179.

[4a] Capitals are used for Canon Tables if the reference is to the *artistic form*; small letters, i.e., canon tables, when merely the *numerical tables* of concordance of the gospels is meant.

that birds disport themselves among the tendrils in a manner still naturalistic in spite of the tendency of the Celtic artist to transform them into lacertines. Furthermore, the rinceau in this arch is bordered by two strips of "rope" ornament, perhaps another of Bruun's non-Celtic motifs.[5] (Pl. III).

The mere presence of such a classical scheme of decoration is enough, it seems to me, to make us seek with Bruun for Continental manuscripts which may have been the prototypes for the Book of Kells. These are a more plausible source than a derivation from the ornaments of the crosses of North England. However, the most cogent peculiarities of the Book of Kells which make inevitable the assumption of a Continental model are not those of ornamentation or of style but concern the structure of the book and its iconography.

KELLS AND LINDISFARNE

The mention of the possibility of an iconographical prototype for the Book of Kells will call to mind its great rival in splendor among the manuscripts of the Celtic style, the famous Lindisfarne Gospels, which exhibits much more quickly its dependence on its Continental model. Here the South Italian or, better, Greek prototype is apparent to all eyes, since the artist of the Evangelist portraits in the English book attempted to copy not only the iconography but also the style of his model. Not so with the creators of the Book of Kells, who have to a great degree succeeded in translating everything into the Celtic stylistic idiom, thus rendering stylistic criticism nearly helpless in detecting the prototype. However, the model is firmly imbedded in its copy, even to its errors, and when disengaged will be seen to be very different from the gospel book which was the original of the Canons and Evangelists of Lindisfarne, and very much richer in its iconographical structure.

The two manuscripts, Kells and Lindisfarne, stand so preëminently at the apex of Celtic art that, even though often compared, it is fruitful to relate them once again. In technical skill and power there is little to choose between the manuscripts. The cross and the initial pages before each of the gospels in the two manuscripts so resemble each other that anyone could be excused for confusing them at first glance. Indeed, the ornamentation of both seems to proceed from the same scriptorium in, perhaps, the earlier and later phases of its history. Yet to the attentive observer the differences will ultimately become the chief interest in the comparison. One of these, the abundance of the foliaceous ornament in Kells and the total lack of it in Lindisfarne, we have already noted. More important, and less noticed, is the difference in coloration of the two manuscripts. In the summer of 1930 I had the privilege of having in my hands for study both manuscripts within a week. I deliberately concentrated my

---

[5] J. Brøndsted, *Early English Ornament* (Copenhagen, 1924), Fig. 71 and p. 85. Examples of the classical rinceau can be seen in the mosaics of Ravenna (cf. A. Colasanti, *L'Arte bisantina in Italia*, Pl. 13) and also on the Chair of Maximianus (*ibid.*, Pl. 45). The rope ornament can be seen on the architrave over the figure of St. Luke on fol. 129ᵛ of MS. 286, Corpus Christi, Cambridge (Pal. Soc., Ser. I, vol. II, London, 1873–1883, pl. 44).

attention on this matter of the color and was surprised to note how little they resembled each other in this point. Since the color reproductions in Millar [6] and Sullivan [7] are sufficiently accurate to carry the differences, the reader can make the comparison for himself. He will note the almost total absence of strong yellows and strong blues in the Lindisfarne book, while these very colors are stressed in Kells. Crimson is used sparingly in the English book, while it plays a large part in Kells. The yellow in Kells is largely used for borders, as if it were a substitute for gold frames (cf. in Sullivan Pls. I, II, V, VII, VIII, etc.), although of course gold is absent in both manuscripts, as is usually the case in Celtic illumination. (The few exceptions in Lindisfarne are noted by Millar.[8]) These divergencies in general coloration suggest a difference in the scriptoria which produced the manuscripts, and a difference of coloration in the models used by each.

Divergent as the color effects of the two manuscripts certainly are, the chief difference between them is iconographic. And this begins at once in the very feature, common to these two manuscripts, which distinguishes them from all other insular Celtic gospel books, i.e., the elegantly decorated arched Canon Tables, or tables of concordance of the passages similar in the several gospel writers. The decoration of these lists of numbers, giving the parallel gospel passages, by means of architectural columns or strips of ornament joined by arches and included under a larger containing arch is probably ultimately of Syrian-Greek origin. Its appearance in both Lindisfarne and Kells is to be traced to the Continental models on which both these manuscripts rest.[9] But, as I have said above, these models were in themselves very different and this difference can be best seen in a comparison of the Canon Tables.

The Canon Tables of Lindisfarne [10] are very simple, consisting of flat strips of ornament, in place of columns, with capitals and bases of interlace. These are joined by simple arches, and the whole is contained under a large arch which is decorated with birds, interlace, lacertines, or Celtic frets. In the space between the arches is the title, in capitals, of the particular canon table whose numbers occur below. The Canon Tables of Kells (Pls. II–XI) are much more elaborate, although based, as we have seen, on the same system. The smaller arches are decorated with ornament like the larger ones and bordered also with colored strips. The great arches are all set within squared-off corners of elaborate ornament, which give a rectangular shape to the whole page. The most distinguishing and important feature of all, unique in Celtic manuscripts, is the inclusion, under the big arches, of the beasts of the Apocalypse which are the symbols of the Evangelists whose works are compared in the tables below. The distribution

[6] *Op. cit.* Color plates of 26ᵛ, 29, and 139.

[7] Sir Edward Sullivan, *The Book of Kells* (2nd ed., 1920).

[8] *Op. cit.*, p. 27.

[9] Arthur Kingsley Porter, *The Crosses and Culture of Ireland* (New Haven, 1931), p. 50. Eusebius composed his tables of concordance most probably in Caesarea, Palestine, for use in Greek Gospel MSS. The earliest preserved dated example of the scheme of decoration under series of arches occurs, by chance, in the Syriac Gospels of Rabula, A.D. 586. The canon tables of the Greek gospels in the British Museum (Add. 5111) which show the same kind of decoration are probably earlier.

[10] Millar, *op. cit.*, Pls. IV–XIX.

of these winged beasts to the four Evangelists is that popularized in the West by
St. Jerome, namely, the man or angel for St. Matthew, the lion for St. Mark,
the bull or calf for St. Luke, and the eagle for St. John. In these Canon Tables
each beast is supposed to be over the column of passages from the Evangelist it
symbolizes and thus pictorially serves as a title.

The question arises, then: Where did this new and surprising iconography of
the "Beast Canon Tables," which so distinguishes Kells from Lindisfarne, originate? Did the Celtic artist of Kells originate it, or did he copy it from a model?
Indeed, it is the problems which arise from the study of the Canon Tables of
Kells which will in the end give us the clues for the solution of the entire history
of the manuscript. Let us therefore study more minutely these interesting first
folios of Kells.

The Canon Tables of Kells

At the present time the Book of Kells is preserved as MS. A.1.6 in the Library
of Trinity College, Dublin. But the first twenty-three folios are kept separate
from the rest of the manuscript in a safe. They are at present unbound but
suffered the same cropping as the rest of the manuscript at the time of a previous
binding. It is not my purpose in this article to discuss the original arrangement
of these loose folios or the foliation of the rest of the Book of Kells except in so far
as it is necessary to deal with the problem raised in connection with the Canon
Tables. However, it is a fact that the foliation has not been seriously disturbed.

The beginning of the book is lost and undoubtedly contained the letter of
Jerome to Pope Damasus beginning *Novum Opus*. Folio 1ʳ today contains in its
first framed column (Pl. 1) the last six names of the *Interpretatio ebreorum nominum
secundum Matheum*. These lists of explanations of Hebrew names occur in Irish
Gospels[11] and also in Continental manuscripts.[12] The right-hand column of the
folio instead of being left blank is filled out with two panels to be looked at sidewise (the only such twist in the Book of Kells) which portray the four symbols
of the Evangelists in anthropomorphic form, i.e., with human hands. This peculiar feature is obviously not part of the decoration planned for in advance but
one of the afterthoughts of the decorators of Kells when the text did not fill up
the two columns reserved for it and already decorated before the writing was
put in. This is one of the several indications that many of the pages were decorated with frames before the scribe wrote in his text.

Folio 1ᵛ (Pl. 11)[13] is the beginning of the Beast Canon Tables described in
general terms above. I shall not call attention to all the details, but merely those
to be used in the following discussion. First it is necessary to point out that the
writing of the numbers was done after the decoration was finished and fits with

[11] Fol. 31ᵛ of *The Book of Armagh* (Dublin, 1913), ed. John Gwynn.
[12] Poitiers, Bibl. de la Ville, MS. 17, fol. 29ᵛ.
[13] For the consecutive comparison of the canon tables and the symbols of the Evangelists which follows, it will be well for the reader to have the text of these tables of concordance before him. Cf. J. Wordsworth and H. J. White, *Novum Testamentum Domini Nostri Jesu Christi latine* (Oxford, 1889), pp. 7–10, or the
editio minor of the same, edited by White (Oxford, 1911), pp. xvii–xx.

difficulty into the columns left for it, since the artist had inserted the little figure who sits on the first xcviii (*sic*) of the text, as well as other ornaments in the columns. This page contains half of the first canon table, wherein the works of all four Evangelists are compared; consequently, in the space above, all four symbols are represented. The calf, however, has legs partly like a bird.

Folio 2^r (Pl. iii) faces and is complementary in its decoration to the opposite page. That is to say, the Canon Tables start on the verso of a folio so that the scheme of decoration calls for similar designs on the two pages which lie before the eye when the book is open. This scheme is rigidly preserved throughout except in one important instance. The page before us is the conclusion of the first canon table; so therefore all four beasts are represented, each over the column proper to its Evangelist. The scribe who crowded the first page of the canon tables with his numbers, on this second and concluding page of the first canon table finishes too soon, so that the artist, perhaps afterwards, is compelled to fill out the bottom of the columns with ornament.

Folio 2^v (Pl. iv) is the beginning of the second canon table, in which are compared the gospels of Matthew, Mark, and Luke. Hence, above the columns are presentations of the symbols: angel, lion, and calf. It is to be noted that the calf has the body of an eagle as in fol. 1^v. The Celtic artist in his native propensity for hybrid animal forms has indulged himself in this case as if in ornament. But the *heads* are those of the beast correct for the Evangelist whose work is compared in the columns immediately below. The artist indicates the beast required by means of the head. The body is, for this purpose, of secondary importance to him. The scribe in this canon table has most inconveniently doubled his columns of numbers for each gospel. They were separated later by means of a narrow strip with no base. This doubling was done by the scribe to insure enough room on the three pages of decoration prepared in advance by the artist for the very long second table of concordance.

Folio 3^r (Pl. v) continues the second canon table, again with two columns of numbers between the strips of ornament. The half-circle bases at the foot of these numbers were added later and overlap the writing. The beasts under the arch are the three proper for this canon: angel, lion, and calf.

Folio 3^v (Pl. vi) concludes the second canon table, which compares Matthew, Mark, and Luke. The beasts are correct as far as their heads are concerned, i.e., angel, lion, and calf, but it is to be noted that the artist has formed hybrids as before, since the lion has the body of a calf and the calf has that of a lion. However, the principle obtains that the *heads* are always the correct ones to identify the gospel in the column below. Now it happened that because of his crowding and doubling the columns of numbers on foll. 2^v and 3^r, the scribe finished the second canon table on this page after nine lines. He then proceeded to write in the *whole of the third canon table*, which compares the gospels of Matthew, *Luke*, and John. In order to complete this he was forced to write numbers below the bases of the decorated panels of this page.

Folio 4^r (Pl. vii) contains the numbers for the fourth canon table, in which are compared the gospels of Matthew, *Mark*, and John. That there should be no doubt about this the scribe has written in the arch above, MATHEUS, MARCUS, IOHANNIS. This he did because he noticed that the beasts below do not conform to this canon table. The symbols, identified by their heads, are angel, calf, and eagle. The calf, it is true, has the body of a lion. But the head is unmistakable with its horns, and, as we have noticed, the artist made no mistakes with his symbols, as far as the heads are concerned, in any of the previous canon tables. The explanation of the difficulty is very simple. This page, decorated by the artist in advance of the scribe, was to have contained the third canon table, which compares the gospels of Matthew, *Luke*, and John and which consequently called for the symbols, angel, *calf*, and eagle. The scribe who wrote in his numbers of the canon tables after the decoration was completed, fearful of expanding beyond the limits of the decorated folios already prepared, crowded his work, as we have already noticed, on foll. 2^v and 3^r and had thus already written out the third canon table on the opposite page. The artist therefore has made no error at all. It is the scribe who is one canon table ahead of the illustration.

This confusion of the text and illustration proves one very fundamental point. The artist did not make up the illustration of the canon tables from the text but copied the "Beast Canon" illustration of an earlier gospel book which on this folio had the third canon table in its proper order and with its proper beasts. The scribe of Kells fills in the numbers later and perhaps after the model used by the artist had disappeared, since, if the model were before the eyes of the scribe, he could have easily consulted its spacing and made the text and the illustration agree.

Folio 4^v (Pl. VIII), which contains the numbers for the fifth canon table, has no representation of the beasts at all! Consequently the scribe thought it necessary to indicate by inscriptions above the frame that this long table is a comparison of the parallel passages peculiar to MATHEUS and LUCAS. Although there is quite enough space under the great arch for the necessary angel and calf the artist has omitted them. The style of ornamentation of this and the next folio (Pl. IX) is the same as the rest of the Canon Tables of Kells. There is no change of artist at this place. Suddenly the series of Beast Canons is interrupted after the fourth canon, or, so far as the illustrations go, after the third canon. And the *reprise* of the iconography on the next folio, which is the complementary page ornamentally to the preceding, will serve only to give more significance to this break.

Folio 5^r (Pl. IX) contains the text of the sixth canon (Matthew, Mark), the seventh canon (Matthew, John), and the eighth canon (Luke, Mark). This calls into play all four symbols of the Evangelists, and all four are represented by the artist of Kells, but the arrangement of the beasts is here different from all the other Canon Table pages. They are not all represented under the great arch as formerly. Two, the angel and the eagle, are used as spandrels of the great arch in order to square up the page. Thus it happens that this page not only does not conform to the general scheme of the Beast Canons, but, in this feature of the spandrels, does not agree with its decorated conjugate page opposite (fol. 4^v). It is, then, the only exception to this symmetry in the Canon Tables in Kells. Why did the artist not put in the beasts for fol. 4^v and why in fol. 5^r does he put two in the spandrels instead of all under the great arch? The beasts themselves on this last folio are unlike those under the arches in the other Canon Tables. The eagle is anthropomorphic, with human hands. Such a form was used in the panels which, obviously, were added to fill up a blank column in the page before the Canons (fol. 1^r), but the anthropomorphic form never occurs among the symbols in the other canon tables, hybrid though many of them are. The angel on our folio carries a wand with a flower head in place of the book universally held by the symbols of Matthew under the arches. The lion and the calf are heraldically affronted and so highly stylized as to make fairly naturalistic the appearance of these symbols elsewhere in the Canons. Why this new set of Evangelist symbols so different from the beasts in the rest of the Canons? Again, the last two pages we have been considering have circles of ornament at the bases of the long decorative panels instead of the more structural half circles, obviously the stylization of a column base, used in all the other pages of the Canon Tables thus far. Why does the artist change from stylized architecture to a freer decorative invention at just this place?

The answer to all our questions can be but one. The pictorial model on which the artist of Kells depended for the Beast Canons was defective after the third Canon. Left to his own resources after the model failed the artist of Kells invented the circular decoration in place of column bases, omitted the beasts altogether on fol. 4^v, but supplied them on fol. 5^r as best he could from other sources,[14] thus spoiling his symmetrical ornamental scheme. Perhaps he intended later to supply the beasts also in the unfinished panel of 4^v, but before this could be accomplished his work had ceased, as we shall immediately see.

Folio 5^v (Pl. x) is suddenly very simple. It contains the numbers for canon nine (Luke, John) and for the part of canon ten which records the passages unique in the gospels of Matthew and Mark. These numbers are disposed in squares bordered by simple frames of yellow and violet. Thus the whole scheme of decoration and its technical style have completely changed for the worse from fol. 5 recto to its verso. The Canon Tables of Kells were interrupted in their manufacture after the artist had finished 5^r. Later, perhaps in another place, they were finished in this meager style. Nothing is lost or torn out, since this change is on the verso of fol. 5 and not on a new folio. That the Book of Kells is an unfinished manuscript is seen on many pages and has frequently been noticed.[15] But in no place is the interruption so clearly seen as in the Canon Tables, finished finally in so niggardly a fashion by another painter after many pages of splendor by the first artist.

Folio 6^r (Pl. xi) contains the final numbers for canon table ten in which are recorded the passages peculiar to Luke and John. The style of ornamentation

[14] The ultimate source of anthropomorphic symbols used twice in the Book of Kells and unique, as far as my knowledge goes, in Celtic illumination is a subject that I must forego in this paper.

[15] Sullivan, *The Book of Kells*, pp. 11, 13 ff.

is the same as that of the previous page and brings to an inglorious close the set of Canon Tables.

The verso of this folio and the recto of the next (on the verso of which is the figure of the Virgin and Child) [16] were originally blank but now contain a series of records regarding the property of the Church of Kells. These were copied into the Book of Kells, presumably for safekeeping, in the second half of the twelfth century as O'Donovan thought.[17]

Such are the Canon Tables of Kells, considered chiefly from the point of view of their iconography. From the description the following points become clear:

1. The Canon Tables of Kells are based on an earlier Gospel book which had canon tables under small arches contained in turn under a large one. Under these arches were the symbols of the Evangelists used as a pictorial title, i.e., the "Beast Canons."

2. The set of Canons in this model contained only six pages and was defective after the beast picture for the third canon, or, since the text of the next canon was probably written in, after the *fourth* canon so far as the *text* was concerned.

3. The artist of Kells continued on his own initiative after the fourth canon, intending to do his best without the model. He made up beasts for fol. 5ʳ but left fol. 4ᵛ unfinished, as can be seen by the poor ornament, added later, in the spandrels and blank panel under the arch (partly filled later by a poor border and containing now a panegyric on the Book of Kells in the handwriting of Gerald Plunket).[18] Before the artist could fill up these spandrels and panel either with ornament or with beasts from another source, the decoration of the canon tables was suddenly arrested.

4. The last two pages of the Canon Tables, of simpler and totally different work, were completed later in some inferior scriptorium after the marvelous artist of the earlier pages was no more available.

But what is the source of the Gospel book which served as the model for the Beast Canons of Kells? What was the style and structure of this model? These questions we can answer to some degree of satisfaction by a study of the iconography of the Beast Canons.

THE ICONOGRAPHY OF THE BEAST CANONS

The pictorial decoration of the canon tables with the symbols of the Evangelists over the columns of concordance in order to identify the gospels is a complicated iconography. It occurs infrequently in western illumination and not at

---

[16] Zimmermann, *op. cit.*, Taf. 168.

[17] James F. Kenney, *The Sources for the Early History of Ireland* (New York, 1929), p. 753.

[18] "The work doth passe all men's conyng that now doth live in any place. I doubt not . . . anything but that ye writer hath obtained God's grace. G. P." Cf. Sullivan, *op. cit.*, p. 6.

all in the East,[19] although the arched Canon Tables were originally a Greek form, as we have noticed.

It was a difficult thing for any set of artists and scribes to copy accurately this complicated iconography. The chances for error are very great, and we have already noted some of the mishaps in the Book of Kells. But it will be this very complication and error which will enable us to trace the descent of manuscripts, since the copying of error in iconography, as in text criticism, is a sure way of exhibiting consanguinity.

Of the manuscripts possessing the Beast Canons which date before the eleventh century, by far the most accurate are the Spanish Bibles. The earliest one with a complete set of canons with the beasts is MS. 6 in the Cathedral Archives of León, which dates A.D. 920[20] (Pls. XII–XIII). In this set of Canons the artist has made one blunder and the scribe two. On fol. 150[v] in the third page of the second canon the lion and the angel are interchanged — an easy error, since the symbols are anthropomorphic. On fol. 151[r] the scribe has continued the title of the preceding canon table instead of writing MATHEUS, LUCAS, JOHANNES of the third table. Again, on fol. 153[v] he has interchanged the names JOHANNES and LUCAS. Otherwise the text and the illustration are accurate in agreement — quite a feat. The canons in this manuscript are extended with little cramping, i.e., they run from fol. 148[v] to include 154[v], or, in all, thirteen pages. The number of intercolumniations varies with the canon tables: four where four gospels are compared, three where three gospels, and two for the canon tables in which only two gospels are equated. This is the most normal and simple arrangement, and, because of this, scribe and artist committed fewer blunders. Another Spanish Bible also at León, but in San Isidoro (Cod. 2), dates A.D. 960 and has a full set of Beast Canons before the New Testament.[21] This is even more extended than the set in the Bible of A.D. 920 filling seventeen pages instead of thirteen (foll. 396[v] to 404[v] inclusive). The result is that I have been able to detect only one error between illustration and text. On fol. 398[v], the third of the pages giving the text of the second canon table, both the symbols and the titles of the columns have been reversed for Mark and Luke. As we observe, the more pages used for the canon tables the fewer are the errors. So we can conclude that the most fruitful cause for confusion between illustration and text was the cramping of the Beast Canons into fewer pages than the original had. This was the reason for some of the difficulties in Kells, as we have seen. In other words, the more extended series of Beast Canons is closer to the original.

We must therefore hold that these two Spanish manuscripts are based on very complete and excellent earlier models. If the principle obtains that the fewer the errors, the closer are we to the original iconography, then we must conclude

---

[19] By singular exception there is a fourteenth- to fifteenth-century Greek Gospel book on Athos (Watopedi MS. 247), which shows the beasts under the columns of concordance, obviously an addition from western sources.

[20] J. D. Bordona, *Manuscritos con pinturas* (Madrid, 1933), I, p. 176, Figs. 169–170.

[21] Dom Henri Quentin, *Mémoire sur l'établissement du texte de la Vulgate* (Rome, 1922), pp. 325 ff. and Fig. 41.

that the Beast Canons were copied in Spain in a purer form than elsewhere. Hence we must entertain the possibility that Spain was the home of this iconography or at least its distributing center. This we must hold in spite of the fact that these Spanish Bibles are later in date than all the other manuscripts we shall consider.

Until the eleventh century the Beast Canons are preserved elsewhere only, to my knowledge, in incomplete or in erroneous forms. We have already studied one of these examples, both incomplete and erroneous, in the Book of Kells. Three other early examples need detain us for only a moment. One is the important eight-century gospel book in the Vatican (Barb. lat. 570) which has the anthropomorphic symbols under the arches of the first canon table only (fol. 1ʳ).[22] In this the artist has confused the symbols of Mark and Luke, or is using some other system of distribution to the several Evangelists than Jerome's. Another incomplete set of Beast Canons is that in the Gospels in the Treasury of the Church of Maeseyck, which are usually dated also in the eighth century.[23] Where the text of the canons has been written in, it does not agree with the beasts; e.g., on fol. 2ʳ the text is that of the second canon, while the four beasts show that the first canon was intended.[24] Elsewhere in the manuscript there is a picture with the sequence, angel, lion, eagle, and calf,[25] which is inconceivable as a headpiece for any canon or set of canons. In fact, all is here thoroughly confused. What may be an excerpt from the Beast Canons occurs on the first page of the set of canon tables in an eight-century Gospels in the Bibliothèque de la Ville of Autun (MS. 4).[26] In the columns at the top of the page are the four symbols of the Evangelists used as capitals and flanking a standing figure of Christ. Below, as bases to the columns, are four seated Evangelists and John the Baptist pointing out the figure of Christ immediately above him. The text in the column above John the Baptist refers to the passage in John's Gospel (I: 29) which relates this scene. The other columns above the heads of the Evangelists contain the verses of Sedulius[27] appropriate to each Evangelist and his symbol. The page is obviously a compiled picture made up of several elements of which the first page of a Beast Canons may be one.

These three manuscripts are what remains of the copies of the Beast Canons which date before the period of the Carolingian Renaissance, and all three are incomplete or full of errors.

BEAST CANONS IN THE ADA SCHOOL

The fullest copies of the Beast Canons in early manuscripts other than the Spanish Bibles are those which fall next to be considered in this treatise in order of date. They are found in the Gospel books of the Carolingian Renaissance.

[22] Zimmermann, op. cit., Taf. 317a and pp. 300–302, where the MS. is assigned to the south of England.

[23] Ibid., Taf. 318–320 and pp. 303–304, where again a south-English provenance is given.

[24] Ibid., Taf. 318b.   [25] Ibid., Taf. 319b.

[26] Zimmermann, op. cit., Taf. 329–331 and pp. 308–309. Here the MS. is dated ca. 780 and assigned to a French provenance.

[27] Sedulii opera omnia, ed. Iohannes Huemer, C.S.E.L., vol. x (1885), pp. 41–42.

But of all these manuscripts this iconography occurs in only one school, i.e., the Ada School, which flourished in the lifetime and under the patronage of Charlemagne, whose putative sister, Ada, ordered one of the gospel books.[28] The other Carolingian schools, Tours, Reims, Franco-Saxon, St. Denis (Corbie), know nothing of the Beast Canons except for two manuscripts of the last-mentioned school; the Codex Aureus of St. Emmeran, now in Munich, which, in this feature, is a direct copy from a Gospels of the Ada School,[29] and the Bible of St. Paul's in Rome, with its sporadic beasts in a few Canons.

In the Ada School itself there exist only two manuscripts with the Beast Canons: (1) the Gospels in the British Museum, Harley 2788, and (2) the Soissons Gospels of the Bibliothèque National, Paris (lat. 8850), whose Beast Canons were copied in the Codex Aureus of St. Emmeran, as we noted above.

THE BEAST CANONS OF THE HARLEY GOSPELS

The Canon Tables of the Harley Gospels occupy eleven pages, i.e., from fol. 6^v to fol. 11^v inclusive (Pls. XIV–XVI). The great arches which enclose the titles of the canons and the beasts of the Evangelists are set within spandrels of ornament which square out the page — a feature unusual in the Canon Tables of the Ada School, but occurring in elementary form also in the Gospels ordered by Ada herself (Trèves, Stadtbibliothek MS. 22) (Pl. XVI. 4). The titles of the canon tables in Harley as well as the text are all written in gold, in keeping with the sumptuous use of this metal throughout this manuscript. Under each great arch and surmounting the title is a highly ornamental cross in gold. In front of the title of each canon is a small cross of equal arms. These crosses also can be paralleled in the Ada School, again in the first page of the Canons of the Gospels of Ada (Pl. XVI. 4).

The most interesting feature of the Canon Tables of the Harley Gospels is the change that occurs suddenly at the beginning of the fifth table. The first six pages have, as columns, flat strips of paneled ornament with flat, highly decorated bases, in these features resembling again the manuscript of Trèves. But from the fifth canon to the end we see a new system. The columns are now three-dimensional and are painted to represent the veining of colored marbles. The bases are shaded to indicate their plastic character and are composed of a number of debased classical moldings. In the great arches above, the system of decoration also changes at the fifth canon. Whereas in the first six pages the ornament is flat, with interlace, lozenges, and linear rinceaux, the last five pages exhibit a more plastic repertory of overlapping scales, shaded acanthus leaves, and perspective "double axe" ornament.[30] Likewise, in the same place, the

---

[28] H. Janitschek in the *Trierer Ada-Handschrift* (Leipzig, 1889), pp. 72–107, discusses this manuscript and gives the division by schools of the manuscripts of the Carolingian Renaissance.

[29] A. M. Friend, "Carolingian Art in the Abbey of St. Denis," *Art Studies*, 1923, p. 72. Georg Leidinger in his sumptuous publication, *Der Codex Aureus der Bayerischen Staatsbibliothek in München* (1925), curiously failed to notice this copying, a fact which, I feel, would have fundamentally changed his discussion of this MS.

[30] R. B. O'Connor, "The Mediaeval History of the Double-Axe Motif," *American Journal of Archaeology*, XXIV (1920), 151–170.

flattened-out leaf capitals consistent with the paneled strips which serve as columns in the former part of the Canons change in the latter part to a plastic and more naturalistic acanthus variety to match the marbled columns below. Again, in the arches of the last pages of the Canons are seen a number of imitations of classical gems replacing the simple lozenges used to punctuate the ornament of the arches of the first six pages.

The explanation of this change is obvious. Clearly the model used at first by the artist of the Harley Gospels was defective after the fourth canon, so that from the fifth canon onwards he was forced to use the Canons of another gospel book as a basis of his work. It was this new model that had the marbled columns and the plastic ornamental system with the gems. Its other characteristics can be inferred from a study of the last five pages of the Canons of Harley.

The change in model can be seen most vividly in the iconography of the Beast Canons. In the first six pages there are no errors at all in the relationship of the symbols of the Evangelists and the numerical tables below. The Canons start on the verso of a leaf. Folios 6^v and 7^r are devoted to the first canon table with its four beasts. The next three pages (foll. 7^v, 8^r and 8^v) contain the long second canon table with the proper beasts: angel, lion and bull. However, the scribe begins the third canon table at the bottom of the last of these pages. The beasts for the third canon table, i.e., man (the Evangelist seated before his lectern), bull, and eagle, are at the top of the next page (fol. 9^r) with its proper title in golden capitals, and the correct names for the Evangelists over their columns of numbers, *Mattheus, Lucas, Iohannis*. But since the scribe had already started the third canon on the previous page, he finishes it in the middle of this page we are considering and immediately starts the fourth canon table which compares Matthew, Mark, and John. By dint of crowding and writing below the bases of the columns, he manages to put in the whole of the fourth canon on this page.

On fol. 9^v (Pl. xv. 3) comes the change in the model we have already described so far as the ornamental system is concerned. In the spandrel between the arches, immediately and significantly, new elements appear. The whole background is painted, not left in plain vellum as hitherto. In place of the single title we have a *tabella ansata* supported by an angel. The bull, required by the fifth canon (Matthew, Luke), refuses to notice his decorative obligation to support his side of the new *tabella ansata* but complacently crouches over his column of text. The decorative cross perches precariously on top of the intruding label. On the next folio, 10^r, the label is again represented as a *tabella*, possessing weight, which is supported at one end by the angel; on the other, an uninterested lion has had his wings manipulated by the artist into an attempt at support for the label. These, of course, are the proper beasts for the sixth canon (Matthew, Mark). On this page the scribe has also written in the short seventh and eighth canons (Matthew, John and Luke, Mark).

Therefore the next page (fol. 10^v; Pl. xvi. 1) starts with the ninth canon, in which are compared the gospels of Luke and John, as can be seen in the large title and in the inscriptions at the head of each column of numbers. The beasts, however, do not agree with this canon. Above the columns entitled *Lucas* are two winged bulls, as there should be, but over the columns of John's share of the concordance are two wingless angels instead of the eagles proper to this Evangelist. The substitution was caused by the presence of the *tabella ansata* above, which requires and must originally have had human or angel supporters. The bulls repeated and adapted from the earlier portion of the Canon Tables (notably the bull on fol. 9^r) pay no attention to the weighty object over their heads, since in their immediate model there was no such object to command their interest. Consequently they leave the heavy work to the angel supporters, much to the detriment of the balance of the *tabella ansata*, which originally must have been symmetrically held by an angel at either end. Indeed, by simply transposing the first angel and bull the balanced order of the model is immediately restored. This symmetrical arrangement, however, was of course made impossible by the necessity of placing the first of the bulls over the column referring to Luke. From this we see that the intrusion of the *tabella ansata* carried with it its own angel supporters and thus plays havoc with the iconography of the Beast Canons.

Folio 11^r has that part of the tenth canon table which gives the passages peculiar to Luke, while fol. 11^v gives the passages found only in John. In each case, having only one gospel to deal with, there was no need for the artist to attempt to balance two beasts. Hence the *tabella ansata* is omitted, and we see the single beast proper for each of these tables (Pl. XVI. 2, 3).

From this description of the Canon Tables of the Harley Gospels the following facts emerge:

1. The model used in the first pages had the beasts correctly placed above the tables for the first three canons. The fourth canon was written in under the numerals for the third canon and hence had no beasts. At this point, i.e., after six pages, the model abruptly ceased. Since the canons started on a verso page, the artist of Harley was left suspended between the recto and verso of his fol. 9.

2. He then used another model to continue his canon tables. This new Gospels possessed the marbled columns, the plastic decoration, and the gems. In the spandrels between the arches were represented a *tabella ansata* carrying the title of the canon and supported by two angels, all displayed against a colored background. This new model *had no symbols of the evangelists.* Only the angels supporting the *tabella* could be used as the symbol of Matthew. The artist of Harley, wishing to complete his iconography of the Beast Canons, saw exactly this possibility. So on fol. 9^v he copied the *tabella* of his new model. He uses one of its supporting angels as the symbol of Matthew. For the symbol of Luke required for the fifth canon he uses one of the bulls of his first model but forgets to give the beast the book always held by it in earlier pages. On the next page, i.e., fol. 10^r, the artist again used the angel supporting the *tabella* as a symbol of Matthew. This time he has himself to supply the lion for the symbol of Mark in the sixth canon. Again he forgets to give the beast its book. The confusion on fol. 10^v is caused by the fact that the ninth canon table (Luke, John) calls for

no angel, symbol of Matthew. But angels there are as the inevitable supporters of the *tabella ansata*. The bulls, supplied from the earlier canons, are again deprived of the book by the forgetfulness of the artist, although the hoof, in one case, is raised as if to support it.

Thus, to explain the peculiarities and errors of the Canon Tables of Harley, we must assume the existence of two earlier manuscripts. One, which we will call X, had the Beast Canons and the flat paneled decoration. The other, to be denominated Y, had the canon tables with the *tabella ansata* and its supporting angels, as well as the plastic decoration, marbled columns, and gems.

It will be more advantageous to deal first with Y and later with X, which, however, will become more important for us in connection with the Canon Tables of Kells.

The Canon Tables of the Lorsch Gospels

The type of the second model, Y, used by the artist of the Harley Gospels can be seen in the rich and beautiful Canon Tables of the Lorsch Gospels, another fine manuscript of the Ada School. The first part of this Four Gospels is preserved in Gyulafehérvár (Karlsburg), Roumania. The rest, i.e., the gospels of Luke and John, is in the Vatican (Pal. lat. 50). The Canon Tables in the first part occupy twelve pages, i.e., pages 13–24 (the manuscript is paged, not foliated). Thus they begin on the recto of a leaf. The columns are, in every case, marbled and have molded bases of a debased classic type. The capitals are forms of acanthus leaves plastically treated, while the ornament of the great arches shows perspective motifs — leaves, meanders, "double axe," etc. A number of the arches are studded with imitations of gems. Most interesting for us is the treatment of the titles of the various canons in the spandrels under the great arches (Pls. xvii–xviii). These titles are inscribed on *tabellae* of various shapes, usually supported by angels in various attitudes. On page 13 of the Gospels, the first of the two devoted to the first canon table, two flying angels support a *tabella ansata* recalling fol. 9ᵛ of the Harley manuscript. The fifth canon of Lorsch on page 20 (Pl. xviii. 1) has a *tabella* of quatrefoil shape supported by two angels running along the tops of the smaller arches in a most animated fashion, quite in the style of the angel on fol. 9ᵛ of Harley. Page 24 of the Lorsch Gospels (Pl. xviii. 2), the last page of the Canons, has two very beautiful angel supporters for the sexfoil panel of the title. The graceful poses of these winged figures obscure, for the moment, the fact that their raised arms no longer support anything, thus making their gestures meaningless, whereas their cousins in fol. 10ᵛ of Harley (Pl. xvi. 1) really support the *tabella*. The "error" in the gestures of the angels in this page of Lorsch can be explained by the simple fact that in the original picture on which this is based, the two angels held a *tabella ansata*, the "handles" of which projected into the hands now so futilely raised in the copy. In this point, i.e., of actual support, the angels of the page just cited in the Harley Gospels are closer to the original than Lorsch since they make better sense.

Thus it becomes apparent that, close as the Canon Tables of Lorsch may be to those of the latter part of Harley, we cannot assume that the artist of Harley copied or adapted the pertinent pages of Lorsch. Rather we are forced to conclude that there existed a common model, i.e., our Y. This model throughout most of its Canon pages was decorated with *tabellae ansatae* supported by angels or winged figures quite in the classical manner, e.g., the title page of the Chronograph of A.D. 354.[31] To this model the artist of Harley was as faithful as his desire to continue the iconography of the Beast Canons allowed him to be. The artist of Lorsch, on the other hand, unencumbered by Beast Canons and anxious to give variety, changed the old *tabella* forms into new quatrefoil and sexfoil tablets but, in one instance, forgot to change the poses of his angel supporters to suit the new shapes.

There is another point which makes the assumption of a common model behind Harley and Lorsch essential and the theory of direct copying of Lorsch by Harley untenable. The backgrounds of all the spandrels under the arches in Lorsch are simple uncolored vellum. But the artist of Harley has in two instances (foll. 9ᵛ and 10ᵛ) painted colored backgrounds behind the *tabellae ansatae*. Since this is contrary to all the other Canon pages in Harley, the artist is surely in this point copying what he found in his model Y. Thus the presence of these colored backgrounds in Harley, omitted in Lorsch, as we noted, and the "error" in the poses of the angel supporters in Lorsch establish the existence of the common model Y, a prototype for both manuscripts.

THE BEAST CANONS OF THE SOISSONS GOSPELS

The only other example of the Beast Canons in the Ada School is the set in the Soissons Gospels (Paris, Bibl. Nat. lat. 8850),[32] the most beautiful and richest Beast Canons in the range of manuscript illumination. The artist was extremely resourceful and adapted his artistic elements into a surprising unity. But, unified as his work is, his models can be detected nevertheless. The Canons start on the recto of a folio and occupy twelve pages (foll. 7ʳ to 12ᵛ). This is the arrangement and number of pages used in the Lorsch Gospels. The text of the numbers under the arches for the longer tables breaks with the same numerals on the same folios in both these manuscripts. For this and many other reasons we can know that the artist of the Soissons Gospels had the great Lorsch Gospels under his eyes and adapted it for his purposes. For instance, in the Canon Tables occur the same motifs of ornament, the same birds, and the same gems. Also the capitals of the columns in both manuscripts show the same little caryatid men embedded in the acanthus (cf. fol. 10ᵛ of Soissons with page 13 of Lorsch, Pls. XIX. 2 and XVII. 1). Most resourceful and clever is the way the artist disposes the beasts of the Evangelists in his spandrels and makes them work artistically, holding up scrolls and labels with their feet and wings. For instance, on fol. 7ᵛ

[31] J. Strzygowski, *Die Calenderbilder des Chronographen vom Jahre 354* (Berlin, 1888), Taf. III.

[32] A. Boinet, *La Miniature carolingienne* (Paris, 1913), Pls. XIX, XX; A. Goldschmidt, *German Illumination*, Pl. 31; H. Janitschek, *Die Trierer-Ada Handschrift*, Taf. 31. Since these canon tables were quite exactly copied in 870 by the Codex Aureus of St. Emmeran, the iconography of the whole set can be seen in Georg Leidinger's publication of this codex.

(Pl. xix. 1) the angel holding the open book with the title is adapted from the angel holding the cartouche in page 16 of Lorsch (Pl. xvii. 2) and now serves as a symbol of Matthew with the other three symbols for the first canon table. The other three beasts are all made to help hold up the book — the lion with his paws, the bull below with his wings, while the eagle goes out of his way to be responsible for his share by reaching out a wing to hold up the title. This preoccupation of the beasts with the books, scrolls, etc., on which the titles are written in these canon tables shows the determined attempt on the part of the artist of Soissons to make artistic and iconographic sense out of his materials. The result is that the Beast Canons are correct in iconography except in one place. This is, significantly, the fifth canon table fol. 10ᵛ (Pl. xix. 2), where there are no beasts at all. The omission is filled by a medallion, containing a standing figure of Christ, supported by two angels. This decorative feature was inspired by the same page and the same canon table of Lorsch, i.e., page 20 (Pl. xviii. 1). The artist of Soissons knows, of course, that the fifth canon comparing Matthew and Luke requires a bull as well as an angel, so he very disgracefully gives one angel a pair of horns! He does this because he has before him another model which is the real cause of the peculiar iconography of this page.

This model was none other than the Harley Gospels. At the fifth canon in this manuscript, fol. 9ᵛ (Pl. xv. 3), we noted the intrusion of the *tabella ansata* with its supporting angel and the use of a colored background behind the tablet to set it off. Also we noted that the bull has no real part in this composition, refusing to help support the tablet above. The large cross above the title, usual in Harley, is, on this folio, enclosed in a shaded medallion, like a globe, set above the *tabella ansata*. The little gold cross with the equal arms, which always stands before the titles of the Harley Canons, is here left out of the *tabella ansata*, since in the tablet of Harley's model, Y, it did not exist. But it is present nevertheless as a detached element against the colored background to the left of the tablet.[32a] In the same fifth canon the very intelligent artist of Soissons tries to make artistic sense out of this page of Harley. Inspired also, as we have said, by the picture for the same canon in Lorsch (Pl. xviii. 1) with its quatrefoil supported by angels, he translates Harley's mixture into a new composition (Pl. xix. 2). The large cross with its globe-like medallion in Harley he enlarges into a figure of Christ holding a cross staff and standing in front of the globe of the firmament with its stars. This globe is supported by two angels like the quatrefoil in Lorsch. But the pose of the angel to the left is copied directly from the single angel of Harley, i.e., the symbol of Matthew. The same angel reversed takes the place of Harley's lazy bull to support the other side of the globe but in the substitution takes on the horns of the animal he replaces. The *tabella ansata* of Harley becomes a strip for the title underneath the globe of Christ. And most significantly of all, the little gold cross existing alone outside the tablet in Harley becomes in Soissons the single floating star in the background on the left of the spandrel, a unique feature, otherwise so difficult to explain.

[32a] Unfortunately hardly visible in reproduction on Pl. xv.

Thus there is no doubt that the Canon Tables of the Soissons Gospels are based on those of Harley. Since this copying shows itself to be from that part of Harley which was done after its first model, X, failed, it is awkward to hold that the truncated X and not Harley was the direct inspiration of the Beast Canons of Soissons.

Another significant detail will show that the artist of Soissons had Harley before him. One of the most striking features of the Harley Canon Tables is the use of spiral columns on their last page, fol. 11ᵛ (Pl. XVI. 3). These spiral columns have double acanthus capitals in the middle of them. But what is more interesting are the little nude men in white who actively disport themselves in a spiral band bounded by a vine tendril, climbing upward to the top of the columns. On fol. 7ᵛ (Pl. XIX. 1) of the Soissons Gospels we see all this copied, the spiral columns, the capitals in the middle of the shafts, the little nude men, climbing upwards along the vine tendrils, painted in white.

Thus for the Canon Tables of Soissons we have to assume only two models, Harley and Lorsch, on the basis of which the really excellent artist composed the most lively and beautiful set of Beast Canons in the history of illumination. From this set are later descended many other fine examples mediated in one line, probably through the almost exact copy of Soissons made in St. Denis for Charles the Bald, i.e., the Codex Aureus of St. Emmeran (Munich, Staatsbibl. lat. 14000), to Bavarian book illustration.[33]

The relation of the existing Carolingian manuscripts containing pictured Canons and the models X and Y which we found necessary to assume can be expressed in the following stemma:

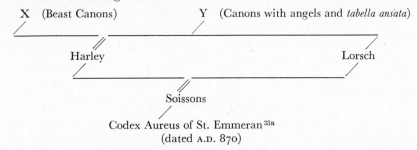

X (Beast Canons)   Y (Canons with angels and *tabella ansata*)

Harley   Lorsch

Soissons

Codex Aureus of St. Emmeran[33a]
(dated A.D. 870)

From this stemma it can be clearly seen that the iconography of the Beast Canons in Carolingian art was derived from one single gospel manuscript, X. It must now become our business to find out what further we can know about this important lost document. Are there any traces of its existence other than its copy in the first six pages of the Harley Gospels' Canon Tables?

KELLS AND ADA

In the description of the Beast Canons of the Book of Kells, we saw that the artist of this splendid manuscript was dependent for this feature on an earlier

[33] E. F. Bange, *Eine bayerische Malerschule des XI. und XII. Jahrhunderts* (Munich, 1923).

[33a] To save reference to a discussion irrelevant to the Book of Kells, the very incomplete Beast Canons of the Bible of St. Paul's are not considered in this article.

gospel book as a model. Because of the errors and difficulties of Kells we were compelled to infer that this model had only six pages of decorated canons and broke off suddenly after the picture for the third canon table. Although the text of Kells completes the fourth canon within its six pages, there is no picture for this canon, so there could have been none in the model.

Likewise in our study of the Canons of the Harley Gospels we were confronted with exactly the same state of affairs. The first model containing the Beast Canons ceased suddenly after six pages, or after the picture for the third canon table. Again in Harley, as we saw in Kells, the text for the fourth canon table was completed within the six pages, but again there is no picture for this canon table. The next picture in Harley is for the fifth canon table.

Now by a comparison of the pertinent pages of the Canons in Kells and Harley, we can explain more exactly one of the errors in Kells. On foll. 8^v and 9^r in Harley (Pl. xv) we see that while the scribe started the third canon table (Matthew, *Luke*, John) at the bottom of the last page of the preceding canon, the bulk of it is on fol. 9^r, so that the beasts on this folio are, correctly, man, bull, and eagle. The fourth canon (Matthew, *Mark*, John) is then written complete but crowded under the third and has, consequently, no beast picture. In Kells on foll. 3^v and 4^r (Pls. vi and vii) the scribe likewise started his third canon table on the page which has the end of the second. But in this case, instead of running it over to the next page, he *finished* it on the same page on which he began it. Thus the fourth canon (Matthew, Mark, John), which should have been subsidiary on the next page (fol. 4^r), is moved up to the heads of the columns, making nonsense of the beast picture which in the model of Kells was surely intended to illustrate the third canon table (angel, calf, eagle). As we said before, it is the scribe of Kells, and not the artist, who departs from the model and thus creates error. Consequently in this comparison of the Canons of Harley and Kells, it is Harley which explains the true state of the model of Kells.

A further comparison of the Canon Tables of Harley and Kells brings to light other similarities. The Canons of both manuscripts begin on the verso of a folio. The pages which face one another in each manuscript have reciprocal decoration. We have noted this already in Kells. In Harley the sets of folios, 6^v and 7^r, 7^v and 8^r, 8^v and 9^r, have the same decoration of arches, columns, capitals, and bases on the facing pages. This reciprocity does not obtain in the rest of the Canon Tables of Harley and consequently must have been in the model, X, for the first six pages. Again both Kells and Harley have triangular decorated spandrels over the main arches to square out the page, a feature unusual in both Celtic and Ada School manuscripts.

When we consider how few were the manuscripts which possessed the Beast Canons (all the Carolingian Gospels with this feature are derived from one manuscript) and when we tabulate all the peculiar agreements in structure and in "error" between the Canon Tables of Kells and Harley, we can come to only one conclusion. The model of Harley and the model of Kells were the same manuscript. The chance for just these errors and similarities occurring independently in an iconography so complicated as the Beast Canons is an impossibility. We know, therefore, that Kells as well as Harley is a copy of our manuscript X.

We have still further proof, this time in connection with the portraits of the Evangelists. The portrait of John in the Harley Gospels, fol. 161ᵛ (Pl. xx), shows the Evangelist, frontal, seated, dipping his pen in an inkwell with his right hand while with his left he holds up, most inconveniently, an open book. Behind him over the back of his throne is draped a cloth of honor in many folds. The pose of this Evangelist, holding out the book grasped from below, is *unique* in the many sets of Evangelist portraits in the Gospels of the Ada School. In Harley itself this portrait in its decoration differs from all the other three Evangelists in that each of the columns which flank John is bordered by heavy colored strips which destroy its third dimensional character, turning it into a panel. The columns flanking the other Evangelists are plastic and simply marbled.[34] Turning to the Book of Kells, fol. 291ᵛ (Pl. xx), we see John in exactly the same pose as in Harley. With his right hand the Evangelist reaches down to dip his very long pen with its foliate top into the inkhorn at his foot. With his left hand he holds up a book, grasped from below, but this time conveniently closed. Behind the Evangelist can be seen the folds of the cloth of honor over the back of his throne. It is to be noticed that in all the Celtic gospel books this pose of an Evangelist is *unique*, confined to Kells. The similarity of the portraits of John in Harley and Kells extends to the colors of the garments of the Evangelist. In Harley John is clad in a purple pallium shaded with gold and worn over a golden tunic with red folds.[35] In Kells the Evangelist wears a purple pallium with red folds over a tunic done in shades of variegated yellows to imitate gold. The folds of drapery are indicated with red lines.[36] This is one of the many places in Kells where yellow is used to imitate gold.

The similarity of the portraits of John in Harley and Kells, combined with their uniqueness in their two schools, confirms the connection between these manuscripts already shown in the Beast Canons. The common model, X, which we must assume, evidently had a portrait of John in just this pose and coloration. Whether he was bearded and whether his book was open or closed we cannot know surely, since our two copies disagree in these points.

The other Evangelist portraits in Harley have no counterparts in Kells, but if the difference which I pointed out between the treatment of the columns which flank them and of those which flank John means anything, we can assume that, so far as the portraits are concerned, Harley derived only John from X and took the other three Evangelists from Y, or some other source. Certainly the negative evidence from Kells confirms this hypothesis.

But the only other Evangelist portrait surviving in Kells, Matthew, fol. 28ᵛ (Pl. xxi), betrays also its dependence on its Continental model. Matthew is

[34] Boinet, *op. cit.*, Pl. xiii for Luke; Goldschmidt, *op. cit.*, Pl. 36, for Matthew; British Museum, *Reproductions from Illuminated Manuscripts*, Ser. iii (1910), Pl. iv, for Mark.

[35] *Catalogue of Ancient Manuscripts in the British Museum. Part II. Latin* (London, 1884), p. 24.

[36] Sullivan, *op. cit.*, Pl. xviii.

seated in frontal pose, on a cushioned bench with drapery over it. Over his
head is a great arch resting on squares of ornament as capitals.[37] The shafts of
the columns are peculiarly bent at right angles out from the capital. Then, pro-
ceeding downward, these shafts end in circles of ornament which serve as the
bases of the columns. This stylization of capitals and bases of columns we have
already noticed in the Canon Tables of Kells, foll. 4ᵛ and 5ʳ (Pls. VIII and IX).
In the spandrels above the great arch, foliaceous ornament, deriving from an
acanthus leaf, decorates the triangle which squares out the picture as in the Harley Gospels. The most significant feature of the portrait, however, is the peculiar
semicircular structure behind the Evangelist. This runs up into the great arch
with its counter curve and is surmounted by a molding with little red tongues.[38]
What kind of model the artist of Kells had before him for the portrait of Matthew
can be best seen in the Evangelist portraits of the Ada School. If we confront the
Kells portrait with the portrait of Matthew from the Gospels of Ada, fol. 15ᵛ
(Pl. XXI), we see the Evangelist seated under the great arch supported by columns, and behind him is the architectural hemicycle, running up into the arch,
so frequently placed behind the Ada School Evangelists. The peculiar semi-
circle in Kells is now seen to be an adaptation of the hemicycle niche of the Ada
portraits. The little red tongues in the molding of this feature in Kells are really
the semicircular-headed windows which decorate the top of the hemicycle in
which the Evangelist sits. Thus the "setting" for the Evangelist in both Kells
and Ada is the same. These arches and hemicycles, which are to be derived ultimately through the medium of Greek gospel books from the theater of Antioch,
are to be found, in Carolingian art, only in the Ada School or its descendants.

Thus it becomes apparent that the artist of Kells has copied another of the
Evangelist portraits in his model, X, but it is one that the artist of Harley re-
jected, in favor perhaps of those of Y. Indeed the use of yellow in the great arch
above the head of the Evangelist in Kells[39] suggests the golden strips which
served as moldings in the same arch of X. The symbols of the Evangelists, the
eagle and calf over the throne and the lion (twice) over the hemicycle, in the
Kells portrait are the addition of the Celtic artist who was accustomed to a page
with these four symbols in front of each gospel.[40]

The third, so-called Evangelist, portrait in the Book of Kells, fol. 32ᵛ (Pl.
XXII), is not an Evangelist at all but is a portrait of Jesus Christ, as Gerald
Plunket inferred when he wrote the words (now erased) *Jesus Christus* in the unfinished spandrels over the main arch.[41] The structure of the Book of Kells
makes this clear. In front of each of the four gospels were (1) great cross page
with symbols of Evangelists, (2) portrait of the Evangelist seated, (3) great Initial page highly ornamented. The gospel of Matthew was peculiar in having

[37] A. K. Porter, *op. cit.*, p. 50.

[38] Sullivan, *op. cit.*, Pl. v.

[39] *Ibid.*, color plate.

[40] Zimmermann, *op. cit.*, Taf. 190, 245. Cf. also John Gwynn, *The Book of Armagh* (Dublin, 1913),
fol. 69ᵛ and fol. 91ʳ.

[41] Sullivan, *op. cit.*, p. 13.

two great initial pages. One of these is for the beginning of the gospel, *Liber generationis* (fol. 29ʳ) and the other (the most magnificent initial in Kells) for the beginning of the gospel proper, i.e., after the genealogy, *XPI autem generatio* (fol. 34ʳ). Immediately in front of this splendid initial is the finest of the cross pages in Kells (fol. 33ʳ) and, in front of this cross page, the portrait we are considering (fol. 32ᵛ, i.e., facing the wonderful cross page).[42] Since there is no reason to suppose that the structure of Kells has been tampered with at this place, our picture is surely a portrait of Jesus Christ motivated by the text and placed here to go with his great initial on fol. 34ʳ. Thus not only did each of the four Evangelists have his cross page and elegantly ornamented initial, but Christ also had His, and these are significantly the most splendid of all. Christ is represented seated, since the cushioned bench is seen behind him. The book, held in his left hand, which is not visible, is pressed down into the drapery over his left knee. He is *not* holding the book with a veiled hand, as seems probable at first sight. His right hand is raised in blessing. Over his head is a great arch supported by bent columns, with bases and capitals stylized as in the case of the portrait of Matthew. The spandrels over the arch are unfinished, but in the model of Kells they contained the peacocks and vases which the Celtic artist has now placed on top of the shoulders of his bent columns. How closely the artist of Kells can follow his model even in details is shown by the presence of the little tassels at the ends of the pallium worn by Christ. These are the characteristic decorations of this garment in classical times and are continued in Byzantine gospel books.[43]

The most significant feature of the iconography, however, which in itself would identify this portrait as Christ and not one of the Evangelists, is the presence of four angels, two on either side, originally next to Christ since the columns in the model were really under the capitals. These angels have wings of various sorts, including the one who, though still an angel, crosses his wings like a seraph. The iconography of Christ seated on a throne surrounded by angels occurs in the Ada School. The Lorsch Gospels show him thus (Pl. XXIII) with a choir of eight angels in attitudes of praise, in the form of busts disposed in a circle which also contains medallions of the "Four holy beasts figuring the men who narrated the sacred gifts of Christ the Healer," as the inscription says. This picture of Christ with the angels and symbols of the Evangelists in Lorsch (page 36) is opposite the great initial page of Matthew's gospel. This position is intentional, since the decoration of the two pages is exactly the same.[44] The portrait of Matthew is placed several pages earlier (page 26) before the Prologue for Matthew's gospel. Thus in the Lorsch Gospels, as in the Book of Kells, the portrait of Matthew precedes the picture of Christ surrounded by the angels.

But the picture of Christ and eight angels in Lorsch contains also the four

[42] Sullivan, Pls. VIII and IX.

[43] E.g., statue of Sophocles in the Lateran, Rome; St. John, fol. 13ʳ, Athos, Stauronikita MS. 43. Cf. K. Weitzmann, *Die byzantinische Buchmalerei*, Taf. XXX. The Lindisfarne Gospels also follow the Greek model in this respect; cf. Millar, *op. cit.*, Pls. XXIX and XXXIII. Another example from Kells is the pallium of St. Matthew (Pl. XXI).

[44] Goldschmidt, *op. cit.*, Pl. 41.

Beasts of the Evangelists, while the Kells miniature has only Christ and four angels. This seeming discrepancy in iconography can be only partially explained. It will be remembered that on the first folio of Kells (Pl. 1) the original artist filled out a blank column after the end of the Hebrew names with two panels of anthropomorphic symbols which have to be looked at sidewise and have no business in that place. Clearly they are transferred from some other position which they must have occupied in the model used by this artist. Now all four of these beasts hold up their books as if they were offering them to some person. For the symbols of the Evangelists this person can only be Christ. Therefore we can be justified if we restore them to the model of the picture of Christ enthroned with the angels, particularly since this is the only picture of Christ enthroned copied in Kells. The missing four angels (missing if we assume there was any significance other than decorative in the number eight in the circle around Christ in Lorsch) may also have escaped in Kells to another page. Perhaps in the great initial page immediately following the portrait of Christ, the three angels to the left of the bar of the X of XPI[45] may originally have belonged to this portrait, but, taking into account the number of instances detached angels appear in Kells, this hypothesis has little cogency. It is more likely that, in the picture of Christ, the four angels balanced the four Beasts.

It is safe to assume therefore that the model of Kells, our X, possessed a page on which was a portrait of Christ enthroned, holding a book, accompanied by four angels grouped in pairs. To him four anthropomorphic symbols of the Evangelists, represented likewise in pairs, were offering their gospel books. This page thus showed the same iconography that we have seen, in even more schematic form, in the Lorsch Gospels.

This picture in Lorsch seems to be unique in the schools of Carolingian illumination.[46] In contemporary or earlier illumination, the iconography we are considering occurs in but one example and only partially in that. This is a very important, but little known, gospel book in Poitiers (Bibliothèque de la Ville, MS. 17),[47] which cannot for paleographical and stylistic reasons date later than the beginning of the ninth century, and which seems to me to have been painted before this time. On fol. 31^r, directly before the beginning of the gospel of Matthew, is the only miniature in this volume (Pl. XXIII).[48] It is of interest to note that it is placed after the canon tables with their gold and silver arches and after the argument, the breves, and the explanation of the Hebrew names for Matthew's gospel; i.e., it is preceded by all the prefatory matter for Matthew. In the miniature, Christ, bearded with a green beard and clad in a silver tunic and golden pallium with the folds of drapery indicated in red, is seated on a multi-

[45] Sullivan, *op. cit.*, Pl. IX.

[46] Adolf Schmidt, *Die Miniaturen des Gerokodex*, pp. 58 ff. Wilhelm Koehler, "Die Tradition der Adagruppe und die Anfänge des ottonischen Stiles in der Buchmalerei," *Festschrift zum 60. Geburtstag von Paul Clemen* (Düsseldorf, 1926), pp. 268 ff.

[47] Catalogue général des Mss. des Bibl. Publ. de France — Departements, Tome XXV, pp. 4–5. On f. 1^v is a note dated 1635 which allows us to believe that this Gospels was then in Sainte-Croix de Poitiers.

[48] Ch. Cahier, *Nouveaux Mélanges d'archéologie. Tome II. Ivoires, miniatures, émaux* (1874), pp. 111–113.

colored throne. He holds a book in his left hand; the drapery over his left knee hides part of the book, as in Kells. He raises his right hand in a gesture of speaking. On either side in medallions are the four anthropomorphic symbols of the Evangelists who offer their gospel books to him open at the very passages quoted by St. Jerome in his preface, *Plures fuisse* (taken from his commentary on St. Matthew),[49] to explain why each beast symbolizes each gospel. Thus do the anthropomorphic symbols seek to explain their hybrid forms to Christ.

In this example of the enthroned Christ, the use of anthropomorphic beasts and the fact that Christ has a beard bring us nearer to the model of Kells than to the picture in Lorsch. On the other hand the enrichment of the angels, absent in Poitiers, associates the Celtic and the Lorsch gospel books. In any case it is clear that in these three manuscripts — Poitiers, Kells, and Lorsch — we are dealing with copies, however imperfect, of the same picture, particularly when we note that in all three Gospels the picture is placed and regarded as a frontispiece for Matthew alone and not as a frontispiece for the whole gospel corpus. Thus it seems sure that in X, the model of Kells, a portrait of Christ surrounded by adoring anthropomorphic beasts and angels came after the portrait of Matthew and that in this arrangement the artist of Kells accurately reproduced his model. To the portrait of Christ he added the sumptuous cross page[50] in pure Celtic ornament in order that Christ should have at least equal honor with the four Evangelists whose portraits in Celtic gospel manuscripts frequently possess this additional feature.

There is no doubt that fol. 32ᵛ of Kells (Pl. XXII) is a portrait of Christ. Above his head is a cross of equal arms. This is not a misplaced cross-nimbus but a feature independent of Christ's figure, associated by the artist of Kells with the yellow arch above, since the cross is formed from the very molding of the arch itself. This cross of equal arms is found again in the frontispiece of the seated Christ in front of the tenth century manuscript of the Carmen Paschale of Sedulius, MS. 176 (126), in the Plantin Museum in Antwerp.[50a] The structure of this poem, which is a versification based on the Four Gospels, makes this page equivalent to a frontispiece for a Gospel Book from which, as a model, it was undoubtedly taken. In this portrait of Christ, on top of the back of the throne we see the same cross with equal arms as in Kells. Turning again to the Poitiers Gospels (Pl. XXIII) we note above the throne of Christ the arrangement of the words ΦѠϹ-ΖѠΗ to form the same cross of equal arms now enclosed in a square. Indeed this use of the cross shape for these words of Light and Life is a feature borrowed ultimately from Syria. A processional cross, datable in the sixth century, which was in the collection of Gustave Schlumberger[50b] has these words inscribed on the equal arms of a little cross, surmounting the larger cross. In this Syrian

---

[49] Wordsworth and White, *op. cit.*, pp. 11–14.

[50] Sullivan, *op. cit.*, Pl. VIII.

[50a] Paul Clemen, *Belgische Kunstdenkmäler* (Munich, 1923), Bd. I, Abb. 19. J. Denucé, *Musaeum Plantin-Moretus, Catalogue des Manuscrits* (Antwerp, 1927), pp. 135–137.

[50b] Gustave Schlumberger, "Monuments byzantins inédits," in *Florilegium . . . Melchior de Vogüé* (Paris, 1909), pp. 555–559.

example the little inscribed cross is enclosed in a circle exactly as in the Sedulius manuscript in Antwerp. Once again, then, the Poitiers Gospels explains the peculiar features in the portrait of Christ in Kells. We can be fairly certain that the model of Kells had the cross of equal arms (inscribed ΦШC-ZШH?) above the throne of the bearded figure of Christ. The comparison of Kells and Poitiers proves conclusively the identification of fol. 32ᵛ of Kells as a portrait of Christ.

The Model of Kells

In the foregoing pages with their rather minute comparisons we have established the fact, it seems to me, that the Book of Kells and the Harley Gospels are based on the same manuscript so far as their iconography is concerned. From the study of the portraits in Kells we have been able to reconstruct the iconography of other pages of this model which the artist of Harley did not copy. It will be convenient now to recapitulate the results of our investigation and describe this model as a manuscript.

The model of Kells, our manuscript X, had the following structure and pictures:

1. A set of canon tables decorated with columns and arches. In the spandrels between the arches were the beasts (not anthropomorphic) proper to each canon. The great arches were squared out with exterior spandrels of ornament. These canon tables began on the verso of a leaf and continued for six pages, when they suddenly ceased at the beginning of the fifth canon. There was no picture for the fourth canon, which was written under the end of the third. The rest of the Canon Tables were unfinished, rather than lost, since the Canons stopped on the recto of a leaf.

2. The portrait of Matthew seated, frontal, under an arch supported by columns and in front of a semicircular exedra.

3. A portrait of Christ enthroned, flanked by angels and anthropomorphic symbols of the Evangelists offering their gospels. These creatures were arranged in pairs. Above Christ's head, or above his throne, was a cross of equal arms, perhaps inscribed ΦШC-ZШH. This picture was in front of the gospel of Matthew but placed after the portrait of this Evangelist.

4. Possibly the portrait of Mark in front of his gospel. (The portrait in Kells is absent; consequently we cannot tell whether the original was defective here or not.)

5. Possibly the portrait of Luke in front of his gospel. (Again in Kells both the portrait and the cross page have disappeared, removing our evidence.)

6. The portrait of John in front of his gospel, seated, frontal, probably under an arch and possibly with a semicircular niche behind him.[51]

---

[51] In Kells there are several pictures other than those of Christ and the Evangelists. Did the model X have also pages with pictures of the Virgin and Child, the Hymn on the Mount of Olives, the Temptation, the Crucifixion, etc., which are or were in Kells? If so, X was a very rich manuscript indeed. But it is an hypothesis that is difficult of proof. Another feature which may have been in the model X is a peculiarity of Harley which seems to be reflected in Kells. This is the use of a little Evangelist, seated in profile in front

Thus we become aware of the existence of a very rich lost manuscript of the Four Gospels, certainly of Continental Latin origin. From our study we see also that the closest iconographic affinities of this manuscript are with the gospel books of the Carolingian Ada School.

We have said that the powerful artist of Kells so effectively translated his model into his own Celtic idiom that stylistic criticism was helpless to detect the prototype. But now that we have reason to know the iconographical structure of this model by means of another method of criticism, we may attempt to discern its style. Since this lost manuscript was copied by both Harley and Kells and since iconographically it is very close to the Ada School, we have several means of determining its stylistic peculiarities. Clearly, X is either an Ada School Gospels dating earlier than Harley or it is an earlier manuscript of some other provenance used in the scriptorium which produced the Ada School.

The stylistic points we can detect in X either by a study of Harley and Kells or by a comparison between them are the following:

1. The use of foliaceous ornament in the arches and columns, particularly of the rinceau (Kells, foll. 2^r and 4^r).

2. The great arches over the portraits with decorated spandrels to square out the page (Kells, foll. 28^v and 32^v, and Harley, fol. 161^v).

3. The decoration of these spandrels with peacocks, chalices, and acanthus leaves (Kells, same folios).

4. The use of gold for the moldings of the arches, columns, and frames. (In Kells done in bright yellow to imitate gold. This can be seen best in the color reproductions in Sullivan: Pls. I, V, VII. This yellow is particularly noticeable in the Canon Tables.)

5. The use of gold for the drapery of the portraits with red to indicate the folds (Harley 161^v and Kells 291^v, illustrated on Pl. XX).

6. The great scalloped nimbi placed around the head of the Evangelists. (Kells, foll. 28^v and 291^v, where the effect is almost that of a cross nimbus. These can be paralleled in the Ada School Gospels, particularly in the Ada manuscript itself, fol. 15^v, Pl. XXI.)

7. The large heads with staring eyes of the portraits and the chalky whiteness of the flesh parts. (Again best paralleled in the Ada manuscripts, particularly in the portrait of John, fol. 153^v of the Gospels in Abbeville, Pl. XXIV.)

8. The heavy beards worn by the Evangelists and Christ in Kells may well have been in the model X. In the Ada School the tendency after the Lectionary of Godescalc (A.D. 781–783)[52] is towards a beardless type, but the beard persists in single Evangelists in the later examples of this school, e.g., Lorsch and Soissons. Christ is always beardless in the Ada School, even in the early manuscript

---

of his lectern, in place of the angel in the beast picture for the third canon table (fol. 9^r, Pl. XV). In Kells in the same beast picture (fol. 4^r, Pl. VII) the angel is seated in profile holding a book, while, in front of him, the pot of flowers may be the Celtic artist's adaptation of the lectern. The substitution of an Evangelist for the angel can be seen also in the Beast Canons of Soissons (fol. 11^v).

[52] Boinet, *op. cit.*, Pls. III, IV.

of Godescalc, but we have illustrated the bearded Christ in the almost contemporary Poitiers Gospel (Pl. XXIII), which, moreover, occurred in the same iconographic connection as the bearded Christ in Kells.

From the stylistic point of view the model of Kells, X, is seen to be a splendid and sumptuous book, richly ornamented and decorated in gold. The presence of the Beast Canons stamps the book as a western and not a Greek production. Now in the West we know of no such complicated, sumptuous, and gilded book decoration until the time of Charlemagne and since all the affinities, stylistic and iconographic, are with the Ada School we must conclude that X was a gospel book made in the scriptorium which produced the splendid manuscripts of this style for the great Frankish king.

It remains only to place X in the sequence of the manuscripts of the Ada School. The earliest we know of is fortunately datable. The Lectionary of Godescalc was made A.D. 781–783, as we infer from the dedicatory poem written by Godescalc for Charlemagne.[53] The bearded Evangelists and the large heads with their staring eyes in this manuscript would seem to link it at once with the model of Kells, but one has only to compare the pictures of Godescalc with the description we have made above of X, to realize that our lost manuscript was a far richer and fuller production than the Lectionary of Godescalc. It resembles much more the later manuscripts of the Ada School. Yet X must date before Harley and Soissons, since they copied it.[54] Unfortunately the date when the Harley Gospels copied X cannot be accurately determined. Harley is usually dated about 800 A.D.[55] To my mind this date is too late by several years. But until my friend, Professor Wilhelm Koehler, has written the volumes on the Ada School in his great publication of Carolingian manuscripts, it is premature and presumptuous of me to assert this earlier dating with any degree of assurance. The lost gospel book, X, was produced, then, in the Ada scriptorium anywhere between A.D. 781 and A.D. 800. In any case it belongs among the earlier productions of this famous atelier.

The miniature in the manuscripts of the Ada School which X may most closely have resembled in style is to be found in the purple Gospels at Abbeville (Bibl. de la Ville MS. 4 [1]) which by tradition was the gift of Charlemagne to Angilbert, who was abbot of St. Ricquier from 790 to 814. In any case this book was mentioned in 831 in the inventory of the treasury of St. Ricquier.[56] In this splendid manuscript the four Evangelist portraits are the sole miniatures.[57] These are not consistent in style. Unique and most archaic is the portrait of John on fol. 153ᵛ (Pl. XXIV). The large head, the staring eyes, and the chalky flesh recall the manuscripts of Godescalc and Kells. The columns which support the great arch are paneled with broad strips resembling the columns which flank the por-

---

[53] Janitschek, *op. cit.*, p. 85.
[54] Cf. Stemma of Beast Canons at the end of this article.
[55] Goldschmidt, *op. cit.*, Pl. 35; *Catalogue of Ancient Manuscripts in the British Museum, Part II, Latin*, p. 22.
[56] Goldschmidt, *op. cit.*, Pl. 42.
[57] *Ibid.*, Pl. 43, and Boinet, *op. cit.*, Pl. x.

trait of John in Harley (Pl. xx). The shoulders of the great arch are squared out with painted spandrels decorated with acanthus and chalices. John is seated frontally on his throne, in front of a rectangular exedra or niche. The background is really a platform (the ancient stage) that has been cut back into by the niche. The whole is seen from above, so that the floor of the platform is visible. In order to represent the perspective of the niche the artist of Abbeville has colored the floor of the platform and the various faces of the wall in violently contrasted lightings. At the top of the wall, carried back around the niche, is a square molding. The effect, seen best on the left, is as if a paneled strip started out horizontally from the capital of each column and then turned sharply downwards at right angles, changing its lighting violently at the angle. This effect is induced by the fact that the platform seen in perspective from above is exactly the same width as the receding face of the niche below it and because the top of the strip starts off exactly on the level of the abacus of the capital. Something very like this must have occurred in one of the Evangelist pictures of X, the model of Kells, since it inspired the Celtic artist in his portraits of Matthew and Christ to run his flanking columns in these miniatures (Pls. xxi and xxii) horizontally from the square capitals towards the figure and then turn them down sharply at right angles. The result in the case of Matthew is that the cushions of the bench on which the Evangelist sits are outside the columns. A similar result would ensue in the portrait of John in Abbeville if the bright receding faces of the niche were mistaken for supports and carried down with the posts for the back of the chair. The hemicycles and niches used as backgrounds for the Ada School Evangelists thus became fertile inspiration for the decorative invention of the artist of Kells, and, flattening out, as he does, the architectural features of his model, he turned the rich plastic portraits of X into the superb designs of his own masterpiece. Again the rich variety of ornament, including rinceaux and interlace, in the manuscripts of the Ada School must have been very congenial to the temperament of this Celtic master.

Thus, by reference to the portrait of John in the Abbeville Gospels we see how the very violence of the style of an early Ada manuscript explains the seemingly "pure" invention of the Celtic artist. Surely the style of the lost Ada Gospels copied by Harley and Kells cannot have been very different from that of the portrait of the fourth Evangelist in the sumptuous Gospels presented by Charlemagne to Angilbert perhaps very early in his abbacy.

The Date and Provenance of Kells

Since X, the model of Kells, was an early product of the Ada scriptorium and since it must have been used by the artist of Harley in the same atelier on the Continent before it departed to the Celtic world beyond the sea, it follows that its insular copy must date later than the Harley Gospels. Therefore the Book of Kells was written and decorated after *ca.* 800, or, if I am correct in dating Harley earlier, after *ca.* 795.

The determination of the *terminus ante quem* for the Book of Kells involves a study of its provenance. Here the Canon Tables again will give us the necessary clue, as we shall see.

The earliest historical reference to the Book of Kells is in the Annals of Ulster, *sub anno* 1007. "The great Gospel of Columcille was wickedly stolen in the night out of the western sacristy of the large stone church of Kells, the chief relic (*mind*) of the western world, on account of its wrought shrine. That gospel was found after two months and twenty nights, its gold having been taken off, and a sod over it." [58] That it was still in Kells in the twelfth century is attested by the contents of the manuscript itself, since on foll. 6ᵛ and 7ʳ, immediately following the canon tables, are copied, in a twelfth-century hand, the charters regarding the property of the Church of Kells. The Abbey of Kells was surrendered to the Crown by its last abbot, Richard Plunket, in 1539. Later the Book of Kells passed into the hands of Gerald Plunket, possibly a kinsman of the last abbot. It was he who correctly identified the portrait of Christ, writing in the empty spandrels the words *Jesus Christus*. The manuscript was then acquired by James Ussher, Bishop of Meath, and came into the Library of Trinity College, Dublin, when his collection was acquired in 1661.

There cannot be any doubt that the Book of Kells was the chief treasure of the Abbey of Kells from the eleventh century until the dissolution of the monasteries, since in it the records of the property of the Church were transcribed for safekeeping on the blank pages following the Canons. One of these pages was originally left blank for a very particular reason, which we can discover.

The Canon Tables of Kells (Pls. II–XI) show two breaks in their sequence, as we have pointed out. The first break was caused by the failure of the Beast Canons in the model X after the fourth canon table, i.e., between foll. 4ʳ and 4ᵛ. The artist of Kells continued on his own responsibility for two more pages of superb ornament. Then suddenly between foll. 5ʳ and 5ᵛ the splendid artist ceased his work. His last two pages contained the fifth, sixth, seventh, and eighth canons. The canons are continued on 5ᵛ and 6ʳ within the poverty-stricken yellow and violet frames, written in black ink different from that used in the earlier canons. Since there are no longer any arches or ornament to fill up the page, the new system of Canons allows the writing to fill the entire page. Consequently the remaining canon tables, the ninth and the long tenth, were easily transcribed on two pages, whereas if the splendid ornament of the earlier Canons had been continued, three pages would have been necessary. This leaves fol. 6ᵛ blank, and on this the charters of Kells were later transcribed. (Folio 7ʳ is the back of the portrait of the Virgin and Child, and the backs of the portraits in Kells were originally left blank.)

Thus the change in the decoration of the canon tables left blank a page which the original artist intended as his last or eleventh page of Canons. This would bring the number of his decorated pages up to the number used in Harley, and this is the number, by calculation from the model X, that it would have to be,

---

[58] James F. Kenney, *The Sources for the Early History of Ireland* (New York, 1929), p. 641.

since the third and fourth canon tables were crowded on the same page in both. We can, therefore, be fairly sure that the vellum was prepared by the artist of Kells for the three pages he never got to do.

The pages were prepared, but after the master hand ceased no one could continue except in the paltry and crowded fashion of foll. 5ᵛ and 6ʳ, with their virtually undecorated strips of yellow and violet. The manuscript we are looking at is the last work of a great school, a great scriptorium. Folios 5ᵛ and 6ʳ were never painted in the scriptorium that produced the rest of the Book of Kells. The manuscript was taken before it was finished to some artistically inferior monastery where the canon tables were completed for liturgical use only. Some cataclysm must have stopped suddenly the decoration of this splendid manuscript and destroyed the great scriptorium which produced it, thus rendering its completion in the same style by others impossible.

This is exactly what happened, according to the history of the Church of Kells. Cenannus (the town of Kells) did not become ecclesiastically important until the headquarters of the Columban *paruchia* were established there in 807–814.[59] The headquarters were suddenly shifted to Kells from the monastery at Iona by the monks fleeing the Northmen. The Vikings plundered Iona in 802 and 806, and destroyed it so completely that it never recovered its former prestige. By 814 the abbot of Iona was established at Kells,[60] and after this the abbots of Kells were regarded as the heads of the *paruchia* of St. Columba (i.e., of all the churches founded by this saint).

Thus it is clear that the Book of Kells was being written and decorated on the island of Iona in the great monastery founded by St. Columba. It was in process of completion when suddenly the Northmen swooped down upon the monastery. The splendid scriptorium was dispersed. The sumptuous model X was probably stolen or destroyed. The hand of the artist of Kells is never seen again in any illuminated Celtic manuscript. The fleeing monks took his glorious unfinished gospel book with them to Kells, where later they completed the necessary canon tables as best they could, and added elsewhere in the volume their meager washes of violet and yellow, contrasting so pathetically with the superb ornament produced in the great scriptorium at Iona, now forever destroyed.

Therefore the work on the Book of Kells, which must have consumed years of labor in decoration and was still unfinished when the Northmen destroyed the possibility of its completion, can be dated between the years *ca.* 795 and 806. That this "chief relic of the western world" was made in Iona many scholars have said before me. The latest and not the least is the late F. C. Burkitt who says of the Book of Kells, "It was doubtless written at Iona itself. . . . There is nothing to suggest that Kells was written in Ireland itself; no doubt it was taken from Iona to Kells, where the monks retired when they deserted Iona."[61]

The close connection between the decoration of the Book of Kells and the

---

[59] Kenney, *loc. cit.*

[60] Kenney, p. 445.

[61] Kells, Durrow and Lindisfarne, *Antiquity*, March 1935, pp. 33–37.

Gospels of Lindisfarne, which has so frequently been remarked, is indeed most reasonable, since the Church of Lindisfarne was a daughter of the Columban foundation in Iona. The manuscripts are both products, so to speak, of Iona. The difference between them is caused partly, no doubt, by their difference in date but chiefly by the difference between their models. The Gospels of Lindisfarne is based on an early and simple Greek gospel book; the Book of Kells on a rich and sumptuous manuscript, the product of the scriptorium of the Ada School under the patronage of Charlemagne.[62] Bruun was quite right. The Book of Kells *was* "produced under the influence of the early *renaissance* which commenced in the Frankish Empire under the reign of Charlemagne."[63]

[62] I have been able to find no direct connection in history between Iona and Charlemagne. The only document which might have any bearing on the situation is the well-known letter of Alcuin to his master Colcu, who undoubtedly was a Celtic teacher associated with some monastic establishment in Britain. The letter was written by Alcuin on the Continent to Northumbria in A.D. 790. Later in the same year Alcuin is in Northumbria and writes back to the Continent to his pupil Joseph, indicating that Colcu, who was also the master of Joseph, is with him. "Sanus est magister vester Colcu; et sani amici tui, qui apud nos sunt." The letter of Alcuin to Colcu is sufficiently interesting in connection with our problem to transcribe partially:

"Benedicto magistro et pio patri Colcu Alcuine humilis levita salutem. . . . Misi caritati tue aliquid de oleo, quod vix modo in *Britannia* invenitur, ut dispensares per loca necessaria episcoporum ad utilitatem honoris Dei. Misi quoque quinquaginta siclos fratribus de elemosina Karli regis — obsecro, ut pro eo oretis — et de mea elemosina quinquaginta siclos; et ad australes fratres Baldhuninga triginta siclos de elemosina regis et triginta de elemosina mea; et viginti siclos de elemosina patrisfamilie Ariede et viginti de elemosina mea; et per singulos anachoritas tres siclos de puro argento; ut illi omnes orent pro me et pro domno rege Carolo, ut Deus illum conservet ad tutelam sanctae sue aeclesiae et ad laudem et gloriam sui nominis. Exaudiat vos omnipotens Deus, pro sancta sua aeclesia intercedentes, et proficere faciat in salutis eterne prosperitate" (E. C. W. Wattenbach et E. L. Duemmler, *Monumenta Alcuiniana*, 1873, pp. 166–168 and 170–172).

From this we gather that Colcu habitually lived in Britannia where the particular oil was not to be found. So Alcuin sends him some. Charlemagne sends gifts to the brothers of Colcu's monastery as well as to other monks and single anchorites. There is no mention of gifts of manuscripts. The site of these Celtic monastic foundations is not determinable except they are in Britain. So there is no reason to identify Colcu with the famous teacher of Clonmacnois in Ireland. The name Colcu is a fairly common Celtic name. Simeon of Durham in his *Historia Regum* mentions the death of "Colcu presbyter et lector" under A.D. 794, but there is no identification of him with Alcuin's master. The name Colcu occurs among the monks of Iona in Adamnan's *Life of St. Columba* (Lib. II, cap. VII, and Lib. III, cap. XV) and may have been a usual name later on in this community. But there is no reason to connect the monastic establishment to which Charlemagne sent gifts with Iona except that they both could be described as being situated in *Britannia*.

[63] It is with singular pleasure that I dedicate this work on the great Irish gospel book to the memory of my friend, Arthur Kingsley Porter, whose wide interests touched with distinction so many fields but none with more than the archaeology of that most delightful of all countries, Ireland, where he elected to spend so much of his time during his last years. To another friend, Wilhelm Koehler, I am indebted for much of the knowledge of the Carolingian illumination here touched upon and for timely assistance by means of indispensable photographs which have made possible this article.

STEMMA FOR THE BEAST CANONS

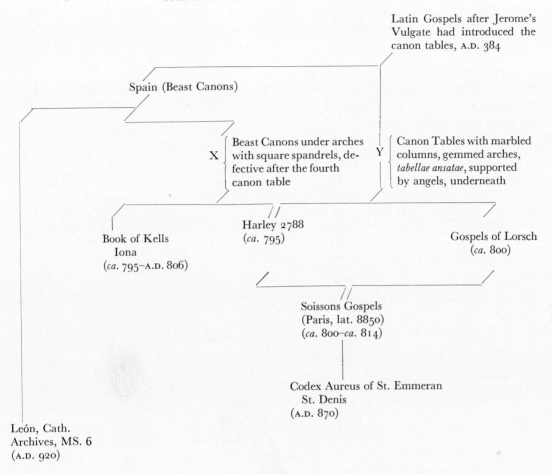

Latin Gospels after Jerome's
Vulgate had introduced the
canon tables, A.D. 384

Spain (Beast Canons)

X { Beast Canons under arches
with square spandrels, defective after the fourth
canon table

Y { Canon Tables with marbled
columns, gemmed arches,
tabellae ansatae, supported
by angels, underneath

Harley 2788
(*ca.* 795)

Book of Kells
Iona
(*ca.* 795–A.D. 806)

Gospels of Lorsch
(*ca.* 800)

Soissons Gospels
(Paris, lat. 8850)
(*ca.* 800–*ca.* 814)

Codex Aureus of St. Emmeran
St. Denis
(A.D. 870)

León, Cath.
Archives, MS. 6
(A.D. 920)

PL. I. THE BOOK OF KELLS, FOL. 1ʳ

PL. II. THE BOOK OF KELLS, FOL. 1ᵛ

PL. III. THE BOOK OF KELLS, FOL. 2ʳ

PL. IV. THE BOOK OF KELLS, FOL. 2ᵛ

PL. V. THE BOOK OF KELLS, FOL. 3ʳ

PL. VI. THE BOOK OF KELLS, FOL. 3^v

PL. VII. THE BOOK OF KELLS, FOL. 4ʳ

PL. VIII. THE BOOK OF KELLS, FOL. 4ᵛ

PL. IX. THE BOOK OF KELLS, FOL. 5r

PL. X. THE BOOK OF KELLS, FOL. 5ᵛ

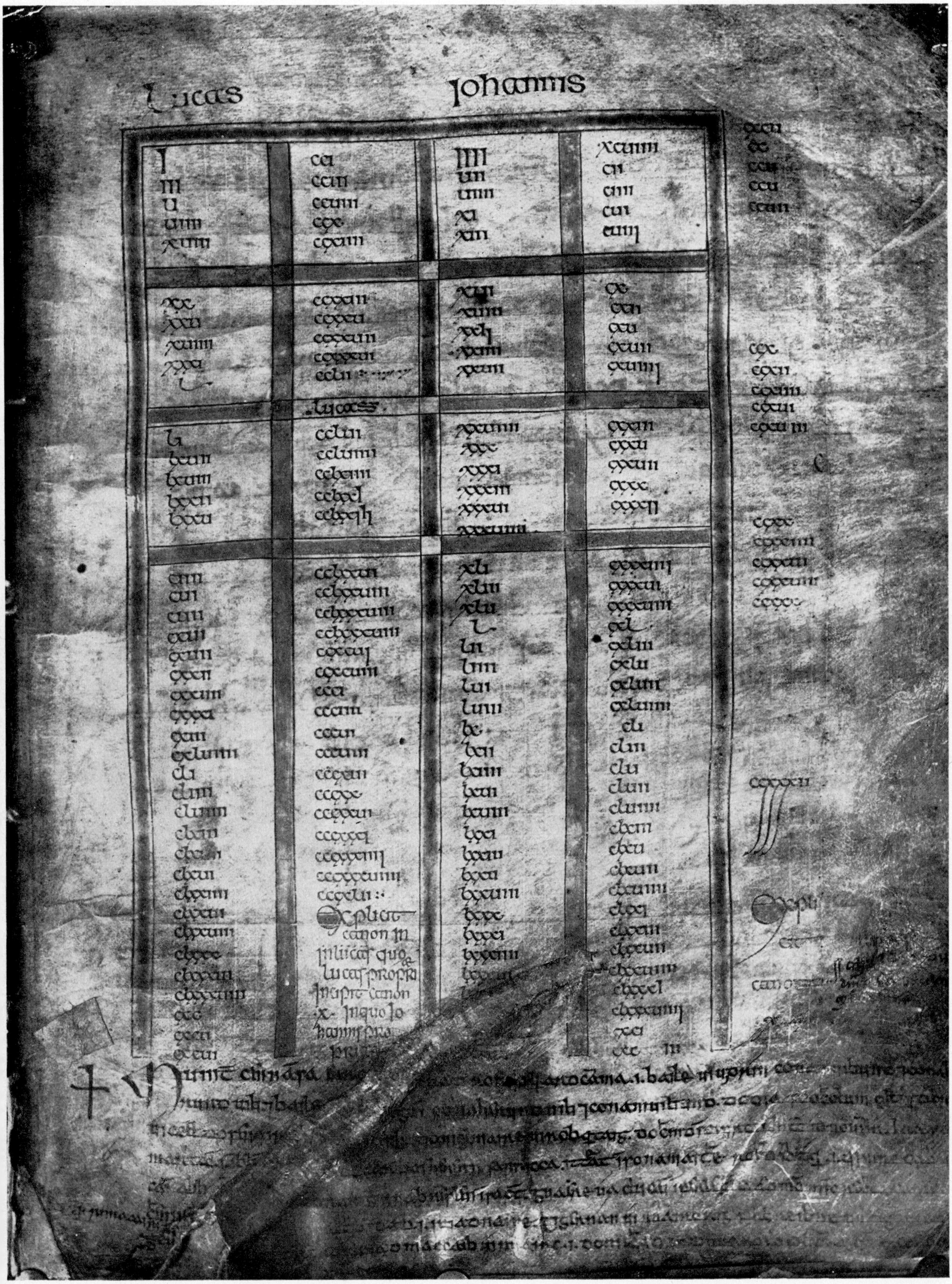

PL. XI. THE BOOK OF KELLS, FOL. 6r

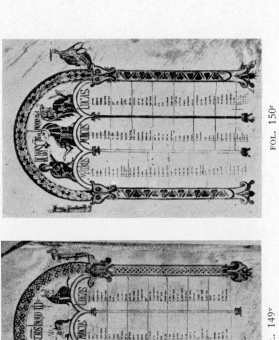

FOL. 150r

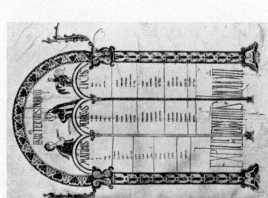

FOL. 151r

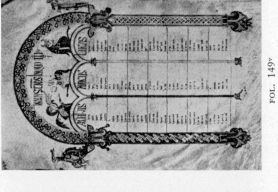

FOL. 149v

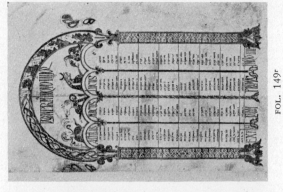

FOL. 149r

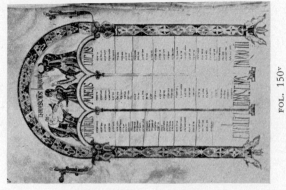

FOL. 150v

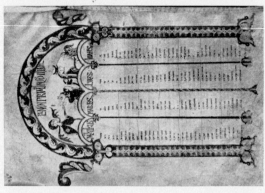

FOL. 148v

PL. XII. LEÓN, CATHEDRAL ARCHIVES, MS. 6, BIBLE A.D. 920

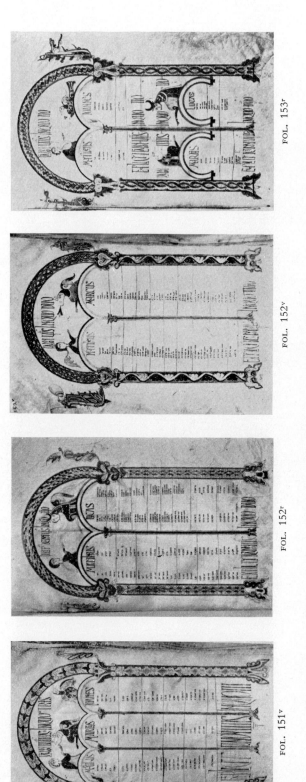

FOL. 153ʳ

FOL. 152ᵛ

FOL. 152ʳ

FOL. 151ᵛ

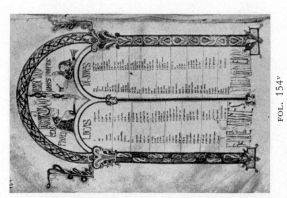

FOL. 154ᵛ

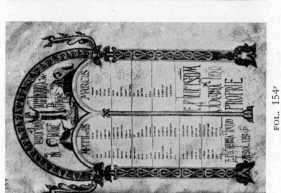

FOL. 154ʳ

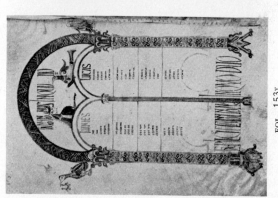

FOL. 153ᵛ

PL. XIII. LEÓN, CATHEDRAL ARCHIVES, MS. 6, BIBLE A.D. 920

FOL. 6ᵛ

FOL. 7ʳ

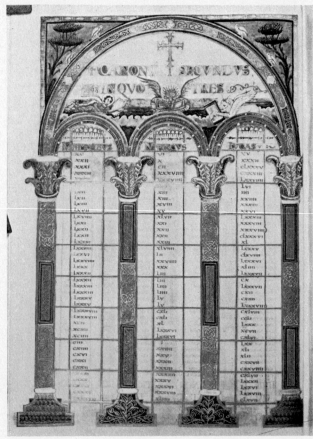

FOL. 7ᵛ

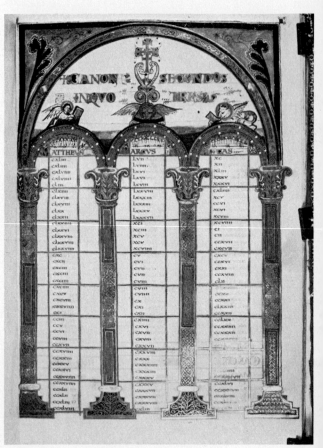

FOL. 8ʳ

PL. XIV. BRITISH MUSEUM, MS. HARLEY 2788

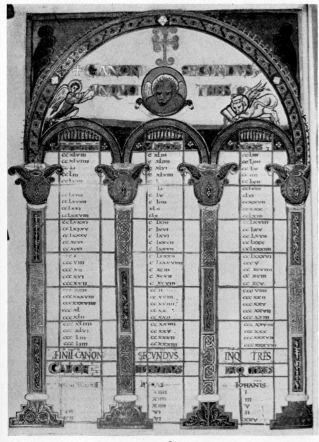

FOL. 8ᵛ

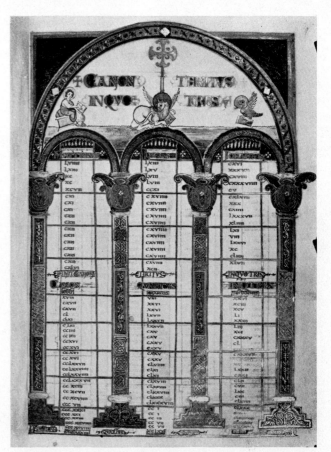

FOL. 9ʳ

FOL. 9ᵛ

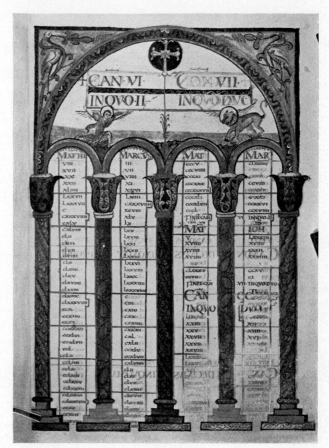

FOL. 10ʳ

PL. XV. BRITISH MUSEUM, MS. HARLEY 2788

[657]

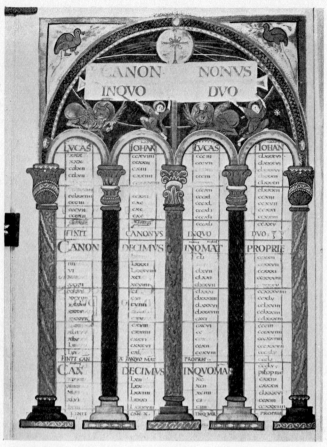

FOL. 10ᵛ

FOL. 11ʳ

FOL. 11ᵛ

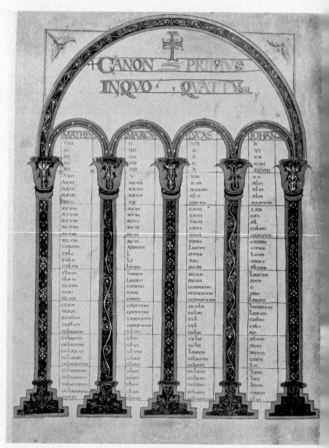

FOL. 6ᵛ

PL. XVI. BRITISH MUSEUM, MS. HARLEY 2788. TRÈVES, STADTBIBLIOTHEK, MS. 22. ADA GOSPELS

PAGE 13

PAGE 16

PL. XVII.   KARLSBURG (GYULAFEHÉRVÁR), BATTHYÁNEUM.   GOSPELS FROM LORSCH

PAGE 20

PAGE 24

PL. XVIII.   KARLSBURG (GYULAFEHÉRVÁR), BATTHYÁNEUM.   GOSPELS FROM LORSCH

[660]

PL. XIX. PARIS, BIBLIOTHÈQUE NATIONALE, LAT. 8850. SOISSONS GOSPELS, FOLS. 7ᵛ, 10ᵛ

PL. XXI. THE BOOK OF KELLS, FOL. 28ᵛ. TRÈVES, STADTBIBLIOTHEK, MS. 22. ADA GOSPELS, FOL. 15ᵛ

PL. XXII. THE BOOK OF KELLS, FOL. 32ᵛ

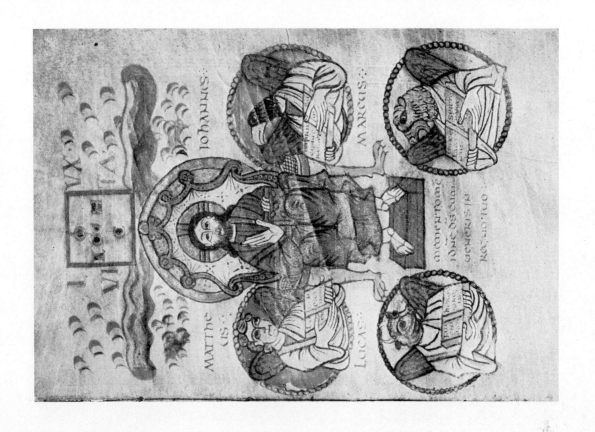

PL. XXIV. ABBEVILLE, BIBLIOTHÈQUE MUNICIPALE, MS. 4 (1). GOSPELS OF CHARLEMAGNE, FOL. 153ᵛ

THE PSALTER IN THE BRITISH MUSEUM, HARLEY 2904

CHARLES NIVER

WITHIN recent years English scholars have turned again to monuments of early England and have restudied a manuscript first published nearly half a century ago. The papers of Sir Ivor Atkins[1] and of Mr. J. B. L. Tolhurst[2] concerning the Missal of Robert of Jumièges which appeared in successive issues of *Archaeologia* are of the highest interest, not only to historians of liturgy and of the church in pre-Conquest times, but also to students of early medieval art. Although Sir Ivor Atkins and Mr. Tolhurst arrived at different conclusions as to the precise monastery for which the Missal was intended, the former assigning it to Peterborough (Northamptonshire), the latter to Ely (Cambridgeshire), the results of their investigations agree insofar as they established East Anglia rather than Winchester (Hampshire) as the location of the scriptorium where the manuscript was written. The evidence brought forward was liturgical and historical, dealing with the calendar, litany, and special prayers of the Missal, and the clues which these could furnish regarding its origin. Another study in the same field is that made by Miss Meta Harrsen[3] of the Gospels formerly at Holkham Hall (Norfolk) and now Pierpont Morgan Library, MSS. 708 and 709.

With the example of these excellent inquiries before one, it seems proper to subject another illuminated manuscript of the period to a liturgical analysis. The document under consideration is MS. Harley 2904 (hereafter cited as *H*), that magnificent tenth-century Psalter[4] of the British Museum in which is a drawing of the Crucifixion (Fig. 1) that has given it a high place in medieval English art. The liturgical data are singularly small. There is no calendar, but merely a litany of saints followed by a few prayers. In spite of this textual poverty, it is possible that certain peculiarities may have escaped the attention of those who have previously commented upon the manuscript.

In order to identify the scriptorium to which the Psalter belonged, we must concern ourselves with the English saints in the litany. These were noted by Sir George Warner and are as follows:[5] Martyrs — Alban, Oswald, Kenelm, Ed-

---

[1] Sir Ivor Atkins, "An Investigation of Two Anglo-Saxon Kalendars (Missal of Robert of Jumièges and St. Wulfstan's Homiliary)," *Archaeologia* (Society of Antiquaries of London: Oxford University Press), LXXVIII (1928), 219 ff.

[2] J. B. L. Tolhurst, "An Examination of Two Anglo-Saxon Manuscripts of the Winchester School: the Missal of Robert of Jumièges, and the Benedictional of St. Aethelwold," *Archaeologia*, LXXXIII (1933), 27 ff.

[3] Meta Harrsen, "The Countess Judith of Flanders and the Library of Weingarten Abbey," *The Papers of the Bibliographical Society of America* (Chicago: University of Chicago Press), XXIV (1930), 1–13.

[4] George F. Warner, *Illuminated Manuscripts in the British Museum*, ser. I–IV (London, 1903), Pls. 7, 8. Eric G. Millar, *English Illuminated Manuscripts from the X to the XIII Century* (Brussels, 1926), p. 73, Pls. 10, 11. Karl Wildhagen, *Studien zum Psalterium Romanum in England und zu seinen Glossierungen* (Halle, 1913), pp. 45 ff.

[5] Warner, *Illuminated Manuscripts*, text preceding Pl. 7. The litany occupies fols. 209[r]–211[v].

mund, Ethelbert; Confessors — Cuthbert, Guthlac, Wilfrid, John [of Beverley (Yorkshire, East Riding)], Chad (Ceadda), Erkonwald, Swithun, Birinus, Judoc, Machutus; Virgins — Etheldritha, Sexburg, Withburg, Werburg.

Before we compare these saints with those in other English litanies, the method to be followed must be briefly explained. In the first place, comparison will not be restricted to manuscripts of the tenth and eleventh centuries. On the one hand, liturgical manuscripts of England belonging to this period are too few in number. On the other hand, liturgical differences throughout the Middle Ages are rather to be found between church and church, monastery and monastery, than between succeeding centuries within the same abbey walls. In the second place, a limitation will be made in the categories of saints to be studied. For instance, the English martyrs invoked in *H* are mostly East Anglian because there were no important martyrs in the south of England before St. Edward the Martyr and St. Elphege. Since the English martyrs of *H* thus appear normally in manuscripts from all parts of England, they can be of little use to us as criteria. The same is true of the four East Anglian virgins of *H*. They lived during the eighth century, they were widely known, and at least three of them are commonly mentioned in litanies from widely separated parts of England.

With the confessors, however, the matter stands differently. In this category — more specifically monastic — East Anglia, Mercia, Kent, and Wessex were all upon an equal footing and could draw richly on their local past. Since it would be natural for each region to favor its own special patrons, we may hope to discover in the choice of confessors the appearance of local cults. Before beginning an analysis of the English confessors of *H*, we may eliminate certain localities from our consideration. Early bishops of Canterbury do not appear in *H*, nor do we find saints peculiar to Glastonbury (Somerset), Malmesbury (Wiltshire), or Worcester. Erkonwald, the lone representative of London, need not detain us. He seems, in fact, a buffer between the five northern saints — Cuthbert, Guthlac, Wilfrid, John of Beverley, Chad — and the southern group — Swithun, Birinus, Judoc, and Machutus — localized in Winchester. Inasmuch as *H* has usually been attributed to Winchester, our inquiry must begin with a review of Winchester litanies.

The two questions calling for investigation are: What is the normal proportion in Winchester litanies of Wessex saints to those from the Midlands and north of England, and which of these groups is given higher rank? For this analysis the following manuscripts of Winchester are available:

The Pontifical of Winchester, called the Benedictional of Archbishop Robert:[6] Rouen, MS. Y 7: New Minster (Winchester), end of tenth century: cited as W^1.

A Miscellany of Prayers:[7] Brit. Mus., MS. Galba A XIV: probably New Minster (Winchester), soon after 1016: cited as W^2.

[6] H. A. Wilson, *The Benedictional of Archbishop Robert* (London: Henry Bradshaw Society, 1903), p. 74. Abbé V. Leroquais, *Les Pontificaux Manuscrits* (Paris, 1937), II, 302.

[7] E. S. Dewick and W. H. Frere, *The Leofric Collectar* (London: Henry Bradshaw Society, 1921), II, 619 ff. Edmund Bishop, "About an Old Prayer Book," *Liturgica Historica* (Oxford, 1918), p. 384 ff.

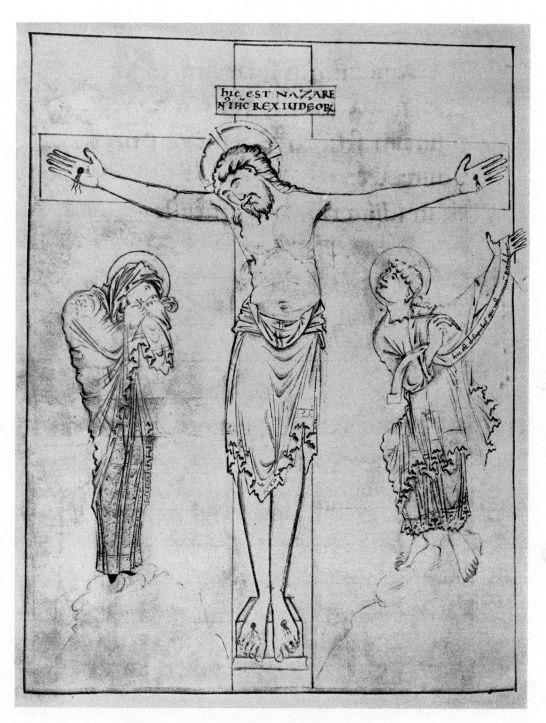

FIG. 1. BRITISH MUSEUM, HARLEY MS. 2904, FOL. 3ᵛ

(*Reduced by approximately one-third*)

A Book of Prayers: [8] Brit. Mus., MS. Titus D XXVI: New Minster (Winchester), 1035–50: cited as W^3.

A Psalter: [9] Brit. Mus., MS. Arundel 60: Old Minster (Winchester Cathedral), c. 1060: cited as W^4.

The Breviary of Hyde Abbey: [10] Bodleian Library, MS. Gough Liturg. 8: New Minster (Winchester), c. 1300: cited as W^5.

The points at issue can perhaps be made clearer by the subjoined table. Here the letter S following a name denotes southern or West Saxon, while the letter N after a name indicates the Midlands or northern England.[11]

TABLE I

W^1		W^2		W^3		W^4		W^5	
Iudoc	S	Guthlac	N	Iudoc	S	Cuthbert	N	Machutus	S
Cuthbert	N	Aethelmod	S	Grimbald	S	Birinus	S	Cuthbert	N
Swithun	S	Entferth	N	Cuthbert	N	Swithun	S	Birinus	S
Grimbald	S	Iudoc	S	Birinus	S	Dunstan		Dunstan	
3 S		Swithun	S	Swithun	S	Aethelwold	S	Swithun	S
1 N		Ywi	S	4 S		Byrnstan	S	Aethelwold	S
		Felix	N	1 N		Elphege	S	Wulstan	N
		Aethelwine	N			Rumwold	N	Edmund	
		Egwine	N			Machutus	S	Richard	S
		Byrnwold	N			Erkonwald		Edward	S
		Grimbald	S			Grimbald	S	Iudoc	S
		Haedda	S			Haedda	S	Grimbald	S
		John [of Beverley]	N			Frithestan	S	8 S	
		Machutus	S			Petroc		2 N	
		Aldhelm	S			Iudoc	S		
		Botulph	N			Guthlac	N		
		Indrahte	S			Congar	S		
		Wilfrid	N			Iwig	S		
		Byrnstan	S			12 S			
		Elphege	S			3 N			
		11 S							
		9 N							

From this tabular view two points are evident. In litanies proper to Winchester, local Wessex saints in every case outnumber those from the Midlands and the North. Secondly, if we consider the first five names in each column,

---

[8] W. de G. Birch, *Liber Vitae: Register and Martyrology of New Minster and Hyde Abbey* (London, 1892), p. 264.

[9] Humphrey Wanley, *Antiquae Literaturae Septentrionalis Liber Alter* (Oxford, 1705), p. 291.

[10] J. B. L. Tolhurst, *The Monastic Breviary of Hyde Abbey, Winchester* (London: Henry Bradshaw Society, 1934), v, Fo. G. 66 ff.

[11] Space does not permit a full discussion of the cults of the individual saints whose names are found in this table and in the following one. The division into a northern and middle group (N) on the one hand, and a southern or Wessex (S) on the other, has been based upon a careful study of the following sources: T. D. Hardy, *Descriptive Catalogue of Materials Relating to the History of Great Britain and Ireland* (London: Rolls Series, 1862–71), vol. 1; Edmund Bishop, "English Hagiology," *Dublin Review*, xcvi (1885), 123 ff.; Richard Stanton, *A Menology of England and Wales* (London, 1887); F. Liebermann, *Die Heiligen Englands* (Hanover, 1889); George Herzfeld, *An Old-English Martyrology* (London, 1900); John Capgrave, *Nova Legenda Anglie*, ed. Carl Horstman (Oxford, 1901); Abbot Gasquet and Edmund Bishop, *The Bosworth Psalter* (London, 1908); Bernhard Fehr, "Altenglische Ritualtexte für Krankenbesuch, Heilige Ölung und Begräbnis," *Festgabe für Felix Liebermann* (Halle, 1921), pp. 31–44; M. R. James, *Suffolk and Norfolk, A Perambulation of the Two Counties with Notices of Their History and Their Ancient Buildings* (London, 1930); Dom Alfons M. Zimmermann, O.S.B., *Kalendarium Benedictinum* (Metten, 1933).

which we may arbitrarily term the honor positions, we find that Winchester saints not only outnumber the others but usually outrank them.

Religious centers of the Midlands and North must now be surveyed in similar fashion for their liturgical customs. A wide range both in time and in place is to be found in the following manuscripts:

The Pontifical of Archbishop Egbert: [12] Paris, Bibl. Nat., MS. lat. 10575: York, eleventh century: cited as Y^1.

A Psalter: [13] Glasgow, MS. Hunterian 229: York diocese, twelfth century: cited as Y^2.

A Manual: [14] Harvard College Library, Widener Collection (fol. 74^v of the manuscript): York, fifteenth century: cited as Y^3.

A Psalter: [15] Rome, Vatican Library, MS. Reg. lat. 12: Bury St. Edmunds (Suffolk), early eleventh century: cited as B.

A Psalter: [16] Cambridge, Corpus Christi College, MS. 53: Peterborough (Northamptonshire), fourteenth century: cited as P.

The confessors found in the litanies of these manuscripts are shown below, the letters N and S denoting, as in the previous table, northern and southern.

TABLE II

Y^1		Y^2		Y^3		B		P	
Cuthbert	N	John [of Beverley]	N	John [of Beverley]	N	Cuthbert	N	Aethelwold	S
Guthlac	N	Wilfrid	N	Wilfrid	N	Birinus	S	Cuthbert	N
2 N		Cuthbert	N	William	N	Botulph .II.	N	Guthlac	N
		Swithun	S	Cuthbert	N	Jurmin .II.	N	Wilfrid	N
		3 N		Swithun	S	Guthlac	N	Swithun	S
		1 S		Edward	S	Dunstan		Dunstan	
				4 N		Erkonwald		John [of Beverley]	N
				2 S		Aethelwold	S	Aidan	S
						Oswald	N	Botulph	N
						Swithun	S	5 N	
						Iudoc	S	3 S	
						Grimbald	S		
						Machutus	S		
						Hyve	S		
						5 N			
						7 S			

A glance at the above table confirms the fact that in the North and the Midlands the same procedure was followed as at Winchester; that is to say, saints from the immediate and surrounding dioceses outnumber those from more distant

[12] W. Greenwell, *The Pontifical of Egbert, Archbishop of York* (Surtees Society, XXVII, 1853), 27 ff.

[13] John Young and P. Henderson Aitken, *A Catalogue of the Manuscripts in the Library of the Hunterian Museum in the University of Glasgow* (Glasgow, 1908), p. 174.

[14] A. S. W. Rosenbach, *A Catalogue of the Books and Manuscripts of Harry Elkins Widener* (Philadelphia, 1918), II, 65; Seymour de Ricci, *Census of Medieval and Renaissance Manuscripts in the United States and Canada* (New York: H. W. Wilson, 1935), I, 1020.

[15] Angelo Mai, *Scriptorum Veterum Nova Collectio* (Rome, 1831), V, 68–69; D. Rock, *Hierurgia* (2d ed., London, 1851), p. 535; New Palaeographical Society, Series II, vol. II, Pls. 166–168; Dom André Wilmart, O.S.B., "The Prayers of the Bury Psalter," *Downside Review*, XLVIII (1930), 200–201. For this last reference I am greatly indebted to Mr. Bernard Peebles.

[16] M. R. James, *A Descriptive Catalogue of the Manuscripts in the Library of Corpus Christi College, Cambridge* (Cambridge, 1912), I, 108, and *A Peterborough Psalter and Bestiary of the Fourteenth Century* (Oxford: printed for the Roxburghe Club, 1921), pp. 14–15.

parts. An exception in the principle of number occurs in the Bury St. Edmunds Psalter, a manuscript in which Winchester influence is very strong. But even here it will be noted that among the first five names local saints are predominant. This method of arranging a litany is thus seen to be uniform in the South, the Midlands, and the North throughout the Middle Ages. Further illustrations and more examples could be given,[17] but it is hoped that the present survey has been sufficiently comprehensive to show not merely a strong tendency but an actual system.

The list of confessors in *H* may now be studied according to these principles. Cuthbert, Guthlac, Wilfrid, John of Beverley, and Chad, the representatives of the North, outnumber the Winchester saints, Swithun, Birinus, Judoc, and Machutus, five to four. But far more significant is the fact that they are marshaled in one group to top the category of English confessors, while those of Winchester stand at the bottom. This arrangement clearly proves that the litany of *H* is closely related to the manuscripts of middle and northern England in Table II, and that it differs radically from the Winchester norm as seen in Table I. We are thus inevitably led to the conclusion that from a liturgical standpoint, *H* is adapted for use in Yorkshire or East Anglia rather than in Wessex.

Thus far our analysis of the litany of *H* has been concerned with the relative number and position of regional saints, an investigation which has led us away from Winchester in the direction of East Anglia and Northumbria. The attempt must now be made to determine the exact religious foundation for which the Psalter was intended. This more restricted problem raises the question: Which single saint in the entire litany is marked above all others for special honor? Now it was the general practice to single out a saint for special veneration in a litany by recourse to the following devices:

1. The saint's name may head the category — i.e., Martyrs, Confessors, Virgins — in which he belongs.
2. Prominence is frequently given by the Roman numeral II, indicating that the saint is to be invoked twice.
3. The name may be written in capital letters to distinguish it from the others.
4. A favored saint is sometimes given importance by means of gold or colored letters.
5. In rare cases the name is followed by the Roman numeral III, signifying a triple invocation.
6. Finally, several of these methods may be combined.

Fortunately, in the litany of *H* such distinguishing marks are to be found. There are three names written in gold letters: St. Mary, St. Michael, and St. Benedict. The first two are in gold uncial letters, the last in gold capital letters. So far as lettering goes, St. Benedict is thus given slightly greater prominence.

---

[17] Research in the subject of litanies contained in English manuscripts has necessarily been limited to some fifty-four printed examples collected from a great variety of library catalogues and publications of manuscripts. To this were added a half-dozen litanies copied from manuscripts now in the United States. In the case of MSS. Harley 2904, Arundel 60, and Cambridge University Library MS. Ff.1.23, photostats were used. If a few inaccuracies occur in some of the printed sources, it is hoped that they will be too slight to affect materially the results which study has revealed.

Furthermore, he heads the list of the confessors. All this was recognized by Warner, who said: "In the Litany special honor is accorded to St. Benedict, and the date is no doubt after the establishment, or revival, of regular monasticism in England in the reign of Edgar (959–975)."[18] But the importance bestowed upon St. Benedict in the litany of *H* is far greater than has heretofore been realized; for after his name has been placed the numeral III, indicating that he was to be invoked three times (Fig. 2).[19] Now a double invocation of

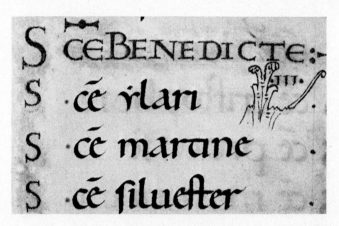

FIG. 2. BRITISH MUSEUM, HARLEY MS. 2904, FOL. 210v

St. Benedict and the placing of the saint at the head of the confessors was quite normal for Benedictine monasteries in general. It is found in *W¹* (Benedictional of Archbishop Robert), mentioned above. A triple invocation, however, was normally restricted to Christ and the Virgin, and was rarely accorded to saints in a litany. This is an extraordinary feature of *H* which merits careful attention.

Referring to the extensive survey of liturgical manuscripts in French libraries made by the Abbé Leroquais, we find in *Les Sacramentaires et les missels manuscrits*

---

[18] Warner, *Illuminated Manuscripts*, loc. cit.

[19] This portion of the litany of *H* reads as follows: "edmunde, ethelberte [then without a break or heading between Martyrs and Confessors], BENEDICTE .III., hilari, martine, sylvester, ambrosi, augustine, hieronyme, Benedicte, gregori, leo, eusebi," etc. In order to explain the omission of a title for the Confessors and the repetition of the name Benedict, we must attempt to reconstruct the scribe's procedure, which may have been as follows. First, with ink, he copied in minuscule script the long list of saints' names. After the word "hieronyme" he wrote "Benedicte" at the bottom of the left-hand column of fol. 210v. The position of "Benedicte" relative to the names of the other Confessors is very high, since it is placed among the Church Fathers. Furthermore, the scribe gave this name special prominence by beginning it with a capital letter. Probably he found the name Benedict capitalized and among the Church Fathers in the prototype before him. After finishing the entire litany in minuscule, the scribe then returned to write with black rustic capitals in the spaces reserved for them the titles heading the various categories of saints. First he wrote *Nomina Apostolorum* and then *Nomina Martyrum*, but when he came to the space left for *Nomina Confessorum* (fol. 210v), he hesitated. Why not put St. Benedict in gold letters at the very top of the Confessors? So he left this space blank and went on to write *Nomina Virginum* in its proper place. Then came the more elaborate lettering in gold majuscules for the words "Maria," "Michael," and (in accordance with his new intention) BENEDICTE, and the columns of *S* beginning *Sce.* (Wherever gold was used, it has subsequently discolored the parchment.) After writing "Sce BENEDICTE" in gold capitals, the scribe added below it the symbol three in Roman numerals to indicate a triple invocation of this name (later someone emphasized this symbol by designing a little floral ornament around it).

The preceding paragraph had already been written when my friend Mr. Bernard Peebles examined a

only one example (II, 146). A Missal of St. Aubert, Cambrai, contains a litany with the invocation, "S. Auberte .III." In the richer material afforded by *Les Bréviaires manuscrits* of the same author the following instances occur: [20]

I, 15. Breviary of Amiens. "S. Firmine, ter."
I, 214. Breviary of St. Géry, Cambrai. "S. Gaugerice .III."
I, 327. Breviary of Langres. "S. Mammes .III."
III, 255. Breviary of St. Victor, Paris. "S. Victor."
"S. Victor."
"S. Victor."
III, 461. Breviary of Senlis. "S. Firmine .III." [21]
IV, 128. Breviary of St. Paul-Trois-Châteaux. "S. Paule, ter."
IV, 141. Breviary of St. Quentin. "S. Quintine .III."

In the monasteries noted above, the triple invocation was by no means *de rigueur*. Usually in the manuscripts from these houses we find the familiar II after the name of the specially venerated saint, or else the latter is given a high position in the litany. One fact, however, is indisputable, according to the examples

---

photograph of the page (fol. 210ᵛ) which has been discussed above. It immediately occurred to him that the second appearance of the word "Benedicte" might well refer to St. Benedict Biscop (d. 691), abbot of Wearmouth, a theory which he was able to fortify by citing the presence of St. Benedict Biscop in several early English Calendars, and also by the more important fact that St. Ethelwold of Winchester (d. 984) had been responsible for a translation of St. Benedict Biscop's relics to his own monastery of Thorney, not far, of course, from Ramsey.

Thus the matter stood — but not for long — for Mr. Peebles followed this observation with a discovery of great significance. On the lower left margin of the page and on the same line as the word "Benedicte" (in black minuscule) there can be seen, although the letters have faded, what appears to be the word "Anniane" written in smaller minuscules by a hand that is probably contemporary with the original hand of *H* and certainly not much later. It would seem that then, as now, the repetition of the word "Benedicte" called for an explanation quite different from that proposed in the first paragraph of this note. "Anniane" in all probability refers to Aniane near Montpellier, and this gloss would therefore have us understand that in this instance "Benedicte" means St. Benedict of Aniane, the great monastic reformer of the early ninth century. The presence of St. Benedict of Aniane in a litany seems to be a great rarity. In the material already cited, upon which this article is based, no other instance can be found. Yet here we have actual documentary evidence that someone in the late tenth or early eleventh century in England thought St. Benedict of Aniane worthy to be included in this high position in a litany. The marginal entry, therefore, is not merely of hagiographical interest. It is important also for the history of the revival of the Benedictine Rule in England during the tenth century.

But let us return to the original scribe of *H*. Surely the word BENEDICTE, written in gold letters and for triple invocation, can refer only to the original bearer of that name, to the founder of the order. As for the repetition of the name lower down on the page and in black ink, we now have three explanations. It may refer to: (1) St. Benedict of Monte Cassino, whose name is repeated here by mistake, or rather by a change of plan; (2) St. Benedict Biscop; (3) St. Benedict of Aniane. In our present state of knowledge, at least, the true intention of the original scribe is a matter difficult to determine.

[20] As this article goes to press, Abbé Leroquais's recently published work, *Les Pontificaux Manuscrits* (Paris, 1937), comes to hand. In it are found four more instances of triple invocations of saints in litanies, all of which refer directly to the dedication of a church:

I, 20. Pontifical of Amiens. "S. Firmine, ter dicatur."
I, 79. Pontifical of Amiens. "S. Firmine, ter."
II, 103. Pontifical of Amiens. "S. Firmine, ter."
II, 338. Fragment of a Pontifical. Usage of Rouen. "S. Petre .III."

[21] Abbé Leroquais does not mention the church in Senlis for which the Breviary was intended. In all probability, however, it was written for the church of St. Firmin, a few miles from Senlis on the road to Chantilly. This church belonged to Saint-Nicolas-d'Acy, a Cluniac priory in Senlis. Cf. Charles Salmon, *Histoire de Saint Firmin* (Arras and Amiens, 1861), pp. 42, 304, 377, 379; *Inventaire sommaire des archives départementales antérieure à 1790* Oise (redigé par Ernest Roussel), Série H, t. II, 424.

which we have cited above. When a triple invocation of a saint does appear, it always points to the dedication of a church to that saint and to the observance of a local cult.[22] Since the same custom was in all likelihood observed in England, we must conclude that H was written for a monastery not merely Benedictine but with a dedication which included St. Benedict. So far as I know, there were only two, St. Benet's, Holme (Norfolk: on the river Bure, northeast of Norwich),[23] founded by King Canute, and the great abbey of Ramsey (Huntingdonshire).[24] St. Benet's, Holme, can be excluded from further consideration because its founding post-dates our Psalter. It is highly probable, therefore, that Ramsey was the monastery to which H belonged.[25]

Ramsey Abbey was founded between the years 968 and 970 by St. Oswald, bishop of Worcester, and by Ethelwine, alderman of East Anglia.[26] The latter

[22] The last example cited in note 20 is especially interesting. Since the Pontifical of Rouen is a fragment and it is only by means of the litany that an identification can be made, we find at last a definite analogy to the problem presented by H. Leroquais, after calling attention to the prominence given to St. Romain and St. Ouen, which indicates the usage of Rouen, goes on to say: "La triple invocation en l'honneur de Saint Pierre apôtre et la place occupée par Saint Benoit, feraient volontiers songer à Jumièges." Now although it is unusual to find a Pontifical adapted to a particular monastery for the use of a visiting bishop, a few other examples do exist — cf. Leroquais, op. cit., I, 15 (Corbie); II, 41 (St. Amand); and II, 229 (Cluny). As for the attribution of this manuscript to Jumièges, if we turn to *Gallia Christiana* (Paris, 1874), XI, 134, we discover that among the Benedictine abbeys of the diocese of Rouen it was indeed Jumièges alone which was dedicated to St. Peter.

[23] William Dugdale, *Monasticon Anglicanum*, ed. Caley, Ellis, and Bandinel (London, 1821), III, 61; Browne Willis, *An History of the Mitred Parliamentary Abbies* (London, 1718), I, 118; J. R. West, *St. Benet of Holme* (Norfolk Record Society, 1932), II, 190.

[24] Dugdale, *op. cit.*, II, 546 ff.; Browne Willis, *op. cit.*, I, 151 ff.; *Historians of the Church of York and its Archbishops*, ed. James Raine (London: Rolls Series, 1879–94), I, II; *Chronicon Abbatiae Rameseiensis*, ed. W. Dunn Macray (London: Rolls Series, 1886); *Cartularium Monasterii de Rameseia*, ed. W. H. Hart and P. A. Lyons (London: Rolls Series, 1884), 3 vols.; W. Page, G. Proby, S. I. Ladds, *The Victoria History of the County of Huntingdon* (London, 1932), II, 187 ff.

[25] Notices of manuscripts existing today which have been identified as belonging to Ramsey Abbey may be found in the following:

Chronicon Abbatiae Rameseiensis, pp. xliv–xlvii; W. de G. Birch, "Historical Notes on the Manuscripts Belonging to Ramsey Abbey," *Archaeological Journal*, N.S., V (1899), 229 ff.; M. R. James, *A Descriptive Catalogue of the Manuscripts in the Library of Corpus Christi College, Cambridge* (Cambridge: University Press, 1912), II, 399; Robert Eisler, *Die illuminierten Handschriften in Kärnten* (Leipzig, 1907), p. 83; Sidney C. Cockerell, *The Gorleston Psalter* (London, 1907), p. 3, n. 1; M. R. James, *The Wanderings and Homes of Manuscripts* (*Helps for Students of History*, No. 17; London: Society for Promoting Christian Knowledge, 1919), p. 69; Sir George F. Warner and Julius P. Gilson, *Catalogue of Western Manuscripts in the Old Royal and King's Collections* (London: British Museum, 1921); E. G. Millar, *English Illuminated Manuscripts of the XIV and XV Centuries* (Paris, 1928), pp. 9–10; Belle da Costa Greene and Meta P. Harrsen, *The Pierpont Morgan Library: Exhibition of Illuminated Manuscripts held at the New York Public Library* (New York, 1934), p. 35, no. 66; Seymour de Ricci, *A Handlist of Manuscripts in the Library of the Earl of Leicester at Holkham Hall* (Oxford: Printed at the Oxford University Press for the Bibliographical Society, 1932), no. 26.

The following manuscripts in the Royal collection are from Ramsey: 2 C.XI, 3 B.XI, 5 F.XV, 7 C.I, 8 C.XVI, 8 D.III, 14 C.IV.

Three Gothic Psalters of Ramsey are now in Corpus Christi College, Cambridge, at St. Paul in Lavanttal, Austria (of this Psalter ten illuminated pages are in the Morgan Library; see the exhibition catalogue referred to above), and at Holkham Hall (Norfolk). The litany of the Cambridge manuscript is mutilated after the enumeration of the first seven martyrs, the litany of the Psalter at St. Paul Lavanttal (cf. Eisler, *loc. cit.*) was added at St. Blasien, and in the Psalter from Holkham Hall the litany is lacking. For information regarding the Lavanttal manuscript I am indebted to Dom Josef Klausberger, O.S.B., and for a careful description of the Holkham Hall Psalter I wish to thank my friend Mr. Edwin C. Rae.

[26] "Vita Sancti Oswaldi, Auctore Anonymo," *Historians of the Church of York*, ed. James Raine (London: Rolls Series, 1879), I, 430; *Chronicon Abbatiae Rameseiensis*, ed. W. Dunn Macray (London: Rolls Series, 1886), p. 39; Wolfgang Keller, "Die litterarischen Bestrebungen von Worcester in Angelsächsischer

endowed the monastery with lands, the former brought to it monks from West-bury-on-Trym (Gloucestershire, on the outskirts of Bristol) to form the nucleus of the new community. The church was completed in 974 and dedicated to the Virgin, St. Benedict, and All Virgins. That the names of the Virgin and of St. Benedict are written in letters of gold in the litany of *H* is thus accounted for. It is not so easy to explain the gold lettering of the name of St. Michael. One can only point out that the Archangel was honored in similar fashion at New Minster in the Benedictional of Archbishop Robert,[27] where he forms company with St. Mary and St. Peter. In any case, from the very beginning, the dedica-tion of Ramsey was abbreviated in documents to the name of St. Benedict alone. This is clear from the fact that the vast majority of gifts and grants of lands to Ramsey were made out "Deo et Sancto Benedicto." [28] The particular veneration shown to St. Benedict is reflected in stories told of Ethelwine. Around this nobleman there later grew up the legend that he chose the location of Ramsey upon the advice of a fisherman to whom St. Benedict had appeared in a dream, and that as a result of this action Ethelwine was cured of a painful malady.[29] Be that as it may, the earliest life of St. Oswald gives us more substantial evidence. This *Vita*, written between 995 and 1005 by a monk of Ramsey, and not long after the alderman's death in 992, contains the following description of Ethelwine at Ramsey: "Celebratis Missarum officiis, exivit tota mentis devotione pede-tentim ad altare Christi et Sancti Benedicti, quasi ad fidele patrocinium. Dilexit praesertim ipsum prae caeteris Sanctis, idcirco multa ei tribuit quia multum eum dilexit." [30] We should expect these sentiments from St. Oswald, who had spent several years at Fleury itself, where the relics of St. Benedict were pre-served. It is interesting to find them expressed by the co-founder of Ramsey, who was only a layman.

In spite of all these signs which point to Ramsey as the home of *H*, certain doubts may arise. For example, other East Anglian monasteries might have shown a more than ordinary devotion to St. Benedict, particularly Ely, Peter-borough, and Thorney, all three founded (or refounded) by St. Aethelwold of

---

Zeit," *Quellen und Forschungen zur Sprach- und Kulturgeschichte der Germanischen Völker*, LXXXIV (1900), 11–21; J. Armitage Robinson, *St. Oswald and the Church of Worcester* (*The British Academy, Supplemental Papers*, V [London, 1919]), p. 37, and *The Times of St. Dunstan* (Oxford, 1923), p. 129.

[27] H. A. Wilson, *The Benedictional of Archbishop Robert*, p. 76. The name of St. Michael is also promi-nent in the Psalter from Winchcomb, now in Cambridge (University Library Ff.1.23). For the special cult of St. Michael in pre-Conquest England cf. Daniel Rock, *The Church of Our Fathers* (London, 1903), III, 135. Rock quotes from Aelfric's *Homilies* (ed. Thorpe, London, 1843), I, 519: "It is now credible that the archangel Michael has care of Christian men. . . . It is done by God's dispensation, that the great heavenly angel is the constant supporter of Christian men on earth, and their intercessor in heaven with Almighty God."

[28] *Chronicon*, pp. 49, 51, 58, 62, 75, 81, etc. At the church council held at Rheims in 1049 there were two English delegates who are described as follows: "Wlfricus S. Augustini Cantuariensis, Alwinus S. Benedicti de terra Anglorum." Cf. Martin Bouquet, *Recueil des historiens des Gaules et de la France* (Paris, 1876), XI, 522; Migne, *Patrologia Latina*, CXLII, col. 1431. Alwinus was abbot of Ramsey, 1043–1080 (cf. *Chronicon*, pp. 170–71). It is thus interesting to note that to a contemporary French chronicler Ramsey was simply "St. Benedict's in Anglia."

[29] *Chronicon*, p. 183 ff.

[30] *Vita Oswaldi*, p. 467.

Winchester, who was the greatest single driving force behind the Benedictine reform in tenth-century England. But if our theory is correct concerning the triple invocation of a saint in a litany, we should have every reason to expect that the local patrons of Ely, Peterborough, and Thorney would receive honor at least equal to that accorded St. Benedict in the litany of *H*, had that manuscript been intended for one of them. This, however, is not the case.[31] The argument *ex silentio*, which as we shall see has further bearing upon the problem of the litany of *H*, deserves careful consideration along with the more valuable positive evidence.

That the extraordinary cult of St. Benedict in England at this period was due primarily to the influence of Fleury is hardly open to question. There were, in fact, three Englishmen who crossed over to France and studied at Fleury itself, later returning to bring back with them the customs of that monastery to England. These men were Osgar,[32] the pupil of St. Aethelwold, St. Oswald of Ramsey and Worcester,[33] and Germanus,[34] a friend of St. Oswald. It would be natural to expect any or all of them to intensify the cult of St. Benedict in England, and it has perhaps been rash to infer that only St. Oswald, as founder of Ramsey, is to be associated with the triple invocation of St. Benedict in *H*. When St. Aethelwold in 963 became bishop of Winchester, it was the Fleury-trained Osgar who succeeded him as abbot of Abingdon (Berkshire). Might not *H*, therefore, have been written at Abingdon under Osgar? Liturgical reasons, however, make this most unlikely. Abingdon was in the diocese of Ramsbury (Wiltshire),[35] and its affiliations were with Winchester rather than with the Midlands and the North, while on the other hand, the litany of *H* has been shown to be characteristic of the North and East Anglia. Furthermore, Abingdon was dedicated to the Virgin alone [36] and could hardly have failed in a litany to show her the same honor as St. Benedict.

St. Oswald, the most famous English alumnus of Fleury, did not confine his Benedictine reforms to Ramsey alone. His episcopal chair was in the cathedral of Worcester, and he founded the small community at Westbury-on-Trym (Gloucestershire)[37] as an experiment in 961, soon after his return from France, and at least seven years before the foundation of Ramsey. In 972 St. Oswald became arch-

---

[31] Ely was dedicated to St. Peter. (Cf. *Liber Eliensis*, ed. D. J. Stewart [London, 1848], p. 110, and Dugdale, *op. cit.*, I, 458.) Peterborough was dedicated to St. Peter. (Cf. Dugdale, *op. cit.*, I, 344.) Thorney was dedicated to the Virgin. (Cf. Dugdale, *op. cit.*, II, 593.)

Gifts to Ely were made out "Domino ejusque genitrici Mariae, et B. Petro Apostolorum principi, nec non S. Aetheldrythae" (*Liber Eliensis*, p. 175). Later the phrase "Deo et S. Aetheldrethae" was the more common form. Land bequeathed to Peterborough was given "Deo et Sco Petro" (cf. Dugdale, *op. cit.*, I, 386). For Thorney we find the phrase "Deo et sanctae Mariae" with reference to gifts (cf. Dugdale, *op. cit.*, II, 601). These formulas should be compared with the words "Deo et Sco Benedicto" referring to Ramsey, as noted above.

[32] *Chronicon Monasterii de Abingdon*, ed. Joseph Stevenson (London: Rolls Series, 1858), I, 129, 344.

[33] *Vita Oswaldi*, pp. 413 ff.   [34] *Vita Oswaldi*, p. 423; *Chronicon*, p. 24.

[35] Geoffry Hill, *English Dioceses, a History of Their Limits from the Earliest Times to the Present Day* (London, 1900), diocesan map for chapter V (909–1066). For the establishment of a diocese at Ramsbury and its relations with Wessex cf. J. Armitage Robinson, *The Saxon Bishops of Wells* (*The British Academy, Supplemental Papers*, IV [London, 1918]), pp. 10, 16.   [36] *Chronicon Monasterii de Abingdon*, p. 258.

[37] *Vita Oswaldi*, p. 424; *Chronicon Abb. Rames.*, p. 29; Robinson, *The Times of St. Dunstan*, p. 129.

bishop of York, and during the following years settled monks at Ripon (York-shire, West Riding)[38] within that diocese. Now the cathedral of Worcester was dedicated to St. Peter (later to the Virgin), Westbury was dedicated by St. Oswald to the Virgin in 961, [39] and the cathedral of York and monastery of Ripon were both dedicated to St. Peter.[40] In the litany of *H*, however, St. Peter receives no distinction whatsoever; his name is not written in gold, nor is it to be invoked more than once. All four establishments just mentioned may therefore be excluded.

We come now to Germanus, the friend of St. Oswald who upon the latter's advice went to Fleury for study. When he returned to England, St. Oswald put him in charge of monks at Westbury-on-Trym.[41] Some years later Germanus was transferred to Ramsey, where he became dean or prior,[42] and in 986 St. Oswald made him abbot of the recently restored monastery of Winchcomb (Gloucestershire).[43] It is our good fortune that three liturgical manuscripts of Winchcomb, all containing litanies, have been preserved. First and foremost is the Sacramentary of Winchcomb,[44] sent as a present from that monastery to Fleury and now in the municipal library at Orléans. In the litany of this manu-script, the names of St. Kenelm and St. Scolastica and the words "Omnes S. Acaunenses" [45] are written in capital letters. The name of St. Kenelm, to whom Winchcomb was dedicated, is to be invoked only once, but the names of St. Peter and of St. Benedict are not only written in capitals but they are each to be invoked three times. Here, at last, is a triple invocation of St. Benedict in an Eng-lish manuscript of the same period as *H*. Thus far it is the only example that has come to hand except the one in the litany of *H*. It is very probable, then, that the two manuscripts are related. A connection between them was, indeed, noted by Dr. Otto Homburger some years ago when he referred to *H* in the following terms: "Schrift und Initialenschmuck sind eng verwandt dem wahrscheinlich in Winchcomb geschriebenen Sakramentar der Bibliothek zu Orléans." [46] Undoubtedly the Sacramentary was written for Winchcomb,[47] which

[38] *Vita Oswaldi*, p. 462. Ernest H. Pearce, "St. Oswald of Worcester and the Church of York," in *York Minster Historical Tracts*, ed. A. Hamilton Thompson (London: Society for Promoting Christian Knowledge, 1927).

[39] H. J. Wilkins, *Westbury College from 1194 to 1544 A.D.* (Bristol, 1917), chapter IX, chart 1: "Dedi-cated to the Apostles Peter and Paul from c. 715 to 717, A.D. To St. Mary in 961 by St. Oswald, Bishop of Worcester."

[40] For York, cf. Dugdale, *op. cit.*, VI (3), 1172; for Ripon, Dugdale, *op. cit.*, II, 131.

[41] *Chronicon*, p. 29; Robinson, *The Times of St. Dunstan*, p. 129. [42] *Chronicon*, p. 40.

[43] *Vita Oswaldi*, p. 435; *Chronicon*, p. 42; Robinson, *op. cit.*, p. 131.

[44] Léopold Delisle, "Mémoires sur d'anciens sacramentaires," *Mémoires de l'Institut National de France* (Académie des Inscriptions et Belles-Lettres), XXXII (1886), 211–218, 367–369; Leroquais, *Les Sacramen-taires et les missels manuscrits* (Paris, 1924), I, 89–91.

[45] Delisle, *op. cit.*, p. 367. "Omnes S. Acaunenses" refers to St. Maurice and the Theban legion who were martyred at St. Maurice near the eastern extremity of the Lake of Geneva. Their prominence in the litany of Winchcomb can perhaps best be explained as due to the literal copying of a prototype of French origin.

[46] Otto Homburger, *Die Anfänge der Malschule von Winchester im X. Jahrhundert* (Leipzig, 1912), p. 5. Homburger has more recently reaffirmed his opinion that *H* is not a product of Winchester, *Art Bulletin*, X (1928), 401, where he refers the reader to his earlier publication.

[47] The name of St. Kenelm appears in the *Nobis quoque* of the Canon of the Mass. Cf. Delisle, *op. cit.*, p. 213, and Leroquais, *op. cit.*, I, 89.

makes it all the more strange that in it the Virgin and St. Kenelm, to whom the monastery was dedicated, are not accorded honor equal to St. Benedict. Does not therefore, this triple invocation of St. Benedict in the Sacramentary cast doubt upon our principle that such a practice indicates a dedication? More important, does not this example at Winchcomb destroy the attribution of *H* to Ramsey? The striking similarity between *H* and the Sacramentary of Winchcomb is best explained by recalling the fact that Winchcomb was doubly exposed to the direct influence of Ramsey. It was St. Oswald, the founder of Ramsey, who resettled the defunct monastery of Winchcomb, and it was Germanus of Ramsey who became Winchcomb's first abbot under the new régime.[48] Nothing could be more natural, therefore, than that Winchcomb should adopt some of Ramsey's liturgical customs.[49] Admitting this *similarity* between *H* and the Sacramentary, an important *difference* assumes special significance. In the three Winchcomb litanies which have come down to us, St. Kenelm, the local patron, is without exception honored above all other martyrs. In the Sacramentary his name is not only written in capitals, it is not only given high position, but it follows directly after St. Stephen, being second in the list of martyrs. The eleventh-century Psalter of Winchcomb now in Cambridge [50] gives St. Kenelm distinction by means of capital letters, and in addition names him first among English martyrs. In the Winchcomb Breviary now at Valenciennes (Nord) we again find the name of St. Kenelm high in the list of martyrs, following directly after St. Sebastian.[51] In conclusion, if *H* had been written for Winchcomb, it is quite inconceivable that the name of St. Kenelm would have been relegated to the position it holds in the litany of that manuscript, namely, *third* in the category of English martyrs, and that his name would have been utterly undistinguished by capital letters or plural invocation. The evidence afforded by the Sacramentary of Winchcomb, therefore, in no way weakens the foregoing attribution of *H*, but on the contrary strengthens it considerably.

The probable date of *H* is indicated by the absence from the litany of certain saints whose cult was peculiar to Ramsey. Because of the character of its

---

[48] Cf. Dugdale, *op. cit.*, II, 297.

[49] Delisle (*op. cit.*, p. 214, n. 3) thinks that the triple invocation of St. Peter in the Sacramentary of Winchcomb refers to a church dedicated to that saint in Winchcomb which was given to the abbey sometime between 1282 and 1314 (cf. Dugdale, *Monasticon Anglicanum*, II, 305). But what evidence is there that this church existed as early as the tenth century? That there was a special veneration for St. Peter at the monastery of Winchcomb is undeniable. In the litany of a Psalter from Winchcomb (Cambridge, University Library, Ff.1.23) St. Peter's name is written in capital letters as are those of St. Mary, St. Michael, St. Kenelm, and St. Benedict, and in a Breviary from Winchcomb (Valenciennes MS. 116) the chief festival of St. Peter is in the same green, red, and blue capitals which distinguish the days of St. Benedict and St. Kenelm. Possibly there were at Winchcomb important relics of St. Peter of which we no longer have record. But what is far more probable is that this cult was borrowed from nearby Worcester Cathedral (dedicated to St. Peter), even as the veneration for St. Benedict seems to have been borrowed from Ramsey.

[50] Univ. Libr., Ff.1.23. J. O. Westwood, *Palaeographia Sacra Pictoria* (London, 1849), no. 41, Figs. 1–2; see also *A Catalogue of the Manuscripts Preserved in the Library of the University of Cambridge* (Cambridge, 1857), II, 312–313; Karl Wildhagen, *Der Cambridger Psalter* (*Hs. Ff.1.23 University Libr. Cambridge*), I, *Text mit Erklärungen* (Hamburg, 1910), and *Studien zum Psalterium Romanum in England*, pp. 50–55; Eric Millar, *English Illuminated Manuscripts from the X to the XIII Century*, p. 112, no. 55.

[51] Leroquais, *Les Bréviaires Manuscrits*, IV, 283.

script, *H* surely falls within the tenth century, a dating which has never been questioned. Consequently, it is by no means surprising not to find in the litany the name of St. Felix, whose remains were translated from Seham (Soham in Cambridgeshire, southeast of Ely) to Ramsey in 1026.[52] For the same reason, also, the name of St. Yvo is absent from the litany of *H*. Not until 1001 was his body removed to Ramsey from Slepe (now called St. Ives, northeast of Huntingdon, in Huntingdonshire).[53] Significant, too, is the fact that St. Dunstan is not invoked in *H*. He died in 988, and, according to Bishop, his cultus began almost immediately after his death and soon became general.[54] This would seem to point to the two decades 970 to 990 as the most likely period during which *H* was written. The absence of two other Ramsey saints makes a more accurate dating possible. The relics of the martyred brothers, Ethelred and Ethelbert, were taken from Wakering (Essex) by the nobleman, Ethelwine, and given to Ramsey.[55] We may assume that if *H* had been written after this translation, their names would surely have appeared in the litany. Now tradition has it that the remains of Sts. Ethelred and Ethelbert were removed during the reign of King Ethelred.[56] The latter ruled from 978 to 1013. Therefore the translation must have taken place between the accession of Ethelred in 978 and the death of Ethelwine in 992.[57] The editors of the *Acta Sanctorum* go so far as to suggest an even closer dating.[58] They note that the Ramsey Chronicle describes Ethelwine's gift as "omnium donationum suarum consummationem." [59] This clearly implies that the translation of the two martyrs took place towards the end of the alderman's life. The festival in honor of the two martyrs in commemoration of their removal from Wakering to Ramsey was observed upon October 17. Now in 986 October 17 fell upon a Sunday, the most appropriate day for such a ceremony as the translation of relics. Although we lack positive proof, it is not improbable that 986 was the actual year of Ethelwine's most important gift. Presumably, therefore, it was before 986 that *H* was written. Although Ramsey was founded during the years 968–970, there could have been little time for writing elaborate books before the building of the church and its consecration in 974. This *terminus post quem* is strengthened by the inclusion of St. Withburg in the litany. She was an anchoress who was buried at Dereham (Norfolk),[60] but her cult in all probability did not begin until after her translation in 974 to Ely,[61] a close neighbor of Ramsey. If, as seems likely, *H* was written at Ramsey within the twelve-year period 974 to 986, its time of origin corresponds closely with the

[52] *Chronicon*, pp. 127–128.

[53] *Ibid.*, p. 114.

[54] Gasquet and Bishop, *The Bosworth Psalter*, p. 27.

[55] *Chronicon*, p. 55. St. Ethelbert, the last martyr invoked in the litany of *H*, is one of the local patron saints of Hereford (Herefordshire), where his relics reposed, and is not to be confused with the brother of St. Ethelred.

[56] T. D. Hardy, *Descriptive Catalogue*, i, 263; Capgrave, *Nova Legenda Anglie*, ed. C. Horstman, i, 431.

[57] W. G. Searle, *Anglo-Saxon Bishops, Kings, and Nobles* (Cambridge, 1899), p. 407.

[58] *Acta Sanctorum*, October, viii (Paris and Rome, 1866), 96.

[59] *Chronicon*, p. 55.

[60] M. R. James, *Suffolk and Norfolk*, p. 13.

[61] James, *ibid.*, p. 14; *Liber Eliensis*, ed. D. J. Stewart (London, 1848), p. 167.

date usually given to the Benedictional of St. Aethelwold, namely, 975 to 980.[62] Although these two manuscripts were certainly written by different hands and in different scriptoria, the general palaeographical similarity has always linked the two books together.[63]

It is at this point that proponents of the old theory that *H* belonged to Winchester may be tempted to argue that although the litany of *H* agrees with East Anglia in general and with Ramsey in particular, nevertheless the book could only have been written and illuminated in Winchester, ordered perhaps by a patron of Ramsey or by a member of that community. This point of view which regards Winchester, the capital, as having a monopoly of literary, scientific, and artistic talent in England during the tenth and eleventh centuries is hardly in accord with the facts. There is, indeed, abundant proof of the culture of East Anglia: Abbo of Fleury, who at St. Oswald's request taught at Ramsey for several years, probably surpassed other scholars in England at that time.[64] His pupil at Ramsey, Byrhtferth,[65] may properly be regarded as a rival in learning of Aelfric of Winchester. Byrhtferth's *Handbōc* or *Computus* was written at Ramsey, and it is an interesting coincidence that the style which is characteristic of the Crucifixion in *H* occurs also in an astronomical work, a tenth-century manuscript of Aratus.[66] Dr. Homburger was the first to show the relationship of these

---

[62] Among the petitions found in the litany in *H* is the following: "ut paganorum saevitiam comprimere digneris." Now it is recorded in the Anglo-Saxon Chronicle that in the year 980, after a long period of peace, the Danes renewed their attacks upon the English coast: "980 . . . in the same year Southampton was ravaged by an enemy fleet, and most of the townsfolk slain or captured. In the same year the district of Thanet was ravaged, and in the same year Cheshire was ravaged by an enemy fleet in the North." (Cf. Margaret Ashdown, *English and Norse Documents Relating to the Reign of Ethelred the Unready* [Cambridge: University Press, 1930], p. 39.) It is, therefore, just possible that these events may have inspired the petition quoted above. If that be true, *H* was probably written between the years 980 and 986.

[63] Cf. Warner, *Illuminated Manuscripts, loc. cit.*

[64] Migne, *Pat. Lat.*, cxxxix, cols. 417–572; Charles Cuissard-Gaucheron, "L'École de Fleury-sur-Loire," *Mémoires de la Société Archéologique et Historique de l'Orléanais*, xiv (1875), 579 ff.; Ernst Sackur, *Die Cluniacenser* (Halle, 1893), i, 274 ff.; Henry Bradley, "On the Text of Abbo of Fleury's *Quaestiones Grammaticales*," *Proceedings of the British Academy*, x (1922); L. Gougaud, "Les Relations de l'abbaye de Fleury avec la Bretagne et les Iles Britanniques (X et XI siècles)," *Mémoires de la Société d'Histoire et d'Archéologie de Bretagne*, iv (1923), 3–30; Max Manitius, *Geschichte der lateinischen Literatur des Mittelalters* (Munich, 1923), ii, 664–672; A. Van de Vyver, "Les Oeuvres inédites d'Abbon de Fleury," *Revue Bénédictine*, xlvii (1935), 125 ff.; N. R. Ker, "Two Notes on MS. Ashmole 328," *Medium Aevum*, iv (Oxford, 1935), 16–19 (a reference which I owe to the kindness of Dr. Hans Meier, Librarian of the Warburg Institute, London).

Bradley (*op. cit.*, p. 1), says that Abbo taught at Ramsey during the years 980–982. According to Charles Gross, *The Sources and Literature of English History* (2d ed., London, 1915), p. 284, Abbo wrote his life of St. Edmund while at Ramsey in 985. Manitius, however, would date Abbo's visit to Ramsey 985/6–988.

[65] Manitius, *op. cit.*, ii, 699–706; Byrhtferth's *Manual*, ed. S. J. Crawford (London: Early English Text Society, 1929); G. F. Forsey, "Byrhtferth's Preface," *Speculum*, iii (1928), 505 ff.; Heinrich Henel, *Studien zum altenglischen Computus* (*Beiträge zur englischen Philologie*, xxvi [Leipzig, 1934]); Van de Vyver, *op. cit.*

The tedious repetitions of Byrhtferth's *Manual* are occasionally relieved by such passages as the following: "When thou, O reverend brother, hearest that the moon is twelve spaces from the sun, then do thou understand that, as if I were to say: 'Byrhtferth the priest stands or sits in the twelfth place after Bishop Eadnoth.'" Cf. S. J. Crawford, *op. cit.*, p. 165.

For the interesting and very plausible theory that Byrhtferth and the anonymous author of the *Vita Oswaldi* were one and the same person, cf. S. J. Crawford, "Byrhtferth of Ramsey and the Anonymous Life of St. Oswald," *Speculum Religionis, Essays and Studies Presented to Claude G. Montefiore* (Oxford: Clarendon Press, 1929), pp. 99–111.

[66] Probably written at Fleury (Van de Vyver, *op. cit.*, p. 143): MS. Harley 2506. Cf. *Archaeologia*, xxvi (1836), Pl. XI, Figs. 4, 8.

two manuscripts, adding, in fact, still another example to the group.[67] The third manuscript, a commentary of St. Gregory on Ezekhiel, contains a full-page drawing of St. Benedict presenting a kneeling monk to Christ enthroned (Fig. 3). This book, which came from Fleury, was first discovered by Professor W. R. W. Koehler in the municipal library at Orléans.[68] Although close in style to the Crucifixion of *H*, the drawing with the exaggerated *cloche* folds of the drapery and the extreme ungainliness of the knees betrays the hand of an inferior artist. Significant, however, is the fact that we find at Fleury the influence of the art of Ramsey, which is not unexpected, considering the close relationship between the two monasteries.[69] The Orléans St. Gregory is perhaps a partial compensation for the loss of that more splendid manuscript, the Benedictional with first lines lettered in gold, which was sent as a present from Ramsey to Gauzlin, abbot of Fleury.[70]

In artistic production East Anglia had already gained a reputation which was to foreshadow the fame of the splendid thirteenth-century Psalters from that region. Ramsey, indeed, had many rivals close at hand in the monasteries of Peterborough, Ely, and Thorney. From the pages of William of Malmesbury Sir Ivor Atkins has extracted the story of how Bishop Wulfstan of Worcester, as a boy, grew fond of a Sacramentary and a Psalter with "capital letters figured in gold" and with "precious initials" which had been written at Peterborough by Wulfstan's teacher, Ervenius, "skilled in writing and depicting anything in colors." [71] To Wulfstan's chagrin Ervenius gave the Sacramentary and Psalter to King Canute, who in turn presented the manuscripts to Cologne "that he might establish a pleasant impression of himself among the German peoples." Some years later Aldred, a friend of Wulfstan, was sent by Edward the Confessor on an embassy to the Emperor Henry III. As he was leaving Cologne to return to England, Aldred was given presents, among them two manuscripts. When Aldred reached the end of his journey and arrived in Worcester, he gave the two books to Wulfstan, for whom he had great esteem. To Wulfstan's great joy, these manuscripts were the very Sacramentary and Psalter which he had cherished as a boy in the abbey of Peterborough! This story is repeated here not only because of what it tells us about the art of East Anglia, but because it furnishes additional evidence of the way in which artistic styles were probably carried from one country to another through the interchange of books.

[67] Homburger, *op. cit.*, p. 5.

[68] Bibl. Mun., MS. 175. See Homburger, *op. cit.*, p. 5, n. 10.

[69] Another instance of what may be the influence of Ramsey upon Fleury is in a manuscript containing various works of Abbo (Berlin, Phillipps MS. 1833). Cf. Joachim Kirchner, *Beschreibendes Verzeichnis der Miniaturen in den Phillipps-Handschriften* (Leipzig, 1926), Fig. 27. An initial *C* on fol. 7ᵛ should be compared with the initials of *H* and of the Sacramentary of Winchcomb.

[70] Delisle thought that Paris, Bibl. Nat., MS. lat. 987 was the very manuscript sent to Gauzlin from Ramsey. The editors of the *New Palaeographical Society*, however, pointed out that this could not be the case, and suggested Winchester. Homburger has given good reasons for their attribution. Andrew of Fleury, *Vita Gauzlini*, 43, ed. P. Ewald, *Neues Archiv der Gesellschaft für ältere deutsche Geschichtskunde*, III (1878), 369; Delisle, *op. cit.*, p. 216 ff.; *New Palaeographical Society*, Ser. I, Pls. 83, 84; Homburger, *op. cit.*, pp. 57–65; Millar, *op. cit.*, p. 107, no. 19.

[71] Migne, *Pat. Lat.*, CLXXIX, cols. 1738, 1739, 1745; Atkins, *Archaeologia*, LXXVIII (1928), 231–232. William of Malmesbury, *Vita Wulfstani*, ed. Reginald R. Darlington (London, 1928), pp. 5, 16.

FIG. 3. ORLÉANS. BIBLIOTHÈQUE MUNICIPALE, MS. 175, FOL. 149ʳ

We have, then, in the story of the Ramsey Benedictional sent to Abbot Gauzlin of Fleury and in the record of the wanderings of two fine Peterborough books actual documentary evidence that East Anglia was quite capable of producing highly treasured manuscripts in the early eleventh century. We have indubitable examples of this art in the eleventh-century Bury St. Edmunds and Crowland [72] Psalters and in the Gospels from Holkham Hall, now in the Pierpont Morgan Library. Is it then unreasonable to suggest that the monastic art which bloomed so magnificently in East Anglia during the early eleventh century might well have had an earlier flowering in the late tenth century? It has already been stated how Mr. Tolhurst and Sir Ivor Atkins have given sound reasons for supposing that the so-called Missal of Robert of Jumièges was written and decorated at Thorney for Peterborough, or at Ely. The same historians believe the Benedictional of St. Aethelwold to be of East Anglian origin. For similar reasons, namely, liturgical content, it has been shown that *H* must have been intended for Ramsey. Now if *H* had been written at Winchester or at any other monastery for Ramsey, we might expect to find a dedicatory inscription recording this fact. That the writing of a manuscript in one monastery for the use of another was rare before the Gothic period is attested by the Codex Egberti,[73] written at Reichenau for Trier, and by the Commentary of St. Jerome on Jeremiah,[74] written at St. Vaast for Cîteaux. In both cases particular care was taken to explain by means of inscriptions within the books what seemed in those times an unusual procedure. Liturgical books were as a rule copied for local use. They were less often made to order. In any case, unless the evidence of palaeography and illumination is overwhelmingly to the contrary, the probabilities are that before the thirteenth century manuscripts were written within the establishments for which they were liturgically intended.[75]

Whether the new English style spread fanwise from a single English center, to be followed immediately with variations in other monasteries, or whether, as is more likely, fresh impulses were received from abroad simultaneously and variously interpreted, is a problem which awaits solution. There is one feature, however, of the Crucifixion in *H* which is characteristic of English art of the period, whatever its ultimate source may be. This is the representation of St. John as actually writing. There are four examples known to me. Two are from

[72] Oxford, Bodleian, Douce 296. The attribution to Crowland (Lincolnshire) was made by Mr. Edmund Bishop and Dr. Frere (see Atkins, *op. cit.*, p. 222, n. 5), and has been followed by Mr. Francis Wormald, *English Kalendars before A.D. 1100* (London: Henry Bradshaw Society, 1934), pp. 253–265.

[73] Adolph Goldschmidt, *German Illumination* (Florence, 1928), II, Pl. 4 (bibliography).

[74] C. Oursel, *La Miniature du XIIᵉ siècle à l'abbaye de Cîteaux* (Dijon, 1926), p. 79.

[75] Somewhat exceptional are the Gospels of Le Mans (Paris, Bibl. Nat., MS. lat. 261), written at Tours for Le Mans (see Wilhelm Köhler, *Die Schule von Tours*, I [Berlin, 1930], 295), and the group of Franco-Saxon Sacramentaries at Rheims, Vienna, Stockholm, Leningrad, Cambrai, and Paris. The latter show unusual identity in decoration combined with great diversity in liturgical usage. Cf. Delisle, *op. cit.*, p. 400, and Carl Nordenfalk, "Ein karolingisches Sakramentar aus Echternach und seine Vorläufer," *Acta Archaeologica*, II (1931), 234–235. Some of these manuscripts, if not all of them, were surely made at one monastery for the use of other monasteries and churches. But there is in this group a stylistic unity in general design and detail which is far less true of those varying adaptations of somewhat similar motifs which we find in English illumination in the tenth century.

FIG. 4. CAMBRIDGE. UNIVERSITY LIBRARY, MS. FF. 1. 23, FOL. 88ᵗ

East Anglia, in *H* and in the Gospels from Holkham Hall in the Pierpont Morgan
Library.[76] A third instance is found in the Psalter from Winchcomb (Fig. 4) to
which reference has already been made, and a fourth example of the motif occurs in the Offices of New Minster.[77] Iconographically, the Crucifixions of the
Holkham Hall Gospels and the Winchcomb Psalter are the most closely related.
Now in only two cases, the Winchcomb Psalter and *H*, do we find the words of
St. John written down, but the inscriptions differ. On the scroll of *H* we read the
verse of the Gospel of St. John, 21 : 24, "hic est discipulus qui testimonium
perhibet," while in the Winchcomb Psalter we read "et ego vidi et testimonium,"
which seems to be an abridgment of John 19 : 35. The Winchester Crucifixion
is iconographically connected with the Holkham Hall Gospels and the Winchcomb Psalter, but Christ is shown as living, not dead, while the sun and moon
are represented as half-length figures instead of as busts within medallions.
Furthermore, the composition in the Offices of New Minster is cluttered up with
inscriptions, and wavy vegetation takes the place of the hilly foreground of the
other examples. The representation in *H* is the earliest, the most simple and
effective, and surely the finest. Was it the prototype to which later artists added
the sun and moon, inscriptions, or the figure of a donor? Or is *H* to be considered the deviation from a more common mode, the variation created by a great
artist? Or finally, does the composition of *H* follow a prototype different from
that behind the other three representations, and is the theme of St. John writing
merely like an English gloss that was freely used? In all likelihood this motif was
derived from some sermon, commentary, or other text.

It is hoped that a solution of some of the problems of iconography and style
in Anglo-Saxon art will be made easier for future investigators through this
attempt to localize *H* at Ramsey. Yet even if that should not be the case, *H* may
have historical associations of unsuspected importance. The rapid cultural
advance made by England in the later decades of the tenth century was undoubtedly brought about by the efforts of that saintly triumvirate, Dunstan,
Aethelwold, and Oswald, of whom the first two have never lacked their meed
of praise. Of them we have tangible reminders in the probable Psalter of St.
Dunstan,[78] and in the Benedictional of St. Aethelwold. Did there ever exist a

[76] Pierpont Morgan Library, MS. 709, fol. iv. *The Pierpont Morgan Library, a review of the growth, development, and activities of the Library during the period between its establishment as an educational institution in February
1924 and the close of the year 1929* (New York, 1930), Pl.VII.

[77] Br. Mus., MS. Cotton Titus D xxvi. Millar, *English Illuminated Manuscripts*, Pl. 24 (a); W. de G.
Birch, "On Two Anglo-Saxon Manuscripts in the British Museum," *Transactions of the Royal Society of Literature* (London, 1878), Second Series, xi, 463–512. Another example of the Crucifixion with St. John writing is on the ivory cover of Morgan MS. 651; Adolph Goldschmidt, *Die Elfenbeinskulpturen aus der romanischen
Zeit* (Berlin, 1926), iv, no. 21, p. 13, Pl. VI; Belle da Costa Greene and Meta P. Harrsen, *The Pierpont
Morgan Library: Exhibition of Illuminated Manuscripts held at the New York Public Library* (New York, 1934),
no. 23, p. 14.

Dr. Goldschmidt (p. 13) says the ivory is probably Belgian of about 1100, and goes on to remark:
"Ungewöhnlich ist der Umstand, dass Johannes das Evangelium schreibend, und zwar mit stark verdrehter
Handstellung, dargestellt ist."

[78] This book is more commonly known as the Bosworth Psalter. Yet Bishop concluded his monumental work on early English calendars — *The Bosworth Psalter* (London, 1908) — with the following words:
"In our opinion therefore this Bosworth Psalter should be assigned to a date corresponding to the earlier

book which belonged to St. Oswald? In an old catalogue of the library at Ramsey there is the following significant entry: "Summa Psalteriorum, omnibus computatis, sine Psalterio Sancti Oswoldi. Centum, per minus centum." [79] Apparently, then, there was a Psalter of St. Oswald, not kept in the library, but probably preserved in the sacristy.   Now if *H* was indeed written and illuminated at Ramsey between the years 974 and 986, may it not be that very book? Unquestionably *H* was intended for some great personage, for it was no mere service book. Could it have belonged to Ethelwine, Ramsey's generous benefactor? Probably not, inasmuch as the monks of Ramsey, who are most lavish in his praise, admit that he was "illiteratus." [80]

If *H* is really the *Psalterium Oswaldi*,[81] it then becomes not merely an important historical document, but also the true spiritual ancestor of those richly decorated Gothic Psalters which made East Anglia one of the chief rivals of Paris in that art which is called illumination.

years of St. Dunstan's archiepiscopate at Canterbury. It was probably written for him, and quite possibly under his direction the artist ornamented it according to his taste" (p. 130).

[79] *Chronicon*, p. 367. The catalogue is contained in Cotton Rolls II, 16, of the British Museum. According to Mlle. Marthe Dulong, who very kindly examined it for me, this manuscript roll is of the early fourteenth century.

[80] *Chronicon*, p. 31.

[81] At the end of the litany of *H* are certain prayers and petitions which have been commented upon by C. A. Swainson in *The Nicene and Apostles' Creeds* (London, 1875), pp. 370–371. He says: "When we come to the intercessions we find a prayer for our king, but none for pope or bishop: we find too a petition 'ut paganorum saevitiam comprimere digneris.' Then there is a special plea for the intercession of St. Benedict. Petitions follow for all Rectors of Churches: for all 'qui mei memoriam faciunt, et se meis indignis orationibus commendaverunt' for my relations and for all 'quorum in communione [misread by Swainson; *H* has *in communi*] mentionem facio.' The manuscript must have been prepared for an Archbishop who had been a Benedictine monk." It is apparently his theory that since the mention of archbishop, bishop, or bishops was omitted from the suffrages of *H*, the psalter was therefore intended for an archbishop himself. If this is true, the possibility that *H* is the *Psalterium Oswaldi* becomes more than ever probable. There are, however, two objections to Swainson's argument. In the first place, is the absence of a prayer for bishop or archbishop really exceptional? There is, as has been shown, sufficient published material at hand regarding the composition of litanies to make possible certain general conclusions, but there is unfortunately not enough evidence available concerning the special prayers which follow after these litanies. As for the phrases quoted by Swainson, they are all found — together with additional prayers — in the Crowland Psalter (Oxford: Bodleian, MS. Douce 296, fols. 120v–121v). In the latter manuscript we find the more usual mention of *episcopos* in the prayers for church and state.

UNE VOÛTE À NERVURES DU XIᵉ SIÈCLE À SIGTUNA

JOHNNY ROOSVAL

L'ÉGLISE de *Sankt Per*, c'est-à-dire de *Saint-Pierre*, à Sigtuna, actuellement à
l'état de ruine, était, originairement (selon mon opinion, depuis 1050
environ), une église épiscopale. L'évêque de Sigtuna est cité encore en
l'an 1134, et, en 1141, on parle d'un *episcopus obsaliensis*. La dignité est donc trans-
mise de Sigtuna à la ville voisine d'Upsala (Vieil-Upsala, situé au nord de la ville
actuelle). Avant de perdre son titre hiérarchique, Sigtuna avait commencé de
descendre de sa position comme première ville commerciale de Svealand. Coupée
dans la fleur de son développement, tout comme Pompéi ou Samarra, Sigtuna a
pu sauver, dans ses ruines nombreuses, une partie précieuse de la civilisation de
notre premier siècle chrétien. Saint-Pierre est une des cathédrales les plus
vénérables, par leur âge, en Suède. En mettant de côté Lund et Dalby, en
Scanie, qui, au moyen-âge, étaient situées en territoire danois, nous voyons en
Saint-Pierre notre cathédrale la plus antique.

Elle est très petite. On voit de suite que c'est le modeste début d'une organi-
sation qui a exigé du temps pour croître. Elle a une longueur extérieure de 38
mètres, environ (Fig. 1). Son successeur comme cathédrale, celle du Vieil-
Upsala, avait, dans son état complet, environ 64 mètres, tandis que le successeur
de cette dernière, lorsque la résidence épiscopale fut transférée à *Nouvel*-Upsala,
c.a.d. la cathédrale actuelle, a 118,7 mètres.

Quoique petite, Saint-Pierre de Sigtuna a une tenue exprimant une force
primitive. Ses murs massifs de granit se groupent autour d'une tour centrale
carrée, qui est encore en assez bon état. L'intertransept est couvert d'une voûte
"en arc de cloître" grossière, qui semble soulagée "par deux arcs de profil
rectangulaire se croisant à angle droit sans clef commune," en partant de et en
retombant sur les quatre coins de la salle (Fig. 2 et 3).

Cette voûte est la chose la plus intéressante de la vieille cathédrale. Pourtant,
elle n'a pas encore été discutée. C'est une forme primitive qui provoque une
étude attentive. C'est apparemment un des incunables de la voûte aux nervures,
une source, peut-être, de notre connaissance des débuts de l'art gothique. On
peut comparer la voûte de Saint-Pierre à celle de Saint-Ours de Loches. Je
viens d'employer, pour la description, les mêmes mots dont s'est servi M. Lambert dans son exposé de la voûte de Saint-Ours.[1] Ce n'est que pour les points de
départ des arcs que les déscriptions diffèrent. A Loches, ils partent "du milieu
des côtés de la salle" c'est de même pour la voûte de Corméry, reproduite dans
notre Fig. 4.

Dans une série d'articles, M. Lambert nous a montré l'importance des

[1] E. Lambert, "Les premières voûtes nervées françaises et les origines de la croisée d'ogives," *Revue
archéologique*, 1933, p. 235.

voûtes du type Loches, qui, dans la chaîne d'évolution, se trouveraient entre un groupe de voûtes mozarabiques de l'Espagne et les voûtes à ogives de la cathédrale de Durham.

Dans cette série, la voûte de Sigtuna semble occuper une place à part qui commande une étude plus approfondie. Ajoutons, à la description de la voûte, qu'elle est faite en moellon et que les pierres des nervures sont taillées sous forme de fer en T, dont la barre entre dans le corps des chapes, ce qui ressort de quelques-unes des pierres dont on peut observer la forme.

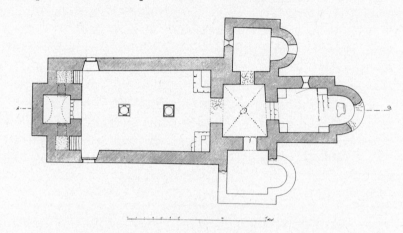

FIG. 1. SIGTUNA, ST. PIERRE, PLAN DE L'ÉGLISE
D'après Henrik Cornell, *Sigtuna och Gamla Uppsala*

Mais il nous faut passer à l'analyse du bâtiment dans sa totalité.

La tour centrale n'a pas d'escalier. On y montait à l'aide d'une échelle, par une porte située dans le mur de l'étage au-dessus de la voûte, et qui donnait sur la nef (Fig. 5). Dans les baies de la tour se profile une colonnette, en forme de deux cônes unis par une boule, attribut caractéristique de l'architecture anglo-saxonne. Aussi, M. Henrik Cornell, auteur de l'étude le plus étendu du groupe d'architecture en question,[2] croit-il que Saint-Pierre ait été conçu d'après un archétype anglo-saxon modifié par des éléments normands. Les deux bras du transept ont l'air de chapelles isolées et ne sont pas alignés avec le carré central (comparer les plans de Sainte-Marie, à Dover Castle, et de l'église de Worth). L'emplacement du clocher, dans le centre de l'église, ainsi que les absidioles, sont, d'après M. Cornell, des éléments normands. Une petite colonne, brisée et trouvée dans l'intérieur de la ruine, et qui probablement a eu sa place dans une des baies de la tour, est ornée avec des reliefs (Fig. 6). J'ai comparé ses animaux à ceux du relief bien connu de l'église d'Ipswich en Angleterre — S. Michel, qui se bat avec le dragon, accompagné d'un animal à quatre jambes — et j'ai trouvé les affinités si évidentes qu'elles indiquent aux deux oeuvres la même époque. Ipswich n'est pas sûrement daté, mais toujours regardé comme appartenant à l'architecture anglo-saxonne,[3] donc avant 1066. Sur une des faces du pied de la

---

[2] Henrik Cornell, *Sigtuna och Gamla Uppsala* (Upsala, 1920).
[3] Julius Baum, *Malerei und Plastik des Mittelalters*, dans la série Handbuch der Kunstwissenschaft, p. 168.

colonne se voient un entrelacement des parties d'un corps de dragon semblable aux entrelacements d'un groupe de pierres runiques qui est regardé comme appartenant au milieu du onzième siècle.[4]

En ce qui concerne la partie ouest, M. Erik Lundberg a procédé récemment, en collaboration avec M. Erik Floderus, à des recherches intéressantes. Ils ont découvert les fondements d'un large vestibule à l'ouest de la façade actuelle, qu'ils interprêtent comme les fondements de deux tours.[5] Tel était donc le plan originaire (Fig. 7). M. Lundberg a aussi trouvé une suture dans l'appareil des façades, immédiatement à l'ouest de la tour centrale. La fabrique a donc été

FIG. 2. SIGTUNA, ST. PIERRE, COUPE LONGITUDINALE
D'après Cornell, ouvrage cité

interrompue après l'achèvement de la tour. Quelque temps après, on a continué le bâtiment en modifiant le plan pour la façade ouest, mais en gardant, toutefois, la plus grande partie des fondements déjà posés.

Si le plan originaire includait vraiment un front d'ouest avec deux tours jumelles, l'église de Saint-Pierre aurait offert, sur une petite échelle, un extérieur du modèle de la Trinité de Caen. Mais il en fut autrement. Le front actuel contient une seule tour. Elle est entourée de deux escaliers, qui, à l'état complet, produisaient probablement l'effet de deux petites tours, appuyées contre celle du milieu. Il n'y a pas de porte dans la partie ouest. Ce "front" est donc tout-à-fait aveugle, tel un grand bouclier protégeant le guerrier. Cette espèce de "Westwerk" — "bâtiment d'ouest" — est une spécialité saxo-westphalienne. (Goslar, Minden, Freckenhorst — voir Frankl, "Baukunst des Mittelalters," dans *Handbuch der Kunstwissenschaft*, p. 85, 93, 180.)

[4] D'après l'autorité du Professeur E. Wessén de l'Académie des Belles-Lettres, de l'Histoire et des Antiquités. Voir *Södermanlands runinskrifter*, publ. de l'Académie sous rédaction de Brate et Wessén, n: 7, 144, 192, 217, 236, 240, 254, 273.
[5] Erik Floderus et Erik Lundberg, dans la périodique *Fornvännen*, 1935, p. 206.

L'étage inférieur de la tour ouest forme une petite chapelle, couverte par une voûte en berceau : elle était probablement destinée aux fonts baptismaux. L'étage supérieur s'ouvre également vers la nef, et on pouvait y accéder par les deux escaliers ; ainsi que l'a montré M. Thordeman, c'était, évidemment, la place d'honneur réservée au roi, disposition qui, en ce qui concerne l'Allemagne, remonte à la loge impériale de la cathédrale de Charlemagne à Aix-la-Chapelle.[6]

FIG. 3. SIGTUNA, VOÛTE DE L'INTERTRANSEPT

La nef était couverte par un comble ouvert, sans plafond, appuyé sur deux colonnes en granit, posées, sur socles très simples et sans bases, dans la ligne centrale du bâtiment.

L'influence anglaise est toute naturelle en Suède, dont la population avait eu beaucoup à faire avec l'Angleterre avant et pendant le XIe siècle. Une grande partie de l'armée avec laquelle Knut de Danemark occupa l'Angleterre, était formée par des suédois, et les résultats matériels de cette expédition, soit les monnaies anglaises, ont été trouvées par milliers dans la terre suédoise.

La forme des monnaies anglaises fut, par la suite, imitée en Suède et, précisément, à Sigtuna, résidence favorite des premiers rois chrétiens. Des monnayeurs anglais y travaillaient au service du roi.

---

[6] Bengt Thordeman, "Sankt Per i Sigtuna," dans le *Fornvännen* (Communications de l'Académie des Belles-Lettres, Stockholm, 1924), p. 204.

Des missionnaires anglais ou d'éducation anglaise jouissaient de la protection de la cour. On distingue, parmi eux, l'évêque Osmund, en raison de son activité artistique en qualité de graveur de pierres runiques.

Osmund, qui était en activité depuis 1020 environ, perdit sa position de chef spirituel et artistique, vers 1057 environ.[7] La mission allemande venue de la métropole de Brème rivalisait avec l'influence de l'église anglaise, et, de 1058 à

FIG. 4. CORMÉRY, VOÛTE DU CLOCHER

1066, ce furent les allemands qui eurent le dessus. Le nouvel évêque de Sigtuna s'appelait Adalward.

En présence de ces faits, on peut donc conjecturer ce qui suit au sujet de l'histoire de Saint-Pierre: Osmund a dirigé les travaux du bâtiment du choeur et de la tour centrale, avant sa défaite en 1057. Ainsi s'expliquerait l'influence anglo-saxonne dans cette partie de Saint-Pierre. Après un intervalle de quelques années, Adalward, membre de la mission teutonique, reprend les travaux interrompus. Il achève l'église. Il raccourcit quelque peu le plan et lui imprime un caractère teutonique. Ainsi s'explique la tour ouest avec ses deux escaliers symétriques. (Ce motif fut, d'ailleurs, souvent appliqué en Suède jusqu'à la fin du XIIe siècle, par exemple, dans l'église abbatiale de Vreta, dans les deux églises visbyennes de Saint-Olof et de Sainte-Marie. Saint-Pierre serait donc, pour la Suède, l'initiateur de cette forme.)

[7] En ce qui concerne la très intéressante histoire d'Osmund, voir Otto von Friesen, "Asmund Kareon," *Svenskt Biografiskt Lexikon*, II (Stockholm, 1920), 375.

FIG. 5. SIGTUNA, LA TOUR CENTRALE

On ne peut guère espérer, pour une époque tellement obscure, voir les conjectures se consolider ou se transformer en preuves. Aussi, non seulement le soussigné, mais chacun de ses savants collègues qui se sont penchés sur les problèmes sigtuniens a-t-il sa chronologie à lui.

Toutefois, il existe une base de calcul qui a été acceptée par tous, élaborée par M. Otto Janse,[8] qui a posé une ingénieuse théorie au sujet de la chronologie interne de la famille des églises romanes en granit avec tour centrale. Il a construit une chaîne d'évolution, basée sur la façon de poser les pierres. On aurait commencé avec un appareil assez régulier, d'après le modèle des églises nor-

FIG. 6. SIGTUNA, FRAGMENT D'UNE COLONNE

mandes ou anglaises. Puis, trouvant cette manière peu convenable au dur granit suédois, on se serait tourné, de plus en plus, vers un appareil cyclopique. Saint-Pierre tient la tête dans cette série. C'est un bel appareil de blocs presque régulièrement carrés, surtout, dans le choeur et dans la tour centrale. La partie occidentale, de son côté, se contente d'un appareil un peu plus rude, constatation qui est en parfaite harmonie avec l'existence de la suture entre les deux périodes du bâtiment de Saint-Pierre qu'a découvert M. Lundberg.[9]

Dans son exposé de recherches récentes à Sigtuna, M. Floderus mentionne non moins de quatre églises en granit dont il a étudié la technique de l'appareil.[10] Par la voie de ses observations, il arrive, par un autre chemin que celui d'Otto Janse, au même syllogisme: Saint-Pierre est la première, les autres ne font que la suivre.

La chronologie *relative* des églises sigtuniennes semble donc bien fixée.

Parmi les auteurs ayant proposé une date *absolue* pour Saint-Pierre, je ne citerai ici que les plus récents. Ainsi, *M. Cornell* propose la date de 1080 environ, en se basant sur plusieurs raisons que nous ne pouvons reproduire toutes ici.

---

[8] Otto Janse, "Ett bidrag till de oornerade granitkyrkornas ålders bestämmelse," dans la revue *Svenska Fornminnes föreningens tidskrift*, XII, 361. Voir aussi le même auteur dans *Gamla svenska städer*.

[9] O.C.   [10] O.C.

M. Thordeman préfère l'époque d'Adalward, soit 1060–1066 environ. C'est, surtout, sur les conclusions de M. Thordeman que je me suis appuyé plus haut. Mais, le fait que l'église a été bâtie en deux périodes, la première, marquée d'un caractère anglo-normand, la seconde, d'un caractère allemand, m'ont forcé de conjecturer les dates de 1050 environ pour la première période, et 1060–1066 seulement pour la seconde.

MM. Lundberg et *Floderus* nous étonnent en prétendant que Saint-Pierre n'ait été bâtie qu'après 1130. Ils la font dériver d'une église norvégienne — Saint-Halvard d'Oslo — qui, d'après M. Johan Meyer,[11] doit dater d'un peu avant 1130. Mais, tout d'abord, le motif de la date de Saint-Halvard est très faible. Les documents nous apprennent seulement qu'un roi norvégien fut

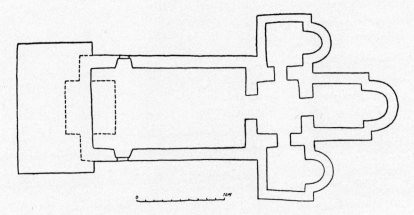

FIG. 7. SIGTUNA, ST. PIERRE, PLAN ORIGINAIRE
D'après les excavations des MM. Lundberg et Floderus

enseveli dans l'église en 1130. On connaît donc le terminus ante, mais non pas le terminus fixus. Puis, ensuite, pourquoi une église sigtunienne doit-elle être subordonnée, artistiquement, à une église d'Oslo? Il n'existe pas, aux XIe et XIIe siècles, d'indices d'une existence d'influences culturelles prédominantes du côté norvégien. Toute autre est la question au XIIIe siècle, pendant la période triomphante du premier gothique norvégien. Ensuite, Saint-Halvard ne ressemble que très superficiellement à Saint-Pierre. Il y a tour centrale et transept, voilà tout. Enfin, si Saint-Pierre datait d'environ 1130–1140, sa partie ouest serait encore plus récente, peut-être de 1150 environ, et, conséquemment, les autres églises de Sigtuna, au sujet desquelles M. Floderus constate, conjointement avec M. Lundberg, qu'elles sont plus récentes que Saint-Pierre (en adhérant à la théorie d'Otto Janse), auraient donc été bâties *après 1150* et, naturellement, avant 1187, l'année du sac de Sigtuna par les mains de pirates esthoniens. La ville qui, selon l'autorité de tous les historiens et archéologues, y compris M. Floderus lui-même, aurait décliné dès le commencement du XIIe siècle, aurait donc, en plein déclin, bâti quatre nouvelles églises de granit en 37 ans! Ajoutons qu'il existe d'autres raisons de réfuter les conclusions de MM.

---

[11] *Norsk Kunsthistorie* (History of Art in Norway, Oslo, 1925).

Lundberg et Floderus, mais celles que nous venons d'exposer paraissent devoir suffire. Il n'y a donc pas la moindre raison de sortir du XIᵉ siècle.

Revenons donc au détail, si intéressant, de la voûte en arc de cloître. Elle constitue un intermédiaire important dans la série de monuments cités dans l'article de M. Lambert, série comprenant, d'un côté, entre autres, des voûtes de la cathédrale de Jaca et de la Santa Cruz de la Seros, en Espagne, une voûte dans l'église Saint-Ours de Loches, dans le clocher de l'abbaye de Corméry, bâtie en 1086, dans la tour septentrionale de la cathédrale de Bayeux, construite entre 1060 et 1080, et, de l'autre, des voûtes situées dans la cathédrale de Durham, vers 1100 environ.

Dans le premier groupe, il s'agit de coupoles en arc de cloître, fortifié par des arcs partant du milieu des murs du carré.

Dans le second groupe, nous nous trouvons en présence de la croisée d'ogives véritable, où, naturellement, les nervures — si elles ne sont que quatre — partent des quatre coins de l'espace vouté.

C'est entre ces deux groupes que se place — par ordre typologique si non strictement par ordre chronologique — la coupole de Sigtuna, qui est une coupole en arc de cloître tout comme les voûtes du premier groupe, mais qui est, en même temps, semblable au second groupe parce que les nervures partent des coins du carré.

Je ne désire pas prétendre que l'évolution ait suivi, géographiquement, un chemin passant par Sigtuna. La petite capitale d'un royaume nordique était par trop périphérique pour jouer un rôle actif dans l'évolution de l'architecture européenne. Mais, elle représente une étape qui, sans sa présence, n'aurait pas laissé de traces. Elle contribue à prouver la connexion existant entre les arts de l'Islam et ceux de l'Europe chrétienne.

Il existe une superstitition, selon laquelle tout travail architectonique et sculptural en pierre, datant d'avant 1100, est suspect. Pour tous ceux qui ont suivi Kingsley Porter dans sa conquête hardie et, finalement, heureuse, du XIᵉ siècle, en Espagne, en Bourgogne et en Italie, l'idée d'une voûte à nervures suédoise, datant du même siècle, n'offre aucune invraisemblance.

Note. Toutes les photographies reproduites ont été mises à la disposition de l'auteur par l'Office de la conservation des monuments de la Suède (*Riksantiquarie Ämbetet*).

SOME MINOR IRISH CATHEDRALS

A. W. CLAPHAM, C.B.E., F.B.A., F.S.A.

THE remarkable character of the prehistoric and early Christian monuments of Ireland has probably been responsible for the almost complete neglect with which many large classes of later medieval Irish buildings have been treated. No general attempt has ever been made to examine the extraordinarily numerous churches and convents of the mendicant orders scattered over the country, and a paper on the evolution of the Irish castle has only recently appeared. The type of structure however which has received least attention of all, is that of the smaller Irish cathedrals. The two cathedrals (Christ Church and St. Patrick) in Dublin and that at Kilkenny are, of course, well known, though the mistaken opinion is still vaguely held in some quarters that the crypt at Christ Church is much earlier than its late twelfth-century superstructure. In regard to the minor cathedrals, however, published information is largely lacking, unless the building incorporates some structure belonging to the earlier age of Irish Christianity.[1]

It is not the purpose of the present paper to attempt in any way to supply this lack, but rather, by calling attention to the interest of the subject, to submit it as a fitting field for future research. In approaching the inquiry it must be accepted, at the outset, that the ordinary development of cathedral-building in England or on the Continent has little or no bearing on the form and structure of these Irish churches. Most of them are insignificant in size and their interest lies largely in their unfamiliar and highly individual forms.

These smaller cathedral-churches of Ireland fall naturally into four types of gradually increasing complexity, which incidentally agree to some extent with their chronological order. The simplest of these types is the single chamber building which is to be found in the group which dates generally from the tenth century. Clonmacnois Cathedral, though largely rebuilt at a later date, seems to represent in plan the church rebuilt in 910. To precisely the same type belongs the cathedral of Scattery [2] (county Clare), of which the dimensions correspond very closely to those of Clonmacnois. Aghadoe Cathedral [3] also is of this type, though actually a building of the twelfth century. To these may be added in all probability the early cathedral churches of Ardmore,[4] Kilmacduagh, and perhaps Glendalough,[5] though all three have various later additions.

The second type displays the simple nave and chancel plan, a plan which

---

[1] T. M. Fallow, *Cathedral Churches of Ireland* (1894), gives a general account of the surviving remains of the minor Irish cathedrals, but the book is in no sense an architectural or archaeological study.

[2] *Journ. R. Soc. Ants. Ireland*, 5th ser., VII (1897), 277.

[3] *Ibid.*, 5th ser., II (1892), 163.

[4] *Ibid.*, 5th ser., XIII (1903), 365.

[5] *Public Works Ireland Report*, 1911–12.

is no doubt as old as the preceding, but its surviving examples in the cathedrals date mainly from the middle of the twelfth century. This was the form of the early cathedral of Tuam (the nave has gone), of the enlarged cathedrals of Glendalough, Ardmore, and Clonfert, and perhaps of others.

Thirdly comes the aisleless cruciform type, not earlier than the thirteenth century, of which the cathedrals of Cashel [6] and Killaloe [7] (Fig. 1) still survive

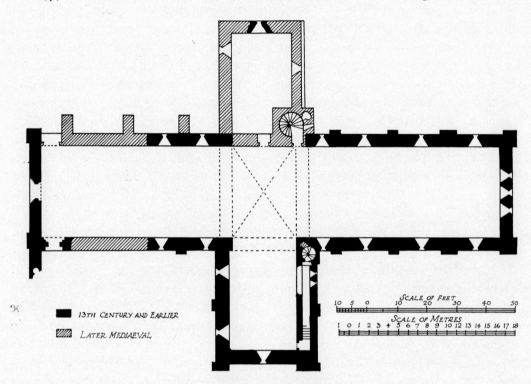

FIG. 1.   KILLALOE CATHEDRAL

largely intact, while that at Kildare [8] has been partly rebuilt; all these have a central tower.

Lastly, the cruciform church with an aisled nave was first introduced at Limerick in the third quarter of the twelfth century and repeated at Cloyne,[9] Armagh,[10] and Newtown Trim [11] in the thirteenth century. Somewhat of the same type was the destroyed cathedral at Waterford [12] in its twelfth-century form and before its thirteenth-century and later extensions.

I do not propose to consider all of these buildings in detail but rather to confine my attention to the half a dozen typical examples with which I am most familiar and to call attention to those later Gothic developments which are dis-

[6] *Ibid.*, 1907–08.
[7] T. J. Westropp, in *Journ. R. Soc. Ants. Ireland*, 5th ser., II (1892), 410, III (1893), 187.
[8] H. N. Craig, *St. Brigid's Cathedral Kildare* (1931). No plan.
[9] *Journ. R. Soc. Ants. Ireland*, 5th ser., VII (1897), 336.
[10] *Ecclesiologist*, XVI, 8 (no plan).
[11] *Arch. Journal*, LXXXVIII (1931), 364.
[12] Sir J. Ware, *History of Waterford* (ed. Harris).

tinctively Irish and which are probably the least familiar to the general student.
Let us then consider in turn the cathedrals of Limerick, Tuam, Kilmacduagh,
Clonfert, Leighlin, and Clonmacnois.

Limerick [13] belongs to the latest development of the minor Irish cathedral
plan. It is a cruciform church (Fig. 2) with an aisleless choir and aisled nave, to
which various chapels and a western tower were subsequently added. Much of

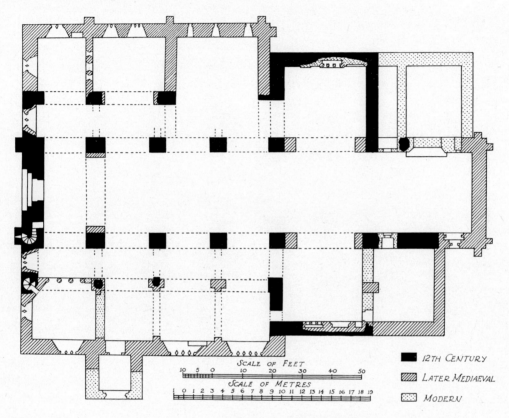

FIG. 2. LIMERICK CATHEDRAL

the structure dates from the second half of the twelfth century, and its characteristics imply that it was put up before the English conquest. The heavy square
piers of the nave, the absence of any provision for a central tower, and the curious
cross-arches formerly dividing the bays of the aisles seem very strongly to imply
that the general design was borrowed from the early Cistercian churches of the
country [14] (a direct introduction from Burgundy), though it is doubtful if any of
the surviving Cistercian churches of Ireland are of as early a date as the cathedral
at Limerick. The arches across the aisles, of which most of the scalloped imposts
still remain, were sprung from a level some feet below the capitals of the nave
arcades, and it seems probable that they represent the skeleton of the well-known

[13] T. J. Westropp, in *Journ. R. Soc. Ants. Ireland*, 5th ser., VIII (1898), 112, gives a good account of the
building and indicates its Cistercian affinities, but the cross-arches of the aisles escaped his attention. Attention may perhaps be called to the series of late fifteenth-century carved misericords which appears to
be English work.
[14] *Arch. Journal*, LXXXVIII (1931), 1.

early Cistercian and Burgundian system of roofing the aisles with a cross-vault
in each bay. At Limerick however only the cross-arches were ever erected, and
these must have supported a high stretch of plain "diaphragm" walling under
the timber roof. Traces yet survive of the high arch opening into the south
transept but there is no evidence that any arch existed on the west of the crossing. This was a common system in the earlier Irish Cistercian churches, where
the high roof of the nave was continued east to the chancel arch. Only one of the
later features of the cathedral need be touched upon; this is the inserted west
tower built upon arches over the west bay of the nave. The tower is narrower
than the nave itself and is thus an example of the type of tower almost universally
employed in the churches of the Irish friaries. These towers, commonly additions

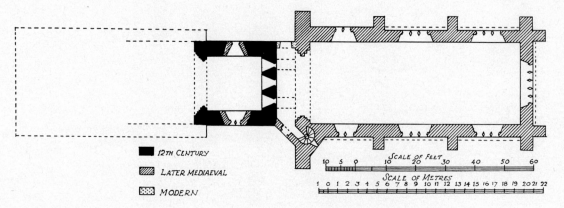

FIG. 3. TUAM CATHEDRAL

to an earlier building, are constructed on two parallel walls with arches, carried
across the building, from the middle of which rises a slender square tower much
narrower in width than the building below. This type of structure seems to have
been copied from English originals in the mendicant orders (examples still survive at Coventry, Lynn Regis, and Atherton) and was almost universal among
the numerous Franciscan and Dominican churches of Ireland. Once well established in the latter country it was adopted here and there by other orders, as
may be seen in the Austin Canons houses at Clare Abbey [15] (near Ennis), Kil-
laghla Abbey [16] (Kerry), Inistoge Priory [17] (Kilkenny), and elsewhere. When
added to the smaller secular cathedrals, this type of tower was more varied in its
position and type, and the examples at Tuam, Clonfert, and Ross are highly
individual.

Tuam Cathedral [18] is little known save for its remarkable Romanesque chancel
arch. As the see of the archdiocese of Connaught it is not a little surprising to

---

[15] *Journ. R. Soc. Ants. Ireland*, 5th ser., x (1900).

[16] *Ibid.*, 5th ser., xvi (1906).

[17] *Ibid.*, 5th ser., vi (1896).

[18] No general account of this cathedral has been published. Notices of the twelfth-century chancel
and arch appear in most general publications on Irish architecture, and it is illustrated in F. Henry, *La
Sculpture irlandaise*.

find that the mid-twelfth-century church seems to have continued to do duty as the cathedral until late in the Middle Ages. This church (Fig. 3) was of the simple native Irish type consisting of a square chancel (about 18 feet) with a nave of proportionate size which has now entirely vanished. Till the building of the new cathedral in 1861–1863, this chancel formed the west porch of the church, the nave having been removed at some uncertain date, perhaps after the fire of 1787. The chancel arch is well known and forms one of the richest examples of Irish Romanesque. The central window of the three in the east wall at that time formed the inner doorway. The late medieval choir (71 feet by 27 feet) is at earliest of late fourteenth-century date and may be of the middle of the fifteenth century, as the papal registers record that the cathedral was in bad repair in

FIG. 4.   TUAM CATHEDRAL. CHOIR FROM
THE SOUTHEAST

1441. The structure (Fig. 4) survives, though the windows have been partly renewed. It has the heavy corbeled parapet, not infrequent in Irish churches of the period, and well-preserved piscina and sedilia. At the west end is a fine lofty pointed arch, the full width of the building, and set on this and the east wall of the early chancel was one of those slender friars' towers (Fig. 5) to which we have already referred. It had been repaired (according to an inscription on the east face) in 1688, but survived until the building of the new cathedral, when it was wantonly destroyed. This is hardly the place to mention the elaborate Italian baroque stall work which now fills much of the building.

Kilmacduagh Cathedral [19] (county Galway) forms the most important structure (Fig. 6) of the group of churches which center around it. The western part of the nave is a megalithic structure probably of the tenth century, and, without excavation, it is impossible to determine if this church was a simple rectangle or if it had a chancel which was removed in the twelfth-century enlargement of the nave. The later medieval alterations to the church consist of the addition of transeptal chapels north and south of the nave and of a new chancel and sacristy. The chancel and south transept are probably works of the fifteenth century, but

[19] *Journ. R. Soc. Ants. Ireland*, 5th ser., XIV (1904), 220.

the north transept is certainly earlier. These transepts, forming adjuncts to the
nave, are again a typical feature of Irish Gothic work; they occur in their most
pronounced and fully developed form in the friars' churches, but until a more
careful analysis has been made of the chronological evidence it is impossible to
say if here again we are to recognize the strong influence of the mendicant orders
on Irish Gothic. Transepts of a precisely similar nature were added to the cathedral of Clonfert, and a single one, on the scale of the friars' transepts, to the cathedral of Ardfert [20] (Kerry). It is clear from the abstracts in the calendar of papal
letters that from 1318 onward constant attempts were made to unite the Con-

FIG. 5. ST. MARY'S CATHEDRAL, TUAM, 1862

naught sees of Kilmacduagh, Achonry, and Annaghdown to the primatial see of
Tuam on the plea of poverty. The separate sees nevertheless survived, and it is
not a little surprising to find the evidence of much late medieval architectural
activity at Kilmacduagh in spite of the avowed poverty of the church.

Clonfert Cathedral [21] (county Galway) is generally known only from its
splendid Irish Romanesque west doorway. This feature entirely deserves its
high reputation, and not its least interesting feature is the pronounced inward
inclination of the jambs, derived from a far earlier tradition and highly remarkable in a structure of the middle of the twelfth century. With the exception of the
west wall the rest of the church (Fig. 7) seems to have been rebuilt on a nave and
chancel plan early in the thirteenth century. To this date belongs the interesting
pair of lights in the east end. The transepts (one roofless and one destroyed), the
chancel arch, and the west tower are late Gothic additions perhaps resulting
from the decayed state of the fabric referred to in the papal letters under 1414.
The tower is yet another instance of the slender friars' towers already referred

[20] A. Hill, *Ardfert Cathedral* (1870).
[21] The best general account of the building (no plan) is in R. R. Brash, *Ecclesiastical Architecture of Ireland* (1875), p. 41. For the twelfth-century west doorway, see F. Henry, *La Sculpture irlandaise*, Pl. 162.

to. At Clonfert, however, the tower is built on two walls running east and west within the west end of the nave, its position being very similar to the corresponding feature at Ross [22] (county Cork).

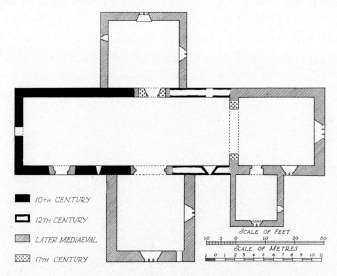

■ 10TH CENTURY

☐ 12TH CENTURY

▨ LATER MEDIAEVAL

▦ 17TH CENTURY

FIG. 6. KILMACDUAGH CATHEDRAL

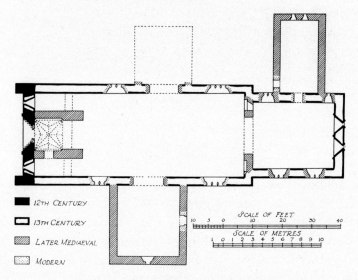

■ 12TH CENTURY

☐ 13TH CENTURY

▨ LATER MEDIAEVAL

▦ MODERN

FIG. 7. CLONFERT CATHEDRAL

Leighlin [23] stands in the barony of Idrone West and the county of Carlow. The early monastery was founded by St. Laserian in the seventh century, presumably at Old Leighlin, a few miles west of Leighlin Bridge over the Barrow, where the cathedral now stands. A castle was built by the bridge by Hugh de Lacy c. 1181, and near here was later founded a Carmelite friary.

[22] T. M. Fallow, *Cathedral Churches*, 68.

[23] There is no published account of this cathedral except in Mr. Fallow's book and in incidental references. There is also no published survey or plan.

In 1248 there was a project [24] to move the cathedral to "a central safe and fit place in the diocese," presumably meaning the east side of the Barrow and within the Pale. This project was seemingly abandoned, and toward the close of the century a new cathedral (Figs. 8–11) was built. It consisted of the long chancel and nave of the present church to which very shortly afterwards the two transepts were added north and south of the nave. The northern one is now roofless and the southern one has been destroyed. They were entered by arches with shafted responds executed in granite. The shafted splays of the eastern windows

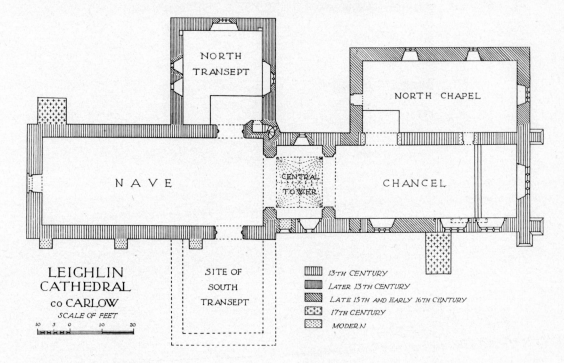

FIG. 8. LEIGHLIN CATHEDRAL

of the chancel and the four-bay sedilia with trefoiled heads are good examples of late thirteenth-century work.

The wealth of the cathedral was increased [25] in 1432 by the annexation to it of the Augustinian Priory of St. Stephen Leighlin which had been vacant for forty years. This priory is not otherwise known.

The late Gothic alterations to the cathedral are ascribed to Bishop Mathew Sanders (1529–1549), whose tomb-slab with a cross and the indent of a brass figure lies in the chancel. The slab has an added inscription to Bishop Thomas Field, 1567. These late alterations include the insertion of the tower in the west end of the chancel, the addition of the large chapel on the north of the chancel and the partial rebuilding of the north and south walls of the chancel itself. The tower is built on four arches set within the earlier walls, and has an elaborately ribbed vault, the plan of which is reproduced exactly as an ornamental design

[24] *Cal. of Papal Records*, I, 242.
[25] *Ibid.*, VIII, 436.

FIG. 9. LEIGHLIN CATHEDRAL FROM THE SOUTHWEST

Photo. H. G. Leask

FIG. 10. LEIGHLIN CATHEDRAL FROM
THE NORTHEAST

Photo. H. G. Leask

FIG. 11. LEIGHLIN CATHEDRAL.
WINDOWS ON SOUTH SIDE
OF CHOIR

on the panels of a sixteenth-century altar-tomb in the nave. The windows in this late work have the usual flowing tracery of that age in Ireland.

The cathedral was thus, originally, of the simple nave and chancel type, to which were added the typical transeptal adjuncts to the nave and the equally typical tower of the friars' type.

Curiously enough the font of late twelfth or early thirteenth-century date is probably earlier than any surviving part of the building. It is square and supported on five shafts.

Clonmacnois Cathedral [26] (county Offaly) is probably the most generally known of all these minor cathedrals, owing to its early associations and the ex-

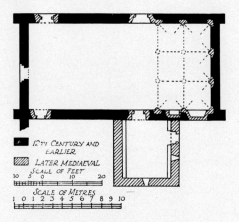

FIG. 12. CLONMACNOIS CATHEDRAL

tent and importance of the other buildings on the site. The church (Fig. 12) is a plain rectangle (62 feet by 28¾ feet) and the presence of buttresses *in antis* at both ends of the building seems to imply that it has preserved its tenth-century plan, though most of the superstructure has been rebuilt. The west doorway is a work of the twelfth century, but the main interest of the building lies in its late Gothic alterations. These consist of the elaborate north doorway inserted by Dean Odo about 1460 and the reconstruction of the choir, probably of the same date. This last work consisted of the insertion of a system of low vaulting, two bays deep and three in the width, and providing a second story or internal gallery at the east end of the church. This vaulted space had open arches toward the west, as is indicated by the surviving remains, but its purpose is highly problematical. One can only suggest that the new high altar occupied the middle of the raised gallery and that it may have been approached by a broad flight of steps in the middle bay of the new structure. This scheme would have certain features in common with the *pontile* in Italian churches, but why it was introduced into this remote and primitive Irish cathedral must remain a mystery.[27]

[26] *Public Works Ireland Report*, 1906–07.

[27] In the preparation of these notes I am greatly indebted to Mr. H.G. Leask for valuable assistance and through him to the Office of Public Works of the Irish Free State for the loan of the plan of Kilmacduagh Cathedral. I am furthermore indebted to Mr. Leask for his personal assistance in the survey of Leighlin Cathedral.

ENGLISH INFLUENCE ON MEDIEVAL ART
OF THE CONTINENT

ADOLPH GOLDSCHMIDT

EVERY country has times of creative power and times of sterility. France had creative years in the Carolingian and Gothic period and in the eighteenth century. Italy's art had its culmination in the time between the fourteenth and the seventeenth centuries, Belgium's and Holland's in the fifteenth and seventeenth, England's from the eighth to the eleventh centuries, during the Gothic period, and in the eighteenth century; Germany holds a prominent place in the tenth and the fifteenth centuries and at the beginning of the sixteenth. England, for instance, for her portraits in the sixteenth century took Holbein from Germany and in the seventeenth Rubens and Van Dyck from Belgium, but in the eighteenth her own art reaches perfection in Gainsborough, Reynolds, and others. Nevertheless one cannot affirm that periods of independent creation and of foreign reception are always identical with those of high and low quality, for often it is the periods of strong reception that lead to an especially high standard.

Apart from the relations between country and country there are two great contrasts in European art which are of a deeper nature, and to the last sources of which it seems impossible to penetrate; these are the differences between Greek or Mediterranean and northern art. In the very earliest manifestations of each there is a certain conformity. In the ornamental work of both regions in prehistoric times we find spots and strokes characteristic of the technique. All these are more or less mere surface-covering patterns intended to reduce the tedium of emptiness and render objects more valuable and pleasing. But while the spirals and wavy lines in the Mediterranean regions developed into plant tendrils, the northern races had a strong inclination to give their ornamental work a distinct dynamic expression. In early Celtic ornament this instinct manifests itself in the swelling and contracting of abstract forms; these seem more than mere lines; they suggest a puffing-up from within and a diminishing in power without actually representing a real living creature (Fig. 1). This manner of expression was accentuated the moment the animal was included in the world of ornament.

The custom of shaping the ends of tools to represent the heads of animals is by no means peculiar to the Nordic peoples. Long before, it had been employed by Oriental and Greek craftsmen, but these workers endeavored to make the animals as naturalistic as possible, whereas in the north the faintest hint seemed to suffice — the slitting of a pointed corner, for instance, would suggest a beak or a snout, and a little circle an eye. The plant, which Mediterranean art very soon came to include in its ornament, was for the northern peoples of the early period not a life-suggesting element like animals or men and was therefore neglected.

The richest examples of the introduction of animals into ornament are to be found in Scandinavian wood carving and Irish or Anglo-Saxon book illumination about the year 700, and in the metal work of both countries. The application is extremely varied; the different parts of animals are either divided or combined to make singular forms, but we almost never come across natural animals in natural proportions. Two crossing waving lines or ribbons, which in their simple form in southern ornament were quite neutral in the direction of their course, when imported into the north soon became filled with dynamic power. Once the line receives a head, anyone contemplating it is forced to fol-

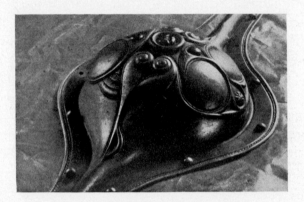

FIG. 1. CELTIC METAL SHIELD
BRITISH MUSEUM

low it in a definite direction. This is shown, for instance, in the ornaments of the Norwegian Oseberg ship (Fig. 2), and equally well and in a still more vigorous and complicated manner in those of Irish and Anglo-Saxon manuscripts. And where the plait-work of the mosaic floors of ancient Roman houses in England was imitated, it grew more complicated and puzzling in order to stir the fancy of the observer.

This Nordic style of ornament, which for the Continent was chiefly represented by the British Isles, because they were connected with it by the Christian religion, a bond which did not exist with Scandinavia, spreads to French soil and becomes part of the art of the Carolingian renaissance of the ninth century, which draws its inspiration chiefly from classic or early Christian models. The new insular current begins to dominate the north of France and the neighboring Rhineland, where it forms the so-called Franco-Saxon style. It is characteristic, however, that the manuscripts of this school accept only the insular ornament, very seldom borrowing the figurative part, while reciprocally the Continental figures exert their influence on English art and change Irish forms of the utmost reduction and stylization into ones more closely resembling nature.

This latter influence increases immensely about the middle of the tenth century and leads to the introduction of classical floral ornament from the Con-

tinent into England. One of the most important examples is the Aethelwold
Benedictional at Chatsworth of about 980. But the French leaf and tendril
forms are not taken over without modification. Through the Anglo-Saxon impulse toward dynamic movement they begin to flourish, to develop exuberantly,
and to cross the frames in the manner of plait-work (Fig. 3). These elongated
leaves, a combination of plant and ribbon, the top of which is curled around,
become a most essential element in the whole of Romanesque art, not only on
the Norman coast of the Channel but throughout Continental floral ornament.[1]

Generally the first step in transplanting was the personal transference by
ecclesiastical or secular leaders, who carried English or Northern French manuscripts into foreign monasteries. In the beginning it was the Irish and Anglo-

FIG. 2. ORNAMENT OF THE OSEBERG SHIP
Oslo Museum

Saxon missionaries who brought Christianity to Germany and founded monasteries in Fulda, St. Gallen, etc., down as far as the north of Italy. These were followed by other northern monks, who carried manuscripts to the new places and
were perhaps miniaturists themselves. Later, when floral ornament had been
developed in England, we can prove that where, according to historical documents, men from England or the Norman shore played a part English ornament
was introduced. Of Citeaux, the mother-monastery of the Cistercians, for instance, we know that the first abbot was Robert of Normandy, and he must have
introduced the style which we find in the ornaments of manuscripts written
there shortly after his time, now in the library of Dijon. The same must be
said of Poitiers in the eleventh century (Fig. 4). In Germany the monastery of
Fulda was founded by Boniface, and the insular script was used there for centuries. The South German monastery of Weingarten, founded by the Guelphs,
received from the Princess Judith of Flanders, who, previous to her marriage
with Guelph IV had been married in England, several Anglo-Saxon manuscripts,
which are now in the Pierpont Morgan Library (Fig. 5). In this way the Anglo-
Saxon style of ornamentation was introduced into Weingarten (Fig. 6).

[1] One may observe a certain inclination toward this development of leaves in the ivories of the so-
called "younger Metz School" (cf. A. Goldschmidt, *Die Elfenbeinskulpturen aus der Zeit der Karolingischen und
sächsischen Kaiser*, Bd. 1, Tf. XXXIV ss.). This is the same school which also in its iconography offers the
starting point for the Aethelwold Benedictional, one of the Anglo-Saxon manuscripts with the new English ornament in question (cf. Otto Homburger, *Die Anfänge der Malerschule von Winchester im X. Jahrhundert*,
Leipzig, 1912). In connection with the investigations of A. M. Friend in Princeton it has been shown that
the locality of these French ornaments also may be Saint-Denis.

FIG. 3. MISSAL, ROUEN MS. Y. 6

FIG. 4. POITIERS MS. 250. VITA S. RADEGUNDIS, SAEC. XI

FIG. 5. PIERPONT MORGAN LIBRARY MS. 709

From Weingarten

In the twelfth century the English style developed a new variation in the form of spiral-shaped leafless stalks with a flower in the middle composed of elongated leaves which clasp the curves of the spiral in an octopus-like manner (Fig. 7). The intervals of the spiral are generally filled in with little human or animal figures or small branches. This ornament grows very popular in rich initials not only in the north of France (Fig. 8) but also in Germany. The regions we have already mentioned, the lower Rhine, Saxony, and also a special group of Franconian and Swabian monastic scriptoria, reproduce these ornaments in the first third of the thirteenth century (Fig. 9). Thus there is a revival of ribbon-

FIG. 6. GERMAN MS. SAEC. XII, FULDA COD. C 1
From Weingarten

like lines in combination with elongated leaves, which in this polyp-like flower produce especially strong associations with muscular animal life by the energy inherent in their manner of clasping. That these stretched leaves play a great part in the capitals of Romanesque architecture is sufficiently well-known. Their existence comes to an end with the early Gothic knob-capital, which represents the most concentrated expression of striving aloft (Fig. 10).

Studying the human figures of the same period, one may observe a certain parallelism. The moment when the English took over from the Continent floriate ornament coincided with their more intense feeling for the naturalness of the human figure, but just as they adapted the style of plants to their own taste so they did in the case of the human figure. They lengthened proportions, gave the figures an attitude as full of movement as possible, and made their garments flutter and the edges run along in narrow zigzag lines.[2] These characteristics may be said to show the same temperament as the complicated lines of the earlier pure ornamental style, though on quite another basis. This Winchester School, so called because some of the earliest manuscripts are attributed to that abbey,

[2] Cf. O. Homburger, *op. cit.*, and G. R. Morey, introduction of the *Catalogue of the Exhibition of Illuminated Manuscripts* held at the New York Library, 1933–1934, pp. xi–xii (a reprint of Morey's article in *The Arts* of April 1925).

FIG. 7. MÜNCHEN COD. LAT. 835. ENGLISH PSALTER

FIG. 8. PARIS, BIBL. NAT. LAT. 11565. FRENCH PSALTER

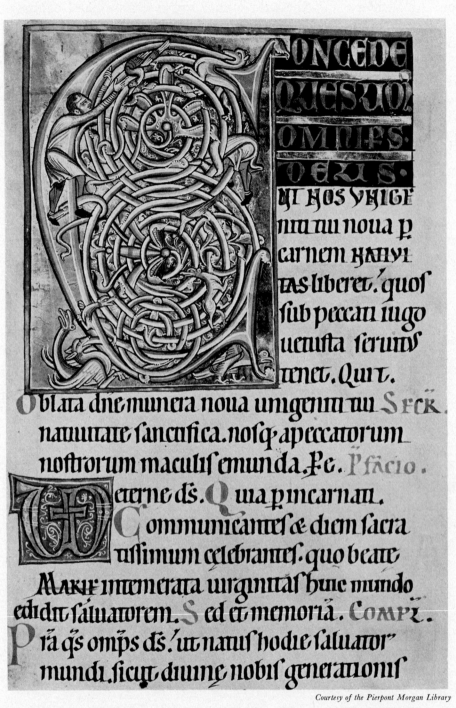

FIG. 9. PIERPONT MORGAN LIBRARY, MS. 710. GERMAN MS.

also extended to other English centers and from there over the north coast of France. And, indeed, the whole region north and south of the Channel becomes more and more entitled to be regarded as a unit in this period. The slender proportions of the figures remain a peculiarity of the work of English artists throughout the following centuries and are probably connected with the slenderness of the English race, though sometimes they attain a length that even in an Englishman would be highly unusual and must be considered a stylistic exaggeration.

It is astonishing with what fineness and conviction many artists in the tenth and eleventh centuries render action, even with this stylization, and how well they contrive to express natural forms, the beauty of heads, with intermittent

FIG. 10. EARLY GOTHIC CAPITALS

pen strokes. Their work represents one of the few really individual styles of the early Middle Ages. Among the best examples are the Caedmon paraphrase in Oxford and the Malmesbury Prudentius in Cambridge. Though the illustrations of the Prudentius depend on earlier models, a comparison of the different manuscripts derived from the same source shows that their style changes according to the country of their execution. These drawings are among the most charming that medieval art has produced; they sometimes approach early Greek art, especially vase painting, though it would be difficult to find any direct connection with real Greek works (Fig. 11). Such creative capacity must be the reason why England shows herself more independent of convention than the Continent in the iconographic sphere. Unusual features in Biblical representations on the Continent are often discovered to have made their first appearance in England, if not in Byzantium.

It is difficult to say what part animals play in the field of ornament in the eleventh and twelfth centuries after having been so distantly related to nature in the early Irish and Anglo-Saxon style of the eighth and ninth centuries. They grow more complete in their bodily construction than they had been in their former connection with the plait-work; nevertheless, as elements of initials or other decoration they continue to be fantastic. The figured initials of northwestern Europe stand in clear contrast to those of Byzantine or Roman origin, a contrast that exists from the beginning of book illumination. If figures appear in the southern ones, they generally have some relation to the text, while those of northwest European descent nearly always are merely a decorative element and have nothing to do with the text. From France the latter enter Spain, to-

Corpus Christi College

FIG. 11. PRUDENTIUS
CAMBRIDGE, CORPUS CHRISTI
COLLEGE MS. 23. FAITH
AND CHARITY

FIG. 12. ENGLISH
PHYSIOLOGUS MS. IN
LENINGRAD. SAEC. XII

gether with the French script, in the twelfth century; on the other hand, several of the South German figured initials — for instance, those of the Hirsau School — as well as Italian ones, contain figures illustrating the text which they introduce. It is difficult to determine whether the rich combination of fantastic animals and floriate ornament in initials of the twelfth century was created in France or whether there, also, England was stimulating. The English material has fewer of this type than the French manuscripts and it is chiefly their early appearance and extensive use on the north coast of France that can plead for England. Perhaps we ought also to take into consideration the English inclination to draw imaginatively unreal animals and demoniacal beings where the purpose is not decoration but the representation of natural objects. The first known version in a European vulgar tongue of the Physiologus, the standard work on animals in the Middle Ages, which was originally written in Greek and then translated into Latin, is in Anglo-Saxon verse. And most of the illustrated Physiologus Romanesque manuscripts were written in England. Their artistic quality is considerable, but, whereas in the early Greek and Latin copies the pictures of the animals correspond to their natural appearance, the English painters often give them quite fantastic shapes (Fig. 12).

This representation of animals and of beings half human and half beastlike reaches its perfection in the twelfth century and seems very characteristic of English taste. The literature of the period also offers examples of this tendency. We know, for instance, the vision that appeared to the Irish knight Tundalus in

FIG. 13. ENGLISH PSALTER
British Museum Tib. C. VI. Saec. XI

the year 1149, which was described by him in his vulgar idiom to a clerk Marcus, who wrote it down in a Latin version. According to this story Tundalus was first translated to Heaven and afterwards to the entrance of Hell, which he saw as the enormous jaws of an animal, with huge teeth between which flames shot forth and seized the condemned. This notion of Hell, which prevailed especially in England, is fixed in numerous pictures of the eleventh and twelfth centuries (Figs. 13 and 14), and was transferred from England to the Continent. In particular, the North German illustrations of Biblical manuscripts adopted it (Fig. 15).[3]

With this are connected all those demoniacal monsters and devilish creatures which Hell sends forth into the world. According to a legend which a writer of the eighth century dedicated to King Ethelbald, St. Guthlac, the hermit of the Isle of Crowland, a place regarded as haunted, was carried up into the air and down to Hell by horribly deformed beings which the author describes in great detail. The beautifully drawn scroll of the twelfth century, now in the

---

[3] Arthur Haseloff, *Eine thüringisch-sächsische Malerschule des 13. Jahrhunderts* (Strassburg, 1897), S. 159 ff. Georg Swarzenski, "Aus dem Kunstkreis Heinrichs des Löwen," *Städel-Jahrbuch*, VII–VIII (1932), S. 274 ff., proves the English influence not only in the iconography but also in the style.

British Museum, which represents this scene (Fig. 16) gives us a nice selection of these demons. Everyone who looks at this composition will be reminded of the print by Schongauer, the Upper Rhenish painter of the fifteenth century,

FIG. 14. WINCHESTER PSALTER. BRITISH MUSEUM, NERO C. IV

who shows St. Anthony in a similar situation (Fig. 17), and it is not at all impossible that some threads connected it with the English tradition found on the Lower Rhine, for there, as we know, a close tie with England existed. There the insular literature of the twelfth century was adapted for Continental use; the poem of Tundalus, for example, has been preserved to us in the Lower Rhenish adaptation of that period.

In the subsequent Gothic period we see that, though the differences between England and the Continent are no longer so marked as before, they are nevertheless decidedly present. Thus the proportions of the English figures are generally slenderer and convey a stronger impression of motion. If similar forms appear in French Gothic, this may not be without English influence. The original difference between the two is well shown by contemporary royal seals. The

FIG. 15. STUTTGART, PSALTER
OF HERMANN OF THURINGIA

FIG. 16. BRITISH MUSEUM HARLEY ROLL Y. 6.
LEGEND OF ST. GUTHLAC

basis of composition is exactly the same, but it is modified according to the different ornamental feeling of the two countries.[4] If we compare the seal of the French king Louis VII, who ascended the throne in 1137, with that of King Stephen of England in 1135 (Fig. 18), we see that in general the same arrangement is kept in both, but the arms of the English king are widely spread and his mantle flutters in many folds far away from the body and the throne, while on the French seal all is kept close together. We find that there is the same difference between the seal of Philip VI of France, who reigned from 1328, and that of David II of Scotland, who ascended the throne one year later. Not only are the proportions in the latter much longer and the movements much more energetic and more strongly opposed, but the arms and legs of the chair are also elongated as far as possible. The extravagant movement of the line is the decisive factor here. One can follow this in English Gothic wall-paintings and manuscripts as well, and, apart from the proportions, we discover, especially in manuscripts, an emphasis on line; the coloring is generally lighter than in France and not so strongly plastic, leaving the drawing more clearly visible, merely touched by color. The faces in the finest English manuscripts have more charm

[4] A. Goldschmidt, "Der angelsächsische Stil der mittelalterlichen Malerei," *Festschrift für Felix Liebermann* (1921), S. 271.

FIG. 17. SCHONGAUER, LEGEND OF ST. ANTHONY

than those in the French ones; the ornaments have more variety and do not show only the ivy-leaf that adorns every French manuscript of the period. Indeed, the French style of the fourteenth century is much more conventional altogether, even in its best examples. Furthermore, the *drôleries* which play such a great part in the tendrils of the margins and which are so full of fantastic invention and of scenes from daily life have their origin in English manuscripts and spread from them throughout France.

The fact that the English of this period had a strong influence not only on the north of France but also on Germany has been shown by Graf Vitzthum,

FIG. 18. SEALS OF FRENCH AND
ENGLISH KINGS

who has proved that the Lower Rhine district, with Cologne as its capital, took the style of its wall-paintings and illuminations chiefly from England, and that this continued up the Rhine as far as Lorraine.[5] Another current passes across North Germany to East Prussia. Robert Freyhan has proved in his publication of the manuscript of Willem of Orlens in Kassel that the illustrations show English style, transferred via Cologne and thus brought to Hessia.[6] Two of the most important German manuscripts of the Apocalypse were painted in Königsberg at the time of the knights of the German order and show distinct traces of English influence,[7] just as the celebrated architecture of the vaults of the same order in Danzig, in Marienburg (Fig. 19), and in Lübeck — usually taken to represent palm trees, impressions which members of the Order received during

[5] Georg Graf Vitzthum, *Die rheinische Malerei zu Anfang des 14. Jahrhunderts* (Habilitationsschrift: Leipzig, 1907).

[6] Rob. Freyhan, *Der Willehalm-Codex der Landesbibliothek in Cassel* (Marburg, 1927).

[7] Toni Herrmann, *Der Bildschmuck der Deutsch-Ordensapokalypsen Heinrichs von Hesler* (Königsberg i. Pr., 1934).

their former residence in the Near East — seem much more likely to have been connected with English architecture, such as the Lady Chapel in Wells cathedral, for instance.[8] And we know that this is not the only architectural design borrowed from England.

This leads us to Gothic architecture in general. The Gothic style had a strong unifying power, and gradually all the European countries followed the

Staatliche Bildstelle, Berlin

FIG. 19. MARIENBURG IN PRUSSIA, PALACE OF THE GERMAN ORDER

forms that were first evolved in northern France and southern England. There have been many discussions as to whether certain elements of Gothic construction, such as the cross-ribs of the vaults, were developed first in England or in France. Though in this question the majority have decided in favor of France, some details would seem certainly to be of English origin and must have been introduced from England to the Continent. One point that strikes us in the English cathedrals is their accumulation of vertical members, not so much in the essential part of the building's construction as in its additional and more decorative elements. The pillars, for instance, are surrounded by many thin

[8] Edward S. Prior, *A Short Chronological History of British Architecture*, p. 29 (illustration).

round shafts which very often give the impression of not being necessarily connected with the ribs, as in Canterbury Cathedral, where through the distinctive black color of their basalt they act chiefly as decorative lines (Fig. 20).

Dehio in his great publication on west European medieval ecclesiastical architecture gives a very good description of the English Gothic and contrasts it with the French. He says that, though it had its origin in the French construction, it very soon changed its character, and that its essence lay not so much in the organic nature of the vaulting as in the secondary aspects. It does not

S. B. Bolas & Co.

FIG. 20. CANTERBURY CATHEDRAL   FIG. 21. DANZIG, VAULT OF THE
          SOUTH TRANSEPT   MARIENKIRCHE

show a *development* in the strictest sense but rather a *succession* of different systems of decoration. He points out the great variety in the shape of arches, from the lancet to the Tudor arch, and their employment alongside one another, while in France the contemporary arches of a building must all conform to the same norm. He speaks of the tracery of the windows, which does not keep within the same limits as the French but as early as in the thirteenth century begins with partitions made by converging arches and continues with wavy lines, intertwining combinations, and quite irregular-looking compositions. The Continent adapted from England the *vescia piscis* (*Fischblase*) and the flamboyant style considerably later. The same is true in the case of vaults: the simple cross-rib soon changes into narrow partitions of fan work and net work, or funnel shape with hanging keystones, as in the Henry VII chapel in Westminster Abbey, and beyond all doubt these complicated forms are the source of the net vaulting that appears on the Continent, first in the Hanse towns along the North German coast (Fig. 21). In England the tracery of the windows spreads as a mere decoration over the walls; the dogtooth and the zigzag moldings inherited from the Norman period still serve as ornament on the pillars between the slender surrounding shafts.

And these as well as the very closely arranged blind arches emphasize the impression that the structural body is covered with a screenlike layer. (Recently even the façade of the cathedral of Strassburg has been associated with the English influence, on account of the net of thin shafts that covers it, and has been compared with the façade of Wells cathedral.)

All these evidences of a fancy that is essentially English are in conformity with those we see in the earlier periods, though they appear under other conditions and on another basis: the inclination toward the use of abstract ornamental forms for expressive linear movement, in the variation of the arches, in the slender parallel shafts, in the complicated lines of net vaulting, and in the narrow grate of screen-shaped wall-arcades.

If, in conclusion, we try to express the result of all these observations, we see that the British Isles represent the North European aspect of the medieval artistic spirit and that a constant influence on the southern element and a constant mingling with southern ingredients produced the richness of medieval art. While it was classical art that reached the climax of illusion in the representation of the external appearance of things, it was the North which by representing movement, by elongating proportions, and by fantastic arrangement gave art the capacity to express those unrestricted innate impulses that make themselves outwardly known. Northern art was responsible for the revitalizing of the tree transplanted from the South, and without this new creative impulse the multifariousness of medieval art would have been impossible.